DIMENSIONS OF DYSLEXIA

Volume One

ASSESSMENT, TEACHING AND THE CURRICULUM

Edited by Gavin Reid

Dimensions of Dyslexia

Volume One

ASSESSMENT, TEACHING AND THE CURRICULUM

Edited by Gavin Reid

Moray House Publications
Holyrood Road, Edinburgh,
EH8 8AQ.

Current and forthcoming titles:

Dimensions of Dyslexia

Vol. 1 Assessment, Teaching and the Curriculum

Vol. 2 Literacy, Language and Learning
Edited by Gavin Reid

Specific Learning Difficulties (Dyslexia)
A Handbook for Study and Practice
Gavin Reid

Open Learning Courses in Specific Learning Difficulties
General Editors – Gavin Reid and Fernando Almeida Diniz

First published 1996
ISBN 0 901580 71 6
© Moray House Institute of Education

Printed and bound in Great Britain by Bell & Bain Ltd., Glasgow

CONTENTS

Section 4:   **Curriculum and Support Approaches**

Section 5:   **Continuing Education**

FOREWORD

JACKIE STEWART
Three-Time World Driving Champion

Dyslexia, or any of the derivative learning disabilities, can be one of the most mentally damaging and painful issues that the young can face. A large percentage of sufferers are abused and ridiculed by their peers, their elders, and even their teachers, in the traditional education system. The anguish and frustration and resulting lack of self-esteem can linger long in a person's life if the correct help and assistance is not forthcoming.

Dyslexia often causes the young to take the easy route – since they are often laughed at and humiliated in the circles in which they would traditionally mix at school and after school – and frequently they are dragged into the 'wrong crowd'. It can lead from truancy and crime, to alcohol and drugs. A life can be ruined or even lost. In an enormous percentage of cases, a young person with a fantastic mind can never reach true potential because they are convinced, due to the insensitivities of others and the inadequacy of the system, that they could never be achievers or successful in anything.

All of this can be avoided by understanding teachers and educators who are prepared to change the system and to accommodate a group of people that require a different kind of education which, in some cases, would only mean 'decimal points of change'. With good communication, the victims of learning disabilities, their friends and peers, could be made to understand that the ability to consume information, by either the written word, the spoken word, or even visual diagrams, cannot be done in the 'traditional manner'. It could also be emphasised that in some cases, those same individuals have skills, talents, and minds, much more expansive than the traditional 'bright' children have. If such a thing were done, humiliation could be avoided, self-esteem could be established, potential developed, a better social life created and pain and suffering avoided.

To a very large extent this difference can be created only by educators and by teachers who are prepared to be shown, and to understand that by doing things a little differently, those young minds can be taught and trained, in a large percentage of cases, to handle most of the challenges of life that otherwise might be immovable obstacles.

In the United Kingdom, it has taken a remarkable amount of time for the traditional education system to recognise that there are special needs within its domain which have to be provided for. The obstinacy of the system to fully appreciate this is extremely frustrating for a sufferer, such as myself, to accept.

What has been achieved at Moray House and what can be achieved in the future with a properly funded programme, will help innumerable people (not only of this generation, but more importantly, future generations) to contribute to and benefit our country and society in general, not to mention the possibility for dyslexia sufferers to be proud achievers.

PREFACE

This two-volume text represents a substantial update and extension to the original Moray House Course Reader *Perspectives on Practice*.

This has been necessary because of the broader scope of the concept of dyslexia and its associated dimensions and the extension of teacher training courses in dyslexia, often now at Post-Graduate and Masters level.

It is fortunate, therefore, that the authors of the chapters in these two volumes were able, despite heavy commitments, to provide the quality of insight necessary both to justify the different dimensions of dyslexia and the higher level of teacher training courses.

The contributors are drawn from a wide area throughout the UK and the United States. The Moray House Centre for Specific Learning Difficulties (Dyslexia) has organised a number of national conferences drawing established international speakers, most of whom have submitted a chapter to this book.

The contributors come from a range of backgrounds incorporating both research and practice, and this is reflected in this two-volume edition.

This book is a team effort in every respect and I wish to acknowledge all those who in some way have participated to achieve this final product. I am sure it will be greatly appreciated by all involved in the area of dyslexia.

Gavin Reid

Centre for Specific Learning Difficulties (Dyslexia),
Moray House Institute, Heriot-Watt University,
Edinburgh.

SECTION 1

INTRODUCTION

ASSESSMENT, TEACHING AND THE CURRICULUM

GAVIN REID

Assessment, teaching and the curriculum are three key dimensions of dyslexia. Each play an important role in facilitating opportunities for the dyslexic child to achieve success at school. The information which can be obtained from an assessment can suggest particular teaching approaches and such approaches should be set within the context of the curriculum. It is appropriate, therefore, that this volume covers these three areas, demonstrating that each one should not be seen in isolation and that every effort should be made to link the three together. They are separated in sections in this Volume, for the convenience of the reader but the contextual and educational considerations which mark their linkage should be uppermost in the mind of the reader.

In Section Two – Assessment – Gavin Reid identifies three essential aspects of assessment: difficulties, discrepancy and differences. In discussing these three factors, the author shows their relevance in the identification of dyslexia. These factors also form the basis of an assessment framework for dyslexia in a later chapter by Gillian Kettles, Karen Laws and Gavin Reid. This framework, which also considers curriculum aspects, gained impetus from development work carried out by a team of educational psychologists from Kent County Council, England, in response to the need to develop some form of structured framework which can assist classroom teachers in the identification and assessment of specific learning difficulties.

Gordon Booth's chapter on "Principles of Assessment' can also benefit teachers by providing a clear rationale for assessment, and Rosemary McGhee in Chapter Four provides some examples of how an assessment can be interpreted in practice.

There is now a great deal of evidence which suggests that phonological processing difficulties are the core difficulty of dyslexia. Rea Reason and Norah Frederickson's chapter on "Discrepancy Definitions or Phonological Assessment?"

provides a definition of phonological awareness and the rationale and content of the phonological assessment battery. They also discuss some of the problems which can result from using discrepancy definitions for the identification of dyslexia.

The role of the educational psychologist and the psychological dimensions of assessment are highlighted by Sionah Lannen and Gavin Reid. This chapter also considers curriculum and teaching factors which should accompany any form of psychological assessment.

Metacognition is an important aspect in both assessment and learning. It focuses on how learners learn and the awareness they have of their own learning processes. This is particularly important for dyslexic children, as they need to have an awareness of the most appropriate learning strategies for them, so that they can maximise their learning potential. Donna Ayres and Karen Morrison in Chapters Seven and Eight discuss factors relating to metacognitive assessment, and provide an interesting insight into the learners' role in assessment.

Rapid advances in educational technology have resulted in an expansion of options and resources in the assessment and teaching of dyslexic children. The major breakthrough on computerised assessment by the research team at Humberside, headed by Chris Singleton, is described in Chapter Nine. This development can be of major significance in early identification and in large scale cost-effective screening.

Another aspect of dyslexia assessment which has been given considerable attention recently is that of listening comprehension. Listening comprehension can be used as an effective measure of the comprehension skills of dyslexic children and in Chapter Ten, Mark Turner, Sarah Geiger and Claire Bedford-Feuell describe some current research in the development of a valid and reliable measure of listening comprehension.

It is important that a comprehensive assessment should be multi-disciplinary to include the perspectives of different professionals. Anne O'Hare in Chapter Eleven therefore provides a detailed perspective of assessment from a medical viewpoint. This kind of information should be seen as complimentary to school-based assessment. It is hoped that this section on assessment provides the reader with a comprehensive insight into the identification of dyslexia and an awareness of current trends in research and practice.

The next section on teaching approaches offers a blend of traditional and established programmes, including new and innovative approaches. This illustrates the dynamic nature of approaches in the teaching of dyslexic children and further highlights that often these approaches are rooted in well-established traditional practices.

Margaret Crombie provides a comprehensive survey of a range of approaches which can be used by the teacher at both primary and secondary stages. Margaret touches on important aspects such as early intervention, planning, materials, the classroom context, information technology and the role of parents.

This is followed by Marcia Henry who provides a detailed overview of the Orton-Gillingham method of teaching dyslexic children. Many of the teaching programmes for dyslexic children being used today are derived from the Orton-Gillingham method. The Orton Dyslexia Society in the USA is a large and well-established organisation which provides an acknowledged leadership in the field of dyslexia. It is fitting, therefore, that Marcia Henry, the current President of the Orton Dyslexia Society, should describe the Orton-Gillingham approach.

This is followed in Chapters Fifteen and Seventeen by two examples of new programmes developed by Helen Calcluth and Verna Dearnley. These provide good examples of structured, multi-sensory approaches based on established principles, yet offering a fresh view of how dyslexic difficulties can be overcome. These programmes, which have been entirely developed by the authors, result from their long experience in teaching dyslexic children and are published for the first time in this volume.

The theory and strategies of spelling are described in the chapters by Alison Duncan and Catriona Collins and Jean Miller. Alison provides a sound research and theoretical framework, which is followed by Catriona Collins and Jean Miller who present some strategies based on their vast experience.

Mathematics can be another area of difficulty for dyslexic children. In Chapter Twenty Elizabeth McKenzie provides some approaches for teaching mathematics, and in the previous chapter, Charles Weedon describes some of the sources of difficulties dyslexic children may experience in mathematics. As well as discussing 'institutional' features, the curriculum and the linkage between language and mathematics, he also pinpoints the principal challenge facing all educators to build upon the hard-won strengths and advantages of current provision, yet at the same time, develop an organisational and curricular flexibility where it is needed.

This view is central to the theme of this volume and indeed to the success of dealing with dyslexia in the classroom.

Emma Vallance's chapter on "Dyslexia and Musical Notation" concludes the section on 'Teaching' and emphasizes how dyslexic difficulties can affect performance in a wide range of areas. Music may well be one of the strengths of dyslexic children, but difficulty in reading music can seriously restrict development in that area. Emma describes the results of a study she carried out in a secondary school and provides useful ideas for the teacher to follow-up.

In Section Three Curriculum and Support Approaches – Sylvia Russell describes how the curriculum can be accessed for dyslexic children through reading, handwriting, spelling, mathematics, and the use of metacognition. Sylvia also provides a case study as an example of how the needs of a dyslexic child can be met. This chapter is followed by an analysis from David Dodds on the concept of differentiation, focusing particularly on the secondary school. David highlights the importance of discussion in helping the dyslexic child achieve some success in different areas of the secondary curriculum.

This is followed by a chapter written by the Learning Support staff at Queen Anne Secondary School, and represents a model of good practice, focusing on the needs of dyslexic children in every area of the school curriculum. The chapter clearly represents a collaborative exercise from a committed learning support department, and highlights many important factors such as the value of co-operation with all teaching staff in the school and the need for an agreed framework of practice within the guidelines suggested by regional policy.

The whole-school theme is followed again in the chapters by Ros Hunter and Morven Brown. Both provide constructive suggestions for accommodating the needs of dyslexic children within the mainstream school. Some dyslexic children, however, respond better to the type of provision found in literacy units, which can be specifically resourced to meet the individual needs of dyslexic children. Alison Fox and Kath Winn describe some the principles and practices associated with the Cedarbank Literacy Unit in West Lothian. This chapter provides the reader with a clear insight into both the internal structure and the teaching procedures of this unit.

Resources which can be used for dyslexic children are increasing at a fast rate. The last two chapters in this section on the "Curriculum and Support Approaches" outline the use of resources in the increasingly important area of information technology and in the final chapter of the section, Anne Philip describes a range of useful resources, based on her long experience in teaching dyslexic children, which can be developed and utilised by the teacher.

The final section in this volume raises issues relating to Continuing Education. This is an area of prime importance, particularly as many dyslexic students have spent a considerable time in developing strategies to help overcome their literacy difficulties, and therefore can do well in further and higher education. It is imperative that the education system provides the opportunity and the support which would allow dyslexic students to thrive. The chapter by Don Mackie provides a general overview of some of the difficulties displayed by adults with literacy difficulties, and Alison Closs, Sionah Lannen and Gavin Reid examine some of the issues relating to helping dyslexic students fulfil their potential. This chapter looks at assessment and the provision of support, and highlights the need for higher education institutions to provide a clear policy and framework of support to accommodate the needs of dyslexic students. This is clearly an important area of staff development.

It is hoped that this volume, which combines three dimensions of dyslexia – assessment, teaching and the curriculum – will provide the reader with a comprehensive overview of the needs of dyslexic learners from pre-school to higher education and how these needs may be met within the education system.

SECTION 2

ASSESSMENT

DIFFICULTIES, DISCREPANCIES AND DIFFERENCES

GAVIN REID

INTRODUCTION

Assessment for specific learning difficulties is a process which considers a variety of different forms of evidence; it should not be portrayed as a rigid formula. A single test or assessment strategy is insufficient since one needs to look for a pattern of evidence which would indicate a specific learning difficulty. It is necessary, therefore, to focus on at least three principal elements: difficulties, discrepancies and differences.

Potential 'difficulties', such as phonological processing, word recognition, sequencing, organisational factors and visual and auditory aspects, should be considered. Attention should also be given to the 'discrepancies' which may be evident, such as that between decoding and reading comprehension, oral and written work and between different subject areas in the school curriculum. At the same time, one must also attempt to adopt a holistic perspective and to identify the child's learning style and reading style preferences. These difficulties, discrepancies and differences can provide a framework for an assessment for specific learning difficulties and also some information to direct the teacher to appropriate methods and programmes.

Ideally, however, the assessment should not be conducted in isolation and strong arguments have been put forward for assessment in conjunction with the curriculum and teaching methodologies (Turner, 1994).

DIFFICULTIES

- **Decoding**

A decoding difficulty is the common factor among the difficulties experienced. It is the problem of decoding the symbols which make up letters of the alphabet, identifying the letter sounds and recognising the word patterns which account for the specific learning difficulty. Poor mastery of letter-sound correspondences is present because of a difficulty in learning the phonetic code.

An assessment therefore needs to focus on phonological factors to assess the child's awareness of sounds and phonological rules (Bradley, 1991; Stanovich, 1991). The decoding difficulty may also be due to segmenting and blending problems. The child would have some difficulty in breaking words down into their component parts and in identifying blends within words. One may also observe sound sequencing errors and indeed other sequencing errors at the letter and word level.

- **Phonological Processing**

There is considerable evidence to suggest that phonological processing difficulties are at the root of these decoding difficulties. Stanovich (1991) suggests there is a lack of phonological awareness, and that the child does not have the ability or awareness to recognise the constituent sound segments which make up words. The phonological-core, variable-difference model (Stanovich, 1988a; Stanovich and Siegel, 1994) claims that virtually all poor readers have a phonological deficit but this is particularly obvious in readers who have an 'aptitude-achievement discrepancy'. Children without such a discrepancy would have more general difficulties.

Mann (1986) sees the phonological problem as one of phonetic coding, implying that the child has difficulty in processing verbal information into the working memory. Mann believes that these memory differences between dyslexic and other readers do not pertain to non-verbal information but to information which needs to be linguistically coded. In a large scale study on cognitive profiles of dyslexic students, it was found that short term auditory memory was a highly significant factor in relation to the difficulties experienced by the sample (Lannen and Lannen, 1995).

There is also some evidence to suggest that auditory perception problems may determine the extent of the phonological processing difficulty (Brady and Fowler, 1985). Interestingly, there is evidence which may rule out the possibility of a generalised auditory perception impairment since Mann also found no difference between dyslexic children and other readers in their perception of non-verbal environmental sounds.

Brady and Fowler (1988) provide evidence for a phonological decoding problem which restricts access to words and names. This type of problem, name retrieval difficulty, does appear to be a significant factor among children with dyslexic difficulties. Stanovich (1985) found that children with dyslexia were slower at naming familiar words from pictures than a control group.

Bradley (1991) identified phonological difficulties particularly associated with rhyming as a key factor in identifying 'high risk' children at the nursery stages. Frederickson (1995) and a team of co-authors have developed a Phonological Assessment Battery (PhAB) which attempts to identify the nature and level of phonological difficulties. This therefore emphasises the importance of phonological factors in assessing for dyslexia.

- **Early Identification**

The issue of early identification is of crucial importance. Early recognition can help to minimise the degree of potential failure by identifying appropriate preventative intervention strategies.

Experimental research in early diagnosis has included areas and skills not necessarily related to reading (Singleton, 1993; Nicolson and Fawcett, 1993). It is necessary, therefore, to recognise the broader perspective of dyslexia and to appreciate that dyslexic children may have difficulty in developing skills and carrying out tasks in activities not directly related to literacy. Such areas can include manual dexterity, reaction times, memory span, non-word repetition, motor skills and balance, awareness of rhyme, visual deficits, automatisation deficits, and picture colour and number naming. These factors have been the focus of on-going research on the development of diagnostic early screening procedures involving the use of microtechnology (Singleton, 1993, 1995; Nicolson and Fawcett, 1993).

Nicolson and Fawcett (1993) contend that early screening, together with appropriate pre-reading support, could help dyslexic children overcome difficulties in literacy acquisition. They argue that microcomputers offer an historic opportunity for the development of diagnostic pre-reading tests. Their present work focuses on the development of an objective and valid 'Dyslexia Early Screening Test' which can be easily and cheaply administered. These tests principally examine performances in a range of activities not dependent on taught skills such as reading.

The Humberside Early Identification Project (Singleton, 1990, 1992, 1993, 1995) provides a good example of a development programme aimed at effective early recognition of dyslexia using microcomputer technology. This has resulted in the development of a commercially available computer programme (KeyStage 1 Cops) which can screen for potential literacy difficulties. The purpose of the tests devised by this project (which includes analysis of children's performances in memory, phonological processing and visual-perceptual skills, is to identify those children who will possibly experience some difficulty in the acquisition of literacy due to some fundamental difficulty in cognition.

Such developments clearly offer some promise in the area of early recognition and can complement some other procedures in early recognition, such as observational assessment (Lannen and Reid, 1993) and formal and informal testing (McGhee, 1993; Evans, 1990). Some attempts at early recognition have centred on the association between phonological awareness and literacy acquisitions (Lundberg *et al.*, 1988; Bradley, 1989, 1992). These studies identify a lack of phonological awareness, such as the inability or difficulty to categorise sounds and recognise and repeat rhyme and alliteration, as being of some significance in early recognition of potential reading difficulties. This has been reinforced by the success of the intervention studies (Bryant *et al.*, 1989; Bradley, 1990, 1992) which introduces training in phonological awareness at an early stage to prevent subsequent reading failure. Bradley's longitudinal study suggests that training children to appreciate the connection between rhyming and letter patterns is effective in helping children develop an understanding of the relationship between phonological awareness and the letters of the alphabet (Bradley, 1988).

VISUAL FACTORS

• **Binocular Control**

Stein and Fowler (1982, 1985, 1993) suggest that a considerable number of children with dyslexic difficulties have an unfixed reference eye, which results in binocular instability, thus impairing progress in reading.

This viewpoint has met with some criticism. Bishop (1989) argued that stable binocular control is acquired as a result of learning to read, rather than as a prerequisite for reading.

Stein and Fowler (1993), however, disputed this and claimed that dyslexic children have in fact less binocular control than a group of younger children matched for IQ and reading age with the dyslexic group. Furthermore, these researchers demonstrated that an improvement in dyslexic readers' binocular control was often followed by reading improvement without any additional tutoring in reading skills. Stein and Fowler therefore argue that unstable binocular control is a feature of dyslexia and a factor which does impede reading.

The responses from the Stein and Fowler research have been obtained through the use of the Dunlop Test (Dunlop, 1972). This test is said to 'indicate the lateral preference of the ocular motor system' and it is argued that it can determine the 'dominant' eye in a binocular situation – that is, by studying the movements of both eyes simultaneously (Stein and Fowler, 1993).

Some criticism, however, has been voiced in the use of this test. The test does have a high level of subjectivity – children have to indicate the movement of a visual stimulus, which they do not directly focus on – which makes it not entirely reliable, especially in inexperienced hands (Stein *et al.*, 1985; Bigelow and McKenzie, 1985). Stein and Fowler (1993), however, did attempt to overcome this in their research design by adaptations to the test providing for more objective responses.

The intervention which, they argued, was followed by improved reading was based on the practice of monocular occlusion. This, they argue, helped to establish a fixed reference eye of binocular control. While they argue that unstable binocular control is a common cause of reading difficulties, they do acknowledge that it is seldom the sole cause. This is an important point to consider since although it has been shown that, for example, visual segmentation skills can be an important aspect in reading difficulties (Johnston, Anderson and Duncan, 1991), phonological aspects also need to be highlighted both in assessment and in teaching (Stanovich, 1988; Goswami and Bryant, 1990).

- **Visual Tracking**

A number of studies have shown a high incidence of right to left tracking of information among dyslexic children. The implication of this is that confusion may occur when the child is trained to read from left to right if this conflicts with his/her natural instincts to read from right to left. This may well account for reversals and misreading of print. It is important, therefore, that a teaching programme emphasises the directional aspect of left to right.

Extensive research (Pavlidis, 1990) suggests that children with dyslexia make more eye fixations and fixate for longer than other children. He suggested that they have less efficient control over eye movements.

- **Visual Sensitivity**

Irlen (1983, 89) claims that some dyslexic children may have scotopic sensitivity (Irlen Syndrome) which results in excessive glare and print distortions when reading. According to Irlen, the treatment for this involves the use of coloured perspex overlays or tinted lenses. The research on this, however, is far from clear cut. Stone and Harris (1991) claim that it is difficult for the dyslexic child to cope with the full range of spectral light, but they argue that the present form of assessment, which takes the form of screening procedures, such as that used by the Irlen Institute, is too subjective. Wilkins (1990) provided evidence for significant improvements in visual acuity in those children who were identified by the screening procedures and subsequently used overlays or lenses. Wilkins (1993) has developed, following extensive research, a range of overlays called intuitive overlays.

A study involving 75 children with specific learning difficulties (Kyd, Sutherland and McGettrick, 1992) presented evidence for visual perceptual dysfunction. Almost half the sample tested positive using the Irlen Screening Test. Subsequent intervention involved the use of appropriate, self-selected, coloured overlays. This was accompanied by significant improvements in reading rate. Similarly, results from an evaluation project of the Irlen overlays and lenses (Wright, 1993) has provided some impressive data on reading rate progress.

Stanley (1994), however, argues that evidence from studies using subjects selected according to Irlen criteria does not necessarily provide support for the Irlen treatment. He cites the study by Scheiman, Blaskey and Ciner (1990) which reports that 95 per cent of 39 subjects identified as candidates for Irlen filters had identified vision anomalies which could be treated by other optometric means. Furthermore, Lannen and Lannen (1995) found that from a sample of 110 students referred for specific learning difficulties, over one third had suspected visual problems.

Pumfrey and Reason (1992) suggest that improvements using overlays can often be due to a 'placebo effect'. They argue that the evidence that dyslexia is primarily due to visual difficulties is not convincing, since much of the literature focuses on language, information processing, and other cognitive aspects such as attention, concentration and memory.

DISCREPANCIES

The identification of discrepancies in ability and performances is an important factor in the assessment of children who may have a specific learning difficulty.

• **Decoding/Reading Comprehension Discrepancy**

Aaron (1989, 1994) presents a case for focusing on the discrepancy between decoding and listening/reading comprehension. Thus, one would expect a child with dyslexia to be poor at decoding and good or relatively better at listening/

reading comprehension. Features of other types of readers can be described using the same decoding/comprehension discrepancy measure. For example, Aaron describes a group, the 'non-specific reading disabled', as being poor at both decoding and comprehension. He also describes a 'hyperlexic' group as displaying a reverse trend from the dyslexic group, being good at decoding but poor in comprehension.

How, therefore, should one attempt to identify a decoding/reading comprehension discrepancy? To test for decoding, words in isolation may be presented, but this is also testing memory for letter and word patterns which may produce some criteria contamination, which would mean that other factors in addition to decoding are being assessed. To eradicate these criteria contamination factors, decoding can be assessed through the use of non-words. By using pronounceable *non-words* based on grapheme-phoneme relational rules, one can obtain some measure of the child's actual decoding ability.

Clearly, it is difficult to obtain a reading comprehension measure if the child has a decoding difficulty. This can be overcome by testing for listening comprehension. Aaron (1989) in a study of school children from six different years found an impressive correlation (0.78) between reading comprehension and listening comprehension. Indeed, among the nine year old group, the correlation was even higher (0.87). Often it is around the nine year age group that concern is quite high in relation to reading progress because by that stage, other factors, such as developmental lag, have usually levelled out and are therefore less influential as a possible cause of the reading difficulty.

The relevance of an effective listening comprehension measure to help in the identification of specific learning difficulties has been highlighted elsewhere (Stanovich, 1991), but it has also been acknowledged that much more development work needs to be carried out to obtain a discriminatory measure between specific learning difficulties and other forms of learning difficulty. In relation to this, promising development work is currently underway (Bedford-Feull, Geiger, Moyse and Turner, 1995) and such measures for assessing listening and reading comprehension can provide, the authors argue, more meaningful classification measures which can be useful to psychological services and exam boards.

•   **Oral/Written Discrepancies**

One may also identify a discrepancy between a child's oral performance and written work or reading fluency. It is, therefore, important to assess the child's oral skills and oral contributions in class in relation to his performance through other modalities. One must, however, bear in mind that some children's oral performance can be affected by other factors such as low confidence and self-esteem, and phonological processing difficulties. Children with a specific learning difficulty may therefore also have a difficulty with oral communication.

- **Curriculum Discrepancies**

Most children display some level of variance in their performances in school between different subject areas. Children with specific learning difficulties, however, may display extreme discrepancies. A discrepancy may be seen, for example, between science subjects and English, or subjects which demand significant amounts of reading. Such children may have abilities at non-verbal problem-solving which can be readily developed in some curricular subjects, although their performance may still be restricted by reading difficulties, since some reading is usually necessary in all curricular areas. To help deal with this, some schools and colleges now provide extensive learning support including readers, scribes and tapes of notes and texts.

DIFFERENCES

Extensive research on learning styles (Dunn and Dunn, 1992) raises the issue of assessing not just the product of learning, but also the process by which learning takes place. It is important, therefore, to appreciate that dyslexic children are all individuals and each will have a specific preference in their learning style. Reid (1992) has tackled the identification of learning styles through an observational schedule which can provide data on the range of learning and contextual factors which can influence children's learning outcomes. Dunn and Dunn (1992) have produced a learning styles inventory, a self-report questionnaire, which has been extensively validated in many countries. Dunn and Dunn's factors include: the environment, including sound, light, temperature and design; emotional aspects which relate to the need for structure and responsibility; sociological aspects, such as student preferences in learning alone or in pairs; physiological factors, such as mobility and time of day; psychological aspects, identifying styles such as analytic (preference to piece details together before attempting to understand the whole) and global (preference for obtaining the overall comprehension of the whole first and then attend to details). Dunn and Dunn found significant differences between the global and analytic groups, and that each group learnt best under different conditions. For example, they found that global learners tend to be less bothered by sound when learning than analytics.

Carbo, Dunn and Dunn (1987) looked at the implications of the Dunn and Dunn model and postulated that no single reading method is best for every child, and that lack of mastery of a reading sub-skill doesn't necessarily indicate a need for that sub-skill. They also found that most primary aged children are global, tactual and kinaesthetic learners and prefer to read in pairs.

The research in learning styles does, therefore, warrant some attention and should be considered in the assessment process. Observational assessment or self-report questionnaires can provide useful information on children's learning which can be complimented by other aspects of the assessment.

CONCLUSION

An assessment should be an all-embracing exercise and should be viewed as a process not a product. All forms of assessment, norm-referenced; criterion-referenced; curriculum-based and metacognitive assessment (where one looks at the process of learning (Reid, 1994)) are of value and all can provide information which can help to identify children with specific learning difficulties and help to provide information which can be useful in the development of support programmes.

There are some key questions one must ask when embarking on an assessment for specific learning difficulties. These include:

- What is being assessed? Is one looking at children's skills, abilities or strategies?
- Why is the assessment taking place? Is it to be diagnostic, prescriptive, predictive or normative?
- How is it to be done? What assessment strategies will be used – norm-referenced, criterion-referenced, observational, metacognitive?
- What will be the effect of the assessment? To what extent will it link with teaching and in what way will it have an affect on the student's self-concept?

Clearly, there are many questions relating to assessment and these are encapsulated in four of the recommendations made following extensive research (Pumfrey and Reason, 1992). These are that:

- Identification procedures should consider the child's previous learning history;
- both normative and criterion-referenced assessment should be supplemented by the observations of pupils, parents, teachers and psychologist;

- attention should be given to strategies, strengths and weaknesses that children bring to their attempts to read and write;
- the symbiotic relationship between assessment and teaching should be appreciated by all practitioners involved with pupils identified as having specific learning difficulties.

These recommendations provide a framework for an assessment. It is important therefore to:

- Obtain a clear rationale of why the assessment is being carried out;
- appreciate the importance of consultancy with parents and other professionals;
- recognise the value of observation and learning styles;
- embrace a range of strategies to identify strengths and difficulties displayed by the child in addition to any discrepancies in perform-ance which may be present.

Consideration of these factors help to ensure that assessment is constructive, productive and positive and will be recognised as an integral element of both teaching and the curriculum.

REFERENCES

Aaron, P. G. (1989). *Dyslexia and Hyperlexia.* Kluwer Academic Publications.

Aaron, P. G. (1994). Differential diagnosis of reading disabilities in Hales, G. (Ed.) *Dyslexia Matters.* London. Whurr Publications.

Bedford-Fuell, C., Geiger, S., Moyse, S. and Turner, M. (1995). Use of listening comprehension in the identification and assessment of specific learning difficulties in *Educational Psychology in Practice,* Vol. 10, No. 4, January 1995, pp. 207-214.

Bigelow, E. R. and McKenzie, B. E. (1985). 'Unstable occular dominance and reading ability'. *Perception,* 14, 329-335.

Bishop, D. V. M. (1989). 'Unfixed reference, monocular occlusion and developmental dyslexia – a critique'. *British Journal of Opthalmology,* 73, 8-5.

Bradley, L. (1988). 'Rhyme recognitions and reading and spelling in young children' in Masland, R. L. and Masland, M. U. (Eds.), *Pre-school presentation of reading failure.* Parkton, Maryland. York Press.

Bradley, L. (1989). 'Predicting learning disabilities' in Dumont, J. and Nakken, J. (Eds.), *Learning Disabilities: Cognitive, Social and Remedial Aspects.* Amsterdam. Swets and Zeitlinger.

Bradley, L .(1991). 'Rhyming connections in learning to read and spell' in Pumfrey, D. D. and Elliott, C. D. (Eds.), *Children's Reading, Spelling and Writing Difficulties: Challenges and Responses.* Neumes. Falmer Press.

Bradley, L. (1992). *Early Identification of Specific Learning Difficulties*. Paper presented at Conference held by Moray House Centre for Specific Learning Difficulties Project, Inverness, June 1992.

Brady, S. and Fowler, A. E. (1988). 'Phonological precursors to reading acquisition' in Masland, R. L. and Masland, M. U. (Eds.), *Pre-school Prevention of Reading Failure*. 204-215. Parkton, Maryland. York Press.

Carbo, M., Dunn, R. and Dunn, K. (1987). *Teaching students to read through their individual learning styles*. Prentice Hall.

Dunlop, P. (1972). 'Dylexia: the orthoptic approach'. *Australian Orthoptic Journal*, 12, 16-20.

Dunn, R. and Dunn, K. (1992). *Teaching Elementary Students through Their Individual Learning Styles*. Allyn & Bacon, Mass.

Evans, A. (1990). Screening at 6+. *Dyslexia Contact*. Vol. 8, No. 1.

Frederickson, N. (Ed.). (1995). *Phonological Assessment Battery (PHAB)*. Research Edition, University College, London. (Now available NFER, Nelson.)

Goswami, U. and Bryant, P. (1990). *Phonological Skills and Learning to Read*. Hove, Sussex. Erlbaum.

Irlen, H. (1983). *Successful treatment of learning disabilities*. Presented at 91st annual convention of American Psychological Association, Anaheim, California.

Irlen, H. (1989). *Scotopic Sensitivity Syndrome*. Screening manual, 3rd Ed. Perceptual Development Corporation.

Johnston, R., Anderson, M. and Duncan, L. (1991). 'Phonological and visual segmentation problems in poor readers', in Snowling, M. and Thomson, M. *Dyslexia, Integrating Theory and Practice*. London. Whurr Publishers.

Kyd, L., Sutherland, G. and McGettrick, P. (1992). 'A preliminary appraisal of the Irlen screening process for scotopic sensitivity syndrome and the effect of Irlen overlays on reading.' *British Opthalmic Journal* 1992: 49: 25-30.

Lannen, C. and Lannen S. (1985). Cognitive profiles and the WISC-R in *Assessment of Specific Learning Difficulties*. Unpublished study, Educational Psychology Services, Riyadh.

Lannen, S. and Reid, G. (1993). 'Psychological dimensions and the role of the educational psychologist in assessment', in Reid, G. (Ed.), *Specific Learning Difficulties (Dyslexia) – Perspectives on Practice*. Edinburgh. Moray House Publications.

Lundberg, I., Frost, J. and Peterson, O. (1988). 'Effects of an exercise program for stimulating phonological awareness in pre-school children.' *Reading Research Quarterly*, 12,3 pp. 263-284.

Mann, V. A .(1986). 'Why some children encounter reading problems: The contribution of difficulties with language processing and phonological sophistication to early reading disability', in Torgeson, J. K. and Wong, B. Y. L. (Eds.), *Psychological and Educational Perspectives on Learning Disabilities*, 133-59. New York. Academia Press.

McGhee, R. (1993). 'Formal assessment', in Reid, G. (Ed.), *Specific Learning Difficulties (Dyslexia) – Perspectives on Practice*. Edinburgh. Moray House Publications.

Nicolson, R. and Fawcett, A . J. (1993). *Early Diagnosis of Dyslexia: An Historic Opportunity?* Keynote address presented at BDA 'Early Diagnosis' Conference, London, June 1993.

Pavlidis, G. T. (1990). Perspectives on dyslexia. *Neurology, Neuropsychology and Genetics*. Vol. 1. Chichester. Wiley.

Pumfrey, P. D. and Reason, R. (1992). *Specific Learning Difficulties (Dyslexia) Challenges and Responses*. NFER Routledge.

Reid, G. (1992). *Learning Difficulties and Learning Styles – Observational Criteria*. Paper presented at S. E. Learning Styles Center, 5th Annual Conference. November 1992. George Mason University, Virginia, USA.

Reid, G. (1994). Dyslexia and Metacognitive Assessment in Links II, Vol. 1, No. 2, pp. 38-43.

Schieman, M., Blasket, P and Ciner, E. B. (1990). Vison characteristics of individuals identified as Irlen filer candidates. Journal of the American Optometric Association, 61, 600-605.

Singleton, C. H. (1990). *Software Developments in Cognitive Assessment and Remediation.* Paper delivered to the British Dyslexia Association Conference 'Advances in Computer Applications for Dyslexics', University of Hull.

Singleton, C. H. (1992). *The Use of Computers in the Early Identification of Dyslexia* Paper presented at Fourth Cambridge Conference, Helen Arkell Dyslexia Centre, April 1992.

Singleton, C. H. (1993). *Early identification of Specific Learning Difficulties.* Paper presented at Specific Learning Difficulties conference, Moray House, Edinburgh, June 1993.

Singleton, C. H. (1995) Computerised screening for dyslexia. Paper presented at Helen Arkell Dyslexia Centre, 5th Cambridge conference, April 1995.

Stanley, G. (1994). Visual deficit models of dyslexia in Hales, G. (Ed.) *Dyslexia Matters.* London. Whurr Publishers.

Stanovich, K. E. (1985). 'Explaining the variance in reading ability in terms of psychological processes: What have we learned?' *Annals of Dyslexia* 35:67-95.

Stanovich, K. E. (1988a). 'Explaining the differences between the dyslexic and the garden-variety poor reader: the phonological-core variable-differentiation model'. *Journal of Learning Disabilities* 21, 590-612.

Stanovich, K. E. (1991). 'Discrepancy definitions of reading disability: has intelligence led us astray?' *Reading Research Quarterly*, XXVI, 1, 7-29.

Stanovich, K. E. and Siegal, L. S. (1994). Phenotypic performance profile of children with reading disabilities: a regression-based test of the phonological-core variable-difference model in Journal of Educational Psychology, Vol. 86, No. 1, 24-53.

Stein, J. F. (1991). 'Vision of Language', in Snowling, M. and Thomson, M. (Eds.), *Dyslexia: Integrating Theory and Practice.* London. Whurr Publishers.

Stein, J. F and Fowler, S. (1982). 'Diagnosis of dyslexia by means of a new indication of eye dominance'. *British Journal of Opthalmology,* 66, 332-236.

Stein, J. F. and Fowler, S. (1985). 'Effect of monocular occlusion on visuomotor perception and reading in dyslexic children' *Lancet,* 13/7/85.

Stein, J. F. and Fowler, S. (1993). 'Unstable binocular control in dyslexic children'. *Journal of Research in Reading,* 16 (1), 30-45.

Stone, J. and Harris, K. (1991). 'These coloured spectacles: what are they for?' *Support to Learning,* vol. 6, no. 3 (1991).

Turner, M. (1994). quantifying exceptionality: issues in the psychological assessment of dyslexia in Hales, G. (Ed.) *Dyslexia Matters.* London. Whurr Publishers.

Wilkins, A .(1990). *Visual Discomfort and Reading.* MRC, APU Cambridge.

Wilkins, A. (1993). *Institute Overlays.* IOO Marketing Ltd., 56-62 Newington Causeway, London SE1 6DS.

Wright, A. (1993). *IRLEN – The Never Ending Story.* Paper presented at the 5th European Conference of Neuro-Developmental Delay in Children with Specific Learning Difficulties, London.

PRINCIPLES OF ASSESSMENT

GORDON BOOTH

THE PURPOSE OF ASSESSMENT

The importance of skilled assessment of any pupil's progress is fully acknowledged today, although in the past, practice in the classroom has often failed to live up to precept. If careful assessment is judged essential for the average school pupil, it is even more crucial in the case of a pupil with specific learning difficulties, whose problems are still frequently misunderstood and are all too often attributed to 'laziness' or 'lack of ability'.

Teachers taking part in a diploma course for the education of pupils with specific learning difficulties volunteered the following reasons for carrying out assessment:

- To diagnose learning difficulties;
- to check on progress;
- to provide feedback to the student(s) themselves;
- to assist with record keeping;
- to explore the pupil's thinking and learning strategies;
- to discover the student's strengths and weaknesses;
- to establish baselines for an intervention programme;
- to monitor the success of a particular programme;
- to enable a report to be written.

These are all valid and important reasons for carrying out assessment and others might well be added. Nevertheless, it is not uncommon for extensive testing to be carried out without the teacher having any very clear purpose in mind – perhaps in the hope that by using a barrage of tests, something of value will emerge to throw light on the nature of the problem and the scale of the task ahead. All assessment should be founded upon a systematic and thoughtful approach, bearing in mind that:

- Each element in a battery of tests should be presented with a specific purpose in mind;

- over-testing is time-wasting;
- testing should be economical and efficient, providing the maximum amount of information in the minimum of time;
- testing should be a positive, enlightening experience for the student and teacher alike;
- the qualitative information elicited may ultimately prove more significant than the quantitative data (the test scores);
- successful assessment depends on an effective relationship between teacher and student;
- assessment should always be used to generate hypotheses.

Assessment is an on-going process which forms an integral part of an educational cycle that will be familiar to most teachers but which is worth re-emphasising schematically.

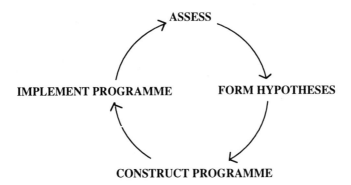

THE RELATIONSHIP

Where on-going assessment forms part of the familiar routine between teacher and pupil, it will be incorporated naturally within the framework of the lesson; and the pupil, just as much as the teacher, should find it a rewarding and illuminating experience. The older student should be helped to understand what the numerical scores mean and be enabled to gauge the degree of progress made, but even the younger child will understand progress made in terms of 'number right this time' by comparison with a previous occasion.

When assessment is being carried out for the first time, possibly in unfamiliar surroundings, care must be taken to establish a friendly, easy relationship. Whatever the age of the pupil or student, he or she should have some understanding of the reason for the testing and should have an opportunity to chat beforehand. Talking about home, family, personal preferences and interests not only helps to place a child at ease but may also provide important information.

Take brief notes unobtrusively, but not covertly, and with a first-time assessment, always double-check basic information such as name, age and address. It is very worthwhile offering a child or young person scope for free drawing in the course of an assessment but, unless time is unlimited, it is generally advisable to tackle much of the more difficult testing first. Obviously, it is important to be aware of fatigue setting in and this forms part of the task of monitoring the child's reaction generally: is there a pattern, for example, of 'high energy, low efficiency' or is the student's output well-paced and methodical?

Indeed, the 'first five minutes' are a vital stage of any new assessment, shedding light on the student's characteristic personality attributes, social attitudes and individual style of approach: whether he is, for example, predominantly outgoing or withdrawn, attentive or distractable, good-humoured or irritable, interested or apathetic, systematic or disorganised in his general approach. At the same time, this information may only be fully obtained once the pupil has settled and established a relationship with the tester.

ATTAINMENT TESTING

Testing is a standardised procedure and every effort should be made to adopt a uniform approach, following the instructions provided in the test manual and, so far as possible, knowing these sufficiently thoroughly to avoid having to refer to them during the test administration. It is obvious that one should ensure the best possible conditions, with a minimum of noise or distraction, and it is important not to feel under pressure of time. On the other hand, there is a tendency for inexperienced teachers to adopt an unduly slow style of testing and this does not encourage interest or high-level attention on the child's part. Despite the need to follow test instructions carefully, it is vital that teachers should be able to exercise their own judgement as to how far to prolong testing or when to intervene and offer a change of activity.

Regardless of the type of test form provided for a specific test, a teacher should establish a systematic personal style of approach to note-taking during testing, remembering that scores form only a small part of the data provided by the child in making his sequence of responses. Pay close attention to – and make a record of – such potentially important details as:

- Varying levels of confidence;
- changes in pace or fluency;
- fluctuations in persistence and motivation;
- indications of altering emotional attitude;
- flexibility of approach and capacity to adopt alternative strategies.

CHOOSING THE RIGHT TESTS

Use tests that are reasonably up-to-date, are well standardised and have proven reliability (implying that the same pattern of results would emerge if the test was repeated) and validity, which indicates that the test contents are appropriate and consistent with the aims of the test. Test manuals should always give clear information about the date of standardisation, the population sample used and technical data concerning reliability and standard error of measurement. Where test norms are provided in the form of reading ages alone, teachers should be aware of the limitations of these and should have some familiarity with alternatives, such as standard scores or centiles.

The range of tests given should, in part, be determined by the stated reasons for referral: i.e. the child's difficulties as perceived by class teacher or parent. However, a child may well have problems in areas of work not mentioned in the referral. For example, because the specific learning difficulties pupil essentially has weaknesses in processing auditory or visual data, computation skills are almost certain to be affected, although this may be obscured by good understanding of number concepts.

Reading should be assessed on more than one dimension: it is important to look at a child's capacity to deal with continuous text and a test such as the **Revised Neale Analysis of Reading** is invaluable in providing separate scores for accuracy, comprehension and speed – but, like any test, it has its limitations and is not particularly suited to the needs of very young or secondary age pupils. A word recognition test (e.g. the Revised Burt) could complement a test of continuous reading and observations made whilst the child reads the passages in the test. Either type of test will afford a great deal more information than simply a set of right and wrong scores: not only will you want to establish generally whether a child:

- Uses a whole word or phonic approach;
- has ability to segment words into syllables;
- shows evidence of useful predictive strategies;

- has a grasp of vowel and consonant digraphs;
- has eye movement problems;

but close analysis of each individual response (especially the incorrect ones) will build up a picture of how the child understands the reading task, what particular tactics are available and not available to him, and which faulty procedures are characteristic of his approach. It is through this analytic technique that one begins to form hypotheses about a child's way of working.

From now on, the tasks for the teacher are to establish where to begin afresh the learning process for the individual pupil and what the key elements of the teaching approach are to be. Neither should ever be a matter of guess-work or random choice but should always emerge from the observed data elicited from the child or student in the course of the assessment, and subsequently organised by the teacher into a meaningful pattern. Scores provide one kind of baseline but qualitative analysis of how the pupil is actually operating or thinking provides the key to the development of a logical and effective teaching programme which aims to build on the child's demonstrated strengths and works to mitigate his weaker abilities.

Both spelling and basic number tests should be given the same detailed error analysis: indeed, the identification of simple operational errors in arithmetic affords the best starting point for a teacher to discover the power of this approach to elucidate what a child knows and does not know, how he thinks, and how he utilises the skills he possesses. With older pupils (or adults) this detective work becomes a real partnership – a mutual voyage of discovery for teacher and student – and should form part of the continuous assessment process which is integral to the interaction of teacher and pupil in any learning situation. Children with specific learning difficulties have an especial contribution to make here and need to be encouraged to talk about how they perceive each learning task: how, for instance, they decipher words in the course of reading, which particular components of a word constitute spelling obstacles for them, or which elements of an arithmetical operation pose particular difficulty.

Written work needs to be a constant feature of the diagnostic interaction between teacher and pupil, always bearing in mind that handwriting output is certain to be slow, effortful and fatiguing for the pupil with specific learning difficulties. Assessment here begins with taking account of basic factors such as body posture, hand preference, pencil grasp and muscle tone; it moves on to scrutiny of letter and digit formation, the spacing between words and the general 'flow' of a child's handwriting. It hardly needs to be stressed that a sample of the student's free writing, no matter how elementary, is essential evidence for a first assessment. It needs the same care in analysis as the responses to formal testing and should always be preserved for future reference.

For younger and older pupils alike, opportunities for free drawing are important, both for relaxation and as a means of comparing executive skills in this area with the youngster's level of conceptual awareness. Detecting a 'mismatch' in this way, between technical skill and intellectual grasp, is fundamental to all diagnostic assessment of specific learning difficulties: it is often dramatically articulated by the pupil himself in a characteristic expression of frustration, 'I should be able to do this but I can't!'

RECORDING

Spoken words are ephemeral and therefore systematic record-keeping is vital, not just at the initial assessment stage but in the course of all interactive teaching which incorporates continuous assessment. Tape-recording has a certain value for later analysis, and also for preserving evidence of a pupil's speed and fluency in reading, but it can be intrusive and should be used with economy and discretion. Effective, economical note-taking throughout a lesson or assessment is more generally useful and has the major advantage of capturing a record, not only of how the pupil has responded, but of one's own moment-to-moment insights, impressions and ideas. These can prove to be of immense usefulness later. You are, after all, aiming to discover which aspects of a child's performance are characteristic features – not just chance occurrences – and it is the recurring elements in the pattern of a child's response which are significant.

After the assessment, take time to review your notes and to sift out the relevant pieces of information. Write these up in a more coherent form, fleshing out your initial thoughts and making preliminary inferences. These will lead either to the formulation of a programme or to the compilation of a complete report for parent or teacher/colleague. In many instances, both will be necessary, to rely mainly on memory is guaranteed to ensure that major gaps in your overall picture will occur.

WRITING UP THE ASSESSMENT

This is an art in itself, to be successfully mastered only through practice. There are certain fundamentals of good report-writing which are self-evident, such as the need to set out test results clearly, adjacent always to the child's chronological age. State accurately the names of the tests and where appropriate, the particular version used. Interpretation of what the test scores imply should follow on logically from this setting out of the basic data and, ideally, your eventual conclusions should be seen to emerge quite inescapably from your interpretation of the evidence. Jargon should be avoided, since reports should be understandable by the intended audience and further explanation from the writer should be unnecessary.

PRE- AND POST-ASSESSMENT CONSULTANCY

Effective, accurate diagnosis depends on objective assessment carried out under the best possible conditions. This does not mean that assessment should be carried out in a vacuum without reference to the information available from teachers and parents, nor that the child's behaviour in the classroom is irrelevant.

Pre-assessment discussion with the class teacher (and possibly head teacher and parent also) will help to clarify or amplify those concerns which should already have been stated in writing. The only caveat is that one should take care to avoid being unduly influenced by strongly-held views that may be quite forcibly expressed in the context of informal conversation. For the same reason, classroom observation is generally best deferred until after the formal assessment is completed: at that point, it helps to illuminate facets of behaviour that cannot easily be judged in the individual setting, such as the child's social and educational interaction with other children, his ability to cope with classroom distraction or the degree to which he is capable of becoming truly 'engaged' in the range of different learning activities. In addition, there is, of course, the opportunity to form a general impression of the classroom's atmosphere and dynamics.

Consultation with teachers and parents following an assessment is essential, possibly at more than one stage. The written report is of fundamental importance, not only as a record of your findings and recommendations but also as a point of reference now and in the future, for all concerned. By itself, however, it is insufficient as a means of communication. Discussion is a two-way process and you will need to know whether the teacher and parent 'recognise' the picture of the child that you have given in your report. If they don't then you have almost certainly not succeeded in your task. Equally, you may wish to have further information on certain points, just as those to whom you are speaking will want you to elaborate on some of your findings and recommendations. 'Listening' on both sides is a basic element of communication and your own role is certainly not to present your report in monologue form!

Successful consultation at this stage will lay the ground effectively for future meetings to review progress and to reassess strategies. Initial discussions with parents are best kept as friendly and informal as possible, without being patronising: they help to establish the kind of trusting relationship that is essential if, in the context of larger multi-disciplinary meetings, true partnership between parents and teachers is to be achieved successfully.

CONCLUSION

Ultimately, your aim is to present a well-rounded and accurate picture of the child in his life-situation, with especial reference to his educational difficulties. This requires great care in the selection of those facts that are relevant and in ensuring that your conclusions actually derive from the evidence uncovered through your assessment. Above all, present your findings honestly, and distinguish fact from fiction and firm conclusions from legitimate but speculative hypotheses which require to be tested out through further exploration and the use of different teaching strategies. Assessment is – or should be – exciting and interesting: intuition and empathy are useful qualities for the teacher but piecing together the jigsaw demands, above all, self-discipline, concentration and a methodical approach.

REFERENCES

Neale, M. (1989). *Neale Analysis*. NFER, Nelson.

Burt, C. (1921). World Reading Test. Revised by Vernon, P. E. (1938-67) as Burt (Re-arranged Word Reading Test). Re-normed by Shearer, E. and Apps, R. (1975). London, Hodder & Stoughton.

FORMAL ASSESSMENT

ROSEMARY McGHEE

BACKGROUND

The learning support service in Grampian operates on an area team basis – a team of learning support teachers who cover a Secondary School and its associated primaries. The team implement a 'float' system which enables a learning support teacher within the team to develop an expertise in specific learning difficulties. It is therefore possible for such a specialist to assess pupils in all of the schools covered by the area teams and either to recommend a course of remedial action to a colleague or, if considered more appropriate, to work with an individual pupil or small groups of pupils in any of the area schools. This system is beneficial to pupils with a specific learning difficulty as continuity can be maintained across the P7-S1 transfer and beyond.

HANDLING REFERRALS

The teacher should, in the first instance, gather all the available information about the pupil. Initially, this will involve discussion with the referring teacher or parent to establish the areas of concern. Access to school reports and, in particular, learning support reports is vital. Well kept records may show a pattern of difficulty emerging before any formal assessment begins. For example, a history of late language development . . . involvement with Speech Therapy, letter reversals continuing long after the infant stages, and persistent problems with blending may all be factors which would contribute to a positive identification of a specific learning difficulty.

Diagnosis of a specific learning difficulty may be described as a 'diagnosis by exclusion', in that all other factors which could be the main cause of the child's difficulties must first be discounted. These factors include poor eyesight, poor hearing, and social and emotional problems. Much of this information (and any evidence of patchy or disturbed school career) will be available from records or should be sought from parents. Concerns about eyesight or hearing should be referred to the medical services. Recent tests should not be replicated unless it is anticipated that they will shed new light on the child's difficulties.

THE ASSESSMENT

Once the educational history and other background factors have been established, the grounds for referral should also be considered before tests which will provide a profile of the pupil's strengths and weaknesses are selected. Once other factors have been ruled out, the diagnosis of a specific learning difficulty, at its simplest, is made when there is a significant discrepancy between an individual's ability in non-verbal and/or oral tasks compared to their attainment in basic reading and writing skills.

In a young pupil, a discrepancy may be quite easy to identify but delayed development caused by a maturational lag may at this stage be the cause of the difficulty. A policy of 'wait and see' is often adopted. Many professionals are reluctant to make a definite diagnosis at the infant stages because classic signs of a specific learning difficulty, such as letter reversals, poor blending skills and difficulty with letter recognition are present in children who later prove not to have a specific learning difficulty.

It would do no harm, at this stage, to use teaching methods proven to work with children who have a specific learning difficulty even if a definite diagnosis has not yet been made. Early intervention has been shown to be more beneficial than later attempts, particularly if the children are spared the trauma of persistent failure. In older pupils, problems of making a clear diagnosis are exacerbated by various compensatory strategies having been adopted by the pupil to cope with or mask their inherent difficulties.

TEST AND TESTING

Tests which provide a Reading Age or Spelling Age when used with tests of ability, such as the British Picture Vocabulary Scale or Raven's Matrices, may indicate a discrepancy between basic literacy attainments and powers of reasoning and general oral ability. Although there is some doubt in relation to the reliability and validity of these tests, they may provide a useful guide to a pupil's ability. Tests should not be administered solely to provide a score but results should be qualitatively analysed to show skills which have been mastered and those which have not. The teacher should note the child's approach to tasks as well as their performance. A programme can be based, at least in part, on the test results.

STANDARDISED TESTS USED IN THE ASSESSMENT OF SPECIFIC LEARNING DIFFICULTY

The following list comprises a selection of some of the more commonly used Standardised Tests. They may be substituted by other tests, depending on their availability and suitability for the pupil involved.

TESTS	PURPOSE
Tests to establish ability level	
Crichton Vocabulary Scale	Measure Oral Linguistic Ability.
Raven's Matrices	Non-verbal test of ability.
Reading Tests	
Neale Analysis (Revised)	Reading in context. A Reading and Comprehension Age within an age range is provided.
MacMillan Reading Analysis	As above.
Word Reading Tests	
Burt	Provide a Reading Age but also an indication of the de-coding strategies which the pupil uses.
Spelling Tests	
Vernon	Provide a Spelling Age but also highlight
Schonell	specific phonic rules which have not yet been mastered.
Arithmetic Test	
Ballard Oral Arithmetic	An arithmetic test is part of the battery of tests which make up Intelligence Tests. Included here to form an overall picture of ability, simple sequencing ability and as a measure of mental agility.
Tests Designed to Diagnose Specific Learning Difficulties	
Bangor Dyslexia Test	Tests areas which researchers have found over the years to indicate a Specific Learning Difficulty. Provides little information which can be of use in planning a remedial programme but seven of the more positive indicators along with other evidence can help in the diagnosis of a Specific Learning Difficulty.

Aston Index
Attempts to provide a profile comparing ability with Reading Age and a profile of the areas of difficulty, i.e. auditory and visual but is poorly constructed and standardised. Recent research (Sutherland and Smith, 1991) has suggested that it is unwise to attempt to make a distinction between auditory and visual causes but that a lack of phonological awareness is more likely to be the root cause of a Specific Learning Difficulty. In practice, it is unlikely that the whole battery of tests would be administered but selected tests can be helpful in profiling strengths and weaknesses.

Form 2 of the MacMillan Reading Analyses can be used as a Listening Comprehension Test. The teacher reads the passage, the pupil is then asked comprehension questions based on the text. A significant difference between Listening Comprehension and Reading Comprehension combined with other indications such as auditory processing difficulties, which give rise to bizarre spelling, would more than likely lead to a diagnosis of a specific learning difficulty.

The Daniels and Diack battery of reading tests is useful in profiling reading difficulties particularly in very young children.

Reversals of letters and words in reading and writing, directional confusion and difficulty in copying written work may indicate mixed laterality. While not thought to be a contributory factor in causing a specific learning difficulty mixed laterality can cause confusions which can exacerbate the difficulty. The Laterality Test in the Aston Index can pinpoint whether mixed laterality is in fact present and steps can be taken to ameliorate the problems caused by the directional confusion.

A good working knowledge of a range of tests and a good understanding of the nature of the condition are essential in order to optimise the assessment process.

FEEDBACK OF RESULTS

The results of the assessment may be recorded in a report as well as being communicated through consultancy and discussions with teachers, school management and parents. Test results should be set out in a clear style which is easy to read at a glance. The report should refer to the test results and give specific examples, particularly where conclusions are being drawn about the nature of the difficulties the child is experiencing. Indications as to further testing required can be made at this stage. This may help to explore more precisely the nature of the specific learning difficulty or in some cases, to suggest that the child's problems are due to some other cause. For example, a motor learning difficulty may be at the root of the problem or perhaps a delay in language development due to frequent hearing loss at an early age may be the source of the difficulty. Whatever the conclusions drawn, recommendations should be made as to the next step.

There now follows an example of the profile of scores obtained after testing a Primary 7 pupil.

PROFILE OF SCORES

Name:	*Andrew*
Date of Birth:	*22/2/82*
Chronological Age at date of Assessment:	*10 years 8 months*
Assessment date:	*2/11/92*

Test results

Schonell Word Reading Test RA	*7.6 years*
Bangor Dyslexia Test	*7+*
Ballard Oral Arithmetic	*Addition 7 years 7 months*
	Subtraction 7 years 7 months

MacMillan New Reading Analysis
Form A used as a Listening Comprehension

Comprehension Age Equivalents	*10:2 to 11:11*
Crichton Vocabulary	*Percentile 10*
	(below average)

Previous test results

Schonell Spelling (8/9/92)	*7.8 years*	
MacMillan Individual Reading Analysis	*Accuracy*	*8.6 years*
	Comprehension	*8.9 years*

Further tests recommended
Raven's Matrices
Auditory Discrimination from the Aston Index

From the test results and from observation of Andrew's approach to the various tasks, it was possible to identify areas of strengths and weaknesses. The conclusions which can be drawn from the test results are that Andrew displays many of the characteristic signs of a specific learning difficulty and that his difficulties would appear to stem from an auditory processing problem. This was evident in his responses to the Crichton Vocabulary Scale. He did not know what 'squabble' meant and kept repeating 'squaggle' despite the target word being presented clearly on several occasions. He also said 'pull' for the meaning of 'brag' suggesting he had confused b/d (drag). The Raven's Matrices were recommended to check on Andrew's non-verbal ability since the results of the Crichton Vocabulary Test do not reflect his general ability level. Since an auditory difficulty seemed to be at the root of his problems, an Auditory Discrimination Test was also recommended. Andrew's score on the Listening Comprehension Test is in the age range equivalent to his chronological age. There is, however, a marked discrepancy between his scores for Reading Comprehension and Listening Comprehension, and understanding of written material is obviously hampered by his reading difficulty. The Bangor Dyslexia Test revealed significant difficulties in sequencing especially months of the year and multiplication tables. Andrew had some difficulty with pronunciation of multi-syllabics but was able to say two of them accurately and with ease. The spelling test did not reveal any 'bizarre' spellings but would suggest that there is little visual memory for words. This may mean that with Andrew's auditory discrimination difficulties, kinaesthetic methods will need to be adopted in order that success may be achieved quickly in the initial stages of a remedial programme. The word reading test highlighted Andrew's difficulty in segmenting words into manageable chunks. Instruction in how to do this successfully will also have to form part of the remedial programme. A small piece of free writing highlighted Andrew's severe literacy difficulties. He appears to have adopted strategies which allow him to operate reasonably successfully in the primary classroom. The main concern is that he may not cope as well in the secondary situation with a resultant loss of confidence and self-esteem.

Piece of free writing for assessment purposes.

Sample of writing by the same pupil from a piece of classwork

> We sow lots of raddits and deaures foxs and lots of uter animals me and kirsty ynslu rest a heid of the curl and see how coud get to that tree then to that thig then to the top of the hill. I waing, I sow Topshs gett out of a cart and the hid on house yack they hid round the cornir. I told kirsty to go and get the culih driver we sow from the top of the hill. I slid down the hill the men were armd with a whip and a n stick then wer damunding munay from fafher. I got uston in my catptlt meud from u forgt sap twig and senps gats it hit the man in the arin I thinek It discolklhd his hand. I pout anuthy ston in my catilplt it hit him in the arin dofof the men droft there wepnus my muthuv hit one of the men over the head with wone of the poms hafe foll of poris the mam was corord n poris. kirsty was dack with the cutil driver he seud you neadid help with to tinckers if lont blick you didnt nead my help after all.

RECOMMENDED PROGRAMME AND TEACHING MATERIALS

Experts in the field of specific learning difficulty have long recommended multi-sensory approaches to the teaching of children displaying the characteristic signs. The main aim must always be to allow the pupil to achieve success as soon as possible in order that the sense of failure compounded over a period to time can begin to be eroded. In Andrew's case, his strength is more likely to be in using visual methods and this should therefore be the starting point. The Charles Cripps 'Hand for Spelling' series combines a handwriting programme with the Look – Cover – Write – Check method of teaching spelling. Drawings on the pages help to jog the memory for specific letter patterns. Blank masters can be used to adapt the method to meet the pupil's needs more precisely. Pupils can make their own mnemonic sentences to aid the memory for particular letter strings.

The vocabulary can be geared to the ability and interest level of the pupil. The kinaesthetic link is added by tracing the word before writing it from memory. There are many computer programmes such as Starspell Plus and Spelltime which have adapted the Look – Cover – Write – Check routine into computer games. They are highly visual and add some variety to the teaching routine. Reading and spelling errors may pin-point the phonic rules which have not yet been mastered. There are many phonics programmes available and an experienced teacher will be able to select the most appropriate one for the age and ability level of the pupil. The Alpha to Omega programme is highly structured and sequential. It need not be followed rigidly but cana be adapted for the pupil's individual needs. Phonic rules are explained, and words are grouped according to letter patterns. Sentences are built up using the phonic rules already mastered and suggestions for games are provided. This is a useful resource for the teacher. Activity Packs have recently been introduced which provide exercises and activities which run in parallel with the text book. The sentences for dictation are useful and it is recommended that the writing of words and sentences has beneficial effects on reading.

The Simultaneous Oral Spelling (SOS) techniques advocated by Gillingham and Stillman can be used as the pupil repeats the dictated words and writes them down. Pupils with auditory processing difficulties must be encouraged to voice the target words. Awareness of the phonology of words makes the detection of phonemes, particularly in consonant blends and terminal sounds, much less of a lottery for the pupil with this kind of difficulty. The Letterland scheme is particularly useful with young pupils in the infant and middle stages. It provides a truly multi-sensory environment in which to learn phonics. Older pupils also enjoy the stories which accompany the phonic rules. It is easier for them if they have started off in the Letterland environment. The 'Reading Direction' is emphasised throughout, thus reducing directional confusion. Rhymes accompany the formation of letters and alongside this, the character specific to each letter can avoid confusion between similar graphemes like b and d, p and q and m and w. Further recommendations in Andrew's case are to improve his segmenting and blending skills, beginning with compound words such as wind-mill, progressing to two syllable words such as pillow and then isolating or blending phonemes in a one syllable word. Segmenting and blending can progress in tandem. Some work on sequences would also be beneficial. Mastery of areas which have had repeated failure in the past increases confidence, and sequences such as the alphabet allow participation in an increased number of activities. For example, using a dictionary, using an index in a book and looking up the telephone directory.

A degree of repeated learning will be necessary and the teacher must be resourceful in applying different methodology in new and interesting formats to keep the pupil's interest until the sequence has been mastered. Around 3 x 20 minute sessions per week will be required to implement this programme. It is often the recognition of the difficulty and the administration of appropriate measures to ameliorate it that proves to be a turning point in the pupil's attitude and consequently this is reflected in their work.

TRANSFER TO SECONDARY

Consultation with Andrew's parents, guidance teacher and class teachers will be essential to smooth his transfer. Observation and recording of Andrew's behaviour in class will highlight how he is coping in the initial stages. In consultation with the above group of people, it may be felt that a period of withdrawal for small group or individual support may be beneficial to support his subject work, help him to organise homework and respond to subject assessments by alternative means. For example, taped essays and responses to tests rather than written.

INFORMAL ASSESSMENT

The majority of pupils referred to learning support teachers for assessment are likely to be unfamiliar to them. Formal assessment is a way of providing a profile of a pupil's difficulties using a limited amount of time effectively.

Teachers with a good background knowledge of specific learning difficulties may be able to carry out much of their assessment on an informal basis. Keeping careful record of reading and writing behaviours can give valuable information about the nature of the difficulties being experienced by the pupils and enable the teacher to respond more precisely to the needs of the pupil.

Records also help to provide an analysis or appraisal of the effectiveness of the various strategies adopted.

CONCLUSION

Assessment in practice utilises, to a great extent, skills in diplomacy and communication. Understandably, parents in particular are anxious to seek an explanation for their child's inability to progress as they had hoped. Some are relieved to find that there is no constitutional cause for their child's problems, others are even more anxious if no precise cause can be found.

Pupils also can exhibit symptoms of anxiety if they feel they may have a specific learning difficulty and this aspect must be carefully considered. Teachers clearly need help in identifying, assessing and planning programmes for pupils with specific learning difficulties. Consultancy, observation or informal assessment will also have a role to play.

It is important to follow up and monitor the pupil's progress. Assessment, therefore, is not a 'one-off' analysis of a pupil's progress, but an enduring and inherent component of learning which can help facilitate effective access to the curriculum for children with specific learning difficulties.

REFERENCES

Ballard Oral Arithmetic – Norms (P. E. Vernon, Scottish Ed. Journal 9.2.40).

Burt, C. (1921). *Word Reading Test*. Revised by Vernon, P. E. (1938-67) as Burt (Re-arranged Word Reading Test). Re-normed by Shearer, E. and Apps, R. (1975). London, Hodder & Stoughton.

Cripps, C. (1992). *A Hand for Spelling*. Cambridge Institute of Education.

Fisher Marriott, *Starspell Plus-*.

Hornsby, B. and Pool, J. (1989). *Alpha to Omega Activity Packs*, Stages 1, 2 and 3. Heinemann Educational.

Key Software, *Spelltime*.

Miles, T. R. (1983a). *The Bangor Dyslexia Test*. Cambridge, Learning Development Aids.

Neale, M. (1989). *Neale Analysis of Reading Ability*. NFER, Nelson.

Newton, M. J. and Thomson, M. E. (1982). *Aston Index LDA*.

Sutherland, M. J., Smith, C. D. (1991). *Assessing Literacy Problems in Mainstream Schooling: A Critique of Three Literacy Screening Tests* – Educational Review, Vol. 43, No. 1.

Raven, J. C. (1993). *Raven's Progressive Matrices and Crichton Vocabulary Scale*. Oxford Psychologists Press.

Vincent, D. and de la Mare, M. (1987). *New MacMillan Reading Analysis*. NFER-Nelson.

Wendon, L.(1985 and 1987). *Letterland Teaching Programme 1 and 2*. Cambridge, Letterland Ltd.

Xavier Educational, *Bangor Hi Spell*.

DISCREPANCY DEFINITIONS
OR
PHONOLOGICAL ASSESSMENT?

REA REASON and
NORAH FREDERICKSON

INTRODUCTION

This chapter considers approaches to the identification and assessment of children with specific learning difficulties. Some of the problems with the commonly used IQ/achievement discrepancy definitions of specific learning difficulties are first discussed. Alternative discrepancy measures based on 'spiky' subtest profiles, performance differences across the curriculum and differences between listening and reading comprehension are also reviewed. Arguments are then advanced for focusing assessment on the phonological difficulties which recent research has implicated in a high proportion of children making slow progress in learning to read. A theoretical causal model of the mechanisms thought to be involved is presented and an assessment battery developed from the model is described. Finally, implications for educational practice are suggested and illustrated through the presentation of an individual case example.

THE NOTION OF DISCREPANCY

A survey conducted by the Division of Educational and Child Psychology of the British Psychological Society reported that 78 per cent of the 882 educational psychologists responding identified specific learning difficulties by assessing discrepancies between abilities and attainments in some form (Pumfrey and Reason, 1991). Although this often involved the use of psychometric test results, there were alternatives that focused on particular aspects of learning, such as discrepancies between well developed use of context and poorly developed recognition of print in the acquisition of literacy. The responses reflected an agreement that the very word 'specific' in specific learning difficulties implied some kind of discrepancy. Children's problems with literacy learning and associated competencies were considered 'unexpected' in comparison with their progress in other areas of learning.

For the purposes of administrative-decision making, attempts have been made to quantify these 'unexpected' discrepancies between literacy achievements and other attainments concerned with conceptual understanding. Psychometric measures have commonly provided the basis for such judgments, i.e. the child's IQ has been used to predict the expected score on a reading test. The difference between the expected score and the child's actual reading score has then been calculated in order to work out how 'unusual' the size of the discrepancy is in relation to test standardisation data. The procedure is outlined by McNab (1994).

Some, including the general public, have had in mind 'bright' children who have made unexpectedly poor progress in acquiring basic literacy skills. Such views are open to accusations of 'elitism'. Consider a hypothetical example of three children aged 10 years. All three have 'reading ages' of about 6 years, but one of them has a 'mental age' of 12 years, the second a 'mental age' of 10 years and the third child a 'mental age' of 8 years. It might now be argued that the child with the highest 'mental age' is the one with the most marked specific learning difficulties and the most pressing claims for additional help. But do not all three children have a need to read and write? And do not all three have the capacity to take advantage of these activities? And can they not all have specific difficulties with the printed word?

Whether any of the children described above, or all three of them, are labelled as having specific learning difficulties depends on society's values and priorities, and on whether that label is required in order to access additional and appropriate help with literacy. These are administrative decisions and ought not to be confused with the purposes of psychological research or educational practice.

As argued by McNab (1994), deciding that a child's specific difficulties are unusually discrepant from his or her ability is quite separate from any diagnosis of specific learning difficulties. The decision is being used as a criterion of eligibility for provision. Consequently, a statistic, rather than observations of particular identifying characteristics, becomes the deciding factor. And we can manipulate that statistic at will. In USA, for example, Frankenberger and Fronzaglio (1991) have found huge variations in incidence depending on the size of the discrepancy required by individual states (i.e. one or two standard deviations). In the context of the Code of Practice on the Identification and Assessment and of Special Educational Needs (DFE, 1994), similar trends are now much in evidence in England and Wales.

The logic of these IQ-achievement discrepancy definitions assumes that individuals with low IQ scores should, of necessity, be poor readers (Siegel, 1989,

1992; Stanovich, 1991). But, children with low IQs who are good readers have demonstrated that this is not the case (Siegel, 1988, 1992). Although IQ and literacy progress are related (Torgensen, 1986), low IQ is not a sufficient cause of poor reading.

A number of studies have investigated differences between children with IQ-achievement discrepancies (dyslexics) and those with poor reading skills but no discrepancy (garden variety) on reading and spelling skills and on cognitive skills related to reading. The research has resulted in a considerable body of evidence, from many countries and with children of different ages, which supports the conclusion that children with reading difficulties of different IQ levels perform similarly on a variety of reading and spelling measures (Friedman and Stephenson, 1988; Siegel, 1988; Rack, 1989; Seidenberg *et al.*, 1985; Share *et al.*, 1987; Felton and Wood, 1992).

According to Stanovich (1991, 1994), discrepancy definitions involving intelligence or ability tests have led researchers and practitioners badly astray. His arguments are particularly pertinent at a time when other researchers, interested in exceptional abilities, have emphasised the multifaceted nature of those abilities and their strong dependence on both environmental and motivational factors (Howe, 1988). The concept of 'potential' and the related concept of 'under-achievement' raise questions about the very nature of the measures used.

ALTERNATIVE MEASURES OF DISCREPANCY

Chronological age vs reading age

Would discrepancies reflecting a contrast between chronological age and reading age (or cut-offs based on percentile rank) be fairer and more 'transparent' than IQ/achievement discrepancies? Unfortunately, there are serious drawbacks relating to test theory and test construction. In the first place, such measures do not take account of the variance of reading scores which increases with age. Secondly, the size of the discrepancy is dependent on the particular test used. Gregory and Gregory (1994), for example, report a study where the Revised Neale Analysis of Reading Ability consistently gave reading ages about nine months below those obtained on the British Ability Scales Word Reading Test. As the two tests did not give comparable results, valid criteria for quantifying the extent of pupils' literacy needs remained elusive. Furthermore, as illustrated by this research, reading is not one unitary process and different tests have been designed for different purposes. This leaves the seeker of measurable discrepancies with the uncomfortable task of deciding which, if any, test to use. Finally, such an approach would group together children whose reading had a whole range of different causes (e.g. poor attendance, intermittent hearing loss, emotional problems, ineffective teaching, weak visual memory, poor phonological skills) rather than those with a particular specific difficulty.

'Spiky' sub-test profiles on tests of ability

Cognitive tests of ability (e.g. the Wechsler Intelligence Scale for Children or the British Ability Scales) have linked the notion of the 'unexpected' to lower scores on particular sub-tests. Discrepancies between sub-test scores have been considered indicative of specific learning difficulties. Elliott and Tyler (1987) have coined the phrase 'spiky profiles' to describe how children with literacy difficulties may obtain depressed scores on some of the sub-scales in the British Ability Scales. The main focus of their work has been to show how different combinations of 'spiky profiles', i.e. different patterns of sub-scale scores, may be indicative of subgroups of dyslexia. This contrasts with the search for a more unitary source of dyslexia.

On the Wechsler Intelligence Scale for Children, low scores on the sub-tests involving arithmetic, information, coding and digit span (the ACID profile) has been considered indicative of specific learning difficulties by *some* practitioners. The evidence for this 'profile' is by no means clear-cut (Kaufman, 1994: Cooper, 1995). A difficulty with statistical techniques that search for factors or clusters in a collection of sub-tests is that the results depend on what variables (sub-tests) have been included in the calculation in the first place. As tests of intelligence or ability are not based on a model of literacy learning, inferences are being made in retrospect about hypothetical cognitive processes which might or might not explain reading difficulties. It would seem obvious that if we are to examine cognitive processes underpinning literacy learning, the measures must have a convincing theoretical foundation, grounded in our knowledge of how children learn to read. The model developed by Frith (1995) provides such a starting point and will be discussed in more detail later in this chapter.

Cross-curricular discrepancies

Another common alternative discrepancy definition involves the use of discrepancies between attainment in different curriculum areas. The idea that children with specific literacy difficulties should not have problems in other subjects, and most particularly not in arithmetic, is a common one. Some studies support this: for example, Silva, MacGee and Williams (1985) found that poor readers and dyslexics did not differ on reading and language measures but the poor readers had lower arithmetics and motor scores than the dyslexics. Yet Siegel and Linder (1984) report that it is relatively difficult to find reading disabled children who do not have problems with arithmetic and Siegel (1990) points out that most individuals with reading problems also have difficulties with computational arithmetic, which involves short term memory, symbolic processing, attention and concentration.

Listening vs reading comprehension

In identifying those children who have specific problems with deciphering the printed text, Stanovich (1991) suggests that measures of intelligence might be replaced by measures of listening comprehension which can then be contrasted with measures of decoding skills. He acknowledges that his is another kind of discrepancy definition but, at least, listening comprehension would have greater face validity in being closely related to the purposes of reading and writing.

Among the groups included by Fletcher *et al.* (1994) was one defined by a discrepancy between listening comprehension and reading comprehension. They found that, compared to groups produced by IQ-achievement discrepancy approaches (children who met the criteria for both the IQ regression and standard score discrepancy methods) the listening comprehension discrepancy method produced a low achievement (non-SpLD) group with more severe language and other cognitive impairments. The definition then worked somewhat, as Stanovich (1986) predicted, with the low achievement group being more like a garden variety group than the low achievement group produced by definitions using IQ-based discrepancies. However, the differences were still small. They acknowledge difficulties with the measure of listening comprehension which they used. Listening comprehension was measured by having the child listen to passages from the Formal Reading Inventory and answer comprehension questions; reading comprehension was measured from the Formal Reading Inventory by having the child read passages silently (equivalent to, but different from, those used for listening comprehension) and answer questions. Although the Formal Reading Inventory is not normed for listening comprehension, because it has four passages of comparable difficulty, it was used for this analysis by creating standardised scores based on the performance of 33 normal children on both. This measure was used because listening comprehension measures with a national standardisation and comparable reading comprehension measures were not available.

Stanovich (1991) points to promising work in progress on listening comprehension which includes that by Aaron (1991); Carlisle (1989); Hoover and Gough (1990); Royer, Sinatra and Schumer (1990); Spring and French (1990). In Britain also, promising work is in progress (Bedford-Feuell, Geiger, Moyse and Turner, 1995; see also Chapter 10 in this volume) which takes account of Siegel's criticism (1989) that currently available reading comprehension tests do not actually measure the ability to read connected text. Rather, she argues that they measure vocabulary, background knowledge, reading speed, and test–taking strategies. Therefore, Siegel holds that reading comprehension measures as they currently exist cannot be appropriately used as measures of reading disability.

Stanovich (1991) also discusses a number of constraints which apply to discrepancies from listening comprehension as well as IQ. There is likely to be under-identification of children with hearing problems or who are unfamiliar with standard English. A further constraint which Stanovich points out, which would affect all aptitude/achievement discrepancy approaches, is the finding that reading itself is a moderately powerful determinant of vocabulary growth, verbal intelligence and general comprehension (Cunningham and Stanovich, 1990). He argues that any discrepancy based conceptualisation is likely to require considerable refinement based on how the act of reading alters the course of development, bringing education related cognitive skills more into line with age.

So the dilemma remains. First, it is possible to have difficulties with both the extraction of meaning from the text and the deciphering of the printed word. Secondly, measures of listening comprehension would have to accommodate the needs of those children whose mother tongue is different from the language of instruction (Cline and Reason, 1993). Thirdly, difficulties with phonological working memory associated with specific learning difficulties may also interfere with tasks involving listening comprehension (e.g. Shankweiler and Crain, 1986). In the light of present knowledge, clear and defensible operational definitions based on discrepancies remain elusive.

THE PHONOLOGICAL CORE VARIABLE

Defining literacy problems in terms of the 'unexpected' tells nothing about the actual nature of those problems. It is a default statement illustrated by the many variations on this theme, first introduced by the World Federation of Neurology in 1968. What is needed is a coherent theoretical basis which allows the formulation of a positive, inclusive definition, rather than a negative, exclusionary one based on children's intelligence or socio-cultural background. One such opportunity is offered by the vast body of research focusing on phonological processes involved in literacy and literacy learning.

First of all, we need to note again that phonological processing difficulties can account for poor progress, independent of IQ. A review of previous studies has led Fletcher (1992) to conclude that there are scarcely any differences in cognitive skills related to reading between children meeting discrepancy as opposed to low achievement definitions. Similar arguments have been presented by Siegel (1992) and Fletcher *et al.* (1994). Stanovich (1988) has suggested that a key to the reading disability experienced by many children is a problem with phonological processing which makes the learning of grapheme-phoneme correspondences very difficult. A wide range of studies provide convincing evidence of the relationship between phonological processing and reading skills:

- Correlational studies have highlighted the association between phonological processing and reading progress in the primary school (Stanovich, Cunningham and Freeman, 1984; Stanovich, Nathan and Vala-Rossi, 1986).
- Longitudinal studies have linked pre-readers' phonological skills with their later acquisition of reading (Bradley and Bryant, 1983; Torgensen, Wagner and Rashotte, 1994).
- Early intervention studies have shown that phonological skills training facilitates the acquisition of reading skills (Blachman, Ball, Black and Tangel, 1994; Cunningham, 1990).
- The inclusion of phonological skills training as part of a comprehensive literacy programme has enhanced the progress of children with reading difficulties (Hatcher, Hulme and Ellis, 1994; Iversen and Tunmer, 1993).

A definition of phonological awareness

Phonological awareness can be defined as sensitivity to sound in spoken language (Gallagher, 1995). Differences have been demonstrated between children who learn to read easily and those who don't. One of the earlier studies (Byrne and Shea, 1979) provides a particularly clear illustration. The study compared children with reading difficulties with those who had made normal progress. All were asked to listen to lists of words being read out to them (so they did not have to read anything themselves) and signal whenever they heard a word which they thought had previously appeared in the list. Overall, both groups were equally accurate in detecting words that had been mentioned previously. But there was an important difference in the errors that they made when they mistakenly thought that they had heard the word previously. The errors or 'false alarms' of the normal readers indicated that they tended to think that they had heard words which **sounded** like the word they had just heard. For example, when they heard the word *fair*, and the word *chair* had appeared in the list previously, they might signal that they had already heard it. In contrast, those identified as having reading difficulties tended to make false alarms in response to words with similar associations or **meanings** to those that they had heard previously. For example, they might signal that they had heard the word *table* when, in fact, the earlier word in the list had been *chair*. They thought of furniture such as *chair/table* rather than rhyme such as *chair/fair/pair*.

Many later studies involving more refined research designs have led to the conclusion that those children who have difficulty with rhyme and alliteration at nursery age later tend to have difficulties with learning to read (Goswami & Bryant, 1990). While this work suggests that proficiency with rhyme and alliteration do not simply develop as a consequence of learning to read and write but are, to some extent, precursors of literacy development, there is also evidence for subtle interaction so that the relationship between phonological awareness and literacy skills is best viewed as a reciprocal one, in which early phonological skill and reading and spelling interact and facilitate each other (Cataldo and Ellis, 1988). Hence, appreciation of rhyme usually occurs prior to formal teaching while attention to the beginnings of words as in 'I spy' games follows more direct teaching (Stanovich, 1994).

Causal modelling

The convincing evidence supporting a phonological 'core variable' in literacy learning and literacy difficulties has led to a causal model described by Frith (1995). The model provides a conceptual framework for considering the impact of phonological processing. It is shown in Figure 1 and is based on the following assumptions:

- Phonological processing competencies are relatively enduring.
- Individuals differ in their development of these competencies.
- Phonological competence is distinct from general cognitive ability.

The model has three levels of explanation: the biological, the cognitive and the behavioural. It also recognises the importance of environmental influences at all three levels. The following are the key points:

- Direct observation can be made at the behavioural level. We can observe how the learner responds to particular assessments and tasks. But, as shown by the model, phonological tests reflect not only phonological ability but are also influenced by other factors.

- At the cognitive level, strengths and weaknesses are inferred from the child's performance at the behavioural level. We must remember,

Figure 1: A Theoretical Causal Model (from Frith, 1995)

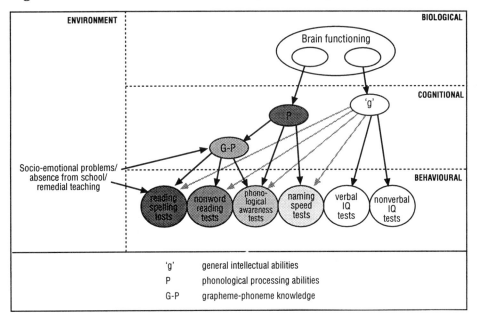

however, that both phonological processing ability and general intellectual ability are hypothetical constructs. They cannot be directly observed but are inferred from the observed behavioural information.

• The biological level involves observations about brain functioning. Influences can be genetic or environmental. In Frith's model, it is assumed that phonological processing difficulties originate at the biological level and that this is likely to have a genetic origin.

The arrows in Figure 1 move from the biological level to 'P' (phonology) at the cognitive level and then to particular tasks assumed to measure 'P' at the behavioural level. General intellectual abilities, 'g', is shown in the model as a separate cognitive component although, as mentioned earlier, it exerts at least some influence on all measures at the behavioural level. Also, as mentioned earlier, environmental variables play an important part. The notation 'G-P' (grapheme-phoneme knowledge) at the cognitive level, combines the influences of teaching and other learning opportunities with the influence of inherent phonological competence ('P').

THE PHONOLOGICAL ASSESSMENT BATTERY (PhAB): RESEARCH VERSION

Based on the Frith model, we can now start to devise tests which tap 'P' at the behavioural level. This was indeed the purpose of an invited research seminar group of practising educational psychologists, educational psychology trainers and leading academics who met at University College London from 1992 to 1994. The collection of papers in Educational and Child Psychology, Volume 12, Number 1, 1995 describes the outcome of their research work. A research version of the resulting Phonological Assessment Battery (PhAB) is also now available (Frederickson, 1995).

Following preliminary pilots of a range of tasks that had been used by researchers in this field, we decided to focus on the initial development and standardisation of five measures:

The Alliteration Test

This test is designed to assess children's ability to identify initial sounds in single syllable words. On each trial they listen to three words and say which two of the three start with the same sound (e.g. ship, *fat, fox*). The test has two forms: the Oral Test and the Picture Test. In the Picture Test, pictures of the named objects are provided and the child may respond by pointing. The Oral Test uses exclusively oral presentations and responses.

The Rhyme Test

This test is designed to assess children's ability to analyse the final 'rime' in single syllable words. (Rimes are the common element in word families, e.g. the 'ate' in gate, mate, plate, skate.) On each trial they listen to three words and say which two of the three 'end with the same sound' (e.g. *made*, hide, *fade*).

The Spoonerisms Test

This test is designed to assess children's ability to analyse the 'onsets' and 'rimes' in single syllable words and to synthesise new words from these components. The Spoonerism test consists of three parts. Part 1 is a Semi-Spoonerism measure where the child is asked to replace the first sound of a word with a new sound (e.g. 'cot' with a /g/ gives *'got'*). Part 2 is also a Semi-Spoonerism measure but here the child replaces the first sound of the first word with the first sound of the second word (e.g. 'die' with 'pack' gives *'pie'*). Part 3 is a Spoonerism measure where the child is asked to exchange initial sounds in two words (e.g. 'sad cat' gives *'cad sat'*).

The Naming Speed Test

This test is designed to assess children's efficiency or automaticity of access to retrieval of phonological coding at the whole word level in long term memory. Two forms of the Naming speed test are provided, each using a different type of stimuli. The Digit Naming Test uses numbers. The Picture Naming Test uses line drawings of five common objects: a table, a door, a ball, a hat and a box. In each case the child is visually presented with a display of 50 items, composed of a random sequence of the stimuli in question (pictures or digits). The child is asked to name the stimuli in sequence as quickly as they can.

The Fluency Test

This test is designed to assess children's efficiency in using phonological codes based on onsets and rimes in accessing and retrieving information from long term memory. For comparison purposes, children's efficiency in using semantic codes is also assessed. Hence, there are three types of retrieval task: Semantic Fluency (e.g. naming animals); Alliteration Fluency (e.g. naming items beginning with /b); Rhyme Fluency (e.g. naming items which rhyme with 'cat'). In each case the child is asked to give as many words as they can in 30 seconds.

It can be seen that the battery of five tests contains a number of component phonological skills:

- Awareness and analysis of onsets and rimes (Alliteration Test and Rhyme Test).
- Search and retrieval from long-term memory of phonological codes based on onsets (Alliteration Fluency) and rimes (Rhyme Fluency).
- Manipulation of phonemic segments (Spoonerism Test).
- Automatic access and retrieval of lexical items on the basis of semantics and phonology (Naming Speed Test).

Initial standardisation was undertaken with a sample of 244 children consisting of a wide range of poor and normal readers covering three chronological age groups of 6, 8, and 10 year olds. The statistical data are reported in the manual and also by Gallagher and Frederickson (1995).

Guide scores were calculated in order to indicate when a child could be considered to have significant difficulty with a particular test in the battery. We must remember, however, that one individual test score can only be regarded as an initial pointer. It needs to be corroborated by low scores on the other tests. In general, the larger the number of tests in the battery pointing in the same direction, and the more careful we have been to eliminate other reasons that could explain exceptionally poor scores (e.g. hearing difficulty or extreme anxiety), the greater the likelihood that we are justified in inferring that there is a general phonological processing difficulty.

The need for caution in using the PhAB guide scores cannot be over-emphasised. The sample from which the scores were obtained is neither sufficiently large (n=244) nor representative to justify the use of the scores for purposes other than as guides to programme planning.

IMPLICATIONS FOR EDUCATIONAL PRACTICE

Children's ability to learn can be affected by a range of reasons, some related to teaching methods, some to adult expectations (school and family) and some to the interaction of these factors with the children's particular aptitudes and approaches. We believe that assessment requires investigation, over time, of the child's achievements and strategies in relation to the reading and writing tasks themselves. Within this overall approach to assessment, we need to question whether, and to what extent, the child's performance on PhAB provides additional information to guide practical teaching plans.

A case example

Stanley is aged 10 years 6 months. On the Wechsler Objective Reading Dimension (WORD) he obtains an Age Equivalent Score for basic reading of 6:3 years and a Spelling Test Age Equivalent Score of 6:6 years (both within the lowest first percentile). Similarly, Stanley makes so many errors on the easiest first passage of the Neale Analysis of Reading Ability that his performance falls well within the lowest first percentile for his age group.

Stanley's literacy performance is, clearly, very significantly behind that required from children of his age. This, in itself, provides comparative data with regard to questions such as 'how bad is bad?'.

Some may now wish to proceed to compare his reading score with a measure of general intelligence, i.e. to determine the extent of discrepancy between the two. On the basis of the research evidence discussed in the first part of this chapter, we would not choose that route, particularly as there is no other evidence to suggest that Stanley's general developmental progress prevents his learning to read.

Instead, we reach for the PhAB because we argue that the tests of phonology are supported by research grounded in a theoretical model of literacy learning. Stanley obtains the following results:

PhAB TESTS   GUIDE SCORE RESULTS

Alliteration	Below the guide score for children aged 5.10-6.11
Naming speed	Age appropriate
Rhyme	Below the guide score for children aged 7.0-8.11
Spoonerisms	Below the guide score for children aged 9.0-10.11
Fluency	Below the guide score for children aged 9.0-10.11

Four of the five test scores are below those expected from children of his age, with Alliteration and Rhyme being very markedly low. The qualitative information obtained from the Alliteration test is particularly revealing, as this was the first test administered and Stanley did not easily understand the instructions. In order to explain why 'pick' and 'pat' should be chosen from the triad 'pick, pat, run', Stanley said that it was because you *picked* stones on the beach and then *patted* your sandcastle. His first and immediate response was to focus on meaning rather than phonology. This tendency accorded well with the research mentioned earlier in this chapter (Byrne and Shea, 1979).

Having understood the instructions, Stanley continued to have serious difficulty in holding the three words in his memory in order to identify and repeat the correct pair. He coped quite well with the test developed for younger children, where he could point to the pictures representing the words and did not have to retain the words in his short term memory. These qualitative observations showed that the easy and automatic identification of alliterative pairs, which is usually achieved quite early in reading development, had not yet been achieved by Stanley.

Now we come to the key question: how far do these observations influence teaching plans? There is a temptation to proceed with some general statements about Stanley needing more detailed work in the area of phonological awareness or phonics. This would not be helpful by itself as the most important ingredient is missing. We need to know in more detail what Stanley has achieved in terms of the literacy curriculum and what teaching/learning opportunities have been provided. Below are some illustrations:

- Stanley can read and spell most initial letters.
- He can spell words such as 'cat', 'pig'.
- Some of his misspellings are quite reasonable alternatives.
- His reading strategy combines cues from pictures and context with the recognition of initial letters.
- Stanley says that reading lots of books is at the top of his list of 'likes' at school.
- His reading record contains plenty of merit points.

School records show the detailed teaching plans that have been made over time. This information demonstrates how hard Stanley has had to work in order to achieve the skills and knowledge listed above while retaining his enthusiasm for the content of books. The PhAB results support these observations in providing a picture of a child who will continue to need much help in developing fluency and automaticity in the phonological competencies involved. But to focus solely on phonology would most certainly be a serious mistake. Growing evidence suggests that teaching plans based on a comprehensive model of reading have larger effects than teaching which addresses only a few components of the reading process (Hatcher, Hulme and Ellis, 1994; Wasik and Slavin, 1993; Reason and Boote, 1994). Within this context better results are achieved where the programmes contain systematic work on the development of phonological skills. (Iversen and Tunmer, 1993; Wilson and Frederickson, 1995).

CONCLUSION

The title of this chapter contrasted discrepancy definitions of specific learning difficulties with phonological assessment of these difficulties. We considered arguments against discrepancies on both empirical and ethical grounds. In essence, we argued that such definitions provided unfair exclusionary criteria rather than promoting an inclusive conceptualisation based on an understanding and analysis of the learning difficulties that may prevent literacy progress. We referred to the convincing body of research demonstrating that phonological processing difficulties could account for poor progress independent of IQ. There appeared to be scarcely any differences in cognitive skills related to reading between children meeting discrepancy as opposed to low achievement definitions.

So how far does the Phonological Assessment Battery (Research Version) take us in offering an alternative? It currently does not provide convenient administrative criteria for determining the allocation of resources. In its present research form, it is intended as a tentative but potentially valuable resource – not as a definitive measure. Rather than being based on IQ-achievement discrepancies, decisions could in future be based on a well standardised version of PhAB and other important measures which can be shown to have a causal relationship to literacy skills development. Although we believe that children with specific learning difficulties demonstrate phonological processing difficulties, these may not be the only underlying cognitive contributors. Other factors, relating perhaps to some aspect of visual information processing or motor skills, may also play a part (Nicholson & Fawcett, 1995).

With regard to educational implications, there is no better alternative than the keeping of careful records of previous teaching and the functional analysis of what exactly the learner has achieved in relation to the literacy curriculum. We would argue that the Phonological Assessment Battery can supplement and extend observations made by teachers through the process of teaching and as such, can support schools in assessing children and drawing up individual educational plans.

REFERENCES

Aaron, P. G. (1991). Can reading disabilities be diagnosed without using intelligence tests? *Journal of Learning Disabilities, 24,* 3, 178-191.

Bedford-Feuell, C., Geiger, S., Moyse , S. and Turner, M. (1995). Use of listening comprehension in the identification and assessment of specific learning difficulties. *Educational Psychology in Practice,* 10, 4, 207-214.

Carlisle, J. F. (1989). The use of the sentence verification technique in diagnostic assessment of listening and reading comprehension. *Learning Disabilities Research,* **5**, 33-44.

Cataldo, S. and Ellis, N. (1988). Interactions in the development of spelling, reading and phonological skills. *Journal of Research in Reading,* 11, 86-109.

Cline, T. and Reason, R. (1993). Specific Learning Difficulties (Dyslexia): Equal Opportunities Issues. *British Journal of Special Education, Research Section,* 20, 1, 30-34.

Cooper, C, (1995). Inside the WISC-III (UK). *Educational Psychology in Practice,*10, 4, 215-219.

Cunningham, A. E. (1990). Explicit versus imlicit instruction in phonemic awareness. *Journal of Experimental Child Psychology,* 509, 429-444.

Cunningham, A. E. and Stanovich, K. E. (1990). Assessing print exposure and orthographic processing skill in children: a quick measure of reading experience. *Journal of Educational Psychology,* 82, 733-740.

Department for Education (1994). *The Code of Practice on the Identification and Assessment of Special Educational Needs.* London: HMSO.

Elliott, C. D. and Tyler, S. (1987). Learning disabilities and intelligence test results: a principal components analysis of the British Ability Scales. *British Journal of Psychology,* 78, 325-333.

Felton and Wood (1992). A reading level match study of nonword reading skills in poor readers with varying IQs. *Journal of Learning Disabilities,* 25, 318-326.

Fletcher, J. M. (1992). The validity of distinguishing children with language and learning disabilities according to discrepancies with IQ: introduction to the special series. *Journal of Learning Disabilities,* 25, 546-548.

Fletcher, J. M., Shaywitz, S. E., Shankweiler, D., Katz, L., Liberman, I. Y., Stuebing, K. K., Francis, D. J., Fowler, A. E. and Shaywitz, B. A. (1994). Cognitive profiles of reading disability: Comparison of discrepancy and low achievement definitions. *Journal of Educational Psychology,* 86, 1, 6-24.

Frankenberger, W. and Fronzaglio, K. (1991). A review of states criteria and procedures for identifying children with learning disabilities. *Journal of Learning Disabilities,* 24, 8, 495-500.

Fredman, G. and Stevenson, J. (1988). Reading processes in specific reading retarded and reading backward 13-year-olds. *British Journal of Developmental Psychology,* 6, 97-108.

Frederickson, N. (Ed.) (1995). *Phonological Assessment Battery (Research Version).* University College London: Educational Psychology Publishing.

Frith, U. (1995). Dyslexia: Can we have a shared theoretical framework? *Educational and Child Psychology,* 12, 1, 6-17.

Gallagher, A. and Frederickson, N. (1995). The Phonological Assessment Battery (PhAB): An initial assessment of its theoretical and practical utility. *Educational and Child Psychology,* 12, 1.

Goswami, U. and Bryant, P. E. (1990). *Phonological Skills and Learning to Read.* Hove: Lawrence Erlbaum Associates.

Gregory, H. M. and Gregory, A. H. (1994). A comparison of the Neale and the BAS reading tests. *Educational Psychology in Practice,* 10, 1, 15-18.

Hatcher, P. J., Hulme, C. and Ellis, A. W. (1994). Ameliorating early reading failure by integrating the teaching of reading and phonological skills: the phonological linkage hypothesis. *Child Development,* 65, 41-57.

Hoover, W. A. and Gough, P. B. (1990). The simple view of reading. *Reading and Writing: An Interdisciplinary Journal,* 2, 127-160.

Iversen, S. and Tunmer, W. E. (1993). Phonological skills and the Reading Recovery programme. *Journal of Educational Psychology,* 85, 1, 112-126.

Kaufman, A. (1994). *Intelligent Testing with the WISC-R.* Chichester: Wiley.

McNab, I. (1994). Specific learning difficulties: how severe is severe? *BAS information booklet.* Windsor: NFER-Nelson.

Nicholson, R. I. and Fawcett, A. J. (1995). Comparison of deficit severity across skills: Towards a taxonomy for dyslexia. In Nicholson, R. I. and Fawcett, A. J. (Eds.) *Dyslexia in Children: Multidisciplinary Perspectives.* London: Harvester Wheatsheaf.

Pumfrey, P. D. and Reason, R. (1991). *Specific Learning Difficulties (Dyslexia): Challenges and Responses.* London: Routledge.

Rack (1989). Reading-IQ discrepancies and the phonological deficit in reading disability. *Paper presented at the biennial meeting of the Society for Research in Child Development, Kansas City, MO,* April.

Reason, R. and Boote, R, (1994). *Helping Children with Reading and Spelling: A Special Needs Manual.* London: Routledge.

Royer, J. M., Sinatra, G. M. and Schumer, H. (1990). Patterns of individual differences in the development of listening and reading comprehension. *Contemporary Educational Psychology,* 15, 183-196.

Shankweiler, D. and Crain, S. (1986). Language mechanism and reading disorder: a modular approach. *Cognition, 24, 1*39-68.

Share, D. L., McGee, R., McKenzie, D., Williams, A. and Silva, P. A. (1987). Further evidence relating to the distinction between specific reading retardation and general reading backwardness. *British Journal of Developmental Psychology,* 5, 35-44.

Siegel, L. S. (1988). Evidence that IQ scores are irrelevant to the definition and analysis of reading disability. *Canadian Journal of Psychology,* 42, 201-215.

Siegel, L. S. (1989). IQ is irrelevant to the definition of learning disabilities. *Journal of Learning Disabilities,* 22, 469-478.

Siegel, L .S. (1992). An evaluation of the discrepancy definition of dyslexia. *Journal of Learning Disabilities, 25,* 618-629.

Siegel, L. S. and Linder, B. (1984). Short-term memory processes in children with reading and arithmetic learning disabilities. *Developmental Psychology,* 20, 200-207.

Silva, P. A., McGee, R. and Williams, S. (1985). Some characteristics of 9-year-old boys with general reading backwardness or specific reading retardation. *Journal of Child Psychology and Psychiatry,* 26, 407-421.

Spring, C. and French, L. (1990). Identifying children with specific reading disabilities from listening and reading discrepancy scores. *Journal of Learning Disabilities,* 23, 53-58.

Stanovich, K. E. (1986). Matthew effects in reading: some consequences of individual differences in the acquisition of literacy. *Reading Research Quarterly, 21,* 360-407.

Stanovich, K. E. (1991). Discrepancy definitions of reading disability: Has intelligence led us astray? *Reading Research Quarterly,* 26, 1, 7-29.

Stanovich, K .E. (1994). Annotation: Does dyslexia exist? *Journal of Child Psychology and Psychiatry,* 35, 4, 579-595.

Stanovich, K. E., Cunningham, A. E. and Freeman, D. J. (1984). Intelligence, cognitive skills and early reading progress. *Reading Research Quarterly,* 14, 278-303.

Stanovich, K. E., Nathan, R. and Vala-Rossi, M. (1986). Developmental changes in the cognitive correlates of reading ability and the developmental lag hypothesis. *Reading Research Quarterly,* 21, 267-283.

Torgensen, J. K. (1986). Controlling for IQ. *Journal of Learning Disabilities, 19,* 452-460.

Torgensen, J. K., Wagner, R. K. and Rashotte, C. A. (1994). Longitudinal studies of phonological processing and reading. *Journal of Learning Disabilities,* 27, 276-286.

Wasik, B. A. and Slavin, R. E. (1993). Preventing early reading failure with one-to-one tutoring: a review of five programs. *Reading Research Quarterly,* 28, 2, 179-200.

Wilson, J. and Frederickson, N. (1995). Phonological awareness training: an evaluation. *Educational and Child Psychology,* 12, 1, 68-79.

PSYCHOLOGICAL ASSESSMENT

SIONAH LANNEN
and GAVIN REID

INTRODUCTION

Assessment is a multi-dimensional exercise which should consider the child, including the cognitive processes which influence learning; the curriculum, focusing on the content and use of resources; and learning style, highlighting the metacognitive aspects of learning. This chapter will examine these three aspects of assessment. It is also important to consider role perceptions between educational psychologists and teachers since such perceptions have clear implications for issues relating to assessment.

ROLE PERCEPTIONS

Some studies have revealed evidence of a mismatch between the perceptions of teachers and educational psychologists regarding the role of the psychologist in assessment (O'Hagen and Swanson, 1981, 1983; Reid, 1990). The teachers in these studies perceived psychologists as a group of professionals with the skills and remit to provide informative, child-focused cognitive assessment. It was felt this could provide additional data in relation to the child's cognitive profile and a clearer explanation of the child's difficulties. Educational psychologists, however, did not perceive the situation in this way, preferring to adopt a consultancy and advisory role. Thus, a mismatch existed.

This, in fact, may well be related to the shift within the profession of educational psychology from an individual child focus to the broader aspect of the educational context within which the child is functioning (Imich and Kerfoot, 1993). Such a shift has resulted in educational psychologists focusing on whole-school issues, perhaps to the detriment of individual child assessments. The role of the educational psychologist in assessment, therefore, may, in fact, reflect the success or otherwise of effectively recognising and addressing both the needs of the individual child and those of the whole-school. How this can be effectively carried out is currently a matter of debate in terms of competing ideologies and restrictive practicalities (Gale, 1993).

Related to the issue of role there is the question of function. Irrespective of the role perceived and adopted by the psychologist in the assessment, the actual function, purpose and outcome needs to be addressed. Examining these issues can be illuminating. It is usually so when practitioners become introspective and ask themselves, 'Just what exactly am I doing? What is the purpose of this and does the expected outcome justify the cost in terms of time and resources?'

Lannen (1993) attempted to find some answers to these questions when she asked a number of teachers and special needs co-ordinators to comment on the function of the educational psychologist in relation to assessment for specific learning difficulties. The responses from this study indicated that the psychologist can perform a key role in assessment. Some of the statements made by this sample of practitioners included the following:

> *"It is important for the teacher to have some knowledge of the child's level of intellectual ability and underlying cognitive skills indicated by formal stand-ardised assessments."*

> *"The inferences highlighted by the psychologist from the assessment can provide a clearer picture of the strengths and weaknesses of the child."*

> *"The consultancy and advice offered by the psychologist informs and highlights practice."*

> *"The outcome of the assessment process involving the teacher and the psychologist can help the teacher develop self supporting strategies for future assessment."*

> *"The psychologist, because of access to a range of information from other professionals and parents, can provide a fuller and more objective perspective to the assessment."*

This study indicates that the educational psychologist does have a key role to play as part of the multi-disciplinary assessment team. This role varies depending on the situation, but can range from formal cognitive assessment to consultancy and advice on curriculum issues and resources.

Attention needs to be directed, therefore, to the nature and the value of the educational psychologist's intervention in each of these dimensions.

COGNITIVE FACTORS

The importance of cognitive processing in relation to competence in literacy is fairly well documented (Seymour, 1986; Snowling, 1990; Dockrell and

McShane, 1993). In relation to dyslexia, it has been asserted that an assessment of such processes can help to provide some identification criteria and a definition and explanation of the difficulty (Singleton, 1993), Seymour, (1986). Seymour provides a useful summary of the psychological processes of learning and their relationship with dyslexia. He discusses three dimensions – the observable behaviours, the cognitive processes and the physiological instantiation. He asserts that the level of competence, the observable behaviours in literacy such as the ability to read and spell, should be distinguished from the cognitive function, the underlying psychological processes which influence the 'level of competence'. Seymour's third dimension relates to the physiological instantiation: physiological aspects related to neural tissue and brain structure. This aspect should be considered by paediatricians but the other two dimensions, competence and cognitive processing, should be addressed by the educational psychologist.

The **competence** dimension may be identified by teachers and psychologists using a combination of standardised and diagnostic tests and other materials such as criterion-referenced assessment and observational frameworks. The **cognitive** dimension, however, is essentially an interpretation of the observations and data stemming from an analysis of the '**competence**' or performance of the child and Seymour argues this can be defined in three of the processing functions of reading: the recognition of familiar graphemic forms; semantic processing – the system based on comprehension and understanding; and phonological processing – the speech production system which contains the vocabulary store. An analysis of these functions provides some explanation and understanding of the child's competence and performance aspects in the acquisition of literacy. Moreover, Seymour's extensive research in this field in relation to the processing functions of dyslexic readers reveals that there can be impairment within elements of the processing system and that dyslexic children can show individual differences and different patterns of this impairment. Seymour asserts that dyslexic children differ in the strategies they use and in the emphasis they give to each processing route, and suggests that an analysis of these factors provide useful guidance for planning support strategies.

COGNITIVE STYLE

A cognitive style is considered to be a reasonably static characteristic (Riding and Douglas, 1993) and can be defined as an individual's characteristic and consistent approach to organising and processing information (Tennant, 1988).

Riding and Cheema (1991) highlight the importance of two principal cognitive styles – Verbal-Imagery and Wholist-Analytic. Further research (Riding and Douglas, 1993) examined the relationship between cognitive style and mode of presentation of learning materials. This study found, for example, that the 'Imagers' improved their learning performance when the material was presented in a text-plus-picture condition and that learning performance for this group suffered when information was presented in a verbal mode. Interestingly, the 'Verbalisers' performed similarly in both the text only and the text-plus-picture conditions. Clearly, therefore, a case can be presented for attempting to acknowledge the cognitive learning style of individuals and not assume that all pupils learn in the same way.

The Wholist-Analytic style of learning would result in the learner processing information in wholes or parts, while the Verbal-Imagery style of learning would be seen in the learner's processing of information either verbally or in mental images.

Children, however, are persuaded to adopt flexibility in the cognitive strategies they use to compensate for difficulties they may encounter with different modes of presentation of learning material. These strategies are flexible and can be learned and developed with practice (Given, Lannen, Nicholson and Reid, 1995). It is important therefore to acknowledge the learner's natural cognitive style and, furthermore, the nature of the learning strategies adopted to deal with the learning task.

Dunn and Dunn (1992) have related learning styles to the classroom situation through the use of a Learning Styles Inventory, which has a high validity and reliability and is used most frequently in learning styles research (Dunn, Dunn and Price, 1975-1989). The variables identified by Dunn and Dunn which help to differentiate student's learning performances are applicable to the classroom because they focus on key learning issues such as how children process, absorb and retain new information. This clearly has implications for individual differences in learning and in learning conditions, including the learning environment. Furthermore, such a focus on learning styles can help to facilitate the individual taking responsibility for their own learning. This indeed appears to be the essence of one such programme developed to encourage self-knowledge in learning (Given, 1993, 1994). Given's programme utilises influential concepts such as self-empowered learning, self-managed learning and reflective learning. Clearly an important role for teachers and educational psychologists is to consider the importance of learning styles, which for dyslexic learners can effectively help to provide self-knowledge to assist in the development of cognitive strategies for life-long learning.

COGNITIVE ASSESSMENT

The implication of the above is that cognitive aspects of the child's profile, such as attention, concentration, memory processes, organisation, comprehension and phonological processing, should be considered during assessment.

PHONOLOGICAL PROCESSING

While there is strong evidence of the link between the above aspects and reading (Dockrell and McShane, 1993; Chasty, 1990) the area of phonological processing is, without doubt, of extreme importance in the development of reading skills, particularly pre-reading skills (Dockrell and McShane, 1993; Stanovich, 1991, 1995).

Awareness of the phonemic structure of words can facilitate the essential grapheme-phoneme correspondences which, studies have shown, are essential for tackling new words (Baddeley *et al.*, 1982; Szeszulski and Manis,1987). Related to this, it has also been shown that awareness of sounds at the pre-reading stage is a good predictor of progress in learning to read (Goswami and Bryant, 1992; Bradley, 1990), and that a sensitivity to and an awareness of rhyme can be related to subsequent development of reading skills and facilitate competence in using the phonemic structure of words while reading, (Bryant *et al.*, 1989). A particularly useful assessment in this respect is the Phonological Assessment Battery (Frederickson (Ed.), 1995) (see previous chapter) which contains the following tests:

Alliteration (oral)
Naming speed (pictures)
Naming Speed (digits)
Rhyme
Spoonerism
Fluency (Alliteration, Rhyme, Semantic).

The authors acknowledge that this test should make a 'clarifying contribution' to identifying 'Phonologically based Specific Learning Difficulties (Dyslexia)', but at the same time, they accept that no 'pure' test of phonological processing exists and one must be aware of other factors which will influence performance.

Nevertheless, the important aspect of phonological awareness can be observed at both the pre-reading stage, by focusing on children's use of sounds and competence with rhyme, and at the reading stage, through analysis of errors. Such observations, therefore, can help in the identification of specific learning difficulties and in the development of targets for a teaching programme.

MEMORY

The role of memory is of considerable importance to reading and to learning and the focus of research has been directed to two aspects in particular: the working memory responsible for processing the information, and the long-term memory in relation to recall. Both processing and recall are important in reading and are areas in which children with dyslexia display difficulties. This is particularly the case on short-term memory tasks in relation to literacy (Jorm, 1983; Stanovich, 1986; Torgeson, 1987). This can be seen in the functioning of the 'articulatory loop', a component of working memory (Baddeley, 1982), which is essentially the verbal rehearsal system and allows material to be processed. This has implications for learning since it has been demonstrated that a competing task can result in 'articulatory suppression' and inefficient use of the working memory.

Furthermore Dockrell and McShane (1993) argue that the links between phonological and memory deficits are significant in the assessment of specific learning difficulties because if there are difficulties converting the printed word into sounds then it follows that difficulties will exist in the storing of these sounds in short-term, working memory. This implies that memory difficulties experienced by children with dyslexia are related to the acquisition of literacy and not necessarily related to other non-literacy areas. Therefore, it follows that the assessment of this function should also involve literacy related tasks.

COMPREHENSION

It has been shown that the reading comprehension level of dyslexic children is in excess of their decoding ability (Aaron, 1989, 1994). At the same time, it might be argued that the decoding difficulty in itself can restrict comprehension. Slow recognition of words can act as a disruptive and influential factor affecting comprehension (Perfetti and Lesgold, 1979). An assessment therefore, should not only ascertain the comprehension level of the child's reading ability but also the reasons for either failing or succeeding at comprehension related tasks.

Clearly, decoding skills in themselves can aid comprehension (Curtis, 1980), but at the same time there is no guarantee that the skilful decoder possesses parity in comprehension (Aaron, 1989; Oakhill and Garnham, 1988). In fact Stanovich (1984) argues that as children reach the end of primary education comprehension replaces decoding as the best predictor of overall reading skills. According to Dockrell and McShane, (1993), semantic and syntactic knowledge at the sentence level are important for comprehension. Thus, an assessment should consider the child's ability to use inference and strategies to facilitate comprehension as well as identifying the child's actual comprehension level.

ATTENTION AND CONCENTRATION

Attention and concentration are implicated in the cognitive processes of the learner in most learning tasks. Other cognitive processes, however, such as memory, may share a reciprocal relationship with attention (Levine, 1995). Levine (1995) sees 'saliency determination' as an important aspect of short-term memory which links memory and attention. This relates to the selection of relevent information from all the stimuli present. Research in memory, particularly that highlighting sensory memory, and the levels of processing model (Craik and Lockhart, 1972; Baddeley, 1988), supports this view, implying that the actual processing of the information and the level to which it is processed aids retention and recall, and that retention and recall can only be accomplished effectively if sufficient attention and concentration are present. It is therefore of some importance to consider attention and concentration factors in an assessment perhaps through recording 'on-task' behaviour or by using a more informal observation technique. (Copeland and Love, 1992; Lerner, Lowenthal and Lerner, 1995).

ORGANISATION

In many ways, organisation holds the key to a number of cognitive processes related to effective learning. It has been demonstrated that organisation of material during learning can aid retention and recall (Buzan, 1993) and that organisational and planning factors are among the principal processing elements in learning, interacting with attention, memory, visuo-spatial ordering, temporal sequential ordering, language, neuro-motor skills, higher order cognition (such as concept formation, problem solving, critical thinking and metacognition) and social cognition aspects (such as social attribution, conflict resolution, prediction of responses and perspective-taking) (Levine, 1995). Organisation in learning can, therefore, have a spin-off effect, enhancing some of the other cognitive aspects of learning. Indeed, many of the successful teaching programmes for dyslexic children display a highly structured pattern and have an organised form of presentation. Organisational ability can be gauged also through observation and by responses in a more formal test, particularly when extended answers are required.

The class teacher can obtain some appreciation of the child's cognitive functioning through observation and the analysis of errors. Thus the child's memory skills, organisational ability, attention and concentration levels are likely to be known to the class teacher or learning support specialist. What additional contribution, therefore, can the educational psychologist bring to this form of assessment? An assertion which may be levelled at the educational psychologist's input is that the information obtained only confirms what is already suspected. This chapter however, asserts that educational psychologists can perform an extended function, both in assessment and consultancy.

WECHSLER INTELLIGENCE SCALE

Perhaps the most widely known test used by educational psychologists which can provide a cognitive profile of the child is the Wechsler Intelligence Scale for Children. This test, which can provide an IQ score and consists of 12 sub-tests (the WISC (III) UK 1993 contains 13 sub-tests), has been the subject of recent criticism concerning its validity, lack of comprehensiveness and particularly when used as a measure of discrepancies between aptitude and attainment (Siegel, 1989; Stanovich, 1991; Stanovich and Siegel, 1994; Conner, 1994 and Cooper, 1995). Conner (1994) furthermore asserts that IQ is not a very satisfactory basis for predicting achievement in literacy. Cooper (1995) asserts that the use of Verbal IQ and Performance IQ is becoming increasingly difficult to uphold, suggesting that this two-factor model is not adequate. The four-factor model Cooper suggests would be more appropriate – verbal comprehension, perceptual organisation, freedom from distractibility and processing speed – than the traditional Verbal and Performance IQ. This alternative four-factor model has, as yet, not been properly validated. The use of intelligence tests, however, does not necessarily imply that the primary aim is to obtain an IQ score. It is fairly well documented that IQ is not a stable measure of cognitive functioning, and indeed there is considerable debate in relation to the notion of intelligence and many different definitions and conceptions of intelligence can be noted (Sternberg and Detterman, 1986).

The sub-tests of the WISC, however, can be regarded as a sample of tests focusing on cognitive skills which can provide some indication of the child's mastery of these skills in relation to the task. Such scores should therefore not necessarily be perceived as a measure of intellectual potential (Anastasi ,1988). However identifying a profile of cognitive skills can be an important aspect of an assessment.

The verbal scale of the test can provide information on the child in relation to general knowledge, comprehension and reasoning, short term memory, concept development, verbal organisation and expression, while visual perception, visual association, spatial and sequencing skills and speed of processing can provide information in relation to the non-verbal (performance) scale. This kind of data, and the accompanying cognitive profile, can be of considerable value and can provide an understanding of the child's learning processes and strengths and weaknesses (Lannen and Lannen, 1995). This will assist in an explanation of the child's performances in the classroom and can also provide guidance for the development of appropriate curriculum materials.

The merits of educational programmes based on the WISC sub-test scores have, however, been questioned and viewed as little more than 'an arbitrary exercise' (Holmes, 1985). Some commentators, though, have successfully provided examples of balanced programmes based on WISC profiles, while acknowledging the need to preserve creativity and individual learning styles (Banas and Wills, 1978; Matarazzo, 1985; Lannen, 1994 and Lannen, 1995).

In relation to children with specific learning difficulties, some evidence exists of a particular cognitive profile based on a child's WISC sub-scale scores (Thomson ,1984, 1989). This profile, although subject to some criticism (Pumfrey and Reason, 1994), indicates that dyslexic children have difficulties with four sub-tests in particular – Arithmetic, Coding, Information and Digit Span, and is sometimes called the 'ACID' profile (Richards, 1985; Miles and Ellis, 1981; Miles, 1994). Additionally, the WISC can provide some data in relation to the child's distractability and anxiety level (Kaufman, 1992).

There is also some evidence that the British Ability Scales (BAS), a similar test to the WISC, can produce responses which highlight a sequential processing deficit – a difficulty which can be associated with dyslexia (Thomson, 1982; Elliot, Murray and Pearson, 1983). The scales of the BAS which may highlight this are Information Processing, Recall of Digits, Basic Arithmetic, Immediate Memory for Visual Recall, and Delayed Memory for Visual Recall.

DIAGNOSTIC USE OF STANDARDISED TESTS

Information which can be used diagnostically can be gleaned from standardised assessment. It is good practice both to provide a permanent record of this information in a formal, written report, acknowledging also the measurable strengths of the child (Collins, 1995) and also to discuss the report informally through discussion and consultancy. In doing so, it is desirable to state how each area of weakness affects the child's self-esteem, social relationships and functioning within the home environment (Gardner, 1994).

The following extracts illustrate this diagnostic use of tests.

CASE STUDY EXTRACTS:

Fig. 1:

'Although Christopher required many of the questions to be repeated on the task of Comprehension, he was able to achieve a score at the 91st percentile. This task, among other skills, measures the ability to process and understand incoming verbal information (his strength in this area was supported by his score on the test of Listening comprehension WIAT (Wechsler Individual Achievement Test). There was, however, a significant difference between his performance on these items and the sub-tests of Vocabulary and Similarities which measure the ability to express ideas verbally and verbal reasoning. I would suggest that Christopher's comparative weakness in the latter skills area is significant in terms of the way he finds it difficult to formulate his thought process verbally and consequently organise his written work effectively and systematically.

This difference between the ability to process incoming information in comparison to outgoing has been found to cause frustration difficulties within the individual as s/he is unable to justify the level of his/her understanding and knowledge through the medium of either spoken or written language.'

Fig. 2:

'The results of the assessment indicate that John is a boy of considerable cognitive ability. He performed exceptionally well on sub-tests measuring both the Verbal Comprehension Factor and the Perceptual Organisation Factor.

John's performance on the tasks which constitute the 'Distractability Factor' was weaker. These sub-tests measure the mental manipulation of numbers/symbols in short-term memory and John's performance suggests a weakness in this form of processing. Once information gets into long term memory, however, John shows strengths in both storage and retrieval.

It must be noted that performance on verbal and perceptual sub-tests can also be adversely affected by distractability and/or anxiety. During the assessment it was noted that John frequently appeared to lose focus, resulting in questions having to be repeated or instruction rephrased.'

Source: Lannen and Lannen (1995)

TEACHING AND CURRICULUM DIMENSIONS OF ASSESSMENT

Cognitive assessment, informal assessment and consultancy can also address issues relating to teaching, resources and the curriculum. The following areas could be identified:

- Reading development/comprehension.

- Spelling/writing skills.

- The development of a confident attitude and independent work habits.

- The development of social interaction skills.

Some suggested methods or approaches to deal with the above difficulties may include the following recommendations:

- Support in a small group within or outwith the classroom situation.

- Individual educational programmes carefully matched to the student's current attainment levels.

- Close liaison between the learning support teacher and class teacher to ensure continuity of curricular and teaching methods.

- The experience of reading meaningful written material in order to increase word identification, knowledge of letter/sound combinations and develop comprehension. 'Taped', 'paired' or 'reading buddies' techniques are all excellent ways of increasing non-visual information such as language structure and inference. These approaches are also excellent for developing tracking skills. The above techniques enable a book higher than the child's actual reading age to be used, helping to overcome the problem of a mismatch between reading ability and interest level.

- A structured approach to spelling/writing skills. Word recognition and use of context cues can be developed by presenting 'word families' or bingo games (where the child listens for the sound e.g. 'p' as in pet, and covers up the sound on his/her card).

  In terms of developing spelling skills, the student would benefit from consolidation at the 'cvc' stage before moving on to consonant blends.

To develop his writing skills, tracking exercises, crossing out letters or words in magazines, 'penmanship' and key-boarding can be useful.

- Social Skills – many of the activities found in social skills 'Circle time' programmes would be appropriate. The 'safe' environment promoted in these group activities encourages children to listen and respond appropriately and is excellent for developing positive social interaction skills.

- Differentiation of the curriculum may be required in terms of:

  Delivery e.g. the task may be presented differently.

  Operations e.g. the student may require a longer time spent on some areas of the curriculum.

  Outcomes e.g. different arrangements for assessment may be needed.

READING COMPREHENSION AND READING SPEED

Listening comprehension gives the reading potential for an individual. Significant under-achievement can be identified, therefore, if one examines listening comprehension scores in relation to other reading criteria. Experience in reading is beneficial in developing reading comprehension.

This can be done through 'taped' reading (following the text while listening to a tape) which is an excellent way of gaining more experience in reading and helps to develop word identification, mediated meaning and fluency. Taped reading is also an excellent way in which to develop the visual tracking/scanning skills which are crucial to reading and studying.

One particular procedure, which has proved successful for reading comprehension, is Reciprocal Teaching. This takes place in a group or 'paired' situation and features guided practice in the application of four concrete strategies aimed at comprehending a section of text. The four strategies are questioning, clarifying, summarising and predicting and have a dual purpose in that they are both comprehension fostering and comprehension monitoring (Baker and Brown, 1984). That is, they enhance comprehension whilst allowing the student to monitor their own learning.

The reading speed of dyslexic students is often slow: they often lose the place when reading. Activities designed to improve tracking skills are therefore useful. Visual tracking skills can be practised using special sheets of nonsense words, prose or unwanted magazines or books. Large print is easiest so the task can be made harder by reducing print size. Tracking combines many skills in one activity – it involves left/right working, orientation, hand/eye co-ordination, sequencing, sound/symbol recognition, word recognition and speed and accuracy of scanning, attention and concentration.

In order to focus a student's attention on to the individual parts of words, a very structured approach to spelling/writing skills will be required, e.g. using a phonic approach either as a lesson (where the children have to find words with the same grapheme/phoneme) or using graded phonic workbooks. Sound symbol associations can also be strengthened in a meaningful way by using a variety of techniques.

For example:

- By presenting word families or bingo games (the child listens for the sound e.g. 'ow' as in cow and covers up the sound on his/her card).

- 'I Spy' is an excellent game for phonic development and can be used for sounds at the beginning, middle and end of words. There are also excellent commercially produced games such as Phonic Rummy (Better Books); Letterland Shuffle (Letterland Ltd.); Spellmaster (Hope Education); Photo Sound Lotto (LDA); Letter Sound Games (GALT); and many more game type activities which the teacher can develop (Kaye, 1984).

- The 'Letterland' system. This combines the structure, progression and multi-sensory teaching approaches that are so important for mastering learning in this area and does it in a way that is great fun – an excellent motivator! (Wendon, 1987).

- There are many other phonic programmes which provide an excellent structure for skills development in this area e.g. Alpha to Omega; (Hornsby and Shear, 1993); the Hickey Multisensory Language Course (Augur and Briggs, 1992); the Slingerland Programme (Slingerland, 1991); Alphabetic Phonics (Cox, 1985); and the Bangor Dyslexic Teaching System (Miles, 1990).

Computer programmes can be used to reinforce phonics (McKeown, 1992; Singleton, 1994). One which has proved very useful is 'Concept Keyboard matching' (Scetlander) which allows the teacher to make up his/her own concept keyboard overlays for alphabet matching exercises. The programme is also versatile enough to allow it to be used for any kind of matching exercise at all ages to reinforce vocabulary, number bonds, multiplication tables and foreign languages.

LEARNING STYLES

The whole area of learning styles and the associated metacognitive aspects of learning styles have received considerable recent attention (Reid, 1994). It is therefore essential that this aspect is considered in psychological assessment.

If, for example, it is found that the student has short-term auditory memory difficulties, it will be necessary to recommend over-learning strategies, which will allow information to be processed into long-term memory.

It is important, therefore, to identify the student's learning style and match it to appropriate teaching strategies. Such strategies, for example, may include:

- Structured learning;
- use of checklists;
- opportunities for creative writing;
- choice of working alone or with others on projects;
- tactile and kinaesthetic resources for learning;
- creative art activities, opportunities for making displays and scrapbooks, dramatic presentations, oral reports and group sharing;
- solving of old problems in new ways, open-ended discussions, self-expressive activities e.g. designing an experiment, keeping a personal journal and acting.

Identifying the learning styles of students (for example, whether they have a visual, auditory, tactile or kinaesthetic preference) can provide a guide for appropriate strategies. The kinaesthetic learner may prefer dramatic presentations, and visual learners may need to learn new skills initially in pictorial form.

Similarly, some children prefer structure while others prefer to work on their own, and are given responsibility for their own learning.

CURRICULUM BASED INTERVENTION STRATEGIES/ WHOLE SCHOOL APPROACHES

Intervention strategies based on the curriculum should be considered, as it places new learning into an appropriate context and helps to facilitate transfer of learning. Examples of curriculum based intervention strategies which can be useful for children with specific learning difficulties include the following:

- Specially prepared or highlighted work sheets;

- teaching the technical vocabulary prior to a lesson;

- providing a tape recording of literature being studied;

- providing a photocopy of notes to save note-taking at speed;

- facility to tape-record notes or 'written work';

- teacher-time to transcribe or to help the pupil transcribe the above tape recording;

- tuition to help to use the word processor effectively;

- study skills to help pupils organise their written work more effectively.

These strategies can provide a framework for helping to meet the individual needs of children within the context of the curriculum.

OBSERVATIONAL ASSESSMENT

Although considerable data can be gleaned from cognitive and formal assessments, observation in the classroom to examine the child's on-task behaviour in the learning context may be as or more, revealing. Clearly, an assessment should consider different facets of learning and there is scope for standardised cognitive and informal observational assessment.

Observational assessment can not only assist in a diagnosis of the difficulty, but it also provides an indication of the student's learning style and learning preferences and gives some direction to intervention in terms of teaching and resources.

A number of arguments can be put forward to support the use of observation in assessment. These include:

- **Flexibility:** observation schedules need not be rigidly criterion referenced. There are no correct or incorrect responses.

- **Adaptability:** the observation framework or schedule can be adapted to different classroom situations and learning situations.

- **Contextual Factors:** observational assessment not only focuses on the learner, but also on the learning context. Thus it provides a more holistic picture than an assessment which is purely child focused.

- **Behavioural Factors:** one is looking at the actual learning behaviour in the learning situation. Formal tests and testing, whilst useful, may produce an 'artificial' response which needs to be taken into account when analysing the test results.

OBSERVATIONAL FRAMEWORK

It is necessary, therefore, to develop an observational framework which looks at the broad range of areas which can relate to some of the difficulties experienced by children with specific learning difficulties.

It is important to gather information which relates to the child, the learning situation and context. The aim is not only to find out **how** or **why** the child is having difficulty, but to gain some insight and understanding into the strategies and processes of learning for that child.

A framework for observational assessment for specific learning difficulties can therefore include the following areas:

- **ATTENTION**
  - Length of attention span.
  - Conditions when attention is enhanced.
  - Factors contributing to distractability.
  - Attention/distractability under different learning conditions.

- **ORGANISATION**
  - Organisational preferences.
  - Degree of structure required.
  - Organisation of work, desk, self.
  - Reactions to imposed organisation.

- **SEQUENCING**
  - Able to follow sequence with aid.
  - General difficulty with sequencing:

        – work,

        – carrying out instructions,

        – words when reading,

        – individual letters in written work.

- **INTERACTION**
  - Degree of interaction with peers, adults.
  - Preferred interaction:
    - one-to-one,
    - small groups,
    - whole class,
  - How interaction is sustained.

- **LANGUAGE**
  - Expressive language:
    - Is meaning accurately conveyed?
    - Spontaneous/prompted
    - Is there appropriate use of natural breaks in speech?
    - Expressive language in different contexts e.g. one-to-one, small group, class group.
    - Errors, omissions and difficulties in conversation and responses e.g. mispronunciations, questions to be repeated or clarified.

- **COMPREHENSION**
  - How does the child comprehend information?
  - What type of cues most readily facilitate comprehension?
  - Use of schema.
  - What type of instructions are most easily understood:
    - written?
    - oral?
    - visual?
  - How readily can knowledge be transferred to other areas?

- **READING**
  - Reading preferences – aloud, silent, alone, paired.
  - Type of errors:

VISUAL, e.g.

– Discrimination between letters which look the same – 'O' 'Q' 'B' 'D' 'T' 'I'.

– Inability to appreciate that the same letter may look different 'R' 'r' 'L' 'l' 'A' 'a'.

– Visual segmentation difficulty – either omitting segments of a word or confusing them with similar looking letters.

– Visual sequencing difficulty – altering the sequencing of letters or groups of letters within words.

AUDITORY, e.g.

– Difficulties in auditory discrimination, with sounds of different frequencies, inability to hear sounds in initial and final position.

• **MOTIVATION/INITIATIVE**

• Interest level of child.

• How is motivation increased? What kind of prompting and cueing is necessary?

• To what extent does the child take responsibility for their own learning?

• What kind of help is required?

• **SELF-CONCEPT**

• What tasks are more likely to be tackled with confidence?

• When is confidence low?

• Self-Concept and confidence in different contexts.

• **RELAXATION**

• Is the child relaxed when learning?

• Evidence of tension and relaxation.

• **LEARNING STYLE**

All learners have a preferred learning style and children with dyslexic difficulties will also have their own individual style of learning. The key phrase is 'individual style of learning', because there will be a variation of learning styles within any group of dyslexic children.

These include the following learning preferences:

- Auditory
- Visual
- Oral
- Kinaesthetic
- Tactile
- Global
- Analytic

It is important therefore to note in observational assessment the preferred mode of learning. Many children will, of course, show preferences and skills in a number of modes of learning. Multi-sensory teaching, therefore, is crucial in order to accommodate as many modes as possible.

- **LEARNING CONTEXT**

When assessing the nature and degree of the difficulty experienced by the child, it is important to take into account the learning context. This context, depending on the learner's preferred style, can either exacerbate the difficulty or minimise the problem. (Reid, 1992.)

Context for Learning:

- Classroom
- Role of Teacher
- Task
- Materials/Resources

The above factors, therefore, need to be observed and matched to the learner's preferred learning style.

- Observe components within a framework for learning.
- Observe some factors within that framework associated with specific learning difficulties.
- Observe preferred styles of learning.
- Acknowledge the importance of the learning context and observe the degree of match or mis-match between the learner and the context.

CONCLUSION

This chapter has attempted to illustrate the importance and the potential involvement of the educational psychologist in the three dimensions of assessment – cognitive, curriculum and learning styles. Such intervention may take the form of formal testing using standardised procedures, informal observation, consultancy on curriculum and teaching issues, and awareness of appropriate resources. Effective assessment therefore should provide for an interaction of these factors in order that a balanced and appropriate assessment can be obtained.

REFERENCES

Aaron, P. G. (1989). *Dyslexia and Hyperlexia.* Kluwer Academic Publisher.

Aaron, P. G. (1994). Differential Diagnosis of Learning disabilities. In Hales, G. (Ed.) *Dyslexia Matters.*

Anastasi ,A. (1988). *Psychological Testing* (6th ed). Macmillan, New York.

Augur, J. and Briggs, S. (1992). The Hickey multi-sensory language course. London, Whurr.

Baddeley, A. D., Ellis, N. C., Miles, T. R. and Lewis, V. J. (1982). 'Developmental and Acquired Dyslexia: A Comparison' *Cognition, 11, 185-99.*

Baddeley, A. D. (1982). 'Reading and working memory'. *Bulletin of the British Psychological Society, 35* pp. 414-416.

Baker, L. and Brown, A. (1984). Metacognitive skills and reading. In P. D. Pearson (Ed.). *Handbook of reading research.* New York: Longman.

Banas, N. and Wills, I. H. (1978). *WISC-R Prescriptions: How to work creatively with individual learning styles.* Academic Therapy Publications, Novats, California.

Bradley, L. (1990). 'Rhyming connections in learning to read or spell'. In Pumfrey, P. D. and Elliott, C. (Eds.) *Children's difficulties in reading, spelling and writing.* Falmer Press.

Bryant, P. E., Bradley, L., McLean, M. and Crossland J. (1989). 'Nursery rhymes, phonological skills, and reading'. *Journal of Child Language* 16, 407-428.

Chasty, H. (1990). *Meeting the Challenges of Specific Learning Difficulties in Reading, Spelling and Writing.* (Pumfrey, P. D. and Elliott, C. (Eds.). Falmer Press.

Collins, C. S. (1995). Specific learning difficulties – why assess? *Scottish Dyslexia Trust News and Views.* Vol. 2, Issue 1. Spring 1995. p4.

Conner, M. J. (1994). Dyslexia (Specific Learning difficulties): Assessing Assessment. In *Educational Psychology in Practice.* Vol. 10, No. 3, October, 1994, 131-140.

Copeland, E. D. and Love, V. L. (1992). *Attention without tension. A teacher's handbook on attention disorders.* 3C's of childhood Inc. Atlanta, Georgia, USA.

Cooper, C. (1995). Inside the WISC-III. UK. *Educational Psychology in Practice.* Vol. 10, No. 4, January 1995, 215-219.

Cox, A. R. (1985). *Alphabetic phonics. An organisation and expansion of Orton Gillingham.* Annals of Dyslexia, 35: 187-98.

Craik, F. I. N. and Lockhart, R. S. (1972). 'Levels of processing: a framework for memory research'. In *Journal of Verbal Learning and Verbal Behaviour,* 11, 268-94.

Curtis, M. E. (1980). 'Development of components of reading skill'. *Journal of Educational Psychology,* 72, 656-69.

Dockrell, J. and McShane, J. (1993). *Children's Learning Difficulties: A Cognitive Approach.* Blackwell.

Dunn, R. and Dunn, K. (1992). *Teaching elementary students through their individual learning styles.* Allyn & Bacon.

Dunn, R., Dunn, K. and Price, G. E. (1975,77,78,79,87,88,89). *Learning Style Inventory*. Price Systems, Box 1818, Lawrence, KS 66044.

Elliot, C. D., Murray, D. J. and Pearson, L. S. (1983). *The British Ability Scales*. Windsor: NFER-Nelson.

Frederickson, N. (Ed.) (1995). Phonological Assessment Battery (PHAB) Research Edition. University College, London. (Now available NFER-Nelson).

Gale, A. A., Analysis of Educational Psychology: Is Educational Psychology up to the Task? *Proceedings of the Annual Conference of the British Psychological Society*. April 1993. Blackpool.

Gardner, P. (1994). Diagnosing Dyslexia in the Classroom: A Three Stage Model. In Hales, G. *Dyslexia Matters*. Whurr, Pub. London.

Given, B. K. (1993). *Breakthrough: A Holistic approach to learning style*. George Mason University, Virginia, USA.

Given, B. K. (1994). Operation breakthrough for continuous self-systems improvement. In *Intervention in School and Clinic*. Vol. 30, No. 1. Sept. 1994, pp. 38-46.

Given, B. K., Lannen, S., Nicholson, M. and Reid, G. (1995). Learning styles – unlocking potential in *LINKS*, Vol. II, No. 1, Spring 1995, pp. 26-31.

Goswami, U. and Bryant, P. (1990). *Phonological skills and learning to read*. Hove, Erlbaum.

Holm, B. J. (1985). A critique of programmed WISC-R remediations. *Canadian Journal of Studies of Psychology*. June 1985, Vol. 1. No. 1.

Hornsby, B. and Shear, F. (1993). *Alpha to Omega* (4th edition). Heinemann Educational.

Imich, A. J. and Kerfoot, S. R. Educational Psychology: Meeting the Challenge of Change. *Proceedings of the Annual Conference of the British Psychological Society*. April 1993, Blackpool.

Jorm, A. F. (1983). 'Specific reading retardation and working memory: A Review'. *British Journal of Psychology*, 74, 311-42.

Kaye, P. (1984). Games for reading. Playful ways to help your child read. Pantheon Books. New York.

Kaufman, A. S. (1992). *Intelligent Testing with the WISC-R*. Joan Wiley, New York.

Lannen, S. (1993). *Perceptions of the Educational Psychologists Role in Assessment*. Unpublished study, Lancashire Psychological Service.

Lannen, C. and Lannen, S. (1995). Cognitive profiles and the WISC-III in Assessment of Specific learning Difficulties. Unpublished study. *Educational Psychology Services*. Riyadh.

Lerner, J. W., Lowenthal, B., Lerner, S. R. (1995). *Attention deficit disorders, assessment and teaching*. Brooks/Cole Publishing C. CA, USA.

Levine, M. (1995). Attention, memory and language variation: A phenoneurological approach to learning disorders. Paper presented at the 5th Cambridge Conference, Helen Arkell Dyslexia Centre. April 1995.

Matarazzo, J. D. (1985). *Computerized clinical psychological test interpretations*. American Psychologist.

McKeown, S. (Ed.). (1992). *IT support for specific learning difficulties*. NCEDT.

Miles, T. R. and Ellis, N. C. (1981). A Lexical Encoding Deficiency. In Pavlidis, G. Th. *Dyslexia Research and its Applications to Education*. Chichester: Wiley.

Miles, E. (1990). *Bangor dyslexia teaching system*. London: Whurr.

Miles, T. R. (1994). Towards a Rationale for diagnosis. In Hales, G. (Ed.) *Dyslexia Matters*. London: Whurr.

Oakhill, J. U. and Garnham, A. (1988). *Becoming a skilled reader*. Blackwell, Oxford.

O'Hagen, F. J. and Swanson, W. I. (1981). 'Teacher's views regarding the role of the educational psychologist in schools'. *Research in Education*, 29, 29-40.

O'Hagen, F. J. and Swanson, W. I. (1983). 'Teachers and Psychologists: a comparison of views. *Research in Education*, 36.

Perfetti, C. A. and Lesgold, A. M. (1979). 'Coding and comprehension in skilled reading and implications for reading instruction'. In Resnick, L. B. and Leaver, P. (Eds.) *Theory and Practice of Early Reading*, Vol. 1. Erlbaum, Hillstate, New Jersey.

Pumfrey, P. D. and Reason, R. (Eds.). (1994). *Specific Learning Difficulties (Dyslexia) Challenges and Responses*. Routledge, London. (5th imp.).

Reid, G. (1990). 'Specific Learning Difficulties: Attitudes Towards Assessment and Teaching'. In Hales G. (Ed.) *Meeting Points in Dyslexia*, BDA.

Reid, G. (1992). *Learning difficulties and learning styles – Observational Criteria*. Paper presented at South East Learning Styles Conference, Virginia, USA.

Reid, G. (1994). *Specific Learning Difficulties (Dyslexia)*. A handbook for study and practice. Moray House Publications, Edinburgh.

Richards, I. L. (1985). Dyslexia: A Study of Developmental and Maturational Factors Associated with a Specific Cognitive Profile. *Unpublished PhD Thesis*. University of Aston, Birmingham.

Riding, R. and Douglas, G. (1993). 'The effect of cognitive style and mode of presentation on learning performance.' *British Journal of Educational Psychology*, 63, 2, 297-307.

Riding, R. and Cheema, I. (1991). 'Cognitive Styles – an overview and integration'. *Educational Psychology*, 11, 193-215.

Seymour, P. H. K. (1986). *Cognitive analysis of dyslexia*. Routledge and Paul Kegan.

Siegal, L. (1989). 'I.Q. is irrelevant to the definition of learning disabilities'. In *Journal of Learning Disabilities*, 22, 5, 577-85.

Singleton, C. (1993). Diagnosis of dyslexia. Paper presented at Moray House Centre for Specific Learning Difficulties Conference. Edinburgh, June 1993.

Singleton, C. (1994). Computers and dyslexia – educational applications of new technology. University of Hull.

Slingerland, B. H. (1971). A multi-sensory approach to language arts for specific language disability children. A guide for primary teachers. Books 1-3. Cambridge, MA: Educational Publishing Service.

Snowling, M. (1990). *Dyslexia: A cognitive developmental perspective*. Blackwell.

Stanovich, K. E. (1986). 'Cognitive processes and reading problems of learning-disabled children: Evaluating the assumption of specificity'. In Torgeson, J. K. and Yong, B. Y. L. (Eds.) *Psychological and Educational Perspectives on Learning Disabilities*. Academic Press, New York.

Stanovich, K. E. (1991). 'Discrepancy definitions of reading disability: Has intelligence led us astray?' *Reading Research Quarterly*, 19, 278-303.

Stanovich, K. E. and Siegal, L. S. (1994). Phenotypic Performance Profile of Children with Reading Disabilities: A Regression-Based Test of the Phonological-Core Variable-Difference Model. In *Journal of Educational Psychology*, Vol. 86, No., 1, 24-53.

Sternberg, R. J. and Detterman, D. K. (Eds.) (1986). *What is intelligence?* Ablex, Norwood, New Jersey.

Szeszulski, P. A. and Manus, F. B. (1987). 'A comparison of word recognition processes for effective use.' *Learning Disabilities Quarterly*, 12, 3-14.

Tennant, M. (1988). *Psychology and Adult Learning*. Routledge, London.

Thomson, M. E. (1982). The Assessment of Children with Specific Reading Difficulties (Dyslexia) Using the British Ability Scales. In *British Journal of Psychology*, 73 (4) (61-78).

Thomson, M. E. (1982). 'Assessing the intelligence of dyslexic children'. *Bulletin of the British Psychological Society* 35, 94-96.

Thomson, M. E. (1989). *Developmental Dyslexia*, (3rd edition). Whurr, London.

Torgeson, J. K., Kistner, J. and Morgan, S. (1987). 'Component processes in working memory'. In Borkowski, J. G. and Day, J. D. (Eds.). *Cognition in special children: comparative approaches to retardation, learning disabilities and giftedness*. Ablex, Norwood, N.J.

Wendon, L. (1987). Letterland teaching programme 1 and 2. Cambridge, Letterland Ltd.

ASSESSMENT OF INTELLIGENCE, COGNITION AND METACOGNITION: REFLECTIONS, ISSUES AND RECOMMENDATIONS

DONNA B. AYRES

METACOGNITION

Researchers believe that the control of cognitive processing depends on one's metacognitive knowledge and the abilities to reflect on and to use this knowledge (Reeve and Brown, 1985). Metacognitive knowledge involves both content and process knowledge: 'declarative knowledge' about one's cognitive processes and 'procedural knowledge' about how to regulate these processes to oversee one's thinking (Brown, 1978; Brown and DeLoache, 1978). Declarative/content knowledge is static and stored in long-term memory. Procedural/process knowledge is strategic, dynamic, and task or situation-dependent (Chi, 1978).

Metacognition is multidimensional: it involves the actions and interactions among: l) the learner's metacognitive knowledge, 2) metacognitive experiences (invoked in situations about it) (Ward and Traweek, 1993).

ASSESSING METACOGNITION

Glaser *et al.* (1987) recommend developing tests that assess the structure/ organisation of the learner's knowledge base, the depth of the learner's initial problem representations, quality of mental models (schemata), efficient use of procedural knowledge, and self-regulatory activities (e.g. self-monitoring). Essentially, this means capturing how a person structures his/her content knowledge, how this knowledge base changes with learning, i.e., how it becomes more reliable, flexible, adaptive, and automatic as the person moves from novice to expert levels of performance (Glaser *et al.*, 1987). Assessors can begin to observe one's control processes.

Definitional and psychometric problems have not stopped researchers from attempting to measure metacognition as the efficiency with which one uses control processes.

Verbal Reports. The efficient use of control processes can be inferred through self-report techniques or through observation, e.g. observing the mouthing of words to infer rehearsal and noting the arrangement of pictures to inform organisation processes in working memory. One way to understand the structure of cognitive processes, then, is to elicit assessees' cognitive processes through think-aloud verbal protocols wherein they are asked to verbalise their thoughts as they work through a problem or task. Kreutzer, Leonard, and Flavell (1975) pioneered the verbal interview procedure in asking subjects to reflect out loud on their performance with everyday memory tasks.

Verbal reports are a form of 'private speech'[1] that becomes self-regulatory as thought and speech interact in such a way that the meaning inherent in speech begins to direct language and the language in turn internalises abstract thought. One's verbalisations are one's thoughts spoken out loud; as they are externalised, they direct action.[2] When one's verbalisations begin to precede rather than follow or accompany action, they begin to mediate action; action becomes voluntary, functional, and potentially automatic in regulating behaviour. As verbalisation serves to mediate behaviour, the child becomes a self-correcting system able to create intentions, form action plans, monitor his own performance, align actual performance with plans, compare the effects of actions, and correct his mistakes (Meichenbaum and Goodman, 1979). As he starts to talk to himself, he becomes increasingly metacognitive; that he talks to himself indicates that he already is.

Research indicates that task demands activate externalised self-talk: the more difficult the task, the greater the amount of self-regulation and vocalised private speech (Anastopoulos and Krehbiel, 1985). Beherend, Rosengren, and Perlmutter (1989) cite research showing that private speech occurred most frequently when children worked on puzzles at or slightly above their cognitive level. Anastopoulos and Krehbiel (1985) further assert that increased cognitive complexity is related to increased private speech production. Fuson (1979) concludes that verbal guidance and rehearsal can direct or prolong one's attention to a task long enough to guide the child through the confusing or difficult aspects of a task. Moreover, the request to think aloud may itself provoke strategy use,

---

[1] 'Private speech' is a term coined by Flavell (1968) to denote an overt verbal utterance made to oneself to guide cognitive performance and to regulate behaviour. Private speech has been referred to an 'inner speech' (Luria, 1961); 'speech for self' (Vygotsky, 1934/1987), 'verbal mediation' (Reese, 1962); 'verbal self-regulation'; or 'self-talk' (Meichenbaum and Goodman, 1979).

[2] As the child verbalises as an afterthought to actions, then utterances begin to accompany actions, then speech starts to guide actions as verbalised plans of action, finally fading into abbreviated speech or inner (subvocal) speech beyond others' audible perception (Berk, 1986).

although metacognitive monitoring will more likely be activated if the subject has not yet automatised the self-regulation activities (Ward and Traweek, 1993).

Analysis of verbal behaviour thus becomes a viable focal point for assessment. Cognitive psychologists have assessed the use of cognitive strategies by having people think aloud as they solve problems presented to them, thus providing a concurrent interview method. This assumes that subjects reveal their cognitive and executive control processes through the 'verbal window' as indirect trace of internal processes, thus reducing the distortion arising from the lag between metacognitive monitoring and the resulting behaviour. By capturing spontaneous and uninterrupted verbalisation, researchers can catch uncensored self-corrections.

Analysis of self-reports has distinguished experts from novices: experts represent the problem more effectively than do novices; they have more subject-matter knowledge and it is hierarchically organised; their more coherent knowledge structure enables them to hold more information in memory and thereby entertain multiple solution hypotheses simultaneously whereas novices operate in a piecemeal fashion, often failing to consider previous information.

The test-taking situation therefore provides an informative occasion for the assessor to probe the assessee's metacognition through observations of how s/he approaches tasks presented during the testing session. Many of the tasks endemic to standardised intelligence testing elicit verbalised private speech as a sign of verbal mediation; moreover, the examiner can solicit verbal reports during task performance in a post-test session aimed at reviewing items or testing to the limits.

Problems with Verbal Reports. A major problem with assessing metacognition involves the fact that metacognition must be inferred. Critics of the verbal report as an inferential method disdain the veridicality and completeness of the verbalisation, claiming that retrospective post-experimental interviews provide the opportunity for the respondent to confuse what s/he actually did during a cognitive processing event with a post hoc rationalisation of it (Cavanaugh and Perlmutter, 1982). The method has its drawbacks: the procedures may disrupt the verbal processing of the task as the person becomes aware during the act of reporting; many deeper-level cognitive processes may be inaccessible ('opaque') to conscious reporting; age, motivation, anxiety, self-disclosure, and verbal ability may confound the results; the examiner's questions and probes might cue subjects to desired responses; the data are difficult to analyse; the procedures have not been standardised; and task difficulty may affect the search for alternative solutions. In addition to ensuring that subjects understood what they were being asked, possessed the verbal skills to express their awareness/

NB

knowledge, and were motivated to provide the information, subjects might report what they inferred they must have been thinking rather than what they actually experienced (Das *et al.*, 1994).

Ericsson (1987), however, posits such verbal reports are valid expressions of thought and an effective inductive empirical method for determining processes which mediate performance but only when the verbalisation are compared to actual performance data. The key to ensuring validity and reliability of the verbal report method, say Ericsson and Simon (1980), is to collect other samples of behaviour (i.e., independent measures) that can check the consistency of the verbalisation. Swanson (1993) recommends behaviourally-anchored verbal protocol coding to improve the reliability and validity of the process.[3] Post-experimental probing that encourages subjects to describe general rather than specific strategies may provide a poor fit to their performance. Verbal knowledge will reflect action more reliably when a strategy has not been automatised; otherwise procedural knowledge becomes unavailable for conscious verbalisation and control by centralised processing resources (Borkowski, Schneider and Pressley, 1989; Cavanaugh and Borkowski, 1979; Das *et al.*, 1964). So, a multi-measure, multi-method approach is indicated.

In spite of their limitations, introspective reports and think-aloud protocols are useful supplements to the direct observation of strategies availed during the performance of some planning tasks. Furthermore, verbalisation itself may lead to more efficient planning through a learning effect, as Das *et al.* (1994) have shown.

Examine Planning Behaviour. Some researchers have turned their attention to planning skills as an indicator of metacognition. Criticising the field of intellectual assessment as represented by common IQ tests for its limited view of

---

[3]Swanson's code includes: a. **Non-strategic.** Subjects recalled idea units, but verbalisations were irrelevant or did not reveal an action sequence (e.g., 'I must remember it,' 'It seemed important'). b. **Visual imagery.** Verbal response in which the context associated with the idea unit is a non-verbal reference such as an object, a picture, or a mental image (e.g., 'I imagined a basketball court in my mind'). c. **Access to long-term memory.** Verbal responses in which previous experience and/or familiarity with the word or idea is associated with the idea unit (e.g., 'I have a friend with the same name'). d. **Advanced organisation**. Verbal responses that refer to the structure of the prose, key words in the prose, or related ideas for logically organising information (e.g., 'I remember that from when I wrote the words on paper in the beginning'). e. **Rehearsal**. Verbal responses in which rote repetition or repetitive naming is associated with an idea unit (e.g., 'I just keep saying the information over to myself). f. **Novel encoding.** Verbal responses that emphasised the salience or unfamiliarity of ideas (e.g., 'I remember that because it is so unusual . . .') (p. 71).

intelligence, Das *et al.* (1994) offer a model – the PASS model (for Planning-Attention-Simultaneous-and-Successive processes) – that focuses on the mechanisms by which information is processed, emphasising how information is processed, not what is processed. Their PASS Model, based on the Luria-Das model (see McGrew, 1986), conceptualises the brain as concerned with three major interlocking systems or 'blocks' of functions designed to capture the use of strategies: – Attention – that maintains alertness, attention, and motivation through processes of activation and arousal to information; one that receives, processes, encodes, and stores information using Simultaneous and Successive information coding; and – Planning – that programs, regulates, and directs mental activity (the executive system); and that is concerned about 'thinking about thinking' or the 'use of strategies to approach tasks' (McGrew, 1986, p. 141).

Attentional tasks require the individual to attend to one aspect of a two-dimensional stimulus while ignoring the other aspect. The person examines and detects the dimensions of the target stimulus and decides to respond to one and not to the other salient competing dimension. Symbol Search on the WISC-III exemplifies an attention task.

Successive processing is serial processing of linguistic stimuli. In successive processing, each bit of information is processed individually, logically, and analytically in sequential fashion. In a successive processing task, the person must appreciate the serial nature of stimuli to reproduce the linearity of events (e.g. repeat a string of numbers in order or reproduce the sequence as presented). Word recall and repetition of digits forward (e.g. the WISC-III Digit Span Forward) are examples of successive processing tasks. The Arithmetic subtest on the WISC-III and WAIS-R measures quantitative reasoning and successive processing to some extent. Word recall tasks also exemplify successive processing tasks.

Simultaneous processing is viewed as parallel or multiple processing – dealing with stimuli holistically. Simultaneous processing functions to integrate or synthesise information all at one time as a meaningful whole. A simultaneous processing task requires the individual to interrelate the component parts of the particular stimulus item to arrive at a correct answer; to do this, the subject must appreciate the interrelationships among all components of the item, i.e., to detect some complete pattern or idea.

It is the third dimension – Planning – which speaks to metacognition. Planning refers to strategy development in problem solving. Planning specifies a function that allows the individual to form plans of action, to carry them out, to inspect performance and regulate behaviour so that it conforms to these plans, and then to compare the effects of these actions with the original intention so as to correct mistakes. Das *et al*, (1994) contend that the planning factor can be assessed through tests that require complex strategies, e.g., Visual Search of Matching Numbers. Factor analyses reveal that planning emerges as a separate factor distinct from attentional, simultaneous, and successive processes, yet one that seems to unite the other three (Das *et al.*, 1994). The Russian neuropsychologist, Aleksandr R. Luria (1973, cited in Das *et al.*, 1994), suggests that 'planning is the essence of human intelligence, as it involves the aptitude for asking new questions, solving problems, and self-monitoring as well as the application of information-coding processes' (p. 17) – particularly important when unique or non-routinised solutions to problems are required. Planning is purposeful behaviour; it redirects behaviour as it links with evaluation of plans in action. Planning is a metacognitive activity (Flavell, 1970).

Current IQ tests are quite limited in scope in relation to the dimensions of the PASS model. As Das and colleagues conclude, 'Unless the four processes are evaluated in tests of intelligence, an abbreviated view of human functioning will continue to misinform psychologists' (Das *et al.*, 1994, p. 127).

Typically, Attention is assessed informally through behavioural observations of the test taker's behaviour during testing. Successive and Simultaneous processing are two basic types of information processing styles traditionally connected with school-like tasks and thus typically incorporated in intelligence testing (Searls, 1985). Most intelligence tests, in measuring verbal/achievement capabilities, thus capture Successive and Simultaneous processing. Planning is not presently assessed because of the lack of practical tests of the behaviours it encompasses. Only the Mazes sub-test on the WISC-III tries to capture this ability explicitly as visual-planning, although Digit Span Backward involves planning processes in requiring the individual to develop some method to convert the order of digits for recall. The WISC Arithmetic subtests also involves planning processes in effecting math computations, i.e., systematic execution of rules, checking one's work, and organising activities in multi-step problems. Proponents of the PASS model argue that existing tests of intelligence do not adequately assess planning formally, which leads to a less-than comprehensive conceptualisation of cognition. Consequently, 'intelligence tests measure only a part of a domain that reflects intelligent behaviour' (Sattler, 1992, p. 78) – not the full spectrum of human abilities.

In fact, Das *et al.* (1994) state that the limited success of current intelligence tests to be sensitive to the deficiencies of many learning disabled children may be the results of their limited view of planning as an aspect of intelligence and the source of the deficit. For example, planning discriminates good from poor readers of comparable IQ: top planners make more inferential statements, question and evaluate their responses, and are better able to infer the author's message in the text, whereas poor planners make fewer inferential statements, do not question or evaluate their responses, and tend to be impulsive, easily frustrated, and unlikely to change their ideas (Ramey, 1985, cited in Das *et al.*, 1994). Reading disabled children are weak in control processes. Learning disabled children may reflect planning deficits in terms of maintaining proper behaviour, following rules, controlling impulses, being disorganised, and failing to complete less structured activities.

Das *et al.* (1994) contend that their PASS processes form a complex and interdependent system, which (1) helps us understand the nature of individual differences, (2) provides a framework within which to conceptualise assessment, and (3) leads directly to theory-based remediation (p. xvii).

The PASS claims to overcome limitations of standardised cognitive batteries with experimental tasks tied directly to the four PASS dimensions via a variety of ways: by content (verbal and non-verbal), presentation format (e.g., memory and motor), modality (visual and auditory), and response format (written and oral).

Thus, planning can be operationalised through simple perceptual-motor tasks, such as the WISC Mazes subtest. Or planning tasks may be inferred from how the assessee analyses a problem, generates a solution, monitors the solution, and modifies the solution if the first one failed. Poor planners look at the page in a disorganised manner, choose incorrect targets impulsively, make many errors, and fail to change their strategy if it is inefficient.

IMPROVING ASSESSMENT OF METACOGNITION DURING TESTING

Change the Object of Measurement. There are ways to utilise current standardised individual testing practices to infer metacognition. The assessor can shift his/her focus to take a more metacognitive stance *vis-a-vis* the object of assessment. Rather than simply look at the total number of word problems an assessee solves, the assessor can examine or infer how the assessee represents the problem information to glean whether s/he is having difficulty with the operations or with the semantic representation of the problem. At various points during task performance, the examiner can ask the assessee questions, making the assessee's think-aloud verbalisation the object of behavioural observation.

McGrew (1986) advises clinicians to combine clinical probes (questioning) with careful observations before, during, and after a person's test performance to infer the use or lack of learning strategies. Questions such as, 'What would you do?'; 'How would you do this?'; 'Why would you do this?'; 'What does it tell you?'; and 'What do you plan to do next?' can elicit a person's metacognitive activity.

Before the testing, the assessor can ask the assessee to make predictions about what comes next in a sequence or the effects of a change in the sequence (as in the WISC Picture Arrangement task). For example, the assessor can ask the assessee to predict her own memory span (e.g. 'How many numbers do you think you can remember in a row?') on the WISC Digit Span subtest or the WJ-R Numbers Reversed subtest. Probes can be added during the test to seek predictions, e.g. by asking the assessee between trials to hypothesise how s/he would act if presented with the task again.

During the testing, the assessor may also observe the assessee's self-talk during test-taking and note whether it is adaptive or maladaptive. Assessors can count the number of plans and hypotheses mentioned by the assessees during the problem-solving task; ask probing questions about how a device, component, or system works and what its purpose is; count the number of errors made or incorrect steps taken; tally the procedures, methods, and skills needed to successfully carry out the plan; and gauge the extent to which the action proceeded in a systematic manner rather than haphazardly or without a sense of a goal structure. In addition, the assessor can question students about their use of metacognitive strategies, i.e. ask them to state the purpose of their activity. In solving mathematics problems, the assessor can ask the assessee to talk aloud as s/he solve the maths problems to note the use of strategies and heuristics, e.g., operating routines, such as drawing a diagram. Examining students' worksheets will reveal information about how they solved their problems. Or, the assessor can ask the assessee to produce a writing sample and then to read it out loud to see if s/he detects and corrects errors as s/he reads (self-monitors).

After the testing session is completed, the examiner can ask the assessee to state how s/he solved these problems or to describe how s/he'd explain to a friend how to do well on the task. Or she can capture the assessee's post-dictions by asking him/her to identify which sequences she could immediately recall after a trial to see how aware s/he is of his/her memory ability and how well s/he has monitored his/her memory proficiency.

Memory tests aid in the measurement of attentional capacity, the use of rehearsal and chunking strategies, and manipulation of information in working memory. So, noting if one chunks strings of digits into groups of two or more or uses the verbal mediational strategy of subvocal rehearsal to facilitate short-term recall may reveal the use of memory strategies.

The assessor can enable the assessee to display metacognitive behaviour. Assessees can be helped to think aloud reliably by being given warm-up tasks where thinking aloud is easy, e.g., mental multiplication or anagram problem solving. Or the examiner can instruct the subject to express verbally all thoughts that come to mind while performing the task.

Change the Method. McGrew (1986) cautions against interpreting standardised IQ subtest results strictly to infer specific cognitive processing abilities because using the sub-test for purposes for which it was not intended may lessen one's certainty about what is being measured by any given task (sub-test). The more appropriate strategy involves seeking alternative assessment methods. Ward and Traweek (1993) highlight the benefits of dynamic or process assessment, in which a child's response to intervention is examined over static assessment, the traditional approach. This shifts the focus from product scores to process measures. Think-aloud procedures are a dynamic assessment tool, which makes observation of a learner's overt verbalisation a form of dynamic assessment.

ALTERNATIVE FORMS OF ASSESSMENT

Alternative theories of intelligence, emanating from the cognitive-developmental perspective, have ushered in a new wave of assessment approaches. These approaches shift the assessment focus away from static models implying permanent deficits toward dynamic forms of assessment that account for students' learning strategies and that imply specific treatment intervention. These approaches emphasise the process of learning rather than its products, seek clues from the students' strategy use, and go beyond diagnosis to contribute directly to the teaching process. Assessment thus accepts as its goals not only identification of what the assessee has learned, how s/he learns, and why learning may be delayed or advanced but also prescription through teaching strategies that match the assessee's profile of strengths and weaknesses to specific remediations (Swanson, 1993). Assessment becomes dynamic.

DYNAMIC ASSESSMENT

Mediated Learning Experiences. Dynamic assessment is concerned with how learning occurs as a result of specific interventions. It assumes that the cognitive system is modifiable through directive instruction and utilises a test-teach-test assessment approach. Vygotsky's theory of the 'Zone of Proximal (potential) Development (ZPD)' provides the foundation for assessing learning as dynamic and interactive. Vygotsky, a Russian psychologist who studied learning disabilities, conceived of the zone of proximal development as that zone between the level of mental functioning revealed by a child when solving a problem alone and that level wherein the child can perform acceptably when given assistance by a more able instructor (e.g. parent or teacher); this becomes the child's level of potential development or learning potential (Vygotsky, 1978). Social influences thus take a prominent role in learning, for they function as 'scaffolds' to transfer control and responsibility for reaching a goal from the adult to the child. Scaffolding helps the learner internalise instructions and self-directed verbalisation and thus enhances the child's awareness of strategies that promote strategic learning. Instruction aimed at assisting the learner to use a concept, skill, or strategy begins to stretch the learner's ZPD; the actual ZPD metric assessing the learner's potential to near-term (proximal) development in the target cognitive domain becomes the test-retest difference. The diagnosis becomes a special form of diagnostic teaching regarding where practical instruction will likely pay off because, given sufficient continuing guidance and practice, the learner becomes able to organise and automatise the behavioural sequences that make up the target skill. As the teacher eliminates explicit instructions, hints, and demonstrations of the skill, responsibility for performance transfers to the learner who, through practice, internalises these new standards of performance, setting the bottom level for a new ZPD.

The challenge for assessment is to relate instructional strategies to the ZPD. This is accomplished by assessing the child's ability, teaching the child a specific concept and evaluating his/her responsiveness, providing the child with accurate feedback, and retesting. Both testing and instructional interventions become customised to match the child's preferred learning strategies. It might be, suggest Glaser *et al.* (1987), that children with an assessed large zone can move quickly through curricula whereas those with a narrow zone might require a slower, more complete instructional agenda. Metacognitive skills may well represent performances that would be needed to realise one's zone of proximal development or to stretch its range.

The larger implication, proposed by Belmont (1989), is that the ZPD provides an attractive alternative to the concept of intelligence as IQ inhering in the child; here IQ is seen as a shared index of general learning potential based on interpersonal interaction with a more competent adult. As static assessments, standardised tests fail to capture the social enterprise of learning in a highly individualistic way. The ZPD, on the other hand, can be identified through a combination of static and dynamic tests. The learner's performance on a standard intelligence test provides information about what s/he has learned to do without assistance. The implications for instruction are self-evident: if the learner's performance is continually re-evaluated, his/her learning efficiency can be improved in relation to instructional demands rather than to a static view of his/her ability levels. Obviously, this method is extremely time-consuming for the assessor.

AUTHENTIC ASSESSMENT OF MULTIPLE INTELLIGENCES

Howard Gardner, a prominent cognitive psychologist from Harvard University, has challenged the concept of a unified intelligence that can be reduced to a single score through objective standardised measurement of isolated and decontextualised tasks. Rather, Gardner identifies intelligence as the capacity for solving problems or creating products in a context-rich, naturalistic setting. Keeping one foot in the abilities paradigm, he fashions intelligence as a broad range of abilities encompassing at least seven different cognitive capacities that cultivate the ability to think. Gardner proposes that each person has capacities in all seven intelligences to varying degrees. While some people possess one or more of the intelligences to an exceptional degree, others appear to lack all but the most rudimentary; most people fall somewhere in between, with some intelligences highly developed and others underdeveloped. Thus, when one finds a student with poor memory, it may reflect the type of memory emphasised in school – linguistic and logical-mathematical memory – not memory associated with other intelligences.

Gardner's list of intelligences include: Linguistic Intelligence (the capacity to use words effectively orally or in writing); Logical-Mathematical Intelligence (the capacity to use numbers effectively); Spatial Intelligence (the ability to perceive and transform the visual-spatial world accurately); Bodily-Kinaesthetic Intelligence (the capacity to use one's whole body to express ideas and feelings); Musical Intelligence (the capacity to perceive, discriminate, transform, and express musical forms); Interpersonal Intelligence (the ability to perceive and make distinctions in the moods, intentions, motivations, and feelings of other people); and Intrapersonal Intelligence (self-knowledge and the ability to act adaptively on the basis of this knowledge) (Gardner, 1983). Intrapersonal intelligence may be akin to metacognition in allowing one to have an accurate picture of his/her own strengths and limitations, needs, and the capacity for self-discipline, self-understanding and self-esteem (Armstrong, 1994). One can infer learning style inasmuch as a learning style may be viewed as 'the intelligences put to work' (Armstrong, 1994).

Gardner does not champion the use of standardised tests to assess these forms of intelligence, although he concedes that the most common standardised tests do provide glimpses of several of the intelligences. The verbal sections of intelligence and achievement tests assess Linguistic Intelligence; the reasoning sections of intelligence tests assess Logical-Mathematical Intelligence; and visual memory and visual-motor tests and some performance items on intelligence tests assess Spatial Intelligence. For example, the Information and Vocabulary subtests on the WISC require linguistic intelligence; the Arithmetic subtest and Similarities (analogies) requires logico-mathematical intelligence; the Picture Arrangement subtest requires spatial intelligence; the Object Assembly subtests infers bodily-kinaesthetic intelligence. Likewise, there is no single test that comprehensively surveys these various intelligences.

Gardner steps away from the traditional paradigm not as much in what he assesses as in how and when he obtains the assessment. Gardner advises assessors to obtain authentic assessments of the intelligences from direct observation in natural settings through criterion-referenced, benchmarked, or ipsative measures rather than through norm-referenced standardised tests, which focus too narrowly on the verbal and logical domains through isolated tasks performed in artificial settings.

Portfolio Assessment. The assessor can move into the natural setting – the classroom – to make the authentic assessment. Authentic assessments require students to demonstrate through performance what they know and understand. Portfolio assessment, wherein the assessor collects samples of the assessee's work over time and across methods, can include measures from all seven intelligences. Exhibitions; investigations; demonstrations; written and oral responses; clinical student interviews (debriefing interviews); journals and anecdotal records; documented observations through audiotapes, videotapes, and photographs; informal tests; and student portfolios containing work samples judged against rating criteria all facilitate performance-based assessment (Armstrong, 1994; Herman, Aschbacher and Winters, 1992). In tackling active and complex tasks, students must apply their prior knowledge and relevant skills. In addition to celebrating the learner's accomplishments and providing a way to communicate progress to the learner, parents, and administrators, the portfolio can help students reflect on their own work and thus build the learner's metacognition.

If standardised tests are used in this milieu, they can be used with relaxed limits beyond the strict administration guidelines, or they can avail think-alouds in conjunction with standardised tests after the completion of standardised protocols. For instance, the assessor can probe student responses, provide opportunities to demonstrate answers in other ways (e.g., through pictures), or probe errors to ascertain how the student is thinking. Armstrong (1994) suggests that one also observe how a student misbehaves in class because his or her acting out behaviour will generally reflect a need for self-expression that, while perhaps unacceptable in class, may represent a more natural form of learning for that child – and thus provide a diagnostic indicator of the student's strengths and learning needs. Or the clinician can pay attention to how the student spends free time and his/her choices of activities and settings to glean preferred ways to learn.

As helpful as portfolios seem for improving classroom instruction (especially for problem-solving strategies and mathematics), questions remain as to whether the psychometric properties of performance assessments are rigorous enough to warrant the curtailment of traditional standardised instruments. There are problems with reliability of raters' scoring, although attempts are being made to improve rater reliability and internal consistency of ratings (Association for Supervision and Curriculum Development, 1993). The use of behavioural checklists and rubrics are examples of such attempts.

Behavioural Checklists. Armstrong (1994) provides checklists that describe typical behaviours for each type of intelligence, which can also be used in authentic settings. For example, the child with Linguistic Intelligence has a good memory for names, places, dates, or trivia and a good vocabulary for his age. The child with Logical-Mathematical intelligence computes arithmetic problems quickly in his/her head, thinks on an abstract level, and has a good sense of cause-effect. The child with Spatial Intelligence reads visual images (e.g., maps, charts, and diagrams) more easily than text and enjoys doing puzzles and mazes. The child with Bodily-Kinaesthetic Intelligence moves, twitches, taps, or fidgets while seated in one spot for a long time, loves to take things apart and put them back together, and displays good fine-motor coordination. The child with Musical Intelligence unconsciously hums to him/herself. The child with Intrapersonal Intelligence builds rapport easily with others. The child with Intrapersonal Intelligence has a realistic sense of his/her strengths and weaknesses, accurately expresses personal feelings; is able to learn from success and failure, and has high self-esteem. The clinician indeed can infer these intelligences from observing the assessee's behaviours during the standardised testing session, although Gardner would implore the assessor to go beyond such cursory inferences and to label them as aspects of intelligence.

Rubrics. Efforts to operationalise Howard Gardner's theory of multiple intelligences have taken hold in some schools in to direct assessment and curriculum development. Gardner advises teachers to collect a lot of detailed, highly idiosyncratic knowledge about how the child's mind works and then use it to guide instruction. Organising the curriculum to facilitate learners' expressions of/ through the seven intelligences (spatial, bodily kinaesthetic, musical, linguistic, logical-mathematic, interpersonal, and intrapersonal) is easier than gaining objective individual assessments limited to the verbal-linguistic and logical-mathematical domains. Gardner promotes the integration of instruction and assessment so that they become virtually indistinguishable. Assessment acknowledges and honours the diversity of intelligence.

The challenge of assessing intelligence as multi-faceted is to ground the assessment in agreed upon standards. The need for reliable portfolio assessment is requiring teachers to be precise about their criteria for evaluating student work within a wide range of task/behavioural sampling, which will help assessors make their assessments. Benchmarking against clear examples of 'best practices' helps. Herman *et al.* (1992) recommend that the assessment process start with specification of the nature of the skills and accomplishments the learner is to develop, specified tasks that illustrate these skills and accomplishments, specific criteria and standards for judging if students reach the standards, and a reliable rating process. Such standards are set by rubrics, agreed upon rules that permit one to evaluate (score) performance. Rubrics developed in concert with students, followed by co-interpretations between student and teacher/assessor, may be a way to move toward this more dynamic form of assessment. Paradoxically, the process of jointly formulating clear models of good work defined by explicit criteria or standards of 'good' fosters students' reflection and critical thinking skills and promotes active learning – i.e. metacognition. For example, asking the student to select her best piece of work from her portfolio and to explain why she chose it both requires and builds reflection.

A rubric may be a checklist or it may reflect the level of explicit criteria captured on standardised assessment instruments, for example, a dimension of effectiveness that is anchored by specific, identifiable and reliable points along a continuum defining quality. For instance, the assessor may ask a student to select a written composition she feels is a particularly good illustration of her ability to communicate or to plan a project. The rubric the assessor uses to evaluate student writing might examine the dimension of organisation within a 5-level range of quality defined as 1 – lacks a clear sense of direction; ideas, details, or events seem strung together in a loose fashion or randomly through to 5 – enhances or showcases the central idea or storyline; the order structure, and presentation of information moves the reader through the text. To evaluate how well a student demonstrates awareness of her own thinking, she may be asked to walk the assessor through the steps of solving a problem, describing what she was expected to do, explaining the sequence of thoughts she used when facing specific steps, recommending ways to improve the problem-solving process, evaluating what she did well and where she needs help, and stating some insights she derived from both the problem-solving exercise and her reflection about it. The assessor's job is to apply a rubric such as the following four-level rubric offered by Marzano, Pickering and McTighe (1993) related to 'Habits of Mind'[4]:

1   Provides a confusing report of the thinking he or she used in completing a task or problem. Cannot describe how performance has been improved.

2   Provides a vague or incomplete description of how he or she thought through a task or problem. Provides only a few ideas about how an awareness of his or her own thinking has enhanced performance.

3   Describes how he or she thought through a task or problem. Provides some ideas about how an awareness of his or her own thinking has enhanced performance.

4   Explains in detail the sequence of thoughts he or she used when facing a task or problem. Provides a detailed analysis of how an awareness of his or her own thinking has enhanced performance. The assessment (rubric) should reveal whether or not the learner knows and understands, i.e. possesses and can demonstrate the capability.

SUMMARY

As long as there are children and learners with individual differences, there will be a need for assessment of learner's strengths and weaknesses. That parents and teachers suspect or denote a difference between academic achievement and aptitude/cognitive ability and want to understand it, means they will seek diagnostic information. And given that academic programs establish selection criteria, there will remain a need for qualifying evaluations based on these differences. Cognitive

---

[4] Marzano *et al.* offer the Dimensions of Learning instructional framework that specifies five dimensions essential to learning: 1) Positive Attitudes and Perceptions about Learning; 2) Acquiring and Integrating Knowledge; 3) Extending and Refining Knowledge; 4) Using Knowledge Meaningfully; and 5) Productive Habits of Mind. Cognitive complexity, cognitive strategies, and metacognition affect all of these dimensions, especially the fifth dimension, which encourages one to be aware of his/her own thinking and to evaluate the effectiveness of his/her actions. The fifth dimension encompasses self-regulation, critical thinking, and creative thinking.

---

testing is not likely to disappear, although its form may change as the technology of psychometrics advances, as models of intelligence and effective cognitive functioning evolve, and as psychometricians, diagnosticians, and teachers adopt more creative, expansive views on what it is they are assessing. The format of assessment will likely enlarge to include additional information garnered from real-world tasks linked to criteria related to what we expect students to be able to do at each level of their learning and development.

Many people question whether or not standardised tests adequately represent student learning and development; they criticise them for being too narrow in content and focus, for emphasising routine and discrete skills over complex thinking and problem solving. To become more holistic, assessors will have to move away from the disadvantages of standardised testing: a stressful milieu; intimidation by scores or percentiles; emphasis on what the assessee cannot do; the separation of testing from instruction and learning; only one chance to answer; a focus on 'the right answer'; esoteric results interpretable predominantly by trained professionals; imposed time limits that may constrain some students' thinking; and attention to lower-order learning skills (Armstrong, 1994).

Broadening one's perspective to encompass alternative forms of assessment becomes a solution. Authentic assessment evaluates the child as a unique learner within natural settings doing familiar things that give him/her a chance to excel. It thus focuses on the student's strengths, provides multiple sources of evaluation captured over time, links assessment with instruction, produces information and results that have practical value, deals with processes as much as with final products, is unobtrusive, involves multiple methods to gather data (creating, interviewing, demonstrating, problem-solving, reflecting, sketching, discussing, and engaging interactively and actively with others and the task), includes higher-order thinking skills as the object of assessment, and provides sufficient time for the student to demonstrate his/her capabilities.

If, indeed, one adopts a cognitive-developmental framework highlighting cognitive and strategic processing, which views the learner as an active participant in the learning process rather than a passive receptacle, then one must expand the forms of meaningful assessment used. A multi-method, multi-measure approach is indicated. Assessment that shifts its attention from static abilities to dynamic cognitive processes will shift from product-oriented measures, including IQ and standardised achievement tests, to process-oriented measures that reflect how students apply skills, processes, and strategies to various learning and problem-solving situations. The shift from the what of assessment to the how and why of assessment enhances the ability of the results of assessment to explain rather than simply describe. Making this shift may also reveal how and why individuals with comparable scores on static IQ tests may have taken different paths to these scores and therefore why particular remediations may succeed or fail to help the learner. Observing and analysing planning behaviour may be a way to initiate the shift.

Assessment information – especially about their use of cognitive strategies – can help students step back and think about what they did well, would and should do differently, and whether or not they need help. As students become aware of their thought processes through journals, probing questioning, goal setting, problem-based learning, guided practice and feedback, and self-assessments, they will be more inclined to transfer their knowledge and strategies to different contexts (Schneider, 1985). In viewing learning as reflective, constructive, and self-regulated, assessment must come to care about how and whether students organise, structure, and use the information they acquire to solve complex problems related to their lives out of school as well as in school. Engaging learners in thoughtful reflection of what constitutes excellent work and how to evaluate their own efforts can aid them in acquiring and applying effective strategies for lifelong learning and thinking. Assessment must therefore provide holistic information about what the learner knows and can do in the real world. The assessment of metacognition becomes important because it helps learners direct their own learning and problem-solving.

In particular, alternative assessments in naturalistic settings provide the opportunity to capture metacognitive behaviour because such settings make it easier for students to demonstrate the full spectrum of their intelligence through tasks that call tor higher-level thinking and problem-solving skills than do standardised tests. Portfolio assessments go beyond linguistic assessment to provide holistic assessment. The assessor's tasks becomes more complicated, nonetheless, for s/he must draw on human judgment for interpretation, not the security of standardised guidelines for testing (Herman *et al.* 1992). The assessor's task also becomes time-consuming and expensive.

Yet if diagnosis is to be aimed at improvement versus simply classification, then assessment must adopt a broader view of student learning and capabilities. The answer is likely a balanced approach to assessment that blends performance assessment with standardised testing. Herman *et al.* (1992) summarise:

> "There is no one right way to assess students . . . We do affirm that performance assessments offer appealing ways to assess complex thinking and problem-solving skills and, because they are grounded in realistic problems, are potentially more motivating and reinforcing for students." (Herman *et al.*, 1992, p. 9).

In fact, the answer is for assessment to become a process and not an end in itself. Just as metacognition expands one's perspective, stretching how we look at assessment will do the same. A way to begin is to take some risk in assessment and pursue multiple forms of measurement and to add additional foci of measurement as suggested here. Carefully and thoughtfully looking for meaningful and reliable indicators of metacognition in the context of standardised cognitive testing is a small stretch but one that can add an invaluable glimpse of learners' strengths and limitations in higher-order thinking skills. It's time to begin – for the sake of both the assessor and the assessee, for each has much to learn and contribute towards the holistic assessment of metacognition.

REFERENCES

Anastopoulos, A. D. and Krehhiel, G. G. (1985, April). *The development of private speech: A review of empirical evidence addressing Vygotsky's theoretical views*. Paper presented at the Biennial Meeting of the Society for Research in Child Development. Ontario, Canada. (ERIC Document Reproduction Service No. ED 257-558).

Armstrong, T. (1994). *Multiple intelligences in the classroom*. Alexandria, VA: Association for Supervision and Curriculum Development.

Association for Supervision and Curriculum Development. (1993). The promise of portfolios. *Update*. 35(7), 1,5.

Behrend, D. A., Rosengren, K., and Perlmutter, M. (1989). A new look at children's private speech: The effects of age, task difficulty, and parent presence. *International Journal of Behavioural Development*, L2, 305-320.

Belmont, J. M. (1989). Cognitive strategies and strategic learning. The socio-instructional approach. *American Psychologist*, 44(2), 142-148.

Benton, S. L. and Kiewra, K. A. (1987). The assessment of cognitive factors in academic abilities. In Ronning, R. R., Glover, J. A., Conoley, J. C., and Witt, J. C. (Eds.), *The Influence of Cognitive Psychology on Testing. Vol. 3. Buros-Nebraska Symposium on Measurement and Testing* (pp. 145-189). Hillsdale, NJ: Lawrence Erlbaum Assoc.

Berk, L. E. (1986). Private speech: Learning out loud. *Psychology Today*, 20(5), 34-42.

Borkowski, J. G., Carr, M., and Pressley, M. (1987). Spontaneous strategy use – perspectives from metacognitive theory. *Intelligence*, 11(1), 61-75 .

Borkowski, J. G. and Cavanaugh, J. C. (1979). Maintenance and generalisation of skills and strategies by the retarded. In Ellis, N. R. (Ed.), *Handbook of mental deficiency: Psychological theory and research*. (2nd ed.). Hillsdale, NJ: Lawrence Erlbaum Assoc.

Borkowski, J. G., Estrada, M. T., Milstead, M., and Hale, C. A. (1989). General problem solving skills: Relations between metacognition and strategic processing. Special issue: Learning strategy instruction. *Learning Disability Quarterly*, 12(1), 57-70.

Borkowski, J. G., Johnston, M. B. and Reid, M. K. (1987). Metacognition, motivation, and controlled performance. In Ceci, S. J. (Ed.), *Handbook of cognitive. social, and neurological aspects of learning disabilities*. (Vol. 2, pp. 147-173). Hillsdale, NJ: Lawrence Erlbaum Assoc.

Borkowski, J. G., Schneider, W., and Pressley, M. (1989). The challenges of teaching good information processing to learning disabled students. *International Journal of Disability, Development, and Education*, 36(3), 169-185.

Brown, A. L. (1978). Knowing where, when, and how to remember: A problem of metacognition. In Glaser, R. (Ed.), *Advances in instructional psychology* (Vol. 1, pp. 77-165). Hillsdale, NJ: Lawrence Erlbaum Assoc.

Brown, A. L., Bransford, J. D., Ferrara, R. A. and Campione, J. S. (1983). Learning remembering, and understanding. In Flavell, J. H. and Markman, E. M. (Eds.), *Handbook of child psychology. Vol. 3: Cognitive development* (4th ed.) (pp. 77166). NY: Wiley. (P. H. Mussen, General Editor).

Brown, A. L., and DeLoache, J. S. (1978). Skills, plans, and self-regulation. In Siegler, R. S. (Ed.), *Children's thinking: What develops?* Hillsdale, NJ: Lawrence Erlbaum Assoc.

Burke, K. (1993). *The mindful school: How to assess thoughtful outcomes.* Palatine, IL: IRI/Skylight Publishing.

Carroll, J. B. (1987). New perspectives in the analysis of abilities. In Ronning, R. R., Glover, J. A., Conoley, J. C. and Witt, J. C. (Eds.), *The Influence of Cognitive Psychology on Testing. Vol. 3. Buros-Nebraska Symposium on Measurement and Testing* (pp. 267-284). Hillsdale, NJ: Lawrence Erlbaum Assoc.

Cavanaugh, J. C. and Borkowski, J. G. (1979). The metamemory-memory 'connection': Effects of strategy training and maintenance, *Journal of General Psychology*, 101, 161-174.

Cavanaugh, J. C. and Borkowski, J. G. (1980). Searching for metamemory-memory connections: A developmental study. *Developmental Psychology*, 16, 441-453.

Cavanaugh, J. C. and Perlmutter, M. (1982). Metamemory: A critical examination. *Child Development*, 53 (1), 11-28.

Chi, M. (1978). Knowledge structures and memory development. In R. S. Siegler (Ed.), *Children's thinking: What develops?* (pp. 73-97). Hillsdale, NJ: Lawrence Erlbaum Assoc.

Chipman, S. F. and Segal, J. W. (1985). Higher cognitive goals for education: An introduction. In Chipman, S. F., Segal, J. W. and Glaser, R. (Eds.), Thinking and learning skills. Vol. 2: Research and open questions, (pp. 1-18). Hillsdale, NJ: Lawrence Erlbaum.

Cohen, R. J., Swerdlik, M. E. and Smith, D. K. (1992). *Psychological testing and assessment. An introduction to tests and measurement.* (2nd. ed.). Mountain View, CA: Mayfield Publishing Co.

Das, J. P., Naglieri, J. A. and Kirby, J. R. (1994). *Assessment of cognitive processes. The PASS theory of intelligence.* Boston: Allyn & Bacon.

Ericsson, K. A. (1987). Theoretical implications from protocol analysis on testing and measurement. In Ronning, R. R., Glover, J. A., Conoley, J. C. and Witt, J. C. (Eds.), *The Influence of Cognitive Psychology on Testing. Vol. 3. Buros-Nebraska Symposium on Measurement and Testing* (pp. 191-226). Hillsdale, NJ: Lawrence Erlbaum Assoc.

Ericsson, K. A. and Simon, H. A. (1980). Verbal reports as data. *Psychological Review*, 87(3), 215-251.

Flavell, J. H. (1968). *The development of role-taking and communication skills in children.* NY: John Wiley & Sons.

Flavell, J. (1970). Developmental studies of mediated memory. In Reese, H. and Lipsett, L. P. (Eds.), *Advances in child development and behaviour* (Vol. 5). NY: Academic Press.

Flavell, J. H. (1979). Metacognition and cognitive monitoring: A new area of cognitive-developmental inquiry. *American Psychologist*, 34, 906-911.

Flavell, J. H. and Wellman, H. M. (1977). Metamemory. In Kail, R. V. and Hagen, J. W. (Eds.), *Perspectives on the development of memory and cognition.* Hillsdale, NJ: Lawrence Erlbaum Assoc.

Fuson, K. C. (1979). The development of self-regulating aspects of speech: A review. In Ziven, G. (Ed.), *The development of self-regulation through private speech* (pp. 135-217). NY: John Wiley & Sons.

Gardner, H. (1983). *Frames of mind. The theory of multiple intelligences.* NY: Basic Books, Inc.

Glaser, R., Lesgold, A. and Lejoie, S. (1987). Toward a cognitive theory for the measurement of achievement. In Ronning, R. R., Glover, J. A., Conoley, J. C. and Witt, I. C. (Eds.), *The influence of cognitive psychology on testing* (pp. 41-85). Hillsdale, NJ: Lawrence Erlbaum Assoc.

Herman, J. L., Aschbacher, P. R. and Winters, L. (1992). *A practical guide to assessment.* Alexandria, VA: Association for Supervision and Curriculum Development.

Hunt, E. (1987). Science, technology, and intelligence. In Ronning, R. R. Glover, J. A., Conoley, J. C. and Witt, J.C. (Eds.), The influence of cognitive psychology on testing (pp. 11-40). Hillsdale, NJ: Lawrence Erlbaum Assoc.

Kreuter, M. A., Leonard, C., and Lavell, J. H. (1975). An interview study of childrens knowledge about memory. *Monographs of the Society for Research in Child Development*, 40 (1). (Series. No. 159).

Luria, A. R. (1961). *The role of speech in the regulation of normal and abnormal behaviour* (J. Tizard, Trans.). NY: Liveright.

Marzano, R. J., Pickering, D., and McTighe, J. (1993). *Assessing student outcomes. Performance assessment using the Dimensions of Learning Model.* Alexandria, VA: Association for Supervision and Curriculum Development.

Mather, N. (1991). *An instructional guide to the Woodcock-Johnson Psychoeducational Battery-Revised.* Brandon, VT: Clinical Psychology Publishing, Co.

McDaniel, E. and Lawrence, C. (1990). *Levels of cognitive complexity. An approach to the measurement of thinking.* NY: Springer-Verlag.

McGrew, K. S. (1986). *Clinical interpretation of the Woodcock-Johnson Tests of Cognitive Ability.* Orlando, FL: Greene & Stratton, Inc.

McLoughlin, J. A. and Lewis, R. B. (1990). *Assessing special students.* (3rd ed.). NY: Merrill/MacMillan.

Meichenbaum. D. and Goodman, S. (1979). Clinical use of private speech and critical questions about its study in natural settings. In Zivin, G. (Ed.) *The development of self-regulation through private speech*, (pp. 325-360). NY: John Wiley & Sons.

Oka, E. R. and Paris, S. G. (1987). Patterns of motivation and reading skill in underachieving children. In Ceci, S. J. (Ed.), *Handbook of cognitive, social, and neuropsychological aspects learning disabilities* (Vol. II, pp. 115-145). Hillsdale, NJ: Lawrence Erlbaum Assoc.

Paris, S. G., Waski, B. A. and Van der Westhuizen, G. (1988). Meta-metacognition: A review of research on metacognition and reading. *National Reading Conference Yearbook*, 37, 143-166.

Pressley, M., Borkowski, J. G. and O'Sullivan, J. (1985). Children's metamemory and the teaching of memory strategies. In Forrest-Pressley, D. L., MacKinnon, G. E. and Waller, T. G. (Eds.), *Metacognition, cognition, and human performance, Vol. 1: Theoretical perspectives* (pp. 111-153). Orlando, FL: Academic Press.

Reese, H. W. (1962). Verbal mediation as a function of age level. *Psychological Bulletin*, 59, 502-509.

Reeve, R. A. and Brown, A. L. (1985). Metacognition reconsidered. Implications for intervention research. Special Issue: Cognitive-behaviour modification with children: A Critical review of the state-of-the-art. *Journal of Abnormal Child Psychology*, 13(3), 343-356.

Sattler, J. M. (1992). *Assessment of children* (3rd. ed.). San Diego, CA: Jerome M. Sattler, Publisher, Inc.

Schneider, W. (1985). Developmental trends in the metamemory-memory behaviour relationship: An integrative review. In Forrest-Pressley, D. L., Mackinnon, G. E. and Waller, T. G. (Eds.), *Metacognition, cognition, and human performance, Vol. 1: Theoretical perspective* (pp. 57-109), Orlando, FL: Academic Press.

Schneider, W. and Pressley, M. (1989). *Memory development between 2 and 20.* NY: Springer-Verlag.

Schroeder, H. M., Driver, M. J. and Streufert, S. (1967). *Human information processing: Individuals and groups functioning in complex social situations.* NY: Holt, Rinehart, & Winston.

Schneider, W., Korkel, J. and Weinert, F. E. (1985). *Metamemory and motivation: A comparison of strategy use and performance in German and American children.* Paper presented at the 68th annual meeting of the American Educational Research Assoc., March 31-April 4, 1985, Chicago, IL. (ERIC Document Reproduction Service No. ED 255 564).

Searls, E. F. (1985). *How to use WISC-R scores in reading/learning disability diagnosis.* Newark, DE: International Reading Assoc. (An IRI Service Bulletin).

Slife, B. D., Weiss, J. and Bell, T. (1985). Separability of metacognition and cognition: Problem solving in learning disabled and regular students. *Journal of Educational Psychology*, 77(4), 437-445.

Swanson, H. L. (1993). Principles and procedures in strategy use. In Meltzer, L. J. (Ed.), *Strategy assessment and instruction for students with learning disabilities. From theory to practice* (pp. 61-92). Austin, TX: PRO-ED, Inc.

Vygotsky, L. S. (1962). *Thought and language* (E. Hanfmann and G. Vakar, Eds/Trans.). Cambridge, MA: MIT Press.

Vygotsky, L. S. (1978). *Mind in society: The development of higher psychological processes.* (Cole, M., John-Steiner, V. and Souberman, E. (Eds. and Trans.). Cambridge, MA: Harvard University Press.

Vygotsky, L. S. (1987). Thinking and speech. In Rieber, R. W. and Carton, A. S. (Eds.), *The collected works of L. S. Vygotsky: Vol. 1). Problems of general psychology* (N. Minick, Trans.). NY: Plenum Press. (Original work published in 1934).

Ward, L. and Traweek, D. (1993). Application of a metacognitive strategy to assessment, intervention, and consultation: A think-aloud technique. *The Journal of School Psychology,* 31 469-485.

Wechsler, D. (1991). *Wechsler intelligence scale for children. Manual.* (3rd ed.). San Antonio: The Psychological Corporation.

Wong, B. Y. (1986). Metacognition and special education: A review of a view. *Journal of Special Education,* 20(1), 9-29.

Worden, P. E. (1987). Commentary: The four M's – memory strategies, metastrategies, monitoring, and motivation. In S. 1. Ceci (Ed.), *Handbook of cognitive, social. and neuropsychological aspects of learning disabilities.* Vol. 11 (pp. 279-302). Hillsdale, NJ: Lawrence Erlbaum, Assoc.

Yussen, S. R. (1985). The role of metacognition in contemporary theories of cognitive development. In Forrest-Pressley, D. L., MacKinnon, G. E. and Waller, T. G. (Eds.), *Metacognition, cognition. and human performance. Vol. 1: Theoretical perspectives* (pp. 253-283). Orlando, FL: Academic Press.

DIAGNOSING THE DIAGNOSIS: CASE STUDIES IN METACOGNITION

KAREN MORRISON

How many ways are there to be aware? As I think about my work as a psycho-educational diagnostician, I am amazed by the levels of awareness that I can have and their usefulness for my skill in identifying what a learner needs in order to learn and perform better. The following are my reflections about how my growing awareness of my role, skill, confusions as an assessor have led me to improve the depth and quality of advice I offer to students in their quest for academic success. Through experience, reflection, and discussions with my colleagues, I have become increasingly aware about the limitations of available psychometric instruments to explain learners' difficulties, and about the benefits of metacognitive awareness to my own practice.

The following account describes how my attempt to probe a learner's metacognition led me to explore and find my own metacognition. It also reveals how what I found illuminated my understanding of my own abilities and limitations as an assessor in addition, it highlights better ways to identify what learners need.

WHAT TRADITIONAL MEASURES REVEAL AND WHAT THEY FAIL TO REVEAL

There is a definite lack of standardised measures available to diagnose metacognition. The complexity of assessing an individual's metacognition is clearly noted in the limited availability of published cognitive and educational tests designed to measure one's awareness of the knowledge, strategies and limitations that are brought to a task. The tests I typically use in conducting a psycho-educational assessment are generally driven by the rigid expectations of school systems for traditional normative procedures and data as the means by which to identify school-related problems. While standardised measures can yield some helpful information, I am frequently left with a myriad of derived scores intended to indicate how a student is performing on specific tasks relative to same age or grade peers – but without any clear insight about **why** a struggle with learning is taking place and how to better teach this child to facilitate her understanding. All too often, traditional test batteries produce profiles that do not reveal cognitive inefficiencies, emotional issues, or ecological factors – aspects that can more fully explain a student's academic and dyslexic difficulties. Without further probing into the **process** of how one approaches specific tasks, I am left at the end of the evaluation with an incomplete picture and unanswered questions, and, therefore, with limited recommendations to help the learner deal with his/her dyslexic difficulties.

I am now aware that there is a gap in knowledge created by a lack of information available just below the surface of testing. I have learned that deeper insight into a student's learning is available by probing how the student approaches the particular tasks in the sub-tests. Through testing-of-the-limits procedures, response analysis, behavioural observations, and direct questioning, I can use traditional content-oriented measures as a means to develop a richer understanding of how the student thinks and the **processes** employed to respond to a question or solve a problem. Through such investigation, I can find information I may easily miss but definitely need. I now consciously look for evidence that the student is or is not using metacognition to understand the task, to ascertain strategies to accomplish it, and to predict and monitor performance. Exploring the depths of testing has now become an integral component of my assessment strategy and has generated information that allows me to identify more specific, meaningful instructional recommendations. Interestingly, I now realise that I did this to some degree although I was not aware of it. Therefore, I utilised metacognitive strategies without being consciously metacognitive.

The following case studies exemplify how I assess for metacognition within a standardised evaluation process to gain a deeper understanding of students' learning struggles. The names in these cases have been changed to ensure confidentiality. My own reflections (metacognition) are presented in boldface type.

The first case study illustrates how the assessment of metacognitive strategies can be informally measured in an applied manner within a specific task domain.

CASE STUDY ONE

Andy: Andy is a 14 year-old who was referred for testing due to a history of mathematic struggles since 9 years old. A traditional standardised test battery revealed average verbal and conceptual skills. Auditory processing was presented as a significant strength. There was nothing in the test scores on the cognitive measures to provide insight about why Andy might experience difficulty with maths; his overall cognitive processing appears intact. **How did Andy perform on the standardised maths tests? I need to look at his scores on the problem-solving and maths tasks.** He consistently demonstrated weak problem-solving skills; he scored at the 28th percentile on the Woodcock Johnson-Revised: Tests of Achievement (WJ-R ACH) Applied Problems sub-test and at the 25th percentile on the Key Math-Revised Problem Solving sub-test. **What does this tell me? Andy doesn't solve word problems very well. He is performing better than only approximately one-fourth of other 14 year-olds (based on test norms and specific tasks). He's struggling, but he and his parents already knew that – that's why he came for testing. I don't think he had to take this test to discover that.**

What else can I glean from these test data? When Andy was required to solve maths word problems involving time, money, and measurement, he failed to consistently identify relevant information from the passage, set up algorithms, and then apply the appropriate operation to solve the problem. **I now know what type of task Andy is having difficulty completing successfully. By *why* is he having difficulty? How can I use this information to help him? I need to look further. Was there a particular *type* of problem with which he had difficulty?** Error analysis revealed difficulty with all types of problems, but further analysis of item content (money, time, measurement) showed no difference in mastery/error rate. **Why is Andy scoring so low? What is happening? He has good reading ability, so why is he not comprehending the relevant information? Was the *mode* of presentation problematic?** The problems were presented both orally and visually, therefore, problems were presented in both modalities.

Was motivation interfering with his performance? Analysis of his behaviour throughout testing suggested that Andy was co-operative and seemed motivated to do well. Interviews with Andy and his parents also indicated that he wants to do well. However, he appeared to have limited confidence in his skills and abilities and, therefore, seemed reluctant to offer a response when unsure of an answer. He reported that he was not good at word problems. Throughout testing, Andy sought structure and feedback for his performance ('Am I timed?' 'Can it be other countries' money?' 'Do you want me to number them?' 'Do you want one on each page?' 'Is this the right way?' 'Can you tell me if I'm close?')

He's motivated but he has negative tapes playing in his head. So what does he do when he encounters a task where there is not an immediate answer or method of attack? What strategies does he use to solve these problems? Is his negative self-talk over-riding effective strategies, or is he simply not availing productive task-specific strategies? On the WJ-R ACH, Andy solved the majority of the problems mentally even though he was given the option to use paper and pencil. Behavioural observations suggested that Andy attacks these problems by rote. When he is unsure of a response, he does not use even fundamental steps to begin to reason through the problem, such as identifying the question being posed.

Was he monitoring his performance? At times, he carried out the first step of a two-step problem. Other times he ignored important information. He does not check the reasonableness of his responses.

What did this analysis allow me as a psycho-educational diagnostician to do that I wouldn't have been able to do otherwise? My analysis led me to conclude that Andy has a learning mindset that learning is simply a rote process of responding from memory with the desired answer. He is not heuristic in his problem-solving approach; he does not use trial and error. If he has not memorised the answer, he lacks a strategy for problem solving. Andy did not use a cognitive strategy such as a problem-solving strategy to tackle problems, nor did he use a metacognitive strategy to plan or monitor his performance. I can offer Andy suggestions that will likely make a difference in his problem-solving skills. For example, I can teach Andy how to ask himself deliberate questions about his approach. He can learn 'metacognitive prompts' that can be incorporated into his problem-solving approach and maths instruction, such as: 'Have I ever encountered a problem similar to this one?' 'What are they really asking here – what do they want?' 'What information is unnecessary?' 'What are the different assumptions I could make?' 'Which strategies seem more likely to work, given my assumptions?' 'What will each of the strategies I have learned get me?'

Since Andy's behaviour seemed to suggest a strong need for structure, the metacognitive strategies can be incorporated into a framework of procedures that will allow him to solve problems in a step-by-step manner. The following instructions become a useful map for Andy: they embed metacognitive and cognitive strategies that he can learn to use.

1. Read the problem thoroughly. Ask, 'What is this all about?' Ensure that you understand all of the definitions and symbols before you attempt to work the problem. (Since cognitive measures indicated that Andy's auditory modality was especially strong, reading the problem out loud can be helpful.)

2. Read the problem a second time. Ask, 'What am I to find here?' Paraphrase the problem in your own words to help you understand

what information is provided and what must be done to solve the problem.

3. Visualise the problem in terms of a picture or diagram. For example, if you are given the word problem, 'Jane owes Betty £50. Mike pays Jane £75 that he borrowed two weeks ago. Sam borrows £30 from Jane. How much money can Jane pay Betty?' Draw the following picture:

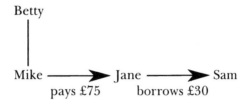

4. Plan how to solve the problem. Decide what process or formula would likely work. (Think about task-specific strategies.)

5. Based on the information given, guess at what a reasonable answer would be. Estimate the answer; this is your prediction.

6. Perform the necessary calculations to work through the problem.

7. Check your work. Compare your answer to your prediction, then check your result against the problem. Is it a reasonable answer?

CASE STUDY TWO

Lynn: The Woodcock-Johnson Psycho-Educational Battery - Revised: Tests of Cognitive Ability (WJ-R COG) is a standardised test that has two separate sub-tests that present 'new learning' tasks. Sub-test 1: Memory for Names presents pictures of space-like creatures one at a time, and the examiner recites each name. After she is introduced to a new space-like creature, Lynn is then shown a separate page that has an array of the space-like creatures and is required to point to the one the examiner names. Similarly, Sub-test 8: Visual-Auditory Learning requires the student to identify up to 28 rebus symbols that are presented within the context of a meaningful phrase or sentence.

Both of these tests require the student to remember, specifically to form and retrieve new visual-auditory associations. Because this type of learning is frequently required in school, these tests can generate information that can be linked to academic tasks. Observations and direct questioning upon completion of the tests give valuable insight into specific strategies the student is employing to remember these associations.

Lynn is 13 years old who was seen for testing due to difficulty understanding concepts and taking tests. Psycho-educational testing revealed above average non-verbal conceptual abilities and above average visual processing speed. Auditory processing and verbal capabilities were within average limits.

Lynn performed significantly better on the Visual-Auditory Sub-test but had considerably more difficulty on the Memory for Names Sub-test where she had to construct meaning. Upon completion of this test, Lynn was questioned as to what she did to remember the information presented. 'I remember that this one' (pointed) 'had little squiggly arms and legs. This one had big eyes. This one had little things that were moving.' I then asked Lynn if she used anything to help her remember the name, she said 'No.' **Had I asked Lynn to reveal if she thought her memory strategy was effective and why, I might have gleaned additional information about her metacognition. I now realise how powerful this additional information would have been to my analysis. I inferred from her comments that she knew that she was not doing a good job. I do not know, however, if she attributed her performance to an ineffective or inefficient strategy.**

While Lynn put forth great effort to remember isolated characteristics of the creatures presented, she had no strategy to connect a space-like creature to the name. She used ineffective memory strategies, although she thought she used a strategy to help her remember. Her strategy focused on remembering isolated characteristics of the space creature rather than associating the name of the creature with its characteristics. She was more successful on the rebus-like task where the associations were meaningful to her and where she did not have to construct the meaning because it was already there. Had she used metacognitive strategies to monitor her performance, she might have discovered that the amount of effort she expended to remember was not paying off and that she should therefore adjust her memory (cognitive) strategy. Without feedback about her performance, she had difficulty turning on her metacognition (her awareness that her memory was or was not good). **While I probed this task directly, I guessed that Lynn used inefficient and ineffective cognitive (memory) strategies as well as no metacognitive (self-monitoring) strategies. I now realise that I should be asking more direct questions about metacognition to assess it.**

What does this information tell me about Lynn's academic struggles?
Lynn uses inefficient strategies to construct meaningful associations. This was also
reflected in measures assessing her ability to store and retrieve educationally
relevant information (science, social studies, humanities). For example, she failed
to consistently recall facts that she should have learned in school. Analysis of her
responses often revealed gaps in factual knowledge about particular subjects.
Gaps in factual knowledge can lead to distortions in concepts; limited conceptual
understanding simply breeds further conceptual limitations because she lacks a
building block foundation upon which to acquire additional facts and constructs.
If she used metacognitive strategies to direct her cognitive strategies, Lynn might
have had greater success in building associations, which would further her
knowledge acquisition. Her ability to integrate details to form the 'big picture' can
provide a conceptual anchor for constructing meaning. Lynn's knowledge
acquisition strategies were inefficient or did not work; they did not provide her
with any meaning-making framework. **I inferred Lynn's strategy deficits from
analysis of how she tackled the more general memory tasks presented in specific
sub-tests, which are presented in new learning type tasks.**

WHERE DO I GO FROM HERE AS A DIAGNOSTICIAN?

What have I learned from this process? I have learned that my own
metacognition can help me just as much as it can help a learner and that I don't
use it enough, just as some students with learning difficulties fail to use their
metacognition. Yet as I reflect on my reflections, I have a better developed sense
of my own metacognition. To this point, I have been operating mostly on an
intuitive level without formally planning and thinking how I will attempt to
evaluate a student's knowledge about his/her own learning. My metacognitive
probing has evolved from experience and a frustration with the limited insight too
often generated from traditional assessment practices. In an attempt to have a
more in-depth understanding of how students learn, I have wanted to 'get inside
their head' to understand how they think. Assessing students' metacognition
enables me to do this.

Examining my own metacognition makes me realise the profound worth of
assessing students' metacognition. But how do I employ more of these assessment
strategies given the time constraints involved in the testing situation and the
expectations of school administrators for traditional data? Yet how can I **not** assess
for metacognition given the insights provided through this process? I am chagrined
as I ponder the countless times I have desired to probe more, but have not done
so because there has been limited time or I have opted for another traditional
measure to validate test scores. As I perused the protocols of my assessees' test

results after the fact, I saw numerous occasions where metacognitive probing would likely have generated additional useful information about the student's learning. Will this influence how I conduct assessments in the future? How could it not? A keener awareness of the assessment process and its nuances will affect my future practice. However, as I negotiate the quest for insight and the reality of time and expectations endemic to the testing situation, I will still have to make compromises. As always, cases will need to be considered on their own individual terms, but I will pay more careful, thoughtful attention to the assessment of metacognition and try not to dismiss the opportunity to gather additional insights and information.

Finally, always seeking to grow professionally and improve my skills as a diagnostician, I am profoundly motivated to learn more about how I can use my own metacognition to refine the process of evaluating dyslexic students' metacognition. I am moved to take a more in-depth look at the literature on dynamic assessment, in particular Reuven Feuerstein's Leaning Potential Assessment Device. What I now realise is that there are ways to glean powerful insights about how people learn and direct their own learning. They are there simply for the looking and the asking.

REFERENCES

Ayres, D. B. (1994). 'Assessment of intelligence, cognition and metacognition: Reflections, issues and recommendations. *Paper presented in partial fulfilment of Ph.D.,* George Mason University, Virginia, USA.

Feuerstein, R. (1979). *The Dynamic Assessment of Retarded Performers: The Learning Potential Assessment Device, Theory, Instruments and Techniques.* Baltimore: University Park Press.

COMPUTERISED SCREENING FOR DYSLEXIA

CHRIS SINGLETON

HUMBERSIDE EARLY SCREENING RESEARCH PROJECT

Humberside Early Screening Research Project is an internationally pioneering five-year research project carried out in the Psychology Department of the University of Hull, over the period 1989 - 1995. The result has been the creation of a new computer-based approach to screening for dyslexia and special educational needs known as KEYSTAGE COPS. The overall rationale for Humberside Project was that early intervention with children identified as being at risk, providing appropriately structured teaching, will prove to be not only more desirable on educational grounds, but also to be more cost effective than waiting until these children have experienced several years of failure and have lagged so far behind their peers that very expensive specialist remediation has to be provided on a withdrawal basis.

The majority of children with dyslexia are not identified until they are about 9 to 12 years of age, by which time they have experienced so much failure that their motivation and self-confidence will have been seriously eroded. The lack of general availability of facilities for identifying dyslexia earlier is a source of considerable frustration for many teachers and psychologists. Without early identification procedures, the teacher may easily assume that the child with reading and or writing problems is lazy or simply requires more time for literacy skills to develop. When children are diagnosed as dyslexic late in the school career, a typical complaint by parents is that they felt there was something wrong from their child's earliest years at school but when they had expressed these misgivings to the teacher, the response had been: 'Don't worry, he/she will pick it up in time.' Needless to say, in these particular cases the child did not 'pick it up' and consequently required specialist remediation some years after the problem was eventually diagnosed. This was often the focus of strong parental resentment and dissatisfaction with the education system, which in such cases is often perceived as having 'failed their child' (Pumfrey and Reason, 1991).

DEVELOPMENTAL PRECURSORS OF DYSLEXIA

At the pre-school stage, many dyslexic children are already showing early signs of their disorder which can be detected by those with experience in this area. The key is usually an uneven developmental profile, particularly in cases where there is a family history of speech or literacy difficulties, or where there is evidence of significant birth difficulties. Characteristic difficulties include one or more of the following:

- Delays in the development of speech and language.

- Difficulties in learning simple patterns of sequential activity, such as remembering the order of simple instructions or reproducing a pattern of coloured beads or bricks.

- Difficulties of fine or gross motor co-ordination.

- High distractibility and poor concentration.

Unfortunately there are no standard or generally accepted objective procedures for identifying dyslexia on the basis of these indicators. In any case, most children with early developmental problems (e.g. speech and language problems) grow out of them in time. Hence, even if a teacher is alert to these early signs and symptoms, this will still usually be insufficient to provide a case for specialist help for the dyslexic child. Schools and Local Education Authorities usually require more 'objective' evidence in order to make special provision. There is therefore a need for objective and formal assessment procedures which are not inordinately costly or time consuming but which are sufficiently reliable to justify taking action.

DISADVANTAGES OF CONVENTIONAL ASSESSMENT PROCEDURES

Conventional diagnosis of dyslexia rests on two main criteria: (i) the *discrepancy criterion* (which implies that dyslexia can only be identified when there is a significant discrepancy between intelligence and attainment) and (ii) the *exclusionary criterion* (that all other potential causes of reading disability should first be excluded). Unfortunately, this has unwittingly has the effect of making dyslexia a condition observed mainly in bright, middle-class children, which has in turn given cause for some professional misunderstanding and disparagement of the condition over many years (Singleton, 1988). It also results in diagnosis being delayed until a 'significant' discrepancy between intelligence and attainment can be demonstrated. In some areas, resourcing policy may force educators and psychologist to ignore a child's problem until that child has slipped below some arbitrary threshold (e.g. two years behind expected literacy skill level). Despite the fact that the child may clearly be falling progressively behind, remediation is not offered until the predetermined threshold is exceeded, with the explanation being given to the parents to the effect that their child's difficulties are not serious enough at the moment for help to be provided. It is clear, therefore, that we have to move to a much more satisfactory definition and more reliable diagnostic criteria if we are to be able to identify dyslexics properly.

The disadvantages of conventional assessment and diagnostic procedures for dyslexia may be summarised as follows:

- They rely on waiting for the child to fail and often come too late in the child's educational career.

- The use of exclusion criteria tends to confine identification to relatively bright, middle-class children. Many children with reading difficulties who come from disadvantaged home backgrounds and/or have emotional problems may be dyslexic but we are unable to give a proper diagnosis if we have to rely upon conventional diagnostic criteria.

- They are relatively expensive and time-consuming: it generally takes four or more hours of an educational psychologist's time to carry out and analyse the necessary tests and compile a report.

- They are not widely accessible: the assessment instruments used are mainly restricted psychological tests and there is a general lack of availability of educational psychologists.

- When based solely on establishing a discrepancy between ability and attainment rather than including assessment of underlying cognitive difficulties, they are of little help to the specialist dyslexia teacher or learning support teacher in formulating an appropriate package of learning activities for the child.

PREDICTING DYSLEXIC DIFFICULTIES FROM COGNITIVE MEASURES

When good and poor readers of matched I.Q. are compared on various psychological measures we typically find differences in underlying cognitive functions subserving memory, phonological processing and sequencing skills. For example, an intensive longitudinal study of reading development (Ellis and Large, 1987) revealed that only three variables (out of a total of 44) reliably differentiated children with specific reading retardation from their better-reading peers when the groups were matched for intelligence. The variables in question were: short-term memory, phonological segmentation (e.g. ability to detect rhyme and alliteration) and reading vocabulary. Comparable results were reported in a large-scale study in Australia (Jorm, Share, MacLean and Matthews, 1986).

A substantial body of research has demonstrated that reading difficulties are, in general, linked to a wide variety of verbal deficits (Perfetti, 1985) and thus such deficits are likely to be encountered much more frequently than deficits in visual-perceptual abilities (Lovegrove and Slaghuis, 1989). However, if children with specific reading disability are compared with children who have more general reading problems, it is in abilities which involve visual processing that differences most commonly emerge (Ellis and Large, 1987). When non-verbal I.Q. alone is controlled in comparison between dyslexic and non-dyslexic subjects, the groups are found to differ mainly on verbal memory and rapid naming ability (Bowers *et al., 1988*). But when verbal I.Q. alone is controlled, differences which show up between the groups tend to be associated with visual and orthographic defects (Willows, 1990). These findings indicate that early identification procedures, as well as tapping underlying verbal deficits, also need to take account of any possible visual defects. Sub-test profiles of individual intelligence scales often reveal the cognitive deficits of dyslexics and point to the main areas of deficit for the dyslexic being in memory (verbal, or visual, or both), sequencing, phonological processing, and overall speed of information processing. Experimental studies of the cognitive deficits of developmental dyslexics have confirmed this view (see Ellis and Miles, 1978, 1981; Gathercole and Baddeley, 1988; Singleton, 1987, 1988; Torgesen, 1985; Torgesen *et al.* 1987).

Phonological processing ability (e.g. being aware of *syllables* and being able to detect *rhyme and alliteration*) is very closely related to early reading development. Children who show good phonological awareness are the ones who are most likely to make the best early progress in learning to read (Lundberg, Olofsson and Wall, 1981). There is now substantial evidence that this type of phonological awareness predicts reading development independently of intelligence and social background, and that children with difficulties in these aspects of cognitive activity are more likely than others to have subsequent problems in learning to read and spell (Bryant and Bradley, 1985; Goswami and Bryant, 1990; Bradley and Bryant, 1983; Fox and Routh, 1983; Lundberg, 1994; Lundberg and Hoien, 1989; Muter, 1994; Olson, Wise and Rack, 1989; Wagner and Torgesen, 1987; Vellutino and Scanlon, 1987).

Hence cognitive precursors of different types of reading disability do exist and can be assessed in young children before beginning to learn to read. In the particular case of the dyslexic, the value of early independent diagnosis would be enormous: instead of *waiting several years for children to fail,* with all the misery and frustration which that inevitably entails, and only then trying to remediate, proper educational provision for these children could be made right from the start. American research has shown that when diagnosis of dyslexia was made in the first two grades of school, over 80% of the students could be brought up to their normal classroom work, while identification delayed until third grade resulted in successful remediation of about only 40% of the students, and if left until the fifth to seventh grade the percentage of successful remediation dropped to 10-15% (Strag, 1972; Badian, 1985). Other studies in Sweden have shown that early identification of children at risk of reading disabilities can result in successful remediation (Lundberg *et al.,* 1980).

THE IDENTIFICATION OF SUB-TYPES OF DYSLEXIA

Teachers of dyslexics are aware that the condition is not a homogeneous one, and that several different types of dyslexia exist. For many years two broad sub-types have been suggested: **auditory dyslexia** and **visual dyslexia**. The visual dyslexic tends to have problems with visual discrimination, visual memory, visual sequencing, left-right scanning and in rapid visual recognition of words. The auditory dyslexic tends to have problems with discriminating speech sounds, in sound blending, auditory sequencing and serial memory, and in phonological awareness. Some researchers also recognise a third type, manifesting in various motor dysfunctions, including speech (articulation) difficulties as well as graphomotor (handwriting) difficulties. There also appear to be 'mixed' types of dyslexia, where sufferers experience combinations of these handicaps (Boder, 1973; Ellis, 1981; Mattis, French and Rapin, 1975; Thomson, 1990).

More recent detailed cognitive research on morphographic and phonographic characteristics of word reading and spelling (Ellis, 1985; Seymour, 1986, 1994) has tended to confirm the existence of at least two broad sub-types involving (a) difficulties with whole word reading (morphographic impairment or visual dyslexia) and (b) difficulties with non-word reading (phonographic impairment or auditory/verbal dyslexia). These sub-types have important implications for teaching and consequently good assessment procedures should be able to give a classification by subtype. The **KeyStage 1 CoPS** suite provides a graphical profile which enables the teacher to distinguish these sub-types of dyslexia, and this can guide the teacher in deciding the extent to which teaching should address 'strengths' or 'weaknesses'.

THE METHODOLOGY OF THE HUMBERSIDE RESEARCH PROJECT

There is, therefore, now a well-established research literature documenting the principal underlying cognitive difficulties associated with the condition, which are in the areas of memory, sequential information processing, phonological awareness, and in some cases, visual-perceptual difficulties. The Humberside Early Screening Research Project used this scientific knowledge of the cognitive precursors of dyslexic difficulties to formulate objective early identification procedures. The precision, objectivity and flexibility of the computer made it an appropriate and cost-effective tool for assessing such cognitive abilities and deficits. A wide range of computer tests was created in order to assess various cognitive abilities, including visual, verbal, associative, sequential and spatial memory skills, also phonological awareness, auditory discrimination, visual processing capacity and other important linguistic and perceptual skills.

The cognitive tests are in the form of 'games' suitable for young children and can be delivered in several short sessions if desired. Several of the games feature a popular and endearing creature from another planet called 'Zoid'. All the tests incorporate attractive graphics and animation as well as high quality digitized speech. A total of 380 children aged 5 years, in 24 schools, were administered these computer tasks, and their literacy, numeracy and intellectual development was followed up over the next three years, using a variety of standarised psychological measures. The follow-up data were then used to determine which of the computer tests were most effective predictors of dyslexia and other learning difficulties.

The aim of this research was to produce a user-friendly computer-based package of tests which will give early indication of many of the children who are at risk of dyslexia and other learning difficulties because of underlying cognitive deficits. Such children might not otherwise be spotted until very much later in their school careers. The tests yield a graphic profile of the child's cognitive strengths and weaknesses which may be pointed out if desired and used in consultation with educational psychologists, learning support staff, and remedial and advisory teachers in formulating an individual learning programme. It is important to note, however, that this system does not necessarily involve labelling children as 'dyslexic' at the age of five years. Rather, the purpose of the tests is to identify children who *are likely to experience significant difficulty in acquiring literacy skills because of underlying cognitive deficits which are known to be associated with dyslexia.* Some of these children may well be giving cause for concern for other reasons (e.g. because they have a history of speech and language problems) but many of them would otherwise be liable to pass undetected for some time. The hope is that such children can be given appropriate teaching and support so that their cognitive difficulties do not significantly retard their literacy development.

SUMMARY OF THE RESULTS OF THE PROJECT

The results of the project showed that the computer tests gave a highly satisfactory prediction of children who later were found to be experiencing literacy difficulties and dyslexia. The computer tests produced data which were normally distributed, giving a good indication of the psychometric integrity of the tests. The computer tests also produced significant correlations with reading development, many of which had higher correlation coefficients than were found between intelligence (verbal and non-verbal) and reading development. Over 80% of children who subsequently were found to be dyslexic or who were experiencing significant reading difficulties were successfully predicted by the computer tests alone on school entry. Structural equation modelling provided confirmation of a statistical and conceptual distinction between verbal/auditory-related tasks and visual/perceptual tasks, thus enabling the identification of dyslexic sub-types, which is further facilitated by the examination of graphical profiles. Various statistical techniques were used to determine which of the computer tests were most effective in predicting later difficulties, and these were selected for the final software suite, into which the norms of the standardised versions were incorporated, so that teachers using the system would be instantaneously able to establish where any given child fell on any of the cognitive components of the suite, in relation to the population norms.

Although the information gleaned from the statistical analysis was the primary factor in determining the composition of the final suite of software, other considerations, such as the attractiveness of the tests to young children, were also taken into account. Eight tests were chosen for the final package (four verbal/ auditory tests, and four visual/perceptual tests), and a ninth test (for colour discrimination) added (See Figure 1). These have been professionally re-programmed for IBM Compatible and Apple Macintosh computers and a version for Acorn Archimedes computers is under development for release in the Autumn of 1995.

The objective has been to create a user-friendly package with menuing system, pupil registration, graphical report mode and facility for print-out of results. The final suite named **KeyStage 1 CoPS** (Cognitive Profiling System for children in KeyStage 1) has been undergoing independent school trials in Humberside and a number of other Local Education Authorities, with extremely favourable responses to the system from teachers and pupils. A number of independent groups are working on the development of appropriate classroom materials for teachers to use with children with various profiles on CoPS. (Note that **KeyStage 1 CoPS** is designed for use with children in Keystage I and so does not assess reading, spelling or numeracy. Versions for older children [**KeyStage 2 CoPS** etc.] currently under development do incorporate literacy and numeracy tests.)

NAME OF TEST	COGNITIVE MODE	PROCESSING SKILLS BEING ASSESSED
Zoid's Friends	Visual	Sequential memory (colours)
Rabbits	Visual	Sequential memory (spatial /temporal)
Toybox	Visual	Associative memory (shape + colour)
Zoid's Letters	Visual	Sequential memory (symbols)
Zoid's Letter Names	Auditory/verbal	Associative memory (symbols + names)
Races	Auditory/verbal	Sequential memory (names)
Rhymes	Auditory/verbal	Phonological awareness (rhyming)
Wock	Auditory/verbal	Auditory discrimination
Clown	Visual	Colour discrimination

Figure 1: Details of tests in the final **KeyStage 1 CoPS** suite 4.

It is intended that the suite will ultimately be made available in versions which would utilise other input devices, such as touch screens, concept keyboards and switches, thus making it accessible to physically handicapped children and to pupils with other disabilities. Further work is underway to develop similar computer-based dyslexia screening and cognitive profiling systems for older children and adults, and in other language versions, including types for children from various ethnic groups where a language other than English predominates. A Swedish version has already been created and will be undergoing national trials in Sweden over the next 12 months.

THE ADVANTAGES OF THE KEYSTAGE 1 COPS SOFTWARE FOR EARLY SCREENING

Computers are now widely used in psychological research for studying human performance on a considerable range of cognitive tasks. The precision, objectivity and flexibility of the computer makes it an ideal tool for assessing cognitive abilities and deficits. When applied to the measurement of certain areas of cognitive activity (e.g. memory) the computer displays a degree of accuracy which is many times better than that shown by a human tester using more primitive equipment (e.g. a stopwatch) and often this can be absolutely critical for a proper assessment of the child's performance. The computer is therefore a natural choice when it comes to designing an efficient and economical programme of screening for potential reading disorders. The feasibility of computer-based assessment techniques in dyslexia has already been demonstrated by a number of research groups in Britain and elsewhere in the world (Singleton and Thomas, 1994).

The advantages of the **KeyStage 1 CoPS** software for assessment of dyslexia may be summarised as follows:

- Greater precision in presenting assessment tasks.
- Greater accuracy in measuring responses.
- Greater objectivity of assessment.
- It can be used much earlier than most conventional methods of assessment.
- It does not require a psychologist to do the assessment.
- It requires only minimal training of teachers or other personnel.
- Children enjoy it more than the conventional assessment methods and so are motivated, which ensures reliable results.
- It gives a detailed picture of a child's cognitive strengths and weaknesses, which can provide important indicators of sub-types of dyslexia, of a child's individual learning styles, and pointers for curriculum development and for differentiation within the classroom.
- It can utilise existing technology in schools so there is no extra expense for schools in purchasing special equipment.
- Once the software has been created and validated it is inexpensive and easy to reproduce for distribution to schools. The program can be used as many times as required without the recurrent expense of test booklets and other costly test materials.

THE KEYSTAGE CoPS GRAPHICAL PROFILE is a unique feature which easily enables the teacher to determine a child's cognitive strengths and weaknesses. Standardised norms provide objective comparison between the child being tested and national reference groups, but the system will automatically assemble norms which enable comparison with the class, the school, with previous years' pupils, or with pupils across the whole Local Education Authority, if desired. Results can be accessed in percentile and/or standard deviation units. Certain cognitive profiles are strongly indicative of dyslexia and these are explained in the Manual. In addition, **KeyStage 1 CoPS** can automatically calculate (based on national norms) the probability that difficulties in literacy and/or numeracy will be experienced by a child later in schooling. The graphical profile can be printed out and filed with a child's school records, and all results can be archived for future reference. Since the graphical profile indicates a child's cognitive assets as well as shortcomings, it gives the teacher important insights into their learning styles, and essential pointers for curriculum development, for differentiation within the classroom, and for more appropriate teaching techniques.

ASSESSMENT REQUIREMENTS OF *THE EDUCATION ACT 1993* AND *THE CODE OF PRACTICE ON THE IDENTIFICATION AND ASSESSMENT OF SPECIAL EDUCATIONAL NEEDS, 1994*

The Education Act 1993, Part 111, places upon Local Education Authorities and Governing Bodies of all maintained schools, the responsibility for identifying and assessing all children with special educational needs '*as early as possible and as quickly as is consistent with thoroughness*' (*Code of Practice on the Identification and Assessment of Special Educational Needs* [Department for Education, 1994] Section 1:4).

The Education Act 1993, specifies that 'The governing body must secure that teachers in the school are aware of the importance of identifying and providing for, those pupils who have special educational needs' (Section 161). The *Code of Practice* says that 'The governing body's report should state the number of pupils with special educational needs and demonstrate the effectiveness of the school's system for identification and assessment' (Section 11:10), and maintains that 'The importance of early identification, assessment and provision for any child who may have special educational needs cannot be over-emphasised' (Section 11:13). It further says that 'To assist in the early identification of children with special educational needs, the school will wish to make use of any appropriate screening or assessment tools.' (Section 11:14). In the case of specific learning difficulties (Dyslexia) the identification should depend on '*clear, recorded evidence of clumsiness or significant difficulties of sequencing, visual perception or auditory or visual recall*' (*Code of Practice*, Section 111:48:iii).

It is clear, therefore, that the intentions of the Education Act, 1993 as reflected in the *Code of Practice* are that much more efficient procedures than hitherto shall be established in schools for identifying special educational needs as early as possible in a child's education, including specific learning difficulties (dyslexia), and that the responsibility for this, in the first instance, lies with the school, its teachers and its governing body. In the case of dyslexia, however, the procedures specified by the *Code of Practice* pose a considerable problem. How are dyslexics to be identified by schools? Only a minority of dyslexics fall into the 2% of children believed to be appropriate for statutory assessment and statementing; many dyslexics, particularly if they are bright, are able to achieve modest progress in early literacy development and may be only 1 to 2 years behind chronological age levels, although this may be far behind what would be expected on the basis of their intelligence. However, the intelligence of such individuals is often not recognised, as teachers frequently rely on written language skills in judging ability and educational potential. Such children are consequently assumed to be 'below average' but not as having special educational needs and therefore tend to 'fall through the net', only to present major educational problems when their special educational needs become apparent later in their schooling. At this relatively late stage, teachers find it difficult to help the child effectively and parents become angry because they believe that their child's special educational needs were not properly recognised and catered for early enough.

A good example would be the dyslexic child with competent visual memory but poor verbal (auditory) memory. Such a child will encounter difficulties in acquiring phonic skills but will be usually able to cope reasonably successfully with early literacy work by relying purely on visual memory (remembering words as whole units but being unable to read or write new or unfamiliar words). This strategy will often be adequate until late in KeyStage 2, when the child can no longer cope with the torrent of new words being encountered on an almost daily basis across the curriculum. At that point, the child's special educational needs (and in particular, their lack of phonic skills) should become apparent but it is difficult to go back to teaching phonics at this stage.

In order to comply with the procedures laid down in the *Code of Practice*, schools need systems for identifying dyslexics early in their schooling. These systems will need to be appropriate for Stages I to 3 of the staged model for special educational needs, and for providing evidence to the Local Education Authorities at Stage 4. Identification based principally on discrepancy between ability and attainment is unreliable and often results in children 'falling through the net'. Nor do schools have satisfactory techniques for assessing difficulties in sequencing, visual perception, or auditory or visual recall, which the *Code of Practice* says should be fundamental indicators of specific learning difficulties and for which there is good research evidence. It is difficult to see, therefore, how schools are going to be able to comply with the new statutory requirements in the identification of dyslexics, without the development and implementation of appropriate and effective systems for this purpose. **KeyStage I CoPS** is designed to meet this need.

CONCLUSIONS

This project has made possible the development of an internationally pioneering scientific approach to cognitive assessment and screening for dyslexia and other special educational needs. The results have been extremely promising and an innovative computer-based system has been developed. It is believed that the system will be very useful for schools not only in identifying potential dyslexics at a much earlier age than hitherto, but also in fulfilling their responsibilities under *the 1993 Education Act* and the *Code of Practice on the Identification and Assessment of Special Educational Needs (1994)*. However, the production of the **KeyStage I CoPS** software suite for use in schools should be regarded not as a conclusion, but as a beginning to this endeavour. What is done after screening is vital. The Manual for the software gives details of interpretation of the test results and graphical profiles, together with recommendations on educational provision for different types of children. It will be important for us to examine how teachers actually use the computer package and what improvements to the system might ensue. It is also essential that schools and Local Education Authorities recognise that teachers need the appropriate skills and resources to help children who are shown to be at risk by the **KeyStage 1 CoPS** software.

For more information about how to obtain KEYSTAGE 1 CoPS or to order a demo disk, or to enquire about training sessions, please contact: LUCID SYSTEMS, 26 Tunis Street, HULL, HU5 1EZ. Tel. and Fax: 01482 - 465589.

REFERENCES

Badian, N. A. (1986). Improving the prediction of reading for the individual child: A 4 year follow-up. *J. Learning Dis.,* 19, 262-269.

Boder, E. (1973). Developmental Dyslexia: a diagnostic approach based on three atypical reading patterns. *Developmental Medicine and Child Neurology* 15, 663-87.

Bowers, P., Steffy, R., and Tate, E. (1988). Comparison of the effects of IQ control methods on memory and naming speed predictors of reading disability. *Reading Research Quarterly,* 23, 304-319.

Bradley, L. and Bryant, P. E. (1983). Categorising sounds and learning to read: a causal connection. *Nature,* 271, 746-747.

Bryant, P. E. and Bradley, L. (1985). *Children's reading problems: psychology and education.* London: Blackwell.

Ellis, N. C. and Large, B. (1987). The development of reading. *British Journal of Psychology*, 78, 1-28.

Ellis, N. C. and Miles, T. R. (1978). Visual information processing in dyslexic children. In M. M. Gruneberg, P. E. Morris and R .N. Sykes *Practical aspects of memory*, London: Academic Press.

Ellis, N. C. and Miles, T. R. (1981). A lexical encoding deficiency: I. Experimental evidence. In G. Th. Pavlidis and T. R. Miles (Eds.) *Dyslexia Research and its applications to education*. Chichester: Wiley, pp. 177-215.

Fox, B. and Routh, D. K. (1983). Reading disability, phonemic analysis, and disphonetic spelling: a follow-up study. *J. Clinical Child Psychology*, 1 2, 28-32.

Gathercole, S. E. and Baddeley, A. D. (1990). Developmental language disorder: Is there a working memory deficit? *Journal of Memory and Language.*

Goswami, U. and Bryant, P. (1990). *Phonological skills and learning to read.* Laurence Erlbaum Associates.

Hoien, T. and Lundberg, I. (1989). A strategy for assessing problems in word recognition among dyslexics. *Scandinavian J. Educ. Research*, 33, 185-201.

Gough, P. B. and Turner, W. E. (1986). Decoding, reading and reading disability. *Remed. and Special Educ.*, 7, 6-10.

Jorm, A. F. (1983). Specific reading retardation and working memory: a review. *Br. J. Psychol.*, 74, 311-342.

Jorm, A. F., Share, D. L., MacLean, R. and Matthews, R. (1986). Cognitive factors at school entry predictive of specific reading retardation and general reading backwardness: a research note *J. Child Psychol. and Psychiat.*, 27, 45-54.

Kirtley, C., Bryant, P., MacLean, M. and Bradley, L. (1989). Rhyme, rime and the onset of reading. *J. Exp. Child Psych.*, 48, 224245.

Lundberg, I. (1994). Reading difficulties can be predicted and prevented: a Scandinavian perspective on phonological awareness and reading. In Hulme and Snowling (Eds.) *Reading Development and Dyslexia* II, 180-199, London, Whurr.

Lundberg, I. and Hoien, T. (1989). Phomenic deficits: A core symptom of developmental dyslexia? *Irish J. Psychology*, 10, 579-592.

Lundberg, I, Olofsson, A., and Wall, S. (1981). Reading and spelling skills in the first school years predicted from phonemic awareness skills in kindergarten. *Scandinavian J. Psychology*, 21, 159-172.

Mann, V A. and Liberman, I. Y. (1984). Phonological awareness and verbal short-term memory. *J Learning Dis.*, 17, 592-599.

Mattis, S., French, J. H. and Rapin, I. (1975). Dyslexia in children and young adults: Three independent neuropsychological syndromes. *Developmental Medicine and Child Neurology* 17, 150-63.

Muter, V. (1991) .The influence of phonological awareness and letter knowledge on beginning reading and spelling development, in Hulme and Snowling (Eds), *Reading Development and Dyslexia*, 4, 45b2, London, Whurr Publishers.

Perfetti, C. A. (1985). *Reading Ability.* New York: Oxford Univ. Press.

Pumfrey, P. D. and Reason, R. (1991). Specific Learning Disabilities (Dyslexia): Challenges and Responses. NFER-Nelson.

Seymour, P. H. K. (1986). *Cognitive Analysis of Dyslexia.* London: Routledge and Kegan Paul.

Seymour, P. H. K. (1994). Variability in dyslexia, in Hulme and Snowling (Eds.) *Reading Development and Dyslexia*, 5, 65-85, London, Whurr Publishers, Ltd.

Singleton, C. H. (1987). Dyslexia and cognitive models of reading. *Support for Learning*, 2, 47-56.

Singleton, C. H. (1988). The early diagnosis of developmental dyslexia. *Support for Learning*, 3, 108-121.

Singleton, C. H. (1990). Software developments in cognitive assessment and remediation. Paper delivered to the British Dyslexia Association Conference '*Advances in Computer Applications for Dyslexics*' University of Hull.

Singleton, C. H. (Ed.) (1991). *Computers and Literacy Skills*, Dyslexia Computer Resource Centre ,Univ. of Hull.

Singleton, C. H. (Ed.) (1993). A Stitch in Time, *Special Children,* January 1993, 30-33.

Singleton, C. H. and Thomas, K. (1994). Computerised screening for dyslexia, in C. H. Singleton (Ed.) *Computers and Dyslexia Educational applications of new technology,* Dyslexia Computer Resource Centre, Univ. of Hull.

Singleton, C. H. (1994). Computer applications in the identification and remediation of dyslexia. In D. Wray (Ed.) *Literacy and Computers insights from research.* UKRA, pp 55-61.

Stanovich, K. E. (1991). The theoretical and practical consequences of discrepancy definitions of dyslexia. In M. Snowling and M. Thomson (Eds.) *Dyslexia: integrating theory and practice* London: Whurr, pp. 125-143.

Strag, G (1972). Comparative behavioural ratings of parents with severe mentally retarded, special learning disability, and normal children. *J. Learning Disabilities.* 5, 52-56.

Thomas, K. V. and Singleton, C. H. (1994). Design strategies and methodological problems in the use of computers for the collection of cognitive data from young children. *Psychology Teaching Review* (in press).

Thomson, M. E. (1982). The assessment of children with specific reading difficulties (dyslexia) using the British Ability Scales. *British Journal of Psychology,* 73, 46-78.

Thomson, M. E. (1990). *Developmental Dyslexia.* Third edition. London: Whurr.

Torgesen, J. K. (1985). Memory Processes in Reading Disabled Children *J. Learning Disabilities,* 18, 350-357.

Torgesen, J. K. *et al.* (1987). Academic difficulties of learning disabled children who perform poorly on memory span tasks. In H. L Swanson (Ed.) *Memory and Learning Disabilities.* Greenwich, Conn: JAI Press, pp. 305-333.

Treiman, R. (1985). Onsets and rimes as units of spoken syllables: evidence from children. *J. Exp. Child Psychology,* 39, 161-181.

Treiman, R. and Baron, J. (1981). Segmental analysis: development and relation to reading ability. In G. C. MacKinnon and T. G. Waller (Eds.) *Readings research: Advances in Theory and practice* Vol. III, New York: Academic Press.

Tyler, S. and Elliot, C. D. (1988). Cognitive profiles of poor readers and dyslexic children on the British Ability Scales. *Brit. J. Psychology,* 79, 493-508.

Vellutino, F. R. and Scanlon, D. (1987). Phonological coding and phonological awareness and reading ability: evidence from a longitudinal and experimental study. *Merrill-Palmer Quarterly,* 33, 332-363.

Wagner, R., and Torgesen, J. (1987). The nature of phonological processing and its causal role in the acquisition of reading skills. *Psychol. Bull,* 101, 192-212.

Willows, D. M. (1990). Visual processes in learning disabilities. In B. Wong (Ed.) *Learning about Learning Disabilities.* New York: Academic Press.

THE ROLE OF LISTENING COMPREHENSION

MARK TURNER
SARAH GEIGER
CLAIRE BEDFORD-FEUELL

INTRODUCTION

Successful reading requires the combination of reading accuracy and reading comprehension. Improving reading comprehension leads to greater access to the whole school curriculum and gives more meaning to the reading process. However, teaching and research frequently emphasises reading accuracy – the correct identification of individual words. This chapter explores reading comprehension. We propose that by assessing the listening and reading comprehension of students, teachers will be able to devise individual programmes to improve reading comprehension. This chapter includes description of practical teaching strategies that use listening comprehension strengths to improve reading comprehension.

THEORY

Students who are identified as having a significant discrepancy between their intellectual ability and reading performance are often defined as having a specific learning difficulty.

Stanovich (1991) considers that measuring the discrepancy between reading ability and listening comprehension is more logical and more relevant for educational purposes than a correlation measure between IQ and reading. He found that listening comprehension correlates with reading comprehension much more highly than full scale or verbal IQ. Hence a discrepancy between reading and listening comprehension would be more likely to isolate a specific decoding problem. Stanovich predicted that students with general learning difficulties would achieve low scores in both reading and listening comprehension. Students with specific learning difficulties would have a listening comprehension measure which is greater than reading comprehension. This may be due to word recognition processes being inefficient and resulting in a lower reading comprehension measure.

Aaron (1991) used a regression equation to predict reading comprehension from listening comprehension test scores. He then identified subjects with reading difficulties based on the discrepancy between their actual reading comprehension and their predicted reading comprehension score. Aaron attributed reading difficulties to poor decoding, poor comprehension or both in combination. His results suggest that this diagnostic procedure has potential utility for identifying specific as opposed to general learning difficulties.

ASSESSING LISTENING COMPREHENSION

A number of assessment methods used in research for the purpose of assessing listening comprehension have associated difficulties. For example, the technique of answering **questions**, used, for example in the Macmillan Reading Analysis, requires the use of particular reasoning techniques (Davey, 1987: Royer, 1986). Teachers often comment on a student's ability to answer a 'comprehension' question when they have been unable to accurately read the text. Some students can make educated guesses at questions without having understood the meaning of the text. Determining and responding to the meaning of questions depends heavily on the ability of subjects to temporarily retain exact meanings of words while sentences are analysed and appropriate responses are planned and executed (Mann, Shankweiler and Smith, 1984).

Free recall is another method of evaluating comprehension; however, it is probable that this method underestimates an individual's grasp of meaning since durability of memory and expressive language factors may contribute to poor performance (Carlisle 1989).

Cloze procedure is also an inappropriate test of listening comprehension as a pupil cannot rerun an oral input with the same facility as they could look forward and backwards in the text to select a word to fill in a blank (Kibby, 1981). Also, the cloze procedure may not be sensitive to the sort of scaffolding of ideas and integration of propositions that is the essential process of formulating a mental model of text meaning (Fuchs, Fuchs and Maxwell, 1988).

One method appeared to have addressed all the above difficulties. Developed by Royer *et al.* (1979) **The Sentence Verification Technique** (SVT) consists of a set of passage and test sentences. A pupil judges, positively or negatively, if the test sentence contains an idea that originates from the passage. A test sentence can be one of four types. These are defined by Royer, Greene and Sinatra (1987) as follows:

1. **Paraphrases**: a sentence which has the same meaning as the original sentence but as many words as possible are changed without altering the meaning of the sentence.

2. **Meaning changes**: highly similar in wording to a passage sentence but different in meaning, specifically with one or two words substituted so that the meaning of the sentence is distinctly different.

3. **Distractors**: a sentence that is different in wording and meaning from any passage sentence but is consistent with the passage theme. This sentence has the same syntactic structure as an original sentence.

4. **Originals**: a sentence taken from the passage.

TEST YOURSELF!

You will be asked to read the passage below. When you have finished reading you will then read the test sentences. Some of these sentences come from the passage or mean the same as a sentence in the passage, but some of the sentences do not come from the passage or do not mean the same as a sentence in the passage.

Now read this passage

Learning to juggle is fun and can be mastered quickly. A juggling ball is easier to hold than a normal ball. As it does not bounce, it is good to play with indoors and outside. Juggling is a skill that will help you to develop speed and rhythm.

Cover up the passage

Some of test sentences below come from or mean the same as sentences in the passage. Some of the sentences do not come from or mean the same as sentences in the passage. If you think the sentence was in the passage or means the same as a sentence in the passage then indicate 'Yes'. If you think the sentence was not in the passage or does not mean the same as any sentence in the passage then indicate, 'No'.

Sentences

1. Juggling is fun and you can soon learn to do it.
2. Learning to juggle is fun, you can master it slowly.
3. A juggling ball is harder to hold than a normal ball.
4. Juggling balls are not hard, they will not break things in the house.
5. As it does not bounce, it is good to play with indoors and outside.
6. Juggling is a skill that will help you to develop speed and rhythm.

7. Jugglers often show their talents in the circus.
8. Juggling is a talent, it helps you to learn quickness and timing.

You will find the answers at the end of this Chapter.

You may wish to read this passage and sentences aloud to a colleague and assess their listening comprehension!

THEORETICAL BASIS OF SENTENCE VERIFICATION TECHNIQUE

The theoretical rationale of the SVT is the assumption of comprehension as a constructive process which results in a memory representation preserving the meaning but not the form of a linguistic message (Carlisle, 1989). Thus, comprehension is a process where the reader or listener constructs an interpretation of the message; interpretation is then stored in long-term memory. Comprehension is measured by assessing the degree to which a reader or listener successfully stores the meaning of a text. Readers and listeners must possess relevant prior knowledge that is appropriately organised to comprehend a text.

The SVT procedure is a measure of whether the reader has encoded the information literally stated in a passage. It is also considered to be sensitive to the integration of text propositions into a meaningful whole. Carlisle and Felbinger (1991) discuss SVTs as a method for assessing passage comprehension that focuses primarily on assessing language comprehension rather than reasoning or metacognitive skills. It would appear that SVTs do not require simple memory for sentences but rather the ability to use text structure to integrate ideas of the passage.

USING SVTs TO ASSESS LISTENING COMPREHENSION

The Sentence Verification Technique has been used to allow listening comprehension to be compared with reading comprehension.

Research was carried out using test materials which had been designed around the parallel forms B + C of the New Macmillan Reading Analysis (NMRA). The students tested were Year 5 and Year 9, MLD, SpLD and controls. It was predicted that there would be significant differences between the listening comprehension scores and the reading comprehension scores of the different groups. It was also predicted that children experiencing specific learning difficulties would score highly on the listening comprehension test.

Audiotapes of the reading passages were recorded and used for the listening part of the test.

Firstly, all students' reading accuracy and comprehension ages were assessed using the NMRA Form A.

Secondly, all students were given a practice passage where feedback on performance was given to teach and check understanding of the sentence verification test procedure.

Thirdly, students either read or listened (via tapes) to the stories from Forms B and C and read or listened to the sentence verification sentences. Half the students listened to stories from Form B and read the stories from Form C; for the other half, this was reversed. Students had to verify whether a sentence was the same as, or meant the same as, a sentence in the story by circling either yes or no on a response sheet. Two of each sentence type (original, distractors, paraphrases and meaning changes) accompanied each passage.

As predicted, there were significant differences between the listening comprehension scores and the reading comprehension scores of the different Year 5 groups at higher text levels. Also as predicted, the students experiencing specific learning difficulties scored significantly higher than the students with moderate learning difficulties on the listening comprehension test.

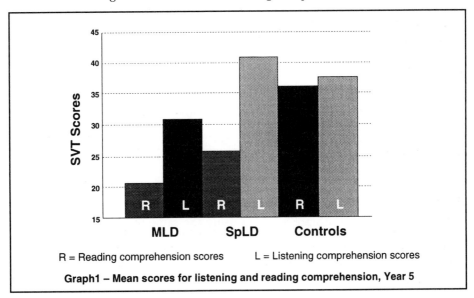

R = Reading comprehension scores   L = Listening comprehension scores

Graph1 – Mean scores for listening and reading comprehension, Year 5

It is of interest to note that children experiencing specific learning difficulties (SpLD) scored significantly higher on the listening comprehension than the reading comprehension test.

It is possible that the SpLD students performed less well on the reading comprehension test than on the listening comprehension test as a result of their poor decoding ability which hindered them from making sense of the text. When listening they achieved a higher score due to their good aural comprehension skills.

There was found to be a significant difference between the listening comprehension and reading comprehension of SpLD students for a more difficult test for the Year 5 group. It is thought that there is potential here to establish a relationship between reading age and listening comprehension ability, such that a significant difference between these two factors could help with the identification of students with a specific learning difficulty. Fluent readers would be expected to have a higher reading comprehension than listening comprehension. This is because if the text is within the reader's decoding ability they are able to scan the text and re-read sections applying their processing skills to understand the text.

To summarise, the SVT test developed in the above study proved to be a valid method to assess listening comprehension and was useful to explore students' individual response differences to listening and reading comprehension. Our research to date suggests that students with specific learning difficulties do respond differently than other students.

LARC Assessment

Due to the potential demonstrated by this small scale study, further listening comprehension materials have been developed. These materials, (named LARC – Listening and Reading Comprehension), consist of two parallel forms of 12 graded passages. Sentences have also been devised using the same criteria as previously specified. LARC can be used from age 5 to age 16 and it is intended that it will offer potential for developing intervention strategies which are established through analysis of error type.

Listening comprehension and reading comprehension are directly comparable because both are assessed using the same technique. Two parallel forms are available.

PRACTICAL AND THEORETICAL IMPLICATIONS

This section offers interventions for students with reading difficulties and also details the implications which listening comprehension research has to enable students to access the curriculum.

Assessing reading comprehension as a measure of comprehension skill

When the new SVT materials were trialed for random selection of year group 2, 5 and 9 students without identified learning difficulties, a correlation of 0.9 was identified between listening and reading comprehension. Aaron (1991) demonstrated a close correlation between reading comprehension and listening comprehension. However, our listening comprehension research suggests differences between reading comprehension and listening comprehension scores in students with specific learning difficulties. When scores were totalled across different groups of students, including those identified as having specific learning difficulties, results gave a correlation between listening and reading comprehension scores of 0.6, a low but significant correlation (Bedford-Feuell, Geiger, Moyse and Turner, 1995).

Recent research using the LARC materials (Chong, Poon and Simons, 1995) suggests that many children do respond equally well to the listening and reading comprehension. However there are some children who do respond quite differently.

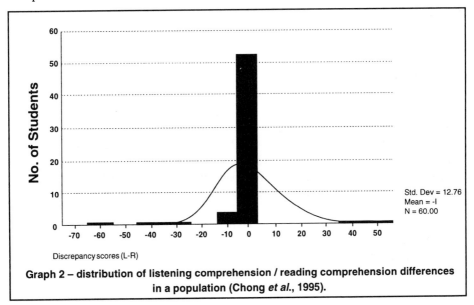

Std. Dev = 12.76
Mean = -I
N = 60.00

Discrepancy scores (L-R)

Graph 2 – distribution of listening comprehension / reading comprehension differences in a population (Chong *et al.*, 1995).

As can be seen in this distribution of listening and reading comprehension differences, a small minority of students achieved listening comprehension scores higher than their reading comprehension scores. Interestingly, a small minority of children appear to have specific listening comprehension difficulties.

Why might differences between reading comprehension and listening comprehension exist?

Specific learning difficulties will limit the ability to read accurately, thus impeding comprehension of what is read. Since standardised tests of reading comprehension demand reading ability, decoding difficulties affect the measurement of reading comprehension. Fluidity of reading is broken, key words are impossible to decode and anxiety can also effect reasoning. Students who have specific decoding difficulties are therefore likely to have more difficulty extracting meaning from text as more attention needs to be paid to decoding words rather than comprehending the text (Perfetti, 1985).

Text difficulty is an important factor. At lower levels of text difficulty, it is more common to have improved performance when reading rather than listening to the text. There must be a difference between the listening comprehension and reading comprehension across a range of text difficulties before such a difference becomes significant.

As a student may be unable to demonstrate good comprehension skills through the use of commonly used reading comprehension tests, an assessment of listening comprehension presents an alternative way to identify comprehension strengths. An assessment of listening comprehension is not affected by decoding difficulties. One of the possible uses of LARC assessments is to identify linguistic skills that may be used in individual education plans to improve reading and writing for meaning.

Outcomes of identifying listening and reading comprehension scores

For the small percentage of students who show a significant discrepancy between their reading and listening comprehension scores on the LARC, the following table suggests some possible interpretations of these discrepancies or performance levels.

LARC assessment outcomes	Listening Comprehension score High	Listening Comprehension score Low
Reading Comprehension score High	Students will have good access to the curriculum assigned. LARC assessment, based on understanding of narrative, correlates with understanding of curriculum information. Need to confirm that curriculum differentiation for high ability is in place.	The opportunity for the student to re-read is important to aid understanding. Possible interventions include repetition of verbal instructions, the use of visual cues, and the use of context when giving verbal explanations. Investigate hearing. There may be social problems resulting in the student withdrawing.
Reading Comprehension score Low	Possible specific reading difficulties. This chapter suggests interventions to utilise good listening comprehension skills to help develop reading comprehension.	Help is required to ensure access to curriculum. Further exploration of possible learning difficulties may be required.

HOW CAN A COMPREHENSION STRENGTH BE USED IN AN INDIVIDUAL EDUCATION PLAN?

Good reading comprehension scores seem to be more important for educational success than reading accuracy measures. Students' reading is enhanced if they are using knowledge of the world and knowledge of language to make sense of the text. Good comprehenders can be taught to use the meaning of a text to make inferences which will help them read particular words and phrases. These comprehension skills can be developed to enable students to use these inferences further thus improving their reading accuracy. Application of listening comprehension skills to boost reading comprehension would allow greater access to the curriculum as a whole.

The following **interventions** aim to boost reading comprehension skills through the development and utilisation of listening comprehension strengths.

Students can be taught to use their comprehension skills through a focus on meaning, at the **word, sentence and passage** level. Importance needs to be placed on raising the student's expectation of acquiring meaning from the text they are attempting to read.

At the word level, it is useful to explicitly teach comprehension of individual key words. This may require exploration of word meaning, how the word is used within a subject or by an author, and potential application in the student's own work. The emphasis, at the word level, should not only be decoding, but also the development of a known vocabulary base. This may be a change from repetitive decoding activities that is often the experience of many students experiencing specific reading difficulties.

At the sentence level, it is necessary for the student to utilise their knowledge of sentence structure so that inferences and expectations can be formed which will aid decoding and comprehension. This can be achieved through a number of different strategies. Explicit teaching of the rules of grammar may be found to be beneficial. Useful interventions may be based on cloze procedure where sentences are written with a key word missing, (these sentences should be grouped so that in one session all the missing key words originate from the same class of word, or part of the word, such as verbs or suffixes). The student is presented with these sentences and in the first instance is expected to provide an educated guess based upon their knowledge of sentence structure. Early in the programme the student may be guided to guess the correct class of word, later using other clues in the passage to gain in accuracy.

At the passage level, reading and listening comprehension assessment would help justify the use of high level narrative, such as 'The Hobbit', to students who demonstrate an above average listening comprehension skill. This helps maintain interest in books and narrative and also encourages the extension of the understanding of linguistic structures and book language.

At the passage level, it is possible to develop good comprehension skills to aid reading accuracy and reading comprehension. A technique known as reciprocal teaching or scaffolding (Moore, 1988), uses a pre-set teacher-pupil dialogue to introduce the theme of the text. One method of carrying out this technique is set out below.

1) Prior to reading a passage of text, the group discuss the title and sub-headings to 'tune in' their background knowledge.

2) The teacher sets a series of questions or tasks to encourage students to:
   - Summarise what has happened so far.
   - Predict what is likely to happen, or what information is likely to be found, what technical words might be used, in the passage to be read.
   - Identify and rehearse difficult, unusual, or technical words in the passage.
   - Seek answers in the passage to a specific question posed.

3) The passage is now read silently by the members of the group, and the teacher leads discussion in respect of the content, its significance and any difficult vocabulary.

4) It may be helpful to finish by reading the text aloud altogether.

5) Once the pattern is clear, the teacher role is taken over by one of the group and he/she takes responsibility for leading the group through each of the bullet points above.

The teacher role is passed around the group members in turn. The teacher may increasingly withdraw from the group and act as a monitor/observer.

It is predicted that students shown to possess good listening comprehension skills will have the potential to make reading comprehension and accuracy gains from this type of programme.

FURTHER USES OF THE LISTENING COMPREHENSION AND READING COMPREHENSION INFORMATION

1. Presenting simple information in written form

LARC results found that reading comprehension scores were usually higher than listening comprehension scores for simple text. This was true for all students tested, including those with specific learning difficulties. This indicates that for easier texts, students are more likely to be able understand a piece of text if they read it rather than if it is read to them. This may be due to the opportunity to reread at leisure. Information from a LARC assessment will yield information regarding the most effective presentation of the curriculum. For example, an individual assessment may demonstrate better access to simple written text rather than simple information presented orally.

This suggests that support time may be used valuably in the production of simplified worksheets which can be read by low reading age students than the use of this support time in class reading aloud of more complex test.

2. Curriculum differentiation and presentation

Analysis of the information gained from LARC assessment may prove that a pupil has access to high level texts if these texts are read to them. This would demonstrate to curriculum providers that complex information and instructions should be presented orally. The LARC results would also suggest a level at which this information should be pitched, providing new information to aid the professional judgement of the teacher.

3. Providing information for requests for examination dispensations

Those requesting exam dispensations may find it possible to use the LARC assessment to demonstrate that a student would have significantly greater access to exam questions if a reader was available to read the examination paper. The comprehension age is critical for examinations. For example, a sixteen year old GCSE student with a reading comprehension age equivalent to the 11 year level, reading accuracy age at nine years, and a listening comprehension age equivalent to 16 years, would be likely to benefit significantly from the use of an amanuensis. In the future, LARC may be admissible evidence for examination boards.

4. Providing information on students who are difficult to assess

It is hoped that teachers of students with expressive language difficulties and/or physical disabilities may be able to gain new information using LARC. The sentence verification technique allows a student to communicate understanding of a piece of text through a 'yes' or 'no' response. Enterprising teachers may be able to devise a number of strategies that would allow students to indicate a positive or negative response. Existing technology and techniques already exist that allow students with cerebral palsy to indicate 'yes' and 'no'. In some cases, LARC assessment may allow teachers and psychologists to test students' strengths that are often difficult to assess.

Error analysis of scientific-type information

LARC assessment may offer formative information regarding the reading style of the student. As detailed in the explanation of the sentence verification technique (SVT), four different sentence types are presented to the pupil (originals, paraphrases, meaning changes, and distractors). When the LARC assessment is completed, responses to each sentence type can be calculated, thus providing further information beyond age equivalence scores. Trialing of the LARC materials indicates that students differ in their responses to sentence types although more research is necessary at this point.

Some students are repeatedly fooled by 'Meaning Changes' but not by 'Distractor' sentences. Analysis and interpretation suggests that the student is highly dependent on decoding words and/or has a good memory for specific words used in the passage. Meaning changes repeat words used in the passage to express a new meaning while distractors use new words. The success of these students in correctly identifying repeated words may be linked to decoding rather than higher level representations of the passage. It is worthwhile to consider how this group of students have responded to the paraphrases which use new words to express an idea originating from a sentence in the passage. This level of diagnostic assessment would potentially offer information to use when writing individual education plans.

Carlisle (1989) has completed work with the sentence types in SVT. She has suggested an analysis of the possible processing problems associated with the sentence types:

- Paraphrase errors – the meanings of the sentences are not computed accurately or completely; the student has trouble recognising the original idea put in a new way.

- Meaning Change errors – the student identifies a test sentence as one already encountered, indicating they may have difficulties with remembering or reading details and noticing text changes which introduce new ideas or themes.

- Distractor errors – the student does not construct a representation of the meaning of the whole passage; pupil is therefore unable to recognise new, albeit related topics.

- Original errors – this suggests more global processing problems. Not expected with Specific Learning Difficulty students.

This type of error analysis is in the theoretical phase of development and further research is required to validate these ideas and the information that they would offer to specialist teachers and psychologists.

FURTHER RESEARCH

It is hoped that the LARC materials will offer new opportunities for assessment and research for teachers and psychologists interested in children's understanding of narrative and its role in the reading process. There is the prospect that once these materials have been standardised, many further correlations and comparisons will be possible. The expectation is that LARC materials will provide further understanding of the reading process in order to help those with reading difficulties.

CONCLUSION

Stanovich (1986) details evidence of 'Matthew effects' which is when students with adequate decoding skills, and students with poorly developed decoding skills develop large differences in educational competence over a relatively brief period of time. Students who quickly acquire the basics of reading ability accelerate the acquisition of further competence compared to students who do not possess adequate decoding skills. Thus, poor readers begin with a disadvantage that inhibits the development of word identification skills which further retards vocabulary development, which further retards knowledge acquisition and so on. This results in an increasing gap in educational competence between students initially having decoding skills and those who do not have them.

The identification of listening comprehension strengths may help students gain access to the curriculum, and inform an education programme that improves reading comprehension. Although the application of listening comprehension to reading development is in its early phases, research is beginning to reinforce the linkages and to suggest practical interventions for teachers.

REFERENCES

Aaron, P. G. (1991). Can reading disabilities be diagnosed without using intelligence tests? *Journal of Learning Disabilities* 24 (3) 178-186.

Bedford-Feuell, C., Geiger, S., Moyse, S., and Turner, M. (1995). Use of Listening Comprehension in the Identification and Assessment of Specific Learning Difficulties, *Educational Psychology in Practice* 10 (4) 207-214.

Carlisle, J. F. (1989). The use of sentence verification technique in diagnostic assessment of listening and reading comprehension, *Learning Disabilities Research* 5 (1) 33-44.

Carlisle, J. F. and Felbinger, L. (1991). Profiles of listening and reading comprehension, *Journal of Educational Research,* 84, 345 - 354.

Chong, S. L., Poon, S., and Simons, M. (1995). Listening and reading comprehension assessment using the sentence verification technique – reliability, diagnostic value and its usefulness. Unpublished project for Msc. Educational Psychology, University College London.

Davey, B. (1987). Post passage questions: task and reader effects on comprehension and metacognition processes, *Journal of Reading Behaviour* 19, 261-283.

Fuchs, L. S., Fuchs, D. and Maxwell, L. (1988). The validity of informal reading comprehension measures, *Remedial and Special Education* 9 (2) 20-28.

Kibby, M. W. (1981). Text review: The degrees of reading power, *Journal of Reading* 24, 416-427.

McKenna, M. C., and Robinson, R. D. (1983). *Teaching Through Text: content literacy approach to content area reading,* Whiteplains, New York, Longman.

Moore, P. (1988). Reciprocal Teaching and Reading Comprehension, *Journal of Research in Reading* 11,1 3-14.

Perfetti, C. A. (1985). *Reading Ability,* Oxford University Press, Oxford.

Reason, R. and Boote (1994). *Helping Children with Reading and Spelling – A Special Needs Manual,* Routledge, London.

Royer, J. M., Hastings, C. N., and Hook, C. (1979). A sentence verification technique for measuring reading comprehension, *Journal of Reading Behaviour*, 11, 355 - 363.

Royer, J. M. (1986). *The Sentence Verification Technique as a measure of comprehension: Validity, Reliability, and Practicality*. University of Massachusetts.

Royer, J. M., and Sinatra, G. M. (1994). A cognitive theoretical approach to reading diagnostics, *Educational Psychology Review*, 6, 81 - 114.

Stanovich, K. E. (1986). Matthew effects in reading: some consequences of individual differences in the acquisition of literacy, *Reading Research Quarterly* 21, 360 - 407.

Stanovich, K. E. (1991). The theoretical and practical consequences of discrepancy definitions of dyslexia, chapter 9 in Snowling, M. and Thompson, M. (Eds. EDS.) London: Whurr *Dyslexia: Integrating to theory and practice.*

Answers to test yourself!

1.	Yes	paraphrase
2.	No	meaning change
3.	No	meaning change
4.	No	distractor
5.	Yes	original
6.	Yes	original
7.	No	distractor
8.	Yes	paraphrase

A DOCTOR'S PERSPECTIVE

ANNE O'HARE

THE ROLE OF THE PAEDIATRICIAN

The doctors who are most commonly consulted with regard to children with specific learning difficulties are those working in Community Child Health and since 1902, local education authorities have been empowered to employ doctors who could periodically examine school children. Obviously, the focus at that time was on conditions such as malnutrition and infection which might impair a child's ability to learn and such considerations are rarely encountered now. The doctor in the school maintains, however, a role in the evaluation of children who are experiencing difficulty learning.

LINKS WITH HEALTH PROFESSIONALS

Since 1974, Community Child Health doctors have been employed directly in the National Health Service, and the speciality has become consultant led. Community Child Health has two major remits:

i) Clinical practice, particularly in developmental medicine, neurology and disability,

ii) Population paediatrics, e.g. educational medicine, which involves health issues relating to the learning environment.

Professional links between Community Child Health and Community Nurses, especially Health Visitors, go back to the latter part of the 19th century.

Links with Primary Care General Practitioners are strengthening, especially since the 1990 National Health Service reorganisation which led to routine immunisations and child health surveillance being conducted largely in general practice, thus releasing Community Child Health doctors to concentrate on other areas such as Special Needs.

Links with hospital services have also increased as a large proportion of community Child Health consultants hold additional hospital appointments over and above their community duties.

Thus, if a child presents in the pre-school years a risk factor for specific learning difficulties, such as speech and language delay, it may be appropriate to alert the school doctor. If the family consult their General Practitioner, either directly because of the specific learning difficulty, or because of related physical disorders such as migraine, they may be referred to the Community Child Health Department. If a child sustains an insult to the developing nervous system which results in a specific learning difficulty, they may be transferred for further assessment and follow-up from the hospital out to the Community Paediatricians. In addition, paediatric therapists frequently consult with Community Child Health doctors.

LINKS WITH OTHER AGENCIES

In addition to these links with Health Service staff, Community Child Health doctors have long-standing links with Social Services, Education and the voluntary sector. Community Child Health doctors are familiar with the demands of working in the community setting. The community is diffuse and complex as a place to work, and much of the work is interdisciplinary and takes place in working environments such as school and social service nurseries which are not under direct medical or health control. Thus, considerable experience of the locality is also needed to build and maintain personal professional contacts (Rogers, 1993).

Taking an appropriate role in the care of children with specific learning difficulties requires skills in communication, assessment and advocacy. Forty per cent of a child's waking life is spent at school and their experiences there contribute to their health and well-being in its widest sense. When a doctor handles a situation with sensitivity, they have much to offer as part of a team involved in assessing and helping a child with a specific learning difficulty. This can be done productively whilst still recognising that the majority of the intervention for such children is educational.

IDENTIFICATION OF CHILDREN WITH DYSLEXIA

Prediction is not the objective of a school medical examination. The primary purpose is to have a considered clinical overview of the child's health status and to consult with parents and teaching staff in the case of children who may give rise to concern. The doctor may have the task of trying to relate the medical findings to the child's functioning. This can be difficult because a child with, for example, a speech and language delay in the pre-school years, may experience difficulty learning to read, but this is not necessarily so (Bax and Whitmore, 1987).

Despite these uncertainties with regard to predicting specific learning difficulties in individual children, there can be a worthwhile contribution from the informed school doctor. Certainly, the Dyslexia Association's view is that 'the contribution from the Health Services is of the highest importance' (British Dyslexia Association 1992). They highlight risk factors to be considered, which involve features such a slow development of speech and language, perceptual difficulties such as those seen in poor shape copying, difficulty sequencing, poor co-ordination and delayed establishment of literacy with a family history of literacy difficulties. How valid then is this advice?

Certainly, a neurodevelopmental examination incorporating these considerations has a relationship to subsequent school progress. Within this broader picture, particular features such as poor auditory discrimination can have an impact on reading progress.

However, Bax and Whitmore's 1987 study of school entrants showed that none of the sub-scores (which included items such as motor score, speech and language score and visual perception score) on their own predicted reading difficulty.

Indeed, it is important to remember that 77% of their clumsy children at school entry had no academic problems at age 7-10 years. However, of the remaining children with poor co-ordination, one quarter did run into significant academic difficulties despite normal intellectual scores.

Bishop (1990) concludes that it is plausible that the left hemisphere of the brain is poorly developed in dyslexics and provides an inadequate substrate for the development of competence in verbally-based skills. Dyslexics as a group have poorer motor skills, which could be a consequence of underlying neurological immaturity. Therefore, it may be possible to identify dyslexic children within the broader group of children with these neurodevelopmental immaturities. Although three quarters of children with these features will have no neurodevelopmental deficit at the age of 10 years, a significant proportion will have under-achieved academically (Gillberg, 1988). Some of the simpler interpretations of risk factors in children such as left-handedness have not stood the test of time, but examining the co-ordination of the hands may reveal the child with mild unilateral brain abnormality which renders the contra-lateral hand clumsy and thus leads to a shift of handedness away from that which would have been genetically determined (Bishop 1980).

There are many aspects in a child's history and examination which merit serious reflection. These are expounded in the following sections and allow the doctor to be alert to children at risk of academic failure. The skill, therefore, required of the doctor is that of arriving at a balanced view and being prepared to facilitate intervention for children where this is appropriate.

DYSLEXIA

For nearly a century there has been intense debate over the mechanisms of dyslexia and whether it exists or not. Initially, the disorder was thought to be visual, and certainly in the medical literature, it was first described by ophthalmologists and termed 'word blindness'. Subsequently in the 1930s the American neurologist Samuel Orton drew attention to the frequent association between reading disability and an underlying disturbance of language. A more recent formulation of dyslexia as a disorder of phonemic awareness has been supported by a wide range of anatomical, neurophysiologial and neuropsychological findings (Roseberger, 1992).

DOES DYSLEXIA EXIST?

Reading skills vary along with intelligence in the normal population, and in addition, dyslexic children fall within the normal distribution of reading skills corrected for ability. That is to say, they do not form a hump at the lower end of the normal distribution (Shavwitz *et al.*, 1992). However, it cannot be concluded that biologically determined reading disabilities do not exist. A similar distribution is seen for intelligence in the mentally handicapped population and yet there is no doubt that many of these individuals have an organic aetiology.

DYSLEXIA AND THE BRAIN

A small number of neuropathological studies in developmental dyslexics have determined that the brain abnormalities are developmental in nature (Geschwind and Galaburda, 1985).

Features include excessive numbers of neurones in the sub-cortical white matter of the left parasagittal region of the brain, and also in the left planum temporale and posterior third of the superior temporal gyrus, suggesting a disorder of neuronal migration. These abnormalities generally fall below the resolution of neuroanatomical brain scanning. However, regional cerebral blood flow techniques in developmental dyslexics in adult life who have deficits in phonological processing have revealed differences from controls with greater asymmetry of function (Rumsy, 1987). Computerised classification of brain electrical activity has also revealed significant differences in functions in the bilateral media frontal lobes and the left posterior quadrant of the brain in dyslexics (Duffy, 1979).

These findings which map function in the brain in dyslexic individuals are compatible with Bishop's theory that dyslexics are characterised by a normal pattern of cerebral lateralisation but that the left hemisphere, which in the majority of people is the language hemisphere, is poorly developed and provides an inadequate substrate for development of competence in verbally based skills (Bishop, 1990).

DYSLEXIA AND GENETICS

Many studies relate a genetic predisposition to dyslexia. The prevalence of dyslexia is variably quoted between 5-10%, with a male to female ratio of 3.5-4 to 1 (Pennington 1990). The sex ratio in familial samples is considerably lower, about 1.8-2 to 1, boys to girls. James 1992 presented evidence that boys are more susceptible to dyslexia as opposed to them being more commonly represented in research through a referral bias. The risk of having an affected father for a dyslexic son is 40%, and for an affected mother is 35%. Dyslexic daughters have a lower risk of having an affected parent, around 17-18%. Twin studies have revealed that 30% of the cognitive phenotype in reading disability is attributable to heritable factors and not due to IQ. The pattern of heritable deficits leads to a growing consensus that dyslexics are more deficient in single word recognition and phonological processing skills than other neuro-psychological factors. A minority of families demonstrate significant linkage between dyslexia and chromosome 15 (Pennington *et al.*, 1987).

It is still unclear whether there is a causal relationship between phonological processing problems and dyslexia. Are the former manifestations of the underlying cause: are they simply correlates of the underlying cause, are they the result of poor reading or are they just incidental to the syndrome?

Certainly, neuro-psychological deficits can be found in adults who have recovered from their difficulties in reading and spelling, and involve deficits in verbal learning and memory, word fluency, temporal order judgments in auditory and visual fields and dexterity in right-sided sequential finger movements (Kinsbourne *et al.*, 1991).

The cognitive phenotype of inherited learning disabilities is complex. Even when mapped very carefully through an affected family there can be a wide range of findings. Such a family had one child with difficulty with phoneme discrimination but relatively intact linguistic processing, whilst another had severe deficits in phoneme analysis and another had generalised deficits across all visual processing tasks. Yet another child had a very specific written spelling disorder and intact reading achievement. Within this family there were, however, similar difficulties across the generations of affected members, on coding digit symbol sub tests (Elbert and Seale ,1988).

THE RELEVANCE OF HEARING, SPEECH AND LANGUAGE TO THE DEVELOPMENT OF READING

The condition of otitis media with effusion (OME) has a part to play in some children who find it difficult to learn to read. This is essentially a process of middle ear catarrh which is very prevalent in pre-school children. Chalmers *et al.* (1989) showed that the presence of a conductive hearing loss, associated with OME at the age of five years in children, led to both depressed articulation scores in their speech and depressed reading scores when they were examined at the age of 7, 9 and 11. In addition, teachers reported behaviour problems more frequently in these children. Obviously the paediatrician in the school needs to ensure that the process is no longer active; if there is a continuing hearing loss in association with middle ear catarrh this requires to be treated in its own right. The more common situation is that there is a lot of past evidence of hearing problems and ear infections, but that at the time that the child presents with problems learning to read the process is no longer active. It is then appropriate for the Paediatrician to advise the teaching staff on this medical background, as it may be pertinent and indicate that the child requires work in the areas which he has missed out on in his pre-school years. He may have poor foundations for his phonological knowledge that he needs to bring to reading.

Dyslexic children are impaired in many language skills to varying extents, and the dominant view is that a central deficit resides at some point in the processes of representing speech sounds and in maintaining and manipulating these phonological representations in memory. Children who can pick odd-one-out words go on to have better reading levels, taking into account their IQ and memory. Children trained in rhyming techniques, particularly if they are linked to the alphabet, do better subsequently in reading and spelling. Many children who are reading deficient have difficulties in short-term memory for linguistic material. Poor readers are less good at repeating a sentence, whereas they are just as good as controls in their comprehension of complex sentences (Shankweiler and Smith, 1984).

Many of these language deficits in dyslexic children will not have been apparent in the pre-school years, but there are some children who before going into school display developmental language delay which has an adverse impact on reading (Silva *et al.*, 1987). Such children are often known to the school doctor when they enter school, and it may be valuable to alert teachers so that they can check whether the child has any difficulties in picking up reading.

PERINATAL CONSIDERATIONS

The Paediatrician seeing a child with a specific learning difficulty may have to consider whether events in the pregnancy, birth and early neo-natal period, might have some bearing on the child's under-achievement at school. Children of low birth weight are known to under-achieve at school, and this is not necessarily associated with a lower intellectual ability (Zubrick *et al.*, 1988). These specific difficulties may be more pronounced in low birth weight children who experience adverse events such as intra-ventricular haemorrhage within the brain. This type of event is very common in pre-term infants, being present in about 50% of very low birth weight infants.

Even low birth weight infants who had an unremarkable course after delivery have delays in verbal comprehension when compared to term children, and problems in phonology are seen in low birth weight children who have experienced illness in the neo-natal period (Largo *et al.*, 1986). In addition, some of the children may have poor visual motor skills (Hunt *et al.*, 1988), and subtle problems in motor development (Marlow *et al.*, 1989).

It is recognised that as a group, low birth weight children can experience difficulties with attention and concentration which have a neurological basis, and are related to effects on the brain of various perinatal events, when the brain has an immature cerebral circulation. These facets of the child's behaviour can compound their academic under-achievement in the classroom.

The Paediatrician will be in a position to evaluate whether perinatal events have contributed to the child's difficulties in the classroom, by considering all the above points.

THE EFFECT OF AN ADVERSE HOME ENVIRONMENT

Learning to read, like any complex behavioural development, is influenced by the child's environment. The Paediatrician may be in a position to judge whether this has had an adverse impact on the child's academic progress. Children who live in crowded homes which lack amenities have lower attainments in reading and mathematics when examined at the age of 16 (Esson *et al.,* 1978). In addition, children in care have lower reading and mathematics attainments than children who have similar socio-economic backgrounds but no experience of care (Esson *et al.,* 1976). Children who are neglected or abused can have more difficulty with speech and language than with cognitive or other development. Auditory and verbal sub-scales of language tests may be the most adversely affected (Law and Conway, 1992).

ACQUIRED DYSLEXIA

Some children experience difficulty learning to read following insults to the central nervous system. These may be quite direct, involving crucial areas for reading such as the left anterior temporal lobe, which leads to deficits in memory skills for auditory-verbal learning (Levine *et al.,* 1981). In other children there is less direct evidence of damage to the brain, but a clear association may be recognised between their condition (e.g. left temporal lobe epilepsy) and their disability in learning to read. In the rare circumstances, where these medical problems are strongly relating to poor progress in reading, the Paediatrician is in a position to assess and advise.

THE ROLE OF MEDICAL MANAGEMENT IN TREATMENT

The Paediatrician can contribute most to meeting the needs of children with specific learning difficulties as part of a multi-disciplinary team. Much of the management and treatment is the province of the education system, but there are several principles which the doctor must bear in mind. These include reducing the child's anxiety, circumventing the handicap, practising areas without disability and direct remedial programme for the disability itself (O'Hare and Brown, 1992). By participating in multi-disciplinary working, the Paediatrician can avoid delivering an assessment which is couched in technical jargon, and may not offer advice of a practical nature. Parents of children with specific difficulties can be all too often met with opposition, when all they need is the reassurance that something is being done, and frequent contact with parents is to be encouraged in this multi-disciplinary working. Morris (1989) also stresses the obvious advantages of new technology for children with specific learning disabilities.

Paediatricians have a scientific training and can help parents, teachers and the community at large to evaluate claims in the treatment of specific learning difficulties. Whilst it is important to remain open-minded, the wholesale endorsement of single explanations and treatments for children with clinical disorders as complex as reading disabilities deserve the doctor's outspoken mistrust (Levine, 1984).

In many instances, the Paediatrician is well placed to contribute to explaining the nature of the child's specific learning disability to the child and the family, and this can often be therapeutic in its own right. There are some specific areas which might be regarded as the remit of the doctor, and controversy remains as to how useful these techniques are to promote children's reading.

THE CONTRIBUTION OF THERAPY SERVICES

The Paediatrician may feel it appropriate to refer the child for assessment and therapy from colleagues in speech therapy or occupational therapy. The contribution of the former is being increasingly recognised and is discussed at some length in other chapters. The occupational therapist may have a particular role for children experiencing difficulty learning to write. Some techniques have been subjected to scientific evaluation and been shown to make a worthwhile contribution to improving the child's situation. Oliver (1990) looked at some special populations of children who had deficits in their writing readiness, and considered that they benefited from individualised instruction which emphasised multi-sensory training. This was especially helpful for children with a difference of 15 points or more between their verbal and performance IQ, and the greatest gains were made by the boys. However, she stressed the unique elements of the writing readiness programme, in that there was co-ordination of direct therapy and on-going classroom orientated remedial programmes, and identified the need for research to evaluate whether other motor components of writing readinesssuch as sitting posture and pencil grip are important treatment modalities.

THE ROLE OF VISUAL TRAINING

This is a most controversial area. Ever since dyslexia 'word-blindness' was first described at the turn of the century, people have been attracted to the idea that vision and visual-perceptual problems were the root cause of reading disabilities. Metzger and Werner (1984) reviewed the literature and found no evidence that children with refractive abnormalities and ocular-motor abnormalities were worse readers than children without these features, and also found no evidence that the perceptual capabilities of children with reading disabilities were any different from those of normal readers. There was no evidence that visual-motor perceptual training produced significant improvement in poor readers, and visual-perceptual skills did not predict poor readers. Whilst visual discrimination test results were different in children who had difficulties learning to read, this was restricted to letter stimuli. However, it does seem sensible to include a test of near-visual acuity in a child having difficulty learning to read. Stewart-Brown *et al.* (1985) taking intelligence into account, found that only children with mild hypermetropia (long-sight) were underachieving at reading in their total group of children with visual deficits. The prescription of spectacles did not seem to alter reading for any of the groups of visually defective children, apart from a trend which did not reach statistical significance in the hypermetropic children. They suggested that it was plausible that the degree of accommodation of the eyes required by these hypermetropic children to read text might have been sufficient to affect their learning to read, and urged that near-vision in such a child should be checked.

There is even greater controversy around the role of orthoptic management in children with reading problems. Stein and Fowler (1985) suggested that 1/6 of dyslexic children may be helped by developing reliable vergance control through establishment of a leading eye. Their technique of occluded spectacles showed a highly significant improvement in reading over chronological age in such children, but it did not appear to help children who had phonemic errors, e.g., children who find it hard to rhyme with simple words or sequence items such as days of the week. Some of this work on unstable binocular control has been criticised but more recently the hypothesis that children who experience frequent visual confusion of text because of unstable binocular control have difficulties discovering the rules and patterns of English orthography has been confirmed (Cornelissen and Bradley, 1994).

The most recent developments in this area of visual-perceptual underpinnings of reading have followed the observation that some individuals are subject to perceptual distortion of text, and yet no longer perceive this distortion when the text has a particular colour. The physiological basis for this remains unclear. Wilkins (1992) has developed a system for ophthalmic precision tinting, and is conducting a multi-centre, double blind, cross-over trial to evaluate the contribution of this therapy in children experiencing difficulties learning to read. In his preliminary work, most of the children who reported abatement of perceptual distortions had either migraine or a family history of migraine, and they picked colours complementary to red. After using their tinted lenses and overlays, the children had fewer headaches and a more positive attitude to reading, but they did not always have improved reading attainments.

MEDICATION

Medication must be seen to have a very limited role in the management of children with specific learning difficulties. This approach is far more popular in the United States where some children with specific learning difficulties would be regarded as suffering from the attention deficit disorder. That is to say, they are developmentally inappropriately inattentive, impulsive and hyper-active. Whilst claims are made for the role of mega-vitamin therapy and exclusion diets, such as the Feingold diet (excluding artificial additives), there is either no benefit demonstrated or the results do not allow one to exclude the effect of a placebo (Haslam *et al.*, 1984). Stimulant therapy, such as methylphenidate, does have place in some hyper-active children. However, in a follow-up of young adults treated for at least three years in childhood with such medications, there was no significant difference in academic outcome, although there was a significantly better outcome for social skills, self-esteem and delinquency rates in young adult life (Hechtmann *et al.*, 1984).

In rare instances, the child with specific learning difficulties may express unusual features which merit further investigation. Such investigations may include neuro-physiological techniques such as electroencephalograms (EEG's), or evaluation of chromosome anomalies. Children with sex chromosome anomalies are frequently intellectually normal, but have an increased rate of problems in auditory perception, receptive and expressive language. Thus, a Paediatrician's opinion, when children run into academic difficulties, may be helpful in clarifying the aetiology of their disabilities.

REFERENCES

Bax, M., Whitmore, K. (1987). 'The medical examination of children on entry to school. The results and use of neurodevelopmental assessment.' *Developmental medicine and child neurology*, 29, 40-55.

Bishop, D. (1980). 'Handedness, clumsiness and cognitive ability.' *Developmental medicine and child neurology*, 22, 569-579.

Bishop, D. (1990). 'Handedness and developmental disorder.' *Clinics in developmental medicine*. MacKeith Press, Oxford, No. 110.

Cornelissen, P., Bradley, L., Fowler, S. and Stein, J. (1994). What Children See Affects How They Spell. *Developmental Medicine and Child Neurology*. 36, 716-726.

Duffy, F. H., Denckla, M. B., Bartels, P. H., Sandini, G. (1979). 'Dyslexia: regional differences in brain electrical activity by topographic mapping.' *Annals of neurology*, 7, No. 5, 412-420.

Elbert, J. C., Seale, T. W. (1988). 'Complexity of the cognitive phenotype of an inherited form of learning disability.' *Developmental Medicine and Child Neurology*, 30, 181-189.

Esson, J., Lambert, L., Head, J. (1976). 'School attainments of children who have been in care.' *Child care health and development*, 2, 339-351.

Esson, J., Fogelman, K., Head, J. (1978). 'Childhood housing experience and school attainments.' *Child care health and development*, 4, 41-58.

Geschwind, N., Galaburda, A. M. (1985). 'Cerebral lateralisation biological mechanisms associations and pathology; a hypothesis and a programme for research.' *Archives of Neurology*, 42, 428-459.

Gillberg, I. C. (1985). 'Children with minor neurodevelopmental disorders: neurological and neurodevelopmental problems at age 10.' *Developmental Medicine and Child Neurology,* 27, 3-16.

Haslam, R. H. A., Dalby, J. T., Radenaker, A. W. (1984). 'Effects of megavitamin therapy on children with attention deficit disorders.' *Paediatrics,* 77, No. 1, 103-111.

Hechtmann, L., Weiss, G., Perlman, T. (1984). 'Young adult outcome of hyperactive children who received long-term stimulant therapy.' *Journal of American Academy of Child Psychiatry,* 23, 261-269.

Hunt, J. V., Tooley, W. H., Harvin, D. (1982). 'Learning disabilities in children with birth weights less than 1500 grams.' *Seminars in Perinatology,* 6, 280-287.

James, W. H. (1992). 'The sex ratios of dyslexic children and their sibs.' *Developmental Medicine and Child Neurology,* 34, 530-533.

Kinsbourne, M., Ruffo, D. T., Gamzu, E., Parma, R. L., Berliner, A . K. (1991). 'Neuropsychological Deficits in Adults with Dyslexia.' *Developmental Medicine and Child Neurology,* 33, 763-775.

Law, J., Conway, J. (1992). 'Effect of abuse and neglect on the development of children's speech and language.' *Developmental Medicine and Child Neurology,* 34, 943-948.

Levine, D., Hier, D., Calvanio, R. (1981). 'Acquired learning disability for reading after left temporal lobe damage in childhood.' *Neurology,* 31, 257-264.

Levine, M. D. (1984). 'Reading disability. Do the eyes have it?' *Paediatrics,* 73, (6, 869-870).

Marlow, N., Roberts, D. L., Cooke, W. I. (1989). 'Motor skills in extremely low birth weight children at the age of 6 years.' *Archives of Diseases in Childhood,* 64, 839-847.

Metzger, R. L, Werner, D. B. (1984). 'Use of visual training for reading disabilities.' *Paediatrics.* 73, (6, 824-828).

Morris, H. (1989). 'Don't Look at the Penguins'. *Special Children,* 29, 7-10.

O'Hare, A. E., Brown, J. K. (1992). 'Learning disorders in disorders of the central nervous system' Chapter 14, in Campbell, A. G. M., Mackintosh, N., (Eds.) *Forfar and Arneils Textbook of Paediatrics* (Edition 4), Churchill Livingstone, 847-854.

Oliver, C .E. (1990). 'A sensory motor programme for improving writing readiness skills in elementary age children.' *American Journal of Occupational Therapy,* 44, 2, 111-115.

Pennington, B. F., Smith, S. D., Kimberlings, W. J., Green, P. A., Haith, M. M. (1987). 'Left handedness and immune disorders in familial dyslexics.' *Archives of Neurology,* 44, 634-639.

Pennington, B. F. (1990). 'Annotation the genetics of dyslexia.' *Journal of Child Psychology and Psychiatry,* 31, 193-201.

Rogers, M. (1993) 'The growing pains of community child health.' *Archives of Disease in Childhood,* 68 (1) 140-144.

Rosenberger, P. B. (1992). 'Dyslexia – Is it a Disease?' *New England Journal of Medicine,* 326, 192-193.

Shankweiler, (1984). 'Repetition and comprehension of spoken sentences by reading disabled children.' *Brain and Language,* 23, 241-257.

Shavwitz, S. E., Escobar, N. D., Shaywitz, B. A., Fletcher, J. M., Makuch, R. (1992). 'Evidence that dyslexia may represent the lower tail of a normal distribution of reading ability. ' *New England Journal of Medicine,* 326, 145-150.

Silva, P. A., McGee, R., Williams, S. M. (1983). 'Developmental language delay from 3-7 years and its significance for low intelligence and reading difficulties at age 7.' *Developmental Medicine and Child Neurology,* 25, 783-793.

Stein, J., Fowler, S. (1985) 'Effect of monocular occlusion on visu-motor perception and reading in dyslexic children.' *Lancet,* 13, 69-73.

Stewart-Brown, S., Haslem, M. N., Butler, N. (1985). 'Educational attainment of 10 year old children with treated and untreated visual defects.' *Developmental Medicine and Child Neurology* 1985, 27, 504-513.

Wilkins, A., Milroy, R., Nimmo-Smith, I., Wright, A., Tyrill, K., Holland, K., Martin, J. (1992). 'Preliminary observations concerning treatment of visual discomfort and associated perceptual distortion.' *Ophthalmology, Physiology, Optics,* 12, 257-263.

SPECIFIC LEARNING DIFFICULTIES: A FRAMEWORK FOR ASSESSMENT

GILLIAN KETTLES
KAREN LAWS
GAVIN REID

There are a considerable number of tests and approaches which can be used to identify and assess children with specific learning difficulties as well as to provide guidance for subsequent teaching and intervention. All forms of assessment, from normative and diagnostic to curriculum-based and metacognitive, although insufficient in themselves to provide a full assessment of a child's learning difficulties, can offer insights into learning programmes from which suggestions can be made about the content and method of teaching. These are not mutually exclusive and can indeed provide a joint framework for assessment upon which an appropriate intervention programme can be based.

An assessment framework can therefore provide a useful guide through the myriad of assessment strategies and tests which can be used to identify and assess children with specific learning difficulties. It is important, however, that such a framework is broad and flexible enough to include diagnosis of the range of difficulties which can be present and how these may affect the learner in different educational contexts. Assessment should not be portrayed as a rigid formula but as an ongoing process which involves gathering a variety of different forms of evidence over a period of time. A comprehensive assessment framework for specific learning difficulties should consider the following:

- The child's strengths and weaknesses.
- The process of learning.
- The curriculum context for learning.

We believe this can be achieved through focusing on criteria relating to difficulties, discrepancies and differences (see Reid, Chapter 2 for a fuller explanation).

CORE AND ASSOCIATED DIFFICULTIES

The phonological core variable model (Stanovich, 1988) highlights the different constellations of cognitive difficulties children with dyslexia may face in addition to the 'core' phonological processing difficulty. This constellation may include sequencing problems, directional confusions, visual and auditory problems, memory difficulties, motor co-ordination and problems with personal and cognitive organisation in a variety of combinations within a continuum from mild to severe (see fig.1). Problems with cognitive organisation may well account for memory difficulties since efficient organisation of material at the retention stage can enhance subsequent retrieval of information.

Fig. 1

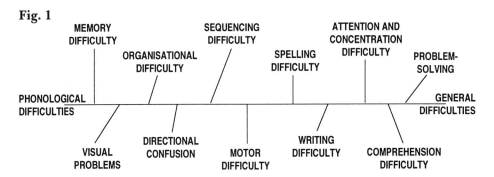

DISCREPANCIES

Identifying patterns of cognitive strengths and weaknesses may provide a useful pointer, indicating the likelihood of a dyslexic problem. This information, however, needs to be supplemented by observing discrepancies in the child's performances across the curriculum.

The principal discrepancy which one should look for is the discrepancy between decoding skills and reading/listening comprehension (Aaron, 1989). A dyslexic child will typically perform poorly on a decoding test, such as that involving the reading of non-words or single words out of context, but perform well on a test which has a significant correlation with reading comprehension. Palmer (1985) found a highly significant correlation between reading comprehension and listening comprehension therefore a test of listening comprehension can be used as a measure of reading comprehension. A dyslexic child would be expected to show a discrepancy between decoding and listening comprehension (Bedford-Feuell, Geiger, Moyse, and Turner, 1995).

Other discrepancies can include those within the sub-test scores of psychometric tests such as the Wechsler Intelligence Scale for Children or indeed between the verbal and performance scales of the same test battery. The dyslexic child's oral performance in class is often discrepant with their written work or reading fluency. Many dyslexic children also show extreme discrepancy performances within different subject areas of the curriculum, for example between Science and English or other subjects which demand significant amounts of reading.

DIFFERENCES

Extensive research on learning styles (Dunn & Dunn, 1992) highlights the importance of assessing not just the product of learning but also the process by which learning takes place. It is important to identify and acknowledge the individual differences of dyslexic children in terms of their cognitive and learning style preferences by commenting on general strengths and weaknesses as well as noting particular aspects of the curriculum which interest and motivate the learner. This can be achieved through self-report questionnaires (Dunn & Dunn, 1992), through dialogue with the student (Hunter, 1993) and by use of an observational framework (Reid, 1992, 1993).

Keefe (1991) identified four higher order factors in learning styles which include: three perceptual responses (visual, auditory, emotive); eight cognitive or information processing styles (sequential processing, simultaneous processing, discrimination, analytic, spatial, memory, categorization and verbal spatial); six study preferences (persistence, posture, mobility, sound, lighting and time of study); and six instructional preferences (verbal risk, grouping, manipulative, temperature, and early and late morning study time).

Carbo, Dunn & Dunn (1986) found that although most primary aged children tend to be more global than analytic, much of the teaching at this stage, including reading programmes, is analytic. Dunn (1993) recommends different ways in which a phonics programme can be introduced and reinforced by acknowledging individual learning style preferences. The range of learning styles can include auditory/visual/kinesthetic/factual analytics and auditory/visual/kinesthetic globals. Auditory analytics, for example, would hear and see the letters first and the sequence of the letters would also be important. Auditory globals, on the other hand, would need to look at the picture simultaneously to the process of reading.

Appreciating the learning style preferences of dyslexic children can help them to develop more effective study techniques and encourage them to take greater responsibility for their own learning. It is, therefore, an important aspect of any assessment.

THE ASSESSMENT FRAMEWORK

The following assessment framework was devised by the authors in response to the needs of mainstream and specialist teachers for some reassurance and control in the identification and assessment of specific learning difficulties. It incorporates and complements existing tests and assessment approaches and can therefore be adapted for a variety of purposes, ranging from initial screening to more detailed assessment and monitoring of progress over time. The following framework is flexible enough to be used by teachers in different educational contexts working with children at different key stages. It may be used to gather different forms of information over a period of time as well as to provide guidance for subsequent teaching and intervention.

We believe a comprehensive assessment framework can be achieved through focusing on criteria relating to difficulties, discrepancies and differences as outlined above. It should include information from the following:

- SENSORY ASSESSMENT
- WORD RECOGNITION TEST
- NON-WORD READING TEST
- SPELLING TEST
- PHONOLOGICAL ASSESSMENT
- MISCUE ANALYSIS
- READING/LISTENING COMPREHENSION TEST
- FREE WRITING
- CURRICULUM INFORMATION
- OBSERVATIONAL ASSESSMENT
- ADDITIONAL RELEVANT INFORMATION

The remainder of this chapter provides an example of a framework for assessment.

1.   DIFFICULTIES

Word Reading Test   Test Used:

Date	Chronological Age	Reading Age	+/-Discrepancy (mths)

Spelling Test   Test Used:

Date	Chronological Age	Spelling Age	+/-Discrepancy (mths)

Bradley Test of Phonological Awareness

Read the following lists of words slowly to the child and ask them to identify the odd one out.
Circle the child's responses below.

Last Sound	**Middle Sound**	**First Sound**
hat mat fan cat	mop hop tap lop	rot rod rock box
doll hop pop top	pat fit bat cat	lick lid miss lip
sun gun rub fun	cot pot hat	bud bun bus rug
hen peg leg beg	fun pin bun gun	pip pin hill pig
fin sit pin win	hug dig pig wig	hem tap had hat
map cap gap jam	red fed bed leg	peg pen bell pet
cot hot fox pot	wag rag bag leg	fish fill fig kick
fill pig hill mill	fell doll well bell	mop dog doll dot
peel weed seed feed	dog fog jug log	seed seal deep seat
pack lack sad back	fish dish wish mash	room food root roof

Number of Errors: Condition 1   Condition 2   Condition 3

Phonological Skills

The Phonological Assessment Battery (PAB) covers this aspect comprehensively (see Chapter 5). Additional information can however be obtained from the following:

1. Ask child to give each letter name and corresponding sound; to offer a word beginning with each sound; and to write the letter corresponding to each sound.

Letter	a	m	t	s	i	f	d	r	o	g	l	h	u
Name													
Sound													
Word													
Writes													

Letter	c	b	n	k	v	e	p	w	j	y	x	q	z
Name													
Sound													
Word													
Writes													

2. Child reads aloud CVC words containing letters from the full alphabet.

Errors													

3. Child reads aloud words with common final consonant blends (tick if read).

Blend	st	mp	nk	nd	ft	sk	ck	nt	ng
Response									

4. Child reads aloud words with common initial blends (tick if read).

Blend	fl	fr	sl	sm	sn	sw	sk	sp	st	bl
Response										
Blend	br	cl	cr	dr	gl	gr	pl	tr	tw	pr
Response										

5.   Child reads aloud words with magic 'e' pattern (tick if read).

Pattern	a - e	i - e	o - e	u - e	e - e
Response					

6.   Child reads aloud words with the following letter combinations (tick if read).

Letters	sh	ch	th	aw	oo	ou	ow	ai	ea	oa	ay	ee	oi	or
Response														

Non-Word Reading Test

Attached is a list of items containing regular spelling patterns which vary in syllable length and complexity. Children should be asked to read aloud each list from 1 to 8. The tester should tick correct responses, record any errors and indicate non-responses (NR) where applicable. Note whether child is affected by syllable length.

List 1	List 2	List 3	List 4
bof	zavil	snep	fomp
cug	cogat	clag	rilt
jid	jefum	drin	hent
kem	radun	twud	jang
wex	woxib	flom	yuld
naz	hesik	bret	zelk
yol	yupog	grap	wilp
hap	nimep	plog	yump
vus	felat	swid	lond
rit	mabup	smug	bamp

List 5	List 6	List 7	List 8
brant	dramep	bamosp	brafeld
clemp	flegom	levunk	clonusp
dwilk	grifut	rudalg	prinalt
frolt	plonad	fonemp	twugimp
glund	swulig	higald	frekont
prand	twapon	vadipt	swalupt
swemp	bletud	donisk	glatong
twing	crovin	gupont	smideng
blomp	smiron	jerupt	pludint
crulk	dwuzet	kalomp	crogamp

2.   DISCREPANCIES

Tests such as the New Macmillan Reading Analysis or Neale Analysis of Reading Ability can be used to complete systematic observation of the child's reading behaviour as well as to identify any discrepancy between reading and listening comprehension skills. Administer chosen test as instructed in the manual, completing miscue analysis and recording child's responses to comprehension questions.

Reading Comprehension   Test Used:

Date	Chronological Age	Comprehension Age	Discrepancy (mths)

Using an alternative form of the same test (eg. Form B of the New Macmillan Reading Analysis) read the passages slowly to the child and record his/her responses to the comprehension questions as before.

Listening Comprehension   Test used:

Date	Chronological Age	Comprehension Age	Discrepancy (mths)

Writing Skills

Arrange for the child to complete a short piece of independent writing. Allow 5 to 10 minutes for completion. Analyse this in relation to the factors below:

Fluency	**Comments**
Speed (Words per Minute)	
Punctuation	
Sentence Structure	
Choice of Words	
Spelling	
Pencil Grip	
Letter Formation	
Size and Spacing	
Attitude to Task	

National Curriculum Attainments*

English

Speaking and Listening	w	1	2	3	4	5	6	7	8
Reading	w	1	2	3	4	5	6	7	8
Writing	w	1	2	3	4	5	6	7	8
Spelling	w	1	2	3	4	5	6	7	8
Handwriting	w	1	2	3	4	5	6	7	8

Mathematics

Using and Applying Maths	w	1	2	3	4	5	6	7	8
Number and Algebra	w	1	2	3	4	5	6	7	8
Shape, Space and Measure	w	1	2	3	4	5	6	7	8
Handling Data	w	1	2	3	4	5	6	7	8

Science										
Experimental and Investigative Science	w	1	2	3	4	5	6	7	8
Life Processes and Living Things	w	1	2	3	4	5	6	7	8
Materials and their Properties.	w	1	2	3	4	5	6	7	8

Comments

*Note: **This can be adapted for the 5-14 Curriculum in Scotland and for any aspect of the school curriculum.**

3.   DIFFERENCES

Research on learning styles highlights the need to assess the process by which learning takes place, not just the actual performance in attainments. It is important to note individual differences in cognitive and learning style by commenting on general strengths and weaknesses as well as on aspects of the curriculum which interest and motivate the learner.

Observational Assessment (Reid, 1992)

The following framework is **not** a checklist but a guide to the type of factors which should be observed in identifying learning strategies, strengths and weaknesses. When completed, this framework should provide you with an overview of the child's learning skills within the context of the classroom.

Interaction	**Comments**
Pupil/Teacher Interaction	
Interaction with Peers?	
Attention/Concentration	
Focus on Task	
Major Sources of Distraction	
Concentration Span in Different Tasks	

Organisational Aspects
Sequence of Activities
Organisational Strategies
Materials and Desk in Order
Teacher Direction

Motor Factors
Handwriting Skills
Body Posture
Colouring
Tracing
Copying

Learning Style
Reliance on Concrete Aids
Memory Strategies
Listening/Auditory Skills
Oral Skills
Visual Approaches
Learning Sequentially
Learning Globally

Emotional Factors
Self-Esteem
Confidence
Motivation
Signs of Tension

Adapted from *Specific Learning Difficulties – An Assessment Framework:* Anderson, J., Heather, A., Kettles, G., Laws, K., Reid, G. (1995). Kent Educational Psychology Service.

This framework has attempted to provide the opportunity for assessment of a comprehensive range of skills and performances within the curriculum. It is also suggested that teachers can utilise this framework in a flexible way. It should however, in its present form, provide them with some guidance on relevant aspects of assessment which can help to identify the difficulties experienced by children with dyslexic problems.

REFERENCES

Aaron, P. G. (1989). *Dyslexia and Hyperlexia.* London, Kluwer Academic Publications.

Anderson, J., Heather, A., Kettles, G., Laws, K., Reid, G. (1995). *Specific Learning Difficulties An Assessment Framework.* Kent Educational Psychology Service.

Arnold, H. (1992). *Diagnostic Reading Record.* Hodder & Stoughton.

Bedford Feuell, C., Geiger, S., Moyse, S. and Turner, M. (1995). Use of Listening Comprehension in the Identification and assessment of Specific Learning Difficulties. In *Educational Psychology in Practice,* 10 (4)207-214.

Carbo, M., Dunn, R. and Dunn, K. (1986). *Teaching Children to Read through their Individual Learning Styles.* Englewood Cliffs, New Jersey, Prentice Hall.

Dunn, R. (1993). *Teaching Students Through Their Individual Learning Styles: A Practical Approach to Learning Styles Training Workshop.* Centre for the Study of Learning and Teaching Styles, St Johns University, Jamaica, New York.

Dunn, R., and Dunn, K. (1993). *Teaching Elementary Students Through Their Individual Learning Styles.* Boston. Allyn & Bacon.

Frederickson, N. (1995). (Ed.). *Phonological Assessment Battery Research Edition* Educational Psychology Publishing, University College London.

Hunter, V. (1993). Strategies for effective learning. In Reid, G. *Specific Learning Difficulties (Dyslexia): Perspectives on Practice.* Edinburgh, Moray House Publications.

Keefe, J. W. (1991). *Learning Style: Cognitive Thinking Skills.* Virginia, NASSP.

Reid, G. (1992). *Learning Difficulties and Learning Styles - Observational Criteria.* Paper presented at South East Learning Styles Conference, George Mason University, Virginia, USA.

Reid, G. (1993). *Dyslexia: Observation and Assessment.* Paper presented at 44th Annual Conference, Orton Dyslexia Society, New Orleans, LA, USA.

Reid, G. (1993). Difficulties, Discrepancies and Differences. In Reid, G. (Ed.) *Specific Learning Difficulties (Dyslexia) Perspectives on Practice.* Moray House Publications, Edinburgh.

Stanovich, K.E. (1988). Explaining the Difference between the Dyslexic and the Garden Variety Poor Readers: The Phonological Core Model. In *Journal of Learning Disabilities.* 21,10,590-640.

SECTION 3

TEACHING

THE ROLE OF THE TEACHER

MARGARET CROMBIE

INTRODUCTION

Provision available to dyslexic children varies widely throughout Britain. There are a few private establishments which offer a very specialised curriculum and teaching geared to meet the needs of a dyslexic population of pupils. At the other extreme, there are schools where the very existence of dyslexic pupils is denied (Thomson and Watkins, 1990; Singleton, 1992). Whether we choose to use the word 'dyslexia' or the term 'specific learning difficulties' is irrelevant to the current chapter. The actual incidence of specific learning difficulties will depend on how we choose to define the problems, but whether we accept a figure of over six per cent (Rutter *et al.*, 1970; Snowling, 1987) or two per cent (Miles, 1991), the reality of the situation dictates that most schools will have a handful of such children. For these children, then, the role of teacher is vital and the responsibilities of the teacher are extremely demanding. Meeting the everyday special educational needs of children with a variety of different problems can never be easy, but it is the teacher who has an important role in determining whether a pupil will thrive or merely survive.

Just what is involved in the role of effective teacher where children with specific learning difficulties are concerned? And what should teachers be expected to provide? All teachers have a responsibility to recognise the signs of such difficulties, to know where to turn for help, and to be able to deal competently with the problems in the classroom situation.

THE PATTERN OF DIFFICULTIES

The initial signs of specific learning difficulties (dyslexia) may not be apparent in the child's early days at school. Sometimes the dyslexic child will learn to identify words by their visual pattern using a look-and-say approach, and it is not till the load on memory becomes too great that the 'reading' process breaks down (Thomson and Watkins, 1990). Sometimes, too, children who do not have specific learning difficulties will show signs, such as b/d confusion, mixed laterality, sequencing difficulties etc., and yet not turn out to be dyslexic (Pumfrey and Reason, 1991). However, if the initial signs do exist, then the teacher should exercise caution and take further steps to establish whether there are grounds for recommending further assessment. Many books on the subject will give a list of indicators of specific learning difficulties (Arkell, 1977; Blight, 1985; Crombie, 1992; Hornsby, 1984; Miles, 1983; Thomson and Watkins, 1990). These include poor reading and spelling; left/right confusion; orientation problems; sequencing difficulties; poor short-term memory; mixed laterality; confusion over punctuation and grammar; difficulty in naming objects; problems with letter formation and a family history of similar difficulties.

Outwith school, the child may be generally quite happy, but difficulties may be apparent when the child is asked to follow a short sequence of instructions, remember a phone number, address or birthday, and the child may be confused over concepts such as yesterday, today, tomorrow, saying, 'I'll do it yesterday'. If there are a significant group of such indicators (six or more), then the role of the teacher at this point is to draw up a programme for intervention in an attempt to accelerate progress and help the child to catch up (Crombie, 1992).

EARLY INTERVENTION

There is good evidence to show that early intervention can be extremely effective. Marie Clay's reading recovery programme (Clay, 1979,1981), although expensive to implement, has proved successful in many countries. She suggests that the best time for intervention is in the child's second year of formal schooling. It is an extremely unfortunate reality of the situation that children often have to fail significantly in learning to read and spell before they will be officially recognised as 'dyslexic'. This may mean that a gap of at least two years has to exist between chronological age and reading and/or spelling ages before a child will be considered 'dyslexic' and in need of some kind of special or specialist help. This size of gap between age and achievement cannot usually exist till a child is in the third year of formal schooling at the earliest. By this time, bad reading habits, mis-spellings and other problems will have become reinforced to a considerable extent, making remediation all the more difficult.

It is important, then, for the teacher to take steps to remedy dyslexic-type difficulties even when no actual diagnosis exists. It may be that in cases of only mild difficulties the child will never be assessed as dyslexic. If, however, difficulties are severe in nature, it is likely that they will require a full diagnostic assessment later, and that specific learning difficulties will become apparent in spite of the best efforts to avoid this. It may be a comfort to know that the difficulties would have been even more severe without intervention, and that without sympathetic help the child might also have developed emotional and behavioural problems.

PREPARATION OF INTERVENTION PROGRAMMES

If the teacher does not feel sufficiently confident to draw up an intervention programme, then it is important to recognise this and to draw in all the help available. Within the school, there may be others who are qualified or at least have a special interest in the field. The learning support teacher, co-ordinator and/or head teacher may be able to give advice and recommend appropriate materials. If the school can request help from local Support Services outwith the immediate school, then their expertise too should be put to use. The advice given should undoubtedly benefit more than just one child: because of the logistics problems of implementation of early intervention for individual pupils, a small group could be targeted. This may include children who have been off ill and missed a significant amount of schooling and children who have come in from other schools or from abroad if they need help in fitting in with the class programme. Any children who are having difficulty in mastering phonic work can be included in the group, so long as it is kept small. The most effective intervention programmes for dyslexic children, it has been found, are phonic and multi-sensory (Hornsby and Miles, 1980; Pumfrey and Elliott, 1990).

While not all the children in the group may actually need multi-sensory teaching, all will benefit from this type of training since it requires children to use all their available senses to aid the learning process. In effect, this means that children should learn to look, say, listen, and write whatever they are attempting to learn. Because the difficulties are mainly in processing symbolic information, this method is particularly effective in learning to read, write and spell, but it is also effective for mathematical knowledge (writing and learning number facts). A considerable amount of overlearning too will be needed for points to become established (Pumfrey and Elliott, 1990).

PLANNING PROGRAMMES

Not all dyslexic children will be spotted early. Often the difficulties only come to light at a later stage. Whether the dyslexic pupil is recognised in the early years of primary school or later, accurate assessment of the pupil's difficulties is essential if individual needs are to be met (Pumfrey and Reason, 1991). The teacher will use this assessment to plan and guide the teaching. A pattern of strengths and weaknesses – along with precise details of phonic knowledge and spelling ability – will enable accurate teaching honed to individual needs. When precise information has been gathered on the points which the child is unsure of, the teacher can then start to build on what the child does know, introducing the points of uncertainty one at a time in a structured, cumulative manner. Advice on planning these multi-sensory programmes should be available, when required, through area specialist teachers and/or educational psychologists.

STRATEGIES AND MATERIALS

In word attack and reading, accurate assessment will require to take into account exactly which aspects of reading the child knows and understands. It will not be sufficient for the child to recognise each letter on one occasion. If the child is really to master the reading process, then responses to symbols must become an automatic process. Digraphs must be recognised as such and not as individual sounds. Blending also has to be practised until it becomes automatic. Often, the simplest way to give reinforcement is through the daily use of flash cards or reading packs to reinforce symbol-sound correspondence. There are a number of phonic-based programmes which are quite suitable for implementing in the classroom. Alpha to Omega (Hornsby and Shear,1993) is structured to the needs of dyslexic children and ready-made flashcards are available to give the necessary practice. The Letterland material (Wendon, 1985 1987), although it appeals more to the younger age group of children, can be extremely useful at later stages. The approach may require to be adapted slightly so that the older pupil will accept the stories and enjoy them, but for the child who has not experienced Letterland at the infant stage, presentation can still be appealing and the learning particularly beneficial to children with different types of learning problems (Bald, 1992).

Reading schemes for dyslexic children need to be selected with care. To give a 10-year-old the same reading book as his young brother who has only been in school for six months could be totally demoralising for the dyslexic pupil. The reading book chosen may well be at the appropriate stage for the dyslexic child's reading level, but in this case would be totally inappropriate for the particular child. It is often best for the teacher to try to find a scheme which is unknown to the other pupils in the class. In this way, comparisons will not be made and the child will avoid the humiliation of being put on an 'infant book'. There are a large range of different schemes available aimed to suit children whose interest age and reading age are discrepant. Schemes such as Oxford University Press's 'Fuzzbuzz' or 'Wellington Square', published by Thomas Nelson & Sons, for younger readers, or for older children the 'Five Minute Thrillers' series from Learning Development Aids will give the pupils reading experiences at their own level of understanding.

SPELLING

The role of the teacher in helping with spelling is to establish good spelling habits from an early stage (Bryant and Bradley, 1985). Learning that spelling is not simply a matter of copying letter by letter is beneficial for all children, but is absolutely essential if the dyslexic pupil is ever to master spelling skills. The use of a LOOK, COVER, WRITE and CHECK routine will encourage the child to think about what he is writing as he does so. He must, however, also learn to say the letters and to rehearse these verbally in his head as he practises the word. Self-checking as well, has to be carried out very carefully as it is very easy for the dyslexic pupil to miss an error. It is also important to match the spelling tasks to the individuals who are learning (Reason and Boote, 1986). Some children may cope with three or four words a day. Others may require to spend a week on two or three words. After children have learned a word, it is important to check that they can remember it, so testing after a few minutes, a day later, and a week later will establish if the word is really known. There is also an aspect that if children know they will be tested they will make a greater effort.

However, in spite of all the effort, the dyslexic child will sometimes be unable to remember the word or words. There will also be errors that seem to persist for ever. Common ones seem to be *whith* for *with, meny* for *many* and *sed* for *said*. It is not always easy to understand why some of the errors persist and why apparently straightforward words prove so difficult for the dyslexic pupil. The teacher should understand that in these cases it is no one's fault that the child has not mastered the words, but with persistence and patience, eventually they usually do come right. It might not, however, always be felt to be worthwhile to expend this amount of effort on each word and the teacher may decide that time spent on dictionary training may be more worthwhile. Often a spelling dictionary or calculator-type Spelling Checker may be more beneficial than the usual dictionary where the dyslexic pupil trying to spell *photograph* may well look under 'f', and wonder why he can't find it. Harrap's English Spelling Dictionary (Wileman-Wileman, 1989) is useful for dyslexic children and is easy enough for most upper primary pupils to master. If the pupil looks up the word by its sound he will see the word printed in blue ink if it is wrong. Alongside is the correct spelling. For example, the child who requires to spell 'said' looks it up under 'sed' and finds it printed in blue. Alongside is the correct spelling in black.

One aspect of spelling which teachers often find difficult is that dyslexic children get words right at one point on the page and get them wrong in different ways at other points on the page. The reason for this is quite simply that the dyslexic pupil does not know when the word is right. In the same way, a dyslexic student who is sent back to his desk to look for his own spelling errors and to correct them may well end up with an even worse attempt than the original. For this reason then, patience and understanding are essential, as is a realisation that asking dyslexic pupils to correct their own mistakes without supervision is often impossible. The class teacher needs to try to set aside a few extra minutes, regularly throughout the day, to ensure that dyslexic pupils get the help they desperately need. This is not always easy to do in a class of mixed-ability children, all of whom have their own very special needs.

THE CLASSROOM CONTEXT

Seating arrangements and classroom planning are very important. Always seat a dyslexic child facing the board as children with these difficulties often become disorientated by having to turn round to copy down work. If the teacher's desk is also positioned by the board, this will avoid the child having to turn round and losing track of the task in hand. Grouping arrangements can be such that the dyslexic child is paired with an agreeable pupil who is prepared to help with reading difficult words, or with finding these in the dictionary. Flexibility of groupings needs to be such that the child is not confined to one group for all activities. If, for example, dyslexic children were to be in the same group for both reading and topic work they might well become disheartened. Often these pupils' oral skills will greatly outpace their reading skills. In a subject which puts reliance on discussion and wider, more general knowledge, the dyslexic child has the opportunity to show knowledge and understanding. This gives an opportunity to boost confidence and increase self-esteem.

Over recent years there has been great and lengthy debate on the pros and cons of withdrawal for individual or small group teaching (Payne, 1991). In my own mind, there is no doubt about the efficacy of the move away from the teaching of a small group outwith the classroom by a teacher who is often unknown to the rest of the class. There does, however, have to be a consideration of what is going to be best for the pupil. Decisions on whether to withdraw or not are sometimes made as a matter of whole-school policy. In this situation, we are not considering the best interest of the individual child. Teachers, and often this will mean head teacher, class teacher and support teacher, should get together to decide what they are aiming to teach and whether it can be achieved best within class or outwith. Accommodation, staffing level and teacher expertise will all play a part in determining the decision to be made, as should the feelings and needs of the pupil.

For instance, for children who have difficulty hearing the individual sounds within words, training in auditory discrimination skills will be necessary if they are ever to learn to spell. To give this training in identifying small differences in sounds in a noisy classroom will be almost impossible. In the same way, it might be a matter of considerable embarrassment to an older pupil to be seen to be practising elementary reading skills in the presence of his or her peer group. There is no easy answer, but it is the role of the child's teachers, in the light of all the facts, to decide what is best and on what occasions a child might be withdrawn.

THE SECONDARY STAGE

Decisions on where structured individual teaching should take place will also have to be made if help is being sought from outwith the school. Support teachers, whether specialists in specific learning difficulties or in the wider range of learning difficulties, should also view the interests of the pupils as being paramount. Often a mixed approach can be best, with the support teacher spending some time in the classroom and some time with the child outwith, to work on specific skills training.

At the secondary stage, however, where specific help is being given in basic reading, spelling and writing skills, it is generally in the best interests of the child for a specialist teacher to carry this out away from the main classroom. There is no way that such basic skills can be taught in the classroom without some degree of embarrassment to the pupil. It is, however, still extremely important for secondary pupils to receive the level of help which they need even when this does mean extraction from another subject. The main difficulty for the specialist teacher, in liaison with secondary subject specialists, is to decide which is the most appropriate subject from which to withdraw pupils. Should we withdraw from the best subject in the hope that the pupil will be able to catch up easily on time missed, or a subject which stresses individualised programmes, perhaps maths, or a subject the pupil is particularly poor at, accepting that he is not likely to make much improvement anyway? Another possibility is to withdraw from non-examinable subjects like social education. Not all pupils, however, will be able to be withdrawn from the most appropriate subject. Demands on the specialist teacher's timetable are likely to be such that compromises will always be necessary. The role of the specialist, however, is to minimise the likely difficulties which might occur through a policy of withdrawing pupils from classes.

Secondary subject teachers also have an important role in furthering the work of the specific learning difficulties specialists and in promoting alternative strategies for those who are totally unable to cope with the demands of the secondary curriculum. Often, when specific difficulties are severe ,the role of the subject specialist is to look for alternative means of presentation. On occasions too, difficulties will be such that a reader and scribe may be needed to give the pupil a fair chance of expressing his knowledge in exam situations. When this is the case, the teacher's role is to give the pupil considerable practice in using these resources, learning to use a reader and scribe to maximum benefit is a skill which has to be practised just like any other. The same applies to the use of tape recorders (Reilly, 1991). Pupils will need considerable practice in using the equipment before they reach the degree of efficiency which is desirable for the exam situation. They need to recognise just how much they have to rewind to get back to the section they wish to hear again or say again. They also have to recognise the right keys for running the tape forward, rewinding etc. All these can be practised and need to be practised if pupils are to master the skills and gain the desired benefits. It is for the teacher to ensure that this is done as often as possible.

The subject teacher can help by providing copies of notes, either by asking a competent pupil to use carbon paper under his work or by photocopying. The use of tape-recorded material too may help in accessing the pupil to novels or other material he might have difficulty in reading. Specialist vocabulary for the pupil's various subjects should be kept handy. If subject teachers write this vocabulary into a pocket-sized dictionary, the pupil can refer to this whenever the need arises (Stirling, 1984). For those whose needs are less severe, most material can be differentiated to a level which will enable the student to cope. Symbolic information can often be given alongside the written words to help these pupils cope. While there may be difficulties in accessing pupils to all subjects at the secondary stage, it is not impossible, and with time and consideration, the needs of the pupils can be met by altering or adapting the means of presentation and responding.

WORDPROCESSING

The use of wordprocessors with the facility to correct spelling can be extremely beneficial to dyslexic pupils once they have reached a certain stage. Generally, this is when work is sufficiently acceptable for an adult to recognise what the words are meant to say. As the computer has been programmed to recognise misspellings, generally it will respond by suggesting various alternatives.

The pupil must, however, have reached a stage where he can recognise the correct version when he sees it on the screen. Small portable wordprocessors with a spelling checker are available for under £100 and for some dyslexic pupils, are a reasonably cheap and easy method of vastly improving the standard of written presentation. Pupils should be given a trial on this type of equipment for a few weeks at least, to ensure that it will be of use before the equipment is purchased. These cheaper machines are generally unable to recognise more bizarre spellings, and wrong spellings of homophones such as 'too' for 'to', but they can still be an enormous asset for dyslexic pupils. For those who have difficulties in producing legible work, the wordprocessor is also of great benefit. Whatever the quality of the spelling, work will always be legible. The need for redrafting, which can be a nightmare for pupils who are likely to introduce new mistakes with every redraft, is eliminated and the teacher can concentrate on correcting the existing errors. The motivational aspect of these machines cannot be underestimated. They present the pupils with a non-judgemental aid to the writing process (Singleton, 1992). For pupils who are all too well aware that the standard of their written work falls considerably short of what the teacher would wish, they can be invaluable.

Teaching typing skills to dyslexic pupils and students can be problematic. Many parents and teachers are concerned that using a computer will involve long hours of routine repetitive exercises of the sort that dyslexic children abhor. Some certainly can learn fast, accurate touch-typing and seem to do so easily. However, most find this difficult and settle for a two- or four-finger 'pick and peck' approach.

This inelegant and inefficient method is sufficiently fast and accurate to meet the needs of most casual use and does not impose an excessive load on the writer. Many teachers put forward the argument that 'proper typing' is a life-time skill and therefore worth the effort. This argument has, until now, revolved round the relative value of effort now and benefits in the future. Technology is already changing this ratio and could make it meaningless in the near future.

Speech recognition programs such as IBM's VoiceType, allow users to speak to the computer and see the words appear on the screen properly spelled and laid out. Current technology relies on moderately high function PCs (at moderately high prices to match) but the prices have been falling and will continue to fall as the technology develops. Within a few years, speech input will be as common as mice and windows are now. This will allow 'writers' to concentrate on the message, not on converting it into key-presses or pen-strokes.

PARENTAL INVOLVEMENT

The involvement of parents in the education process has been well researched and found to be wholly desirable (France, Topping and Revell, 1993; Hewison and Tizard, 1980; Young and Tyre, 1983). The role of the teacher in involving parents therefore is an important one (Acklaw and Gupta ,1991). Parents must feel that they are able to discuss any points of concern. They must also be helped to know how they can best aid their children. Whether this is in providing moral support, paired reading help, or more detailed instruction will depend on the abilities and previous knowledge of the parents.

The attitudes of teachers towards parents will also determine just how much knowledge is gained. Parents should feel sufficiently comfortable to be able to divulge, in confidence, relevant information which may influence expectations and increase the teacher's understanding of the pupil and his background. This will only happen if the parents see teachers as being sympathetic and genuinely interested in the learning needs of their children. For example, if parents themselves are unable to read, teachers would want to know this. It would be a pointless exercise to send out letters inviting such parents to attend a paired reading evening at the school. These parents may also need help in interpreting reports and understanding Records of Needs. All parents can help their children in some way. Often with guidance from the teacher, parents can prove a tremendous resource in aiding the development of the children we all seek to help (Hornsby, 1984).

INVOLVEMENT OF OUTSIDE AGENCIES

In most areas, help is available from outwith the immediate school. This may be in the form of further assessment, advice, direct teaching, support teaching or in-service training, and might involve agencies such as psychological service, support services, colleges or university faculties of education. The type of help provided will vary from area to area, but certainly there should be help in determining the needs of the pupil through psychological services. They will arrange and carry out detailed assessment of needs, and decide, in consultation with school staff and parents, whether the case is sufficiently severe to warrant the opening of a Record of Needs in order to describe what provision should be available for the pupil and to safeguard the pupil's rights in a legal sense. Psychological services can also determine what level of support is desirable and advise on sources of obtaining this help.

As more and more teachers are becoming aware of the types of difficulties faced by dyslexic pupils, the demand for training has increased. Pressure from outside bodies to ensure that pupils' needs are met by staff who have the training to deal with the problems has meant that training agencies are now offering more INSET in response to an increasing demand. Provided the training of pre-service teachers is included, we should in time have a much greater awareness of specific learning difficulties and how teachers can best deal with the problems in the classroom situation.

MOTIVATION

An area which deserves separate consideration in any discussion of dyslexic problems is that of motivation. A pupil who has poor motivation is unlikely to gain much from his time in school. All too often, where there are dyslexic problems, the pupil loses interest over time. This is only to be expected when, no matter how much effort is expended, success is seldom or never achieved. From this point, the pupil seems to be on a downward spiral, avoiding where possible any situation which brings negative feelings of self-concept (Pumfrey and Reason, 1991).

As reading is likely to bring about such feelings, the pupil will try at all costs to avoid reading. Such pupils need all the support and help teachers can offer to bring about a change in attitude which will reverse the downward trend. It is for the teacher to find the strengths of the pupil and give praise and encouragement whenever possible. Through an increase in confidence, the pupil's whole approach to school work may be altered.

CONCLUSION

The key to the success or failure of teaching for dyslexic pupils undoubtedly lies in the hands of the teachers they encounter as they make their way through our schools. A successful programme for dyslexic pupils will provide them with maximum support, encouragement, and opportunity for achievement by whatever means are available. The demands made on dyslexic children must be realistic. Often this will mean accepting much less than the child seems to be capable of orally. However, by a series of small and carefully graded increments ,the dyslexic pupil can often be brought to a very acceptable standard of literacy. Where this is not always possible, an acceptance of the problems and perseverance to keep on trying can be balanced by presenting alternative means of accessing the curriculum. Through careful handling and sympathetic help, dyslexic pupils can then be helped to achieve their potential, however great or humble that may be.

REFERENCES

Acklaw, J. and Gupta, Y. (1991). *Talking with parents of 'dyslexic' children: The value of skilled discussion methods*. Support for Learning, Vol. 6, No. 1, 37-39.

Arkell, H. (1977). *Dyslexia – Introduction – A Dyslexic's Eye View*. The Helen Arkell Dyslexia Centre, Farnham.

Bald, J. (1992). *Love and War in Letterland*. Child Education, Vol. 69, No. 5, 40-41.

Blight, J. (1985). *Practical Guide to Dyslexia*. Egon Publishers Ltd., Baldock.

Bryant, P. and Bradley, L. (1985). *Children's Reading Problems*. Basil Blackwell Ltd., Oxford.

Clay, M. M. (1979). *Reading: The Patterning of Complex Behaviour – Second Edition*. Heinemann, Portsmouth, New Hampshire.

Clay, M. (1981). *The Early Detection of Reading Difficulties*. Heinemann Educational, London.

Crombie, M. (1992). *Specific Learning Difficulties (Dyslexia) – A Teachers' Guide* – Revised, Jordanhill Sales and Publications, Glasgow.

France, L., Topping, K. and Revell, K. (1993). *Parent-tutored Cued Spelling*. Support for Learning, Vol. 8, No. 1, 11-15.

Harris, C. (1978). *Fuzzbuzz*. Oxford University Press. Oxford.

Hewison, J. and Tizard, J. (1980). *Parental Involvement and Reading Attainment*. British Journal of Educational Psychology, 50, 209-15.

Hornsby, B. (1984). *Overcoming Dyslexia*. Martin Dunitz Ltd., London.

Hornsby, B., and Miles, T. R. (1980). *The Effects of a Dyslexia-Centred Teaching Programme*. British Journal of Educational Psychology, 50, 236-242.

Hornsby, B., and Shear, F. (1993). *Alpha to Omega*, – Fourth Edition, Heinemann Educational Books Ltd., Oxford.

Miles, T. R. (1983). *Dyslexia – the Pattern of Difficulties*. Granada, London.

Miles, T. R. (1991). *Dyslexia: Integrating Theory and Practice*. Whurr Publishers Ltd., London.

Payne, T. (1991). *It's Cold In The Other Room*. Support for Learning, Vol. 6, No. 2, 61-65.

Pumfrey, P. D. and Elliott, C. D. (1990). *Children's Difficulties in Reading, Spelling and Writing*. The Falmer Press, London.

Pumfrey, P. D. and Reason, R. (1991). *Specific Learning Difficulties (Dyslexia) Challenges and Responses*. Routledge, London.

Reason, R. and Boote, R. (1986). *Learning Difficulties in Reading and Writing – A Teacher's Manual*. NFER-Nelson, Windsor.

Reilly, J. (1991). *The Use of Tape-recorders to Develop Speaking and Listening Skills*, in Snowling and Thomson, (Eds.). Whurr Publishers Ltd., London.

Rutter, M., Tizard, J. and Whitmore, K. (1970). *Education, Health and Behaviour*. Longman, London.

Singleton, C. (1992). *The Patient Teacher*. Special Children, September, 1992.

Snowling, M. (1987). *Dyslexia – A Cognitive Developmental Perspective*, Blackwell, Oxford.

Snowling, M. and Thomson, M. (1991). *Dyselxia; Integrating Theory and Practice*. Whurr Publishers Ltd., London.

Stirling, E. G. (1984). *Spelling Checklist*. University of Sheffield Printing.

Thomson, M. E. and Watkins, E. J. (1990). *Dyslexia: A Teaching Handbook*. Whurr Publishers, London.

Wendon, L. (1985, 1987). *Letterland Teaching Programmes 1 and 2*. Letterland Ltd., Cambridge.

Wileman, B. and Wileman, R. (Eds.) (1989). *Harrap's English Spelling Dictionary*. Harrap Books Ltd., Bromley.

Young, P, and Tyre, C. (1983). *Dyslexia or Illiteracy? Realising the Right to Read*. The Open University, Milton Keynes.

THE ORTON-GILLINGHAM APPROACH

MARCIA K. HENRY

The Orton-Gillingham approach is a structured, sequential, multi-sensory approach linking visual, auditory, and kinaesthetic modalities. Visual input refers to seeing a letter, letter combination, word, phrase or sentence. Auditory input refers to hearing letter and letter combination sounds either individually, within syllables, or within words. Kinaesthetic-tactile input refers to both hand-arm movements and lip, tongue and throat movements.

The Orton-Gillingham approach stems initially from the work of Dr. Samuel Torrey Orton. From 1925 until his death in 1948, Dr. Orton devoted himself to research and teaching in the field of developmental dyslexia. Orton, a neurologist and psychiatrist, called attention to otherwise normal children who had a specific disability in learning to read. His conclusions were based on his work at the Medical School of the State University of Iowa where he organised an experimental mobile mental hygiene clinic. Here he first studied 'M.P.', a 16 year-old boy in junior high school who had never learned to read (Orton, 1925). Orton recorded his observations that M.P. exhibited '. . . mirror reading, mirror writing and a strong tendency to attempt to read parts or all of a word from right to left and confusion of those letters in which orientation is essential' (p. 581). After intensive study of M.P. and others, Orton coined the term 'strephosymbolia' (twisted symbols) to describe the difficulty these patients had in remembering whole word patterns and the orientation of letters.

Orton was convinced that this reading disorder was the result of incomplete cerebral dominance, but that the effective intervention was educational. While in Iowa, working with reading specialist Marion Monroe, he established the combination of procedures for remedial reading instruction based on visual, auditory, and kinaesthetic linkages, now known as a multi-sensory technique. Orton had concluded that:

> *"In general, the re-education methods which we propose may be said to be based on training for simultaneous association of visual, auditory and kinaesthetic fields; i.e., tracing and sounding the visually presented word and maintaining*

consistent direction by following the letters with the fingers during the sound synthesis of syllables and words."

(Orton, 1928, p. 1098)

In the late 1920s, Orton moved to New York and directed the Language Research Project under the auspices of the New York Neurological Institute. Here, he enlisted the help of Anna Gillingham to further the development of educational intervention as an alternative to regular classroom instruction. Anna Gillingham engaged remedial reading teacher Bessie Stillman to assist in developing a curriculum for reading, spelling, and writing instruction. The goal was to establish efficient word attack habits in reading, writing, and spelling through systematic, well-planned sequences of repetitive drills and to provide the student with thinking patterns to enable him to cope, as far as possible, with the irregularities of the English language (J. Orton, 1964).

During this 'retraining' teachers teach students to link the sounds of the letters with the written symbol. Students also link the sound and symbol with how it feels to form the letter pattern. As students learn new letter patterns, they both read and spell words, phrases, and sentences using these patterns.

Miss Gillingham and Miss Stillman designed this approach for individual one-on-one tutoring, although the approach is now used successfully with small groups of children who have similar learning needs. Together, Gillingham and Stillman wrote and privately published the classic manual entitled, 'Remedial Training of Children with Specific Disability in Reading, Spelling, and Penmanship' (Gillingham and Stillman, 1956). At the time of Gillingham's death in 1964, the manual was in its sixth edition.

Teachers begin by teaching the basic language units, individual letters (graphemes) and their sounds (phonemes). As rules of the language become necessary, they are incorporated into the lessons. For example, when students become introduced to suffixes, they must learn suffix addition rules. While the Orton-Gillingham lessons focus on integrated decoding and spelling instruction, vocabulary development and comprehension strategies are included in most cases.

RETRAINING FOR READING

Teachers present the common consonants and vowels, one or two at a time, they clarify the visual and the auditory patterns, and strengthen their linkage by introducing the motor elements of speech and writing at the same time (Orton,

1966). Children link how the letter looks (visual pathway) with its sound (auditory pathway) and how it feels to form the letter (the kinaesthetic-tactile pathway). Each lesson includes a review of consonant and vowel patterns taught previously, a blending drill to practise putting the sounds together, the introduction of a new consonant or vowel pattern, and numerous opportunities for reading and spelling words and phrases. Children usually end the lesson by reading from a book or magazine suitable for their reading level.

Students who read at a primary level usually first learn the sounds of consonants and vowels and some of the other common letter patterns such as **oo, ee, or, ar, all,** and various consonants blends. They also learn the common rules of the English language such as the final-e rule and when to use -**ck** and -**tch**. Older students, who are reading at third grade level and above, must learn a variety of syllable patterns and the common prefixes and suffixes to add to short base words as in un**like**ly. They then learn the Latin word roots as in in**spect**ion, and the Greek word parts as in **telegraph**. These latter strategies give readers the means to read words of more than one syllable.

RETRAINING FOR SPELLING

Inaccurate spelling almost always accompanies a specific reading disability. A good speller usually has a clear-cut auditory pattern of the spoken word, adequate handwriting to reproduce it, and a dependable visual memory of the particular letter symbols and their sequence in its graphic counterpart (Orton, 1966).

Training for spelling relates closely to reading in the Orton-Gillingham approach. Associations between graphemes and phonemes are learned in both directions: the teacher shows the grapheme and the child gives the sound; and the teacher gives the sound and the child names and writes the letter. Students receive auditory training and direct practice in writing the sounds to dictation. Orton believed that students with a good auditory rote memory could sometimes learn to spell words correctly by saying letter names while spelling aloud. This simultaneous oral spelling (S.O.S.) is an integral part of many of the Orton-Gillingham variations, but in others students move directly from sounds to letters (see Clark, 1988, and Sheffield, 1991, for information regarding program similarities and differences).

Many individuals with dyslexia who learn to read accurately continue to have problems in spelling. Witness the adult dyslexic, a successful banker, who wrote 'Tommorrow were going sking.'

RETRAINING FOR HANDWRITING

Many dyslexics are able handwriters, but many are not. Teachers and students must agree on both the hand and the slant that are natural to the student. Pencil grasp, hand position, and proper placement of the paper are also important. Teachers model letter formation for the child and have the child trace the letter(s), copy the pattern several times, and write from memory. Careful monitoring of letter formation helps to ensure accurate printing and/or cursive writing.

(NOTE: For more in-depth information about the specifics of the Orton-Gillingham approach see Gillingham and Stillman, 1956, and J. L. Orton, 1964. For a thorough explanation of Dr. Orton's research into language disabilities see Orton, 1937.)

LESSON PROCEDURES

Teachers make or purchase 3 x 5 inch cards and print a common grapheme (visual pattern consisting of consonants, vowels, consonant digraphs, vowel digraphs, and other common patterns) on each card. During the first lesson, the student should go through the card deck both visually (student sees card and says sound) and auditorially (teacher says sound and student responds with the spelling). Teachers place the cards that the student knows in one pile and begins introducing new sounds according to a logical sequence. Review is added as often as necessary.

The teacher should be aware of the student's strong and weak learning modalities. Some students may require supplementary work on areas affecting linguistic awareness. These include auditory discrimination and sequential memory, sound blending and segmentation, rhyming, and classification as well as visual discrimination and memory.

Lessons always incorporate card drills, spelling, and reading as students review old patterns or learn new letter-sound correspondences and rules. Lessons usually include the following activities:

I   Card Drills

Visual.   Using commercial or teacher-made cards containing the common letter patterns, teachers show cards one-at-a-time to students. The student responds with the appropriate sound or sounds. If the sound is incorrect, the student should immediately trace the letter(s) on the card to see if this kinaesthetic-tactile reinforcement provides a stimulus for the correct response. If not, the teacher should give the sound, have the student write the letter(s) and say the correct sound simultaneously.

Auditory. The teacher next presents the phonemes (sounds) auditorially. The teacher says the sound and the student replies with the letter name(s). The student repeats the sound for kinaesthetic and auditory reinforcement. Do not allow the student to guess. When the correct response is unknown, the student should be told the correct response while being shown the appropriate grapheme. He then writes the letter(s) while saying the sound aloud.

Blending. Once a word is segmented into syllables or individual sounds, the student must also be able to bring those sounds together as a whole word. The **card blending drills** train students to identify changes in the syllable patterns as the letters change and to gain fluency in reading unknown words (see Fig. 1). The teacher flips the cards to make new real or nonsense words. Cards should be placed in a logical order following the structure of English orthography (the English spelling system).

Therefore, **x** would not come in an initial position and -**tch** would not follow a vowel digraph.

Fig. 1 – Set-up for Card Blending Drills

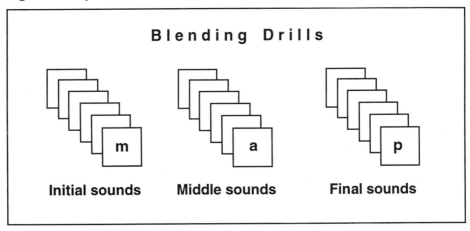

The student should try to connect the vowel sound to the initial consonant sound to prevent choppy blending (i.e. **ma** p - map, **ma** t - mat, etc.). Both real and non-words will appear in the blending drill. The student then says the word as a whole after saying the separate sounds. Once the student blends consonant-vowel-consonant words easily, he can move onto reading word lists. Word lists are more effective than blending drills for reading four, five, and six sound units and for multi-syllabic words (e.g. *stick, blimp, splint, basket,* etc.)

II   Introduction of New Phonograms

The teacher shows the student a card containing a new phonogram. The teacher gives the sound and the student repeats. Many teachers provide a key word – a common noun beginning with the new sound. A model of the phonogram should be written in the student's notebook or paper (make large letters for younger children). The student traces the letter(s) several times, simultaneously giving the sound. He then copies the letter(s) and finally writes from memory, always saying the corresponding sound.

III   Reading

Word lists and phrases. Words containing new and review patterns provide practice reading numerous words. Nonsense words are often included as they are valuable in checking the child's ability to synthesize all sound units. In order to facilitate reading and to discourage guessing, students should be encouraged to isolate the vowel sound first and then to blend from left to right.

Approximately 100 of the frequently used short words do not use traditional letter-sound correspondence. These non-phonetic (rote memory) words such as *one, want, laugh* and *friend* must be memorised.

Oral reading selection. Most lessons end with oral story reading. A book or magazine article or short story appropriate to the child's instructional reading level should be used. The teacher should read the passage before giving it to the student to read the passage. The teacher points out difficult words, phrases and proper names before the child reads the material aloud.

Many students like to use a marker, such as an index card, index finger or pencil to help keep their place. The student should be encouraged to sound out all words which have known patterns. Otherwise, the teacher should give the word to the child.

Some teachers alternate reading with the students. Another useful strategy is to have the child read several paragraphs silently before reading aloud. After reading one or two paragraphs aloud, appropriate comprehension questions should be asked, both at the literal and inferential level. Also, discuss story elements such as characters, setting, and plot with your students. Students reading expository passages should be exposed to the structure of descriptive, sequential, and argumentative-persuasive style.

IV Spelling

Phonetic words. Students should be encouraged to actively sound out phonetic words while spelling. Words, phrases or sentences are dictated based on new and previously presented phonograms. The student should repeat each word, phrase or sentence before writing. The student may benefit from identifying the vowel sound first. Many teachers encourage students to use only letter sounds while spelling phonetic words. Other teachers ask children to say both letter names and letter sounds.

Non-phonetic words. Words that must be rote memorised should first be traced, then copied and later written from memory, while saying letter names. The student should be aware of why the word must be memorised; usually only the vowel sound differs from normal letter-sound correspondence (i.e., according to v-c-e rule, **one** should say /one/).

V Handwriting

Legible writing must be encouraged and developed. Careful attention should be paid to pencil grasp and writing posture as well as to monitoring actual letter formation. Writing practice should be scheduled in the lessons for students having difficulty with either cursive or manuscript letter formation. Hand writing drills may include tracing and copying a model, working at the chalkboard, or drawing large letters on newsprint. Cursive writing generally begins in grade 3. Linkages of certain letters are often difficult. The student may need drill in connecting cursive **br, bl, wn, ol, ve,** and other more awkward connections.

VI Composition

As students are learning more patterns, they should be encouraged to write sentences, paragraphs, and short stories. As students learn new patterns, they are less anxious to rely only on the spelling words that have been memorised. They also are willing to try to spell the words they really want to use, rather than substitute simpler words.

SUMMARY

The Orton-Gillingham approach is a structured, sequential multi-sensory approach linking visual, auditory, and kinaesthetic pathways for learning. This approach encourages systematic direct instruction on the the structure of the English spelling system in a multi-sensory fashion.

These lessons differ greatly from traditional reading instruction and the newer 'whole language' approach. Until the late 1980s, teachers used a basal reading series as the basis for reading instruction. The word analysis component included a phonics strand with drill and practice provided through workbooks. As most dyslexic learners need to discuss the specific concepts, and go beyond phonics to a deeper understanding of language structure, they may not learn to read with this approach.

The whole language approach now in place in most schools suggests that written language is learned as naturally as spoken language. In addition, whole language advocates believe that by being exposed to books and magazines and to opportunities for writing, children will make the necessary phonics generalisations without explicit instruction. Parents and teachers who understand the problem of dyslexia, know that neither of these points provides a logical rationale for dyslexic readers.

In conclusion, the most effective solution is to give children explicit instruction in the structure of English words so that students learn strategies to break the alphabetic code. The Orton-Gillingham approach provides just such instruction. In 1966, Samuel Orton's widow summarised Dr. Orton's contributions to the field of dyslexia:

> *"As early as 1925, he had identified the syndrome of developmental reading disability, separated it from mental defect and brain damage, offered a physiological explanation with a favourable prognosis, and fully outlined the principles of remediation by which, in the past forty years, hundreds – thousands in fact – of disabled readers have been helped to overcome their handicaps."*
>
> (Orton, 1966, p. 119)

To that statement ,we can add an additional 20 years towards the efficacy of the Orton-Gillingham approach. (See McIntyre and Pickering (in press) for research studies supporting the use of this approach for students with dyslexia).

REFERENCES

Clark, D. B. (1988). *Dyslexia: Theory and practice of remedial instruction.* Parkton, MD: York Press.

Gillingham, A., and Stillman, B. (1956). *Remedial training for children with specific disability in reading, spelling, and penmanship.* Cambridge, MA: Educators Publishing Service.

McIntyre, C., and Pickering, J. (Eds.) (in press). *Efficacy of multi-sensory structured language instruction for students with dyslexia and related disorders.* Baltimore: The Orton Dyslexia Society.

Orton, J. L. (1964). *A guide to teaching phonics.* Cambridge, MA: Educators Publishing Service.

Orton, J. L. (1966). The Orton-Gillingham approach. In J. Money (Ed.), *The disabled reader: Education of the dyslexic child.* Baltimore: The Johns Hopkins University Press.

Orton, S. T. (1925). 'Word-blindness' in school children. *Archives of Neurology and Psychiatry,* 14, 581-615.

Orton, S. T. (1928). Specific reading disability - strephosymbolia. *The Journal of the American Medical Association,* 90, 1095-1099.

Orton, S. T. (1937). *Reading, writing, and speech problems in children.* New York: W. W. Norton & Co.

Sheffield, B. B. (1991). The structured flexibility of Orton-Gillingham. *Annals of Dyslexia,* 14, 41-54.

A PHONIC ATTACK STRUCTURED SKILLS PROGRAMME (P.A.S.S.)

HELEN CALCLUTH

BACKGROUND

The programme which will be described in this chapter is a multi-sensory structured phonics programme for children with dyslexic-type difficulties. Recognising the limitations of other similar multi-sensory programmes, this programme, developed by the author, attempts to overcome these through acknowledging the individual needs of children and in particular, the difficulties with auditory discrimination, sequencing and blending displayed by children with dyslexic-type difficulties.

The PASS programme, was developed to tackle the problem of Specific Learning Difficulties in reading and spelling in a practical and viable way within the mainstream school setting. It is designed to be used in a whole-class or group situation and, if used in the early stages, can prevent the specific learning difficulty from becoming severe. Although the programme focuses on the whole-class or small group situation, it can still be tailored to the individual needs of each child. Older dyslexic children and adults can also benefit from the programme.

PROGRAMME

The programme deals only with single syllable phonic words. Reading and spelling skills are taught together through phonics. PASS cards (single letter, blend and digraph cards) are used to make words. The programme is presented in a cumulative, structured, phonic order, with accompanying word lists at each level. The presentation of the structure highlights auditory discrimination skills.

- **Phonic Structure – main programme**

Level A	consonant/vowel/consonant words
Level B	use of k and c
Level C	initial blends
Level D	end blends

Level E	-ck, -ll, -ff, -ss, -zz
Level F	sh, ch, th, qu, wh
Level G	'magic' -e
Level H	w/wh, f/th/v, ng/nk (auditory discrimination)
Level I	oo, ee, ea, ea, ai, ay, oa, ou, aw, au, oi, oy, ow, ow and vowel digraphs with letter -k.

A supplementary programme deals solely with auditory confusions and is used as additional material where a child or group of children have particular difficulty. It deals with:

1 medial vowels
2 endings -t, -d, -k, -p, -b and n/m
3 s blends
4 r/l blends
5 j/d, ch/sh, ch/j, j/dr, ch/tr
6 -ar, -or, -er, -ir, -ur
7 'magic' - e with -re and -ke

• **PASS Cards**

PASS cards have rounded top corners to facilitate easy arrangement for use. They are colour-coded to help establish vowel/consonant awareness and the development of figure ground discrimination for blends and digraphs. PASS cards are used in a multi-sensory way. The learner, therefore, is trained to listen to the speaker and vocalise each sound as he sequentially places the letter cards from left to right. This means that the learner is simultaneously **hearing** the sound and **seeing** the letter card as he **places** it in sequence. This procedure helps to integrate auditory and visual skills and develops automatic sequencing skills.

Examples of words at different PASS levels

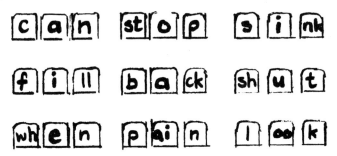

Magic – e cards

Single consonants are colour coded in black, vowels and vowel diagraphs in green, initial blends in red, end blends in purple, and double letters and consonant diagraphs in blue.

The cards can also be used by the teacher to form words for the learner to decode.

In written spelling, the learner must be trained to use a similar multi-sensory technique. He must simultaneously sound aloud each letter or digraph as he writes it, thus assisting in the integration of auditory, visual and kinaesthetic channels.

- **Implementation**

  The programme can be implemented by the class teacher or the school learning support teacher, for an individual child, or a group of children, with specific learning difficulties. It can also be used to advantage in the whole class situation. No specialised knowledge is required to utilise and implement the programme.

  In the whole-class situation, the programme can be used as an effective intervention programme, at Primary 3 or 4 stage. The class is taught, or reminded of, a simple phonic skill or rule, for example, letter 'x' makes the sound (ks), or double -ll, -ss, ff, -zz comes after a short vowel in a one syllable word. The skills are presented in a cumulative structured order. The class is given a simple spelling test to diagnose difficulty in a particular skill. Those who have difficulty in the particular skill, become a selected group to work on the PASS cards. When the selected group has mastered this skill, the class is taught and tested in the next skill in the structure, and a new group with difficulties in this skill selected to work on PASS cards at this level. Selected groups will be different for each PASS level, although there may be a core group of children who require every level. Children with no dyslexic-type difficulties will not be selected by testing procedures and, therefore, will not receive input.

- **Whole Class**

  If the programme is used in the whole-class situation, it gives all children in the class the same known cumulative framework of phonic knowledge, which the teacher can use as a basis for spelling correction in free writing. This is an important aspect of the programme. An error can be pointed out to the child, and he can use his own learned phonic structure to correct the error.

  In the whole-class situation, the programme is not exclusive, and can be used to complement any phonic programme in place in the school. It is also suitable for children familiar with Letterland characters.

  In the classroom situation, the PASS programme can easily become part of the language programme. To fit in with class organisation, PASS cards can be conveniently used with selected groups of children sitting round a table after group activities in reading.

- **Evaluation of the Programme**

  Although in most cases the PASS programme has been used in conjunction with other programmes, the instances where it has been used as the principal means of dealing with the dyslexic difficulty have been well evaluated. Below is an example of one such evaluation following the use of the PASS programme in a whole-class situation.

- **Whole-class Situation**

  A Primary 3 class, in which about one third of the children displayed dyslexic-type difficulties, was chosen for PASS Programme intervention.

Two of these children had been assessed by the School Psychologist as having severe specific learning difficulties, requiring individual specialist input. I worked with the class teacher, on a co-operative teaching basis, for 15 blocks of one and a half hours, from September 1992 to March 1993. The class teacher taught the appropriate teaching point and administered the relative spelling test before each PASS level. On my visits, I implemented the programme with the groups of children, selected at each level, as having difficulty. Only five children required no input.

The Burt Word Reading Test was used for reading assessment. For calculation purposes, it was assumed that below a reading accuracy of 6 years 4 months, an improvement of two words was equivalent to one month. In the class of twenty four children, tested in reading, before and after the implementation of the PASS Programme, the average increase in reading accuracy was 10.5 months in six months. On analysing the results, it was found that the nine children (Group 1), who had marked specific difficulties, that is those who required six or more PASS sessions, had an average increase of 9.6 months: the ten children (Group 2), who had minor difficulties, that is those who required one to three PASS sessions, had an average increase of 15.2 months; and the five children (Group 3) who had no difficulties and no PASS sessions had an average increase of 7.4 months.

Fig. 1

	No. of PASS Sessions	Range of RAs (Sept)	Average Increase in RA (Sept-March)
Group 1	6-13	-6y4m to 6y8m (and 1 RA 7y2m)	9.6 months
Group 2	1-3	6y5m to 8y5m	15.2 months
Group 3	none	6y9m to 9y10m	7.4 months

The PASS Programme in the whole class situation achieved its objective by significantly improving the reading attainments of those children with mild to severe specific learning difficulties (Group 1). It also effected an increase in reading accuracy of better readers, whose very minor problems would normally go undetected (Group 2). This significant increase in RA in Group 2 was not anticipated, and the hypothesis that very minor difficulties, such as occasional difficulty with medial vowels or r/l in blends, can significantly impede reading accuracy merits further investigation. The children who required no input (Group 3) made the progress in reading accuracy at the rate which would be anticipated.

Continuous assessment was used to monitor spelling. Most children in Group 1 made significant progress and the improvement in spelling in other groups was in line with that expected for the age group.

2 2 i 9 2 0
2 b o 2 o m P l u
          D i P   f a g
s i m   d a t
2 e m f a t   9 o s
d r i   e l a
i a h   m i l 2 o t
2 i r   m i 2 m m
s i r f a e

Child X has been assessed by the school psychologist as having severe specific learning difficulties. Above is his PASS test in words with initial blends (Nov. '92) and on the right his attempt at the same words in final assessment (March '93).

spot   trip
stem   pot
brim   flot
brip   glas
pram   twin
slot   k lap
swim   plug
~~----~~
grac   frog
stbr
f loq   cliff

CONCLUSION

From present evaluation, the PASS Programme presents itself as an effective multi-sensory structured phonics programme which can be used to prevent or remediate specific learning difficulties in the individual, group or whole-class situation.

As a multi-sensory programme, it differs from some other commercial programmes, in that the multi-sensory input is implemented only where and when the child requires such input.

As a whole-class intervention programme, it differs from other programmes in which initial screening is carried out and a remediation programme developed and implemented for each child. In the PASS Programme **continuous** screening (spelling assessments) for a structured set of difficulties is an integral part of the programme, and children are selected for intervention in a group situation for particular difficulties, rather than an intervention programme being developed for each child. The programme is, therefore, a much more time-effective and cost-effective exercise.

UNDERSTANDING SPELLING

ALISON DUNCAN

INTRODUCTION

Considerable interest has been shown over the last 15-20 years in the psychology of spelling. Psychologists from a variety of differing backgrounds have been addressing questions such as: What kind of a skill is spelling? Is it a process? How is it acquired? What is its relationship with reading? How is it used? Why do some people lose it and some never seem to acquire it? Evidence has been accumulating from experimental cognitive psychology, from linguistics and psycholinguistics, from neuropsychiatry, from educational and from developmental psychology which contributes to our understanding on the above and other questions regarding spelling.

It is perhaps something of a paradox that while psychologists have been turning their attention to spelling, the teaching profession have largely ignored it (with some very notable exceptions). It is not clear whether the diffidence about teaching spelling has been because teachers do not regard it as important or because they see it as something which will 'sort itself out later' or even because they are unsure of the best way to go about it. However, curricular developments both north and south of the border are likely to put the teaching of spelling back on the agenda for our schools.

The first part of this chapter examines several important questions in the psychology of spelling, concentrating entirely on English orthography which is famous for its complexity and thus has provided an ideal testing ground for cognitive and psycholinguistic theories of spelling.

THE NATURE OF ENGLISH SPELLING

'. . . *to name or set down from memory, in the correct order, the letters of a word.*'

The above has been accepted as a working definition of spelling yet it gives no indication of how the letters of the word were acquired, how they were stored in memory or how they became available for use. The process of spelling involves the recall and reproduction of the one acceptable form for each word and the visual recognition that what one has set down is, in fact, the correct form.

In order to understand this process of mature spelling in English, it is necessary to spend some time exploring how the English writing system works.

Writing is a way of expressing speech in graphic form. It is important to distinguish here between pictograms which express objects or concepts visually (e.g. traffic signs) and true writing which represents units of spoken language.

Early writing systems like Chinese employed one symbol for each word of the language. This probably developed from the earlier picture writing with pictograms becoming more stylised and abstract and gradually coming to be accepted as symbols for words or 'logograms'. Modern Chinese writing is still logographic as is one of the Japanese systems (Kanji). These systems are rather uneconomical since they contain many thousands of symbols which take several years to learn. The acquisition of literacy for Chinese children is then a long slow process which makes considerable memory demands.

A further step was taken by the Phoenicians who converted the Egyptian logographic system of hieroglyphics into a syllabic system. This system works by breaking words into component syllables and employing a separate symbol for each syllable.

The syllabic system was completed around 1500 BC. The Japanese also have a syllabic script (Kana) which is made up of 36 symbols each representing a single syllable. This seems to work well for a language which contains a small number of syllables, but for a language like English, with a large number of syllables, it would be very uneconomic.

It was not until approximately 1000 BC, relatively late in the history of writing, that the Greeks invented the alphabet – a system which employs a different letter or group of letters for every sound in the spoken language. Many writing systems in use today, including our own, use this principle and all modern alphabets are descendants of the Greek version (many via the Roman alphabet).

To spell using an alphabetic system, then, children would have to:

- Be aware that it is possible to segment words into constituent phonemes (e.g. to break up the word cat into 3 phonemes c a t).
- Know that the same phonemes can exist in different words (e.g. that

the only difference between 'cat' and 'mat' are the single sounds 'c' and 'm').

- Be aware of the written symbols (graphemes) which represent each sound of the language.

The alphabetic system of writing would seem an economic system, although one which relies heavily on phonological awareness in writers. In what we might call 'regular' or 'transparent' alphabetic systems, the spelling of a word would convey the words pronunciation and vice versa. Some modern alphabets, like Finnish, Italian and Latvian come very close to this, but most have their irregularities. English is particularly difficult for the writer in that it contains many words which do not readily reveal their written form through their sound, e.g. 'women', 'yacht', 'debt', 'island', 'knight', and many others.

It is interesting that English did not previously contain so many irregularities but that the combined influence of professional scribes, of early Dutch printers and of spelling reformers (whose etymologies were not always accurate), have produced a standardised orthography with more than its fair share of these potential pitfalls for writers. Add to this the fact that, unlike the Dutch and the Germans, we have never reformed our spelling to keep pace with changing pronunciation and we are left with a system which seems to display a tension between the alphabetic demands for transparency and the wish to retain an element of the older logographic principle! The situation, however, is even more complex than that generalisation suggests.

Levels of Representation

English orthography tries in various ways to represent in print differing levels of the spoken language.

i)   **Word Level**
     The placing of spaces between words in print and writing is the most basic way of making writing sensitive to the structure of spoken language at the word level (although some may argue that print has had the reciprocal effect on readers of making them more aware of distinctions between the words in their language).

     Another word level influence is the way in which English orthography can distinguish between homophones e. g.:

bean and been	fair and fare
hear and here	hair and hare
loot and lute	read and reed

It is possible for both alternatives for the above words to be regular if there is more than one regular way of spelling a phoneme. English, however, goes further in supplying:

'two', 'hymn', 'damn',

to distinguish from

'too', 'him', 'dam'.

These alternatives are not rule-governed and would require to be learned as logographs.

Another word level influence (Chomsky and Halle, 1968), is seen in the retention of the silent 'g' in sign and 'b' in bomb which supply clues to the reader that these words are, in fact related to 'signature' and 'bombard' in which the 'g' and 'b' are pronounced.

ii)   Morphemic Level

Words can be divided into smaller units of meaning called morphemes. For example, a word like 'harm' is one morpheme but 'harmful' contains two as do 'harming' and 'harmed' -ing and -ed are known as bound morphemes in that they cannot occur on their own and 'harm' would be the root morpheme.

The plural words 'ropes' 'robes' and 'roses' all have the plural morpheme -'s' in their written form but the careful listener will hear three distinct sounds in their spoken form r o p e s, r o b e z, and r o s i z.

Another example of spelling preserving morphemic identity at the expense of alphabetic transparency is the spelling of past tense verbs,

e.g. 'Flapped', 'soared', 'glided',

would be pronounced as if spelt

'Flapt', 'soard', 'glidid'

but the presence of '-ed' in the spelling of each word points to its grammatical function.

iii)   Phoneme Level

Even at the phonemic level there are, in English, several irregularities and inconsistencies. Some vowels can be spelt in more than one regular way (meat, street, complete) and sometimes two different pronunciations can be used for the same letter strings (mint and pint).

An understanding of English spelling then requires not only phono-logical awareness coupled with a firm grasp of the grapheme-phoneme correspondences, but also a lexicon of ideographs (the highly irregular 'one-offs' like 'island') plus an awareness of the structure of the language at the word and at the morphemic and phonemic levels. The skilled speller also has acquired knowledge of many of the spelling rules which dictate what letter strings may follow which and can estimate the probability that a certain choice among the many possibilities will prove to be the correct one. The study of spelling will in itself contribute to the development of the child's understanding of the language at each of the above three levels.

COGNITIVE MODELS OF SPELLING

An adequate cognitive theory of spelling would have to be capable of explaining four things.

First, how is spelling knowledge acquired? Secondly, how is it stored? Thirdly, how is the knowledge accessed when the writer needs it? And fourthly, how is the knowledge translated into hand, wrist, finger and arm muscle movements?

Much of the work done on spelling by psychologists has concentrated on how we are able to produce the correct letter string for a particular word and on what sorts of errors the normally competent speller makes when she/he is incorrect.

Phonic Mediation
One popular model proposed by neuropsychologists suggests that spelling is dependent upon speaking – that is, the writer starts with the meaning and then accesses the phonemic form of the word she/he wants. Using his/her knowledge of phoneme-grapheme correspondences, she/he creates a spelling for the target word. Models like this, which rely upon speech, are known as phonic mediation models. They have, however, a number of drawbacks, especially with regard to English spelling.

Homophones create problems for such phonic mediation theories. How is the writer to choose the correct spelling for 'won' for example, or 'reign' or 'there' using phonic information alone? The spelling of these and many other English homophones is determined by the meaning. This would suggest the existence of a more direct semantic –> graphemic information route.

Another argument against the importance of sound comes from neuropsychological evidence. Shallice (1981) cites the example of a particular brain-injured patient who could spell correctly over 90% of dictated real words but who could not produce plausible spellings for phonically regular non-words. This was in spite of the fact that he could hear, repeat and read the same non-words. This patient could not assemble spellings from sound, yet he could spell the majority of words whose spellings he had learned before his stroke.

Although the many studies which have used the spelling of non-words in their design (see Frith, 1980) have demonstrated that phonic mediation is always an option for the writer, it seems clear that a quicker, more efficient route must exist for skilled performance.

Addressed Spellings

An alternative to phonically assembled spellings would seem to imply some kind of internal lexicon or long-term store of learned spellings. When we are writing, we start out with the meaning of a word we want. This meaning is stored in some form of semantic code which activates the appropriate graphemic production unit. Ellis (1984) has suggested a graphemic buffer zone which is capable of holding a word's spelling between retrieval and execution, and is also capable of holding the latter part of a word while the earlier portion is being written. Writing is a comparatively slow process and the incorporation of a buffer zone would appear necessary.

The internal lexicon is conceptualised as consisting of abstract work units having several different facets or identities. Every word in the lexicon has a phonological representation which consists of information about acoustic, articulatory and phonemic properties of the word; a syntactic identity specifying characteristic grammatical functions of the word in sentences and a semantic identity – a kind of dictionary definition. All of this is considered to be acquired and known implicitly as a consequence of learning to speak.

In the course of learning to read and write, an orthographic identity is added to the above for each word. This information is not thought of as purely ideographic i.e. memorised rotely as a word shape, but rather it is memorised as a sequence of letters.

Linnea Ehri (1980) has put forward a word identity amalgamation theory to explain how the orthographic information about each word is incorporated into lexical memory. Assuming that beginning readers already know how words are pronounced their task is to assimilate the printed form to the phonological structure they already have in memory. Ehri suggests that they do this by matching at least some of the letters to phonetic or phonemic segments they can detect in the word. These segments serve as slots in lexical memory and are then filled by images of letters seen in the word's spelling. To process and remember the letter-sound correspondences effectively, readers must already be familiar with those letters as symbols for the relevant phonological segments. If at least some of the letter-sound relationships are known and recognised, then there will be enough 'glue' to secure the visual symbol in lexical memory.

The kind of information useful for setting up orthographic memories includes not only information about single letter – sound relationships but also information about more complex functional spelling patterns (Venezky, 1970) about syllabic print – sound structure and about common spelling patterns shared by sets of rhyming words (e.g. air, hair, stair, pair, chair, fair etc.).

As the person's repertoire of printed words grows, he becomes aware of new patterns for mapping speech into writing and his knowledge of orthography as a system for mapping words grows. It is likely that reading and writing contribute to this orthographic knowledge although some of it may develop as a consequence of the explicit teaching of phonics.

When printed words are stored in lexical memory, the orthographic forms are amalgamated with phonological, with syntactic and with semantic identities. Amalgamation occurs as readers practise pronouncing and interpreting unfamiliar printed words while they are reading text for meaning. Once identity amalgamation has taken place for particular words, these words are processed in a different way. They begin to be recognised and produced as whole units (addressed spellings) rather than as letter sequences.

This theory is attractive for a number of reasons. The idea of a multi-faceted word representation which contains the information needed to speak, to understand, to read and to write a word would make a direct semantic-graphemic route to word spelling easy. This linking of orthographic information directly with meaning explains how we can choose the correct spelling for homophones. At the same time, the model does not ignore the importance of the phonological route to reading and spelling, especially for the younger reader and writer.

Bryant and Bradley (1980, 1985) have shown the importance of phonological awareness for children learning to read and write. In particular they have found strong associations between children's ability to segment words phonologically and put them into categories which share a common sound (e.g. cat, rat, hat, bat) and their subsequent reading and spelling ability. By making phonemic segments of words serve as the slots to be filled at the initial acquisition time, Ehri takes account of the importance of phonology for children at this stage. The theory then has a developmental potential which I shall return to later.

One important aspect not yet considered in spelling production is how the knowledge becomes transmitted to the hand/arm. D. Simon (1976) proposes a model compatible with Ehri's in that the internal word store contains a motor memory along with the phonemic, graphemic, syntactic and semantic. This motor memory would presumably become amalgamated with the other facets of the word through repeated experience of writing the word by hand. Cunningham and Stanovich (1990) demonstrate the superiority of handwriting (over both manipulation of letter tiles and typing onto a computer) in establishing early spelling memory. They trained 24 first graders in all three methods having the children pronounce the name of each letter as they set it down and then name the word when they had reproduced it. The handwriting condition proved superior even when the method of post-testing used the computer and the tiles.

Ellis (1982) suggests a progression from the retrieval of a graphemic code from memory to the selection of letter shapes. One factor to be taken into consideration here is whether one is writing in lower or upper case letters. Next one must decide on size of letters and then put together the motor patterns of strokes and directions. Finally comes the execution of these patterns.

Ehri's model refers to the orthographic memory for a particular word being acquired as a visual memory but there are good reasons for supposing that the skilled writer does not rely upon a visual image of each word she/he wishes to write.

To begin with, any normal person who knows how to spell a word can do so in a variety of ways. She/he can write the word in upper or lower case letters using pen and paper or using a blackboard and chalk. The first requires finer wrist and hand movements, the second large, whole arm movements. She/he can spell the word aloud, can type it onto a computer and can produce the word by the manipulation of letter tiles, or even inscribe it in sand by means of the toe or emblazon it on a wall with spray paint! The speller can also recognise the word when it is produced in all of these different ways.

Seymour and Elder (1982) showed that even quite young children are capable of recognising and reading single words which have been arranged in unusual patterns e.g.

The fact that so many different visual images of the same word can be generated and recognised would suggest that a literate person's internal lexicon operates on highly abstract codes. This is not to suggest that visual imagery is never used in generating a word's spelling but rather that most literate people have a quicker, more efficient route. A visual route may be favoured by some and may also be extremely useful in checking a spelling one is unsure of by writing it and scrutinising what one has written.

I would suggest some sort of developmental progression is probable with younger children relying on fairly concrete visual images during the word identity amalgamation period. This will gradually move towards an abstract code as the spelling of certain words are amalgamated in lexical memory with the words' other identities. Once the child has reached the stage of over learning certain words, we can assume amalgamation to have taken place and these words will now be represented in lexical memory by an abstract code capable of generating any of the possible forms the word can take (i.e. printed or cursive script; upper or lower case; typed or written; small or large; on paper or a larger surface and done with the hand, foot or whole arm).

THE RELATIONSHIP BETWEEN SPELLING AND READING

Most information processing models treat reading and spelling as two separate processes (Morton, 1980) – an input and an output process which are quite independent of each other. If this is the case, then learning to read will not automatically, at the same time, lead to learning to spell. There is evidence from young children first acquiring literacy, from skilled performance and from case studies of adult stroke victims to support the separation of the processes.

Bryant and Bradley (1980) observed that young children would often read words which they could not spell and would spell words which they could not read. This was explained by the fact that they preferred to read whole words but wrote by segmenting the target word into phonemes and setting the word down letter by letter. Charles Read (1971) also found that young precocious spellers who wrote before they had been formally introduced to the orthographic system often could not read what they themselves had written.

Fluent readers rarely look closely at words. They use context, syntax and grammar together with their knowledge of the world which they bring to the text. A cursory glance at each word to check whether it fits with the above is usually enough to provide meaning.

Spelling, on the other hand is very different. The writer has a blank piece of paper and has to set down upon it the one acceptable spelling for each word. There are no clues to be gleaned from context and guessing is quite likely to result in a mistake. Children who read efficiently for meaning, but do not look closely at words, are not likely to develop an accurate orthographic memory for words.

Simultaneous Writing and Reading

Spelke, Hirst and Neisser (1976) replicating an older Solomons and Stein Study (1896) have shown that it is possible to read silently with understanding and, at the same time, write words to dictation without loss of efficiency to either task. This would add further support to the idea that reading and writing do not compete for the same physical or mental processes.

However, looking at the evidence from brain-injured patients it has to be said at these injuries to the brain which impair reading tend also to impair writing. One well-documented case study (R. G.) lost his ability to read phonologically after undergoing brain surgery but could still read virtually any familiar word. In marked contrast, R. G. could readily spell phonologically both words and non-words. In this case we see a clear direct word –> meaning route co-existing with intact phonic spelling but impaired phonic reading in one and the same person.

The long-established syndrome known as letter-by-letter reading in which brain-injured patients have lost their ability to recognise words as wholes but rather name each letter in turn as they work through a word has been noted as going along with relatively intact writing (Patterson and Kay, 1983). It has been suggested that these patients, having lost their direct route, are reading via their spelling system.

We are however, still a long way from a full understanding of how the processes of reading and writing interact.

A DEVELOPMENTAL PERSPECTIVE

There would seem to be a body of evidence to suggest that there is a qualitative difference between the strategies used by young children just learning to spell and those used by older children and proficient spellers. Although spelling strategy used will be influenced by the teaching methods a child experiences, there is still enough evidence of differences to justify a developmental perspective on spelling.

The Pre-Literate Child

Before children have been formally introduced to the skills of literacy they do have some conceptions of the nature and purposes of writing. Some young children can even interpret writing in a consistent way, although a way which is entirely different from how literate people interpret writing. We cannot really get a developmental perspective on spelling without some understanding of children's early conceptions of writing.

Lavine (1977) detected a progressive ability to differentiate writing from other marks and symbols amongst pre-school children. By age three, all of her sample of 45 pre-schools could differentiate writing from pictures. Around four years, they began to distinguish writing from writing-like scribbles and by five, some were able to tell the difference between numbers and letters. Of displays of Roman letters, 96% were classified as writing by the five year olds .

Lavine's sample children looked for three characteristics of writing. First the symbols must be arranged in lines. Secondly, a minimum number of symbols must be employed and thirdly a variety of symbols should be used.

Emilia Ferreiro is a developmental psychologist who has worked in Argentina, in Geneva with Piaget and in Mexico City. She has therefore had the opportunity to compare the children of illiterate slum dwellers with those whose homes treat literacy as a valuable and necessary part of everyday life. Her empirical studies (1978, 1982) have supported Lavine's three general points about linearity, multiplicity and variety.

Ferreiro followed a group of 30 children, aged between three and six years for a period of two years, looking in particular at their spontaneous writing. Her evidence suggests something like the following developmental sequence.

i)   The youngest children believe only nouns are capable of being written down. They seem to think that the written word is a representation of the object itself and should reflect some of the qualities and attributes of the object. They are surprised, therefore, that the word 'cat' is shorter than the word 'kitten'.

ii)   Children begin to realise that utterances can be written down but seem to ascribe whole propositions to one symbol, e.g. 'I ate a sweet' is read for 'The girl' in the sentence 'The girl ate a sweet'.

iii)   Nouns in both subject and object position are written down separately, but no separate symbol is needed for the verb.

iv)   All words except the article are capable of having a separate written symbol.

v)   Everything that is said can be written.

Ferreiro asserts that a child discovers syllabic writing when she/he discovers that even a singular referent has more than one letter in its representation. Before their realisation that spoken utterances are written using an alphabetic system, children explore other hypotheses, some of which reflect the historical development of systems of writing.

Early Alphabetic Spelling

At this stage children make their first approximation towards an alphabetic orthography using letter/sound correspondence. In order to do this, they must be able to segment the flow of speech (normally perceived as continuous) to phonemic units. This can prove difficult for some young children and, indeed there is evidence that many children do not begin to develop this ability until they are introduced to to spelling-sound correspondences in school.

Some pre-school children, however, have begun to segment speech into units and make very clever and inventive attempts to represent these units in writing in their own way. Children (like Paul Bisset) who have been introduced to letter names and upper case letters will use these in their attempts to communicate sound on paper – Paul's message 'RUDF' (Are you deaf?) when he could not get his mother's attention is a good example of how this early phonetic writing uses consonants and letter names.

Charles Read's (1970) young creative spellers also used letter names in their early spelling before they had been formally introduced to the alphabetic system, e.g.

UNITDSATS   for United States
LADE   for lady
TIM   for time
U   for you.

The Phonological Speller

At this stage, children are beginning to apply knowledge of the surface phonology of words in their spelling. They have become aware of grapheme-phoneme correspondences and can recognise and make use of the fact that common sounds in different words can be represented by the same letter (e.g. top and tap both begin with 't' and end with 'p').

Evidence for this stage comes from Bradley and Bryant (1985) who noted that younger children, those aged below seven, could often spell words which they could not read. In their study (reported in Frith, 1980) they found that words spelled correctly, but not read were phonetically regular. (The words were 'bun' 'leg', 'mat' and 'pat'.) They suggest that for many young children writing a word is predominantly a matter of alphabetic letters and phonological segments. They make exclusive use of the phonological code.

More evidence for a phonological stage comes from Yuko Kimura who worked with Japanese and English children. The children were given the task of writing down the names of objects in 10 pictures (a spelling task) but also had a concurrent vocalisation task to do at the same time. They had to chant "bla, bla" whilst they were writing. It was found that the task of spelling was considerably harder for the English children than for the Japanese children who were using the Kanji or logographic script. It seems then that English children found their spelling task difficult because the concurrent vocalisation interfered with the phonological strategy they used for spelling.

The idea of a phonological stage is consistent with the experience of many infant teachers who can confirm that a large corpus of spelling errors made by young writers is with phonetically irregular words, e.g. 'coff' for cough 'laff' for laugh 'luv' for 'love' etc.

A Transition Stage

Children begin to move from a reliance on representing the phonemes they detect in words to a recognition and reproduction of common graphemic patterns. Much evidence for the transition stage comes from analysis of children's spelling errors. For example, Beers, Beers and Grant, (1977) found that middle primary children used spellings like 'gait' for 'gate' because they had learnt to represent long vowels with digraphs. It is, however, quite difficult to tell from looking at a child's spelling errors exactly what strategy the child used to generate the particular error.

In the transitional stage that the earlier non-standard phonetic spellings still persist, but alongside new standard spellings. It is interesting to note the child at this stage often seems to know what letters are used in the standard spellings of common words but has not yet mastered the correct sequence, e.g.

ashoer	for ashore
huose	for house
freind	for friend
frist	for first
siad	for said

(Williams, 1974)

The children who made the above errors are showing the influence of standard graphemic patterns although their spelling is far from standard.

Marino (1978) suggested that influences on standard spelling which work at the phonemic, graphemic and morphemic levels represent increasing developmental complexity and are therefore increasingly difficult for children. It would seem reasonable to suppose for example, that an understanding of the relationship between the words 'suggest' and 'suggestion' and of how that relationship is retained in the spelling of 'suggestion' demands a more sophisticated meta-linguistic awareness than does a grasp of letter-sound correspondences. However, there is evidence that children in the early alphabetic or pre-phonetic stage do use morphemic knowledge in their spontaneous spelling. Read (1986) reports that his young creative spellers very quickly moved to using one form for the '-ed' morpheme in the past tense of verbs, regardless of the distinction in pronunciation between, for example:-

'helped'   'hated'   'killed'.

A similar pattern was discernible with the plural '-s' morpheme, with young children quickly learning to apply their morphemic knowledge to spelling and to use '-s' to represent both [s] and [z] sounds.

Marino expected that, from her sample of 180 children in second, third and fourth grade, fewest errors would be phonetic in nature (i.e. would show inaccurate phonology or phoneme –> graphemic knowledge) and most would be morpho-phonemic. She further expected that phonemic errors would begin to decrease at an earlier age, followed by graphemic, then morphemic. The graphemic errors were the only ones which did not fit her prediction, being significantly less frequent than morphemic errors at all stages, but more frequent than phonetic errors only at grades 3 and 4. This may reflect the way in which the graphemic level was defined, the definition including 'varying degrees of abstractness' (pg. 83). A re-analysis of the corpus of errors categorised by Williams (1974) also reveals graphemic errors occurring from six years to eleven years.

Research into spelling might benefit from a clearer definition of the idea of a graphemic error. The graphemic level does not seem to correspond to a linguistic level at all, in the way that the phonemic and morphemic levels do. Any of the spelling rules in English are only graphemic conventions and children may go about learning these in a less predictable fashion than they do to represent the phonological and morphological aspects of their language.

Marsh *et al.* (1980) studied the development of strategies in spelling and their findings lend support to the idea that the transitional period can be fairly lengthy – up to five or six years. Comparing seven year olds, ten year olds and college students they found an overall developmental increase of various strategies. The ten year olds spelled more of the regular CVC words and non-words correct than did the seven year olds, but there was no corresponding increase for the college students. There seems then to be a ceiling for the straightforward phonological strategy of the earlier stage. The second strategy studied (using a final '-e' marker to denote a long vowel) showed the same pattern with ten year olds significantly better than seven year olds but the same as college students. The third strategy was the use of analogy. No seven year olds used this strategy while one third of the ten year olds and one half of the college students did. The ability to spell by analogy would appear to be a later development.

Standard Spelling
In this stage, correct spelling for most frequently used words has become automatic. Using Ehri's model, the orthographic identity of known words has amalgamated with the semantic, syntactic, phonemic and motor identity. One characteristic of the final stage speller is that she/he can use reading of his/her own writing to check on whether words look right. Slips of the pen can, of course, be made by a proficient speller but they rarely go undetected. Spellers in this stage know when they do not know how to spell a word and will therefore be able to go to a reference book to procure a spelling.

IMPLICATIONS FOR TEACHING

If there is a developmental progression in children's spelling, what are the pedagogical implications? Children may arrive in school and begin formal training in literacy at any point in the pre-literacy sequence (see p.201). It is important that teachers of infants are aware of the conceptions which children have about print and writing and of the hypotheses they hold about what can be written and what can be read. Many parents and teachers are unaware of the existence of non-alphabetic writing systems!

Other children, like Read's creative spellers, are already attempting to analyse speech into its constituent parts and working out ways of representing it on paper, using their meagre knowledge of the alphabet and letter names.

Both these groups of children need encouragement to develop their writing, including their spelling, and this will mean that the infant teacher will have to tolerate non-standard spellings. An understanding of spelling processes will help the teacher to do this. Taking a developmental perspective on spelling enables the teacher to look with interest at a child's non-standard spellings for the information they contain about the child's orthographic development. It also enables the teacher to set up spelling goals which are realistic and attainable. Whatever stage the child is at, she/he should be encouraged to enjoy and take an interest in words. There are many games available for children to play with words and a supply of plastic letters would be a useful addition to the infant classroom.

Teaching methods

Margaret Peters' (1967) idea of spelling being 'caught' by children through their exposure to print has been very influential in educational circles. There are some lucky children, high on verbal intelligence scores, good at visual analysis of words with careful but fast handwriting, who do seem to develop standard spelling quickly and with the minimum of teaching. However, many Children need more help. Do cognitive models of spelling have anything to offer the teacher?

The visual approach

Peters (and many others) stress that spelling is basically a visual-motor activity and have therefore developed the LOOK, COVER, WRITE, CHECK method. In this method, the child does not copy words, but writes from memory.

The Multi-Sensory Approach

This approach has been espoused by many different people, but usually for different reasons. Maria Montessori, Samuel Orton and Grace Fernald all recommended multi-sensory teaching. (For a description of the methodology, see Bryant and Bradley, 1985.)

Although many writers (Barr, 1985) are almost apologetic about the multi-sensory approach, calling it eclectic, amalgamation theory provides theoretical support for just such an approach. If lexical memory contains an amalgam of different codes (phonemic, semantic, syntactic, graphemic and motoric) for each known word, then making the different aspects of the word explicit when committing the spelling to memory should make the amalgamation process more efficient.

Lynette Bradley's (1985) version of the multi-sensory approach goes even further and adds simultaneous vocalisation to the process.

There are many more questions about teaching spelling than it has been possible to address here. Before concluding, however, I shall turn my attention to the important area of attitude.

ATTITUDES

Margaret Peters' picture of the good speller was one of a child who is interested in words, careful with them, who enjoys using writing in play and in learning other skills. But what of the child who does not seem to care whether spellings are correct or not? Often an uncaring attitude is covering a sense of failure, hopelessness or bemusement. If we assume an interest in writing to be fairly natural for children in a literate society, then the teacher's job is to foster and encourage this interest, enabling the child to progress. A sense of success is very important to the child's attitude to himself as a speller and the adults who read the child's writing must demonstrate that they value his/her attempts in order to promote the image of the child as a writer.

However, as they get older, children can often see for themselves how good their writing is. Spelling mistakes are a salient feature of children's written work and their visual presence is such that they can easily distract the teacher's or the examiner's attention from the content and style of the piece of writing. The complexity of English orthography has resulted in many children who spell inaccurately and many of them have developed low academic self-esteem.

The claim that problems with spelling and punctuation will largely disappear if content is valued above technical accuracy has not been tested and should therefore be treated with caution. If a way can be found for teachers and parents to help children develop accurate spelling, even with highly irregular words, they will produce much more interesting writing and will communicate with confidence and a sense of personal involvement and achievement.

Moseley (1987) found that poor spellers used significantly more regularly spelt words, used shorter words, relied upon a 'core vocabulary' of high frequency words and developed strategies of repeating the same words to minimise errors.

These children had developed negative views of themselves as spellers and writers and appeared unenthusiastic and uncaring about spelling.

Attitude to spelling, especially for children in the transition stage, who should be experiencing more control and prediction in their orthographic knowledge, would seem to be very important.

REFERENCES

Arvidson, G. (1963). *Learning to Spell*. Wheaton.

Barr, J. (1985). *Understanding Children's Spelling*. Edinburgh. SCRE.

Barr, J. E. and Lambourne, R. D. (1984). Analysing Spelling Performance on a range of purposeful writing tasks. *Educational Psychology*, Vol. 4. No. 4, 297-311.

Beers, C. S. (1980). The relationship of cognitive development to spelling and reading abilities in Henderson, E. H. and Beers, C. S. (Eds.) *Developmental and Cognitive Aspects of Learning to Spell*. Newart, Del.

Beers, J. W., Beers, C. S. and Grant, K. (1977). The logic behind children's spelling. *Elementary School Journal*, 3, 238-42.

Bishop, D. V. M. and Robson, J. (1989). Accurate non-word spelling despite congenital inability to speak: Phoneme-grapheme conversion does not require sub-vocal articulation. *British Journal of Psychology*, 80, 1-13.

Bryant, P. and Bradley, L. (1985). *Children Reading Problems*. Oxford. Basil Blackwell.

Cunningham, A., Stanovich, K. E. (1990). Early Spelling Acquisition: Writing, Beats the Computer. *Journal of Educational Psychology*. Vol. 82, No. 1, 159-162.

Ehri, Linnea (1980). The Development of orthographic images in Frith, U. (Ed.) *Cognitive Processes in Spelling*. London, Academic.

Ellis, A. W. (1982). Spelling and Writing (and reading and speaking) in Ellis, A. W. (Ed.) *Normality and Pathology in Cognitive Functions*. London: Academic Press.

Ellis, A. W. (1984). *Reading, Writing and Dyslexia: A Cognitive Analysis*. London Erlbaum.

Ferreiro, E. (1978). What is written in a written sentence? A developmental answer. *Journal of Education*, 160, 4.

Ferreiro, E. (1980). The Relationship between Oral and Written Language: The Children's Viewpoint in Goodman, Y. M. (Ed.) *Oral and Written Language Development Research: Impact on Schools*, National Council of Teachers of English.

Frith, U. (1980). *Cognitive Processes in Spelling*. Academic Press. London.

Kimura, Y. and Bryant, P. E. (1983). Reading and writing in English and Japanese, *British Journal of Developmental Psychology*, 1, 129-44.

Lavine, L. O. (1977). Differentiation of letter-like forms in pre-reading children. *Developmental Psychology*, 13 (2) 89-94.

Maggs, A., McMillan, K. Patching, W., Hawke, H. (1981). Accelerating Spelling Skills using Morphographs. *Educational Psychology*, Vol. 1, No. 1, 49-56.

Marino, J. (1978). Children's use of phonetic, graphemic and morphophonemic cues in a spelling task (doctoral dissertation, Stale University of New York – Albany) Dissertation Abstracts International, 1979 39(10) 5997A (University Microfilms No. 79-07220).

Marsh, G., Friedman, M., Welch, V. and Desberg, P. (1980). The development of strategies in spelling in Frith, U. (Ed.) *Cognitive Processes in Spelling*.

Moseley, D. (1987). Words you want to learn. *British Journal of Special Education,* Vol. 14, No. 2, 59-62.

Patterson, K. and Kay, J. (1983). Letter-by-letter reading: Psychological descriptions of a neurological syndrome. *Quarterly Journal of Experimental Psychology.* 34A, 411-441.

Peters, M. (1967). *Spelling: Caught or Taught?* London, Routledge.

Peters, M. L. (1970). Success in Spelling, *Cambridge Monographs on Education.* No. 4, Cambridge Institute for Education.

Read, Charles (1970). Pre-school children's knowledge of English phonology. *Harvard Educational Review,* 41, 1-34.

Shallice, T. (1981). *Phonological agraphia and the lexical route in writing.* Brain, 1981, 104, 413-429.

Simon, D. P. (1976). Spelling – a task analysis *Instructional Science,* V 277-302.

Solomons, L. M. and Stein, G. (1896). Normal motor automatisms – *Psychological Review* 3, 492-512.

Spelke, E., Hirst, W. and Neisser, U. (176). Skills of divided attention. *Cognition* 4, 215-230.

Stephens, M. and Hudson, A. (1984). A comparison of the effects of direct instruction and remedial English classes on the spelling skills of secondary students. *Educational Psychology,* Vol. 4, No. 4, 261-267.

Venezky, R. L. (1970). *The Structure of English Orthography.* The Hauge, Mouton.

Williams, A. (1974). A Study of Spelling Errors in Wade, B. and Wedell, K. *Spelling: the task and the learner.* Educational Review Occasional publication. University of Birmingham.

STRATEGIES FOR TEACHING SPELLING

VERNA F. F. DEARNLEY

STRATEGIES FOR TEACHING SPELLING

This collection of guidelines, hints and mnemonics has been acquired through the years, to help children overcome their learning and spelling difficulties.

In setting up the programme, I have given a few working examples, but have omitted long lists of words.

When teaching a child with little or no reading skill, the short vowels 'a' and 'u' are taught as contiguous, the reason being that these two vowels are frequently confused, as are the short 'i' and 'e.' The difference can be emphasised by pointing out the movement of the jaw and lips, when sounding these vowels immediately one after the other; starting with the smile for the short 'i', through 'e-u-a' and dropping the jaw for the final, lip-rounded 'o.'

If a child has difficulty with word-building, I have found it useful to ask him to 'put' the first syllable (or single sound), into his/her left hand and hold it in the closed fist. When the fist is touched, the child repeats the sound held. The second syllable is 'put' in the right fist, and the sounds are produced when the fists are touched in succession, reducing the interval at each repetition, until the whole word is formed.

In teaching a student who is able to read fluently, but has difficulty with spelling, I reinforce those rules which need practise, after pointing out the need to 'protect' a single short, weak vowel from the interaction of another vowel, by the use of a double consonant (VCCV). This double barrier prevents the second vowel changing the sound of the first (VCV), hence the 'protected' vowel. e.g. bite, bitten; gripe, gripped.

TEACHING AIDS

The Edith Norrie Letter Case (1973) is extremely useful in the teaching of spelling and the kinesthetic feedback is invaluable. The letters in the case are printed on small tiles of cardboard, and are divided into labial sounds, sounds that are lingual, and the guttural, velar sounds. Aspirated sounds are black, while the voiced sounds are printed in green. Sounds which may be both voiced and aspirated (e.g. 'th,' 'wh') are printed with a central horizontal green band. The vowels are red, and thus it is possible to illustrate the need for a doubled consonant, to 'protect' a weak vowel, by separating the 'splashes of red'.

Words are built up by the pupil, mouthing the sounds if need be, to discover where in the mouth, the sounds are formed. A word is analysed by looking for the 'red splashes' and the number of spaces between them, and following them. The word may then be covered and typed out on the word-processor, stating the names of the letters as they are typed, as an audial reinforcement. This exercise, in time, may be expanded to the dictation of sentences which are built up, and must be lined up tidily (using a ruler), and punctuated (punctuation symbols are provided in the Letter Case). Again, the sentence may be typed out on the word-processor from memory, to enhance memory recall. Finally, the pupil must return the letters to the appropriate place in the Letter Case.

A further aid in the teaching of non-readers is the Words in Colour system, devised by Caleb Gattegno (1962). In this system each sound is given a colour and, though the shape of the sound may change, the colour remains constant, and the child refers back to a word he knows, to identify the sound by its colour.

Thus the sound of the long vowel 'a,' may be identified in the words p **ai** d, gr **ea** t, st**ay**, v **ei** n, w **eigh** t, str **aigh** t, duv **et**. The shape of the sound may also be identified on the Fidel charts, which are separate charts which list all the shapes of each sound, both vowels and consonants, in columns. The text readers are printed in black and white, the colours being limited to the demonstration charts.

Gattegno has also devised the game of 'Transformations', in which a word is transformed into a final selected word, making one move at a time. A letter may be added to the word, either at the beginning of the word or at the end; it may be inserted into the word, or one of the sounds may be changed. A sound or letter may not be subtracted to aid transformation, but a doubled letter may be reduced to a single letter, i.e. ll may be reduced to a single l.

	is--> glands:	is --> it--> sit --> sat --> sad--> sand--> land--> gland--> glands-->

(i)

	at--> spent:	at--> an--> and--> end--> send--> spend--> spent

The use of a word processor is also invaluable as a teaching aid. With many children it seems that the act of typing the words helps the pupil to 'see' the words more clearly, and the naming in sequence of the letters as they type, reinforces audial memory. Words which present difficulties with medial vowel or consonant placement may be highlighted and the appropriate letters enlarged and printed in bold type to draw attention to them. The word may then be scrolled until it is off screen and the child attempts to reproduce the correct spelling, comparing it with the scrolled back original. Any mistakes can be easily altered, and the final result is presented as a neat and pleasing text. The division of words into syllables can be demonstrated, as can the doubling of consonants when adding a vowel suffix. The bleep of the Spellchecker, draws attention to mis-spelled words, but the tutor should be alert to the misuse of the homophones, their and there, hear and here, and to, too and two, which the processor will accept as correct, as it will poor grammar.

TEACHING PROGRAMME

The phonetic pronunciation of the vowels or of digraphs, is indicated by the bracketed symbol placed immediately following the letters.

BASIC RULES PART ONE

When the non-reader has learned to build simple words and substitute different vowels in these, to change them into other words or nonsense sounds, and to recognise those which are proper English words, the spelling programme begins. The child must have at least a basic ability to read before he can spell.

The teaching programme deals firstly with the consonant-vowel-consonant words, CVC, and the need to protect a weak vowel in a single (Flossy – ff, ll, ss) syllable word, or by a doubled consonant in a two syllable word. The pupil is later introduced to open and closed syllables, in words such as Po-lish and pol-ish.

The 'silent e' words are depicted with the VCV symbol, to show the inter-action of the second vowel on the first; this is used again in words of greater complexity, where the pupil must decide whether the syllable is open or closed to warrant the proximity of the vowels. The Edith Norrie Letter Case is a valuable help in this situation.

The next levels deal with the spelling of words with (k), (j) and (s). Each of these sounds is depicted with a logo.

(k) =

$$k \begin{cases} a \\ i \\ o \\ e \end{cases}$$

(k) =

$$c \begin{cases} a \\ u \\ o \\ l \\ r \end{cases}$$

$$\therefore \quad c \begin{cases} i \\ e \\ y \end{cases} (s) \qquad \text{I cycle to the city centre}$$

(ii)

(j) =

$$j \begin{cases} a \\ i \\ o \\ e \\ u \end{cases}$$

(g) =

$$g \begin{cases} a \\ u \\ o \end{cases}$$

$$\therefore \quad g \begin{cases} i \\ e \\ y \end{cases} (j) \qquad \text{The gentle giant does gymnastics}$$

It is pointed out that initial 'c' is more common than 'k,' in the spelling of English words, mainly because the letter 'c' can be used to produce two sounds, hard and soft, but also because most words with initial 'k' are imported (kayak, kangaroo, Koran). The 'k' word pages are found in the dictionary and held between the finger and thumb of the right hand, the 'c' word pages are held between the finger and thumb of the left hand and the difference in the thickness of the two is noted. When it is pointed out that the initial 'kn' words (which are taught as a separate entity) make up a large portion of 'k' words, it is appreciated that 'c' is the more common initial spelling.

The 'j' and 'g' words are similarly examined. It must be noted that the rule (soft g + i,e,y) holds even as a medial spelling for *(j)* words, engine, energetic, injury, enjoy, with the exception of words derived from the Latin root ject, inject, object, subject, project. (The Latin endings act, ict, ect, uct and nct may be pointed out to the pupil.) It is explained that the 'g' is followed by a silent 'u' after the letter, in words such as guess, guest, guilty, tongue, catalogue, to keep the hard sound of the letter, and to separate it from the softening influence of 'i,' and 'e,' but that the rule got out of hand in the words guard, guarantee, etc.

The spelling of the medial and final *(k), (j), (ch)* are dealt with in greater detail, introducing the French qu and que, and the Greek ch *(k)*; plus the final 'age' *(ij)*, with the 'ege' exceptions, and the 'ridge' and 'ledge' words. Words with the 'ege' ending are taught as a mnemonic; 'it is a privilege to go to college, it would be a sacrilege not to do so'. The only word using ige as an *(ij)* ending being 'vesitige'.

The final syllable *(ch)* tch, ch is taught, (as is the final dge, ge) as a jingle.
'Short vowel, long ending tch (dge); Long vowel, short ending ch (ge)
Vowel already protected, short ending ch (ge)
Remember which, rich, such, much.'

Reference is made to the final 'ture' = *(cher)* in the words picture, furniture, manufacture, which the child will be reading but not necessarily using for writing.

Words are taught in family groups and the exceptions are used for writing practice to reinforce those words which do not conform to the guidelines, unless they are outwith the pupil's needed vocabulary.

At this stage, a short history of the development of the English language is discussed and the fact that it is a living, on-going process, with new scientific words being invented, in addition to words that are still being imported, and re-imported with modifications, from America and the former colonies. Place names dating from the Danish invasion may be pointed out on a map, 'thorpe' (village) Scunthorpe; 'by' (homestead) Derby, Rugby; 'toft' (site of a house) Lowestoft.

The derivation of spellings from the Anglo-Saxons who used the digraph hw, which French scribes transformed into wh, so that hwaer became where, and hwaenne became when, leads to the 'detective's questions' words; when, who, why, where, what, which, whose, whether etc.

The second group of wh words are taught with the exaggerated pronunciation of the *(hw)* beginning: white, whistle, whisper etc.

ADDITION OF SUFFIXES

The addition of suffixes, and the need to double the last consonant if adding a vowel suffix to a CVC ending of the base word is the next stage in the programme. It is emphasised that the spelling of a suffix never changes; any change that takes place must be in the base word or root. This concept is expanded with more able pupils to the placing of stress in words of two syllables, and the need to double the final consonant of the base word when adding a vowel suffix, if the vowel is not already protected by another consonant or by the presence of a double vowel, and if the stress is on the second syllable.

Words ending with 'l' are different,' the final 'l' needs to be doubled wherever the stressed syllable, unless the word ends with a double consonant or has two vowels before the final 'l': excel+ent; cancel+ed; crawl+ed; feel+ing. The suffix 'ly' is added to a base word, without change.

Many dyslexics, particularly those with an audial dyslexia, find it difficult to hear the stressed accent in words. It is necessary to do a great deal of work in this field with clapping rhythms to familiar words, Chris-to-pher, Al-as-dair, Mer-ce-des, De-cem-ber etc. Placing the stress on a different syllable, emphasises the difference in the sound of the word.

Spelling of *(ul)*. The **le** is applied as if it were a vowel suffix (adapted from French elle) therefore the weak vowel must be 'protected' by a double consonant; except for the consonants. S U R M N W V – Simon's Uncle Roger Makes Nice Warm Vests (Elizabeth Wood) which add a final el or al to the base word: e.g. tinsel, duel, barrel, camel, tunnel, towel, travel. Final 's' nearly always adds 'el,' but sometimes adds 'al' in words such as universal, disposal, nasal, dorsal, reversal, and rehearsal.

The spelling of *(sul)* as cil, cel must be treated as a separate category.

The 'schwa' *(er)* sound produced by the combination of r with a vowel as a medial and a final sound is taught, with reference to the placement of the word endings ir, yr; er, re; ur, or and ar.

er: is used for comparatives; or people doing simple jobs; or indicating their origin e.g. villager, Londoner etc. Also after tt: butter, matter.

re: is used for units of measure i.e. metre etc. also for centre and theatre.

ar: is used after l or ll collar, regular (calendar – writing practice)

at
ct   all add or. The or ending is used for people who undergo intensive
it   training to qualify e.g. solicitor, professor, actor, director, inventor.
ess

In addition verbs ending ate, drop the 'e' and add 'or' e.g. calculate – calculator, regulate – regulator.

'our' = ending for abstract nouns.

The pupil is reminded that apart from 'very', a weak vowel keeps its sound if followed by and 'protected' by a 'rr,' in words such as hurry, marry, barrel, sorry, horrid etc.

BASIC RULES   PART TWO

The next level is –

The spelling of *(ee)* 'i' before 'e,' except after 'c,' and the exceptions, protein and seize, and the sound *(ay)* = ei reign, rein, vein.

The spelling of *(sh)* in the initial, medial and final positions follows.

Initial

The 'sh' in simple, mainly Anglo-Saxon words, is first dealt with: shop, shut etc.

The two words that use 's' for the initial *(sh)*: sugar and sure.

The French 'ch' *(sh)* in the words: chef, chalet, chauffeur, champagne.

The Greek 'sch' *(sh)*: schedule, schist.

Final

Most words use the simple 'sh' ending

French words use che: moustache, quiche, panache, cache.

Medial

This is more complicated ground, and the only five common words using the simple medial 'sh,' are taught as a mnemonic.

'It is the fashion for bishops to sit on cushions to eat rashers of bacon with mushrooms.' – 'ship' is a suffix and is added to friendship, worship, kinship etc.

Otherwise medial (sh) may be ti, si, ssi, ci, or xi.

'ian' is a suffix meaning 'one who' and is added to base words which may end with 'c' or 't':

music-ian, opti-cian, magic-ian.   ci = *(sh)*

Egypt-ian, Mart-ian, Alsat-ian.   ti = *(sh)*

'xi' (sh) is not commonly used, nor are the words in the vocabulary of many younger pupils, but must be shown to exist in words such as, anxious, complexion, crucifixion, obnoxious, noxious.

Pupils are taught that 'tion' is used after the long vowels 'a,' 'e,' 'o,' and 'u,' to say *(shun)*.

The consonants 'n,' 'c,' 'p' are also followed by tion. (National Car Park = n,c,p).

The short vowel 'i' is an exception and adds tion, unless the word end is – mission.

-ssion is also used to 'protect' weak vowels 'a,' 'u,' 'e': passion, concussion, expression.

(iii)

'sion' (sh) is used after 'l,' 'n,' 'er,' (the learner sign is used as a mnemonic) also 'ur.'

compul-sion, propul-sion; exten-sion, comprehen-sion; diver-sion, aver-sion.

'ur' words based on the Latin root cur, excursion, incursion.

```
┌─────────────┐
│             │
│      L      │
│             │
└─────────────┘
```

Learner

'sion' (zhun) follows a long vowel as a general rule; the pupil is told to listen for the *(zh)* sound: invasion, persuasion.

It occurs in words with the Latin root 'vis' – vision, division.

The spelling of *(us)* Nouns = **us;** Adjectives = **ous.**

The two categories of *(us)* words are taught separately with reference to the fact that the 'us' group are all nouns, and 'ous' adjectives. To make a noun ending 'our' into an adjective, the letter 'u', in the 'our' is dropped before adding the 'ous' ending: e.g. humour – humorous, glamour – glamorous.

The pupil must also be reminded that to keep the 'c ' 'ang' 'g' soft, in words such as courage and outrage, the final 'e' must be retained, before adding the ous suffix; unless it is changed to 'i' as in the words spacious, and vicious.

The spelling of *(chur), (zhur), (shor).*

Pupils are reminded of the earlier reference to ture = *(cher)* and family groups of words are built up: picture, furniture etc.

They are again reminded that 's' = (sh) in the words sugar and sure, and the words built from 'sure' are taught: assure, insure, pressure.

The same 'sure' pattern is used for *(zhur)* words measure, treasure, leisure, pleasure.

The spelling of *(ah)* **a** (without 'r') followed by ff, ss, st, sk, nce, th, nt, lf, ft.

Mnemonic 'Ask father to take a bath after planting the bulbs and cutting the grass, as we are going to the staff dance at half past nine'.

(The pronunciation of the long **a** varies from region to region and this guideline may not apply in all areas).

The mnemonic showing the different sounds of 'ough', however, is worth pointing out to a poor reader.

'Though the tough plough-boy thought he had cleaned the trough thoroughly, the dirt showed through the clear water.'

The spelling of *(ah/oo)* = *ou* or *ow*.

In the initial position it is 'ou,' unless followed by a single 'l,' 'n,' or 'er.'

(**Learner** logo), when it changes to ow.

ow + l	fowl, growl, howl, prowl	(exception foul)
ow + n	clown, frown, drown, down etc	(exception noun)
ow + er	flower, tower, power, shower.	

Further exceptions to the guideline are   crowd, towel, vowel, bowel

In the final position the *(ah/oo)* is 'ow'   cow, how, now.

The Anglo-Saxon ending ough, in the words plough and bough needs to be taught.

The spelling of (or) = au or aw [apart from words beginning or, orbit, order, etc.]

Initial	Only five words use initial aw. *(or)* awe, awful, awning, awkward, awl.
	All others use au for the initial sound: author, autumn, authority. etc.
Medial	'au' unless followed by a sing 'l,' 'n,' 'er' (**Learner** logo) when it changes to 'aw.'

aw + l	crawl, brawl, drawl [exceptions: haul, caul]	
aw + n	dawn, drawn, prawn, lawn	
aw + er	drawer	

Final   aw   claw, draw, raw, paw, gnaw

Medial   [Anglo-Saxon] augh = *(or)*
                  caught, taught, daughter, slaughter, naughty, haughty
'The farmer caught his naughty haughty daughter and taught her not to slaughter worms.'

Medial   [Anglo-Saxon] ough + t = *(or)*
                  thought, bought, sought, nought, fought.

Medial   [Anglo-Saxon] augh = *(arf)*
                  laugh, draught.

The Latin suffixes 'ary,' 'ery,' 'ory' are added to base words

ary – relates to 'a person,' or 'a thing,' or 'a place connected with.'
          secretary, infirmary, salary, aviary, stationary.
ery – relates to 'an occupation' 'a trade' or 'an art'
          pottery, refinery, bakery, surgery, machinery
ory – 'a place where', 'relating to'
          dormitory, factory, theory, directory, victory.

Pupils are encouraged to exaggerate the sound of the last syllable, to hear which ending to use.

Final   est/ist.
                  'est' is an Anglo-Saxon suffix, and is used for the superlative degree in comparisons.
                          cold colder coldest etc
                  'ist' is a Greek suffix, meaning 'one who believes in ' or 'one who is skilled in'
                          scientist, cyclist, Methodist, Baptist, biologist etc.
The two endings should be taught separately.

Initial   air/aer.
Use 'aer' if the next letter is a vowel: aeroplane, aerial, aerated.
Otherwise use air: airman, aircraft, airsick, airtight.

(iv)

Situation spelling of long vowels: 'a,' 'e,' 'i,' 'o,' 'u,' ' oo,'

LONG V	INITIAL	MEDIAL	FINAL
a	open syll a-pron	open syll fa -tal spa- cious	
a-e	a-te	open syll in va de + er /ed	viol ate infl -ate
ai	ai- d	usually medial p- ai-d m- ai-l l- ai-d t- ai-l	never
ay			1 or 2 syll r-ay displ-ay p-ay Sund-ay
ei		ei always medial v-ei-n v-ei-l r-ei-gn f-ei-gn	1 or 2 syll
ey			th-ey ob-ey pr-ey conv-ey wh-ey surv-ey
eigh	numbers eigh-t eigh-teen	only 2 fr-eigh-t w-eigh-t	sl-eigh n-eigh
aigh		only 1 str-aigh-t	never
ea		only 3 gr-ea-t br-ea-k st-ea-k	

et –   French suffix –   ball-et   duv-et   bouqu-et
ae   Sund-ae

Situation spelling — Long vowels l

LONG V	INITIAL	MEDIAL	FINAL
i	open syll i-tem i-con	open syll fi- nal bi- ble	[never in English words – changes to y] ski=Scan; taxi =taxi-cab
i - e	ice	sp-i-ced adv-i-sed bi- = prefix biped	suffixes - ise, -ize - ice - ine
Anglo- Saxon igh		n - igh - t l - igh - t and rhyming words	h - igh s - igh n - igh
ie			t- ie l- ie p- ie d- ie
ye			b-ye r-ye
y		Greek 'borrowings' hy- drogen ty-phoon	sk-y fl-y tr-y cr-y wh-y my by

I
eye
eigh –   h-eigh-t   sl-eigh-t
is   –   is-land
ais   –   ais-le

Situation spelling — Long vowel u

LONG V	INITIAL	MEDIAL	FINAL
u	open syll u-niverse u-tility	d-u-ty	em-u men-u
u-e	use	1 or 2 syll cu-te vol-ume concl-ude	
ue			c-ue virt-ue d-ue stat-ue contin-ue rev-ue resid-ue
ew	ewe		f-ew cr-ew n-ew vi-ew d-ew dr-ew
eu	=Greek 'good' eu-logy eu-phoria Eu-rope	pn-eu-matic pn-eu-monia f-eu-dal	f-eu li-eu

eue   qu-eue
ieu   ad-ieu   l-ieu
iew   v-iew
hu   ex-hu-me
you
eau   b-eau-ty

Situation spelling - Long vowel e

LONG V	INITIAL	MEDIAL	FINAL	
e	open syll e-mit e-dict	Prefixes be-, de-, ne-, pre-, re-, se-, are never followed by a doubled consonant	m-e w-e	b-e h-e
ee		b-ee-t m-ee-t spl-ee-n thirt-ee-n ex-, suc-, pro + ceed (others use cede)	s-ee b-ee fl-ee	coff-ee toff-ee committ-ee
ea	ea-t ea-st ea-sy	s-ea-t b-ea-t m-ea-t h-ea-t wh-ea-t tr-ea-t	s-ea t-ea	fl-ea
ei		[after c + ei] rec-ei-ve conc-ei-t	never	
ie		bel-ie-ve pr-ie-st	prair-ie	
ey			k-ey mon-ey hon-ey	

i	cl-i-que pol-i-ce ant-i-que un-i-que
eo	p-eo-ple
oe	am-oe-ba
e-e	Latin cede – prec-ede conc-ede rec-ede

Situation spelling — Long vowel o

LONG V	INITIAL	MEDIAL	FINAL
o	open syll o-ver o-pen o-bey	mo-st, po-st, gho-st ho-st	1 or 2 syll g-o pian-o s-o sol-o ech-o
o-e	owe	open syll ho-tel	
ow	ow-n	[$(\bar{o})$ + l, n, er] b-o-w-l s-ow-n bl-ow-er	1 or 2 syll b-ow cr-ow sn-ow fl-ow arr-ow shad-ow wind-ow bel-ow tomorr-ow
oe		goe-s	t-oe d-oe f-oe sl-oe[berry] h-oe r-oe
oa	oa-ts oa-th oa-k	b-oa-t cl-oa-k c-oa-l l-oa-n c-oa-st, t-oa-st, r-oa-st, b-oa-st	
ou		s-ou-l m-ou-ld	

owe
eau   plat-eau   portmant-eau
ough   th-ough
oo   br-oo-ch
ot   dep-ot
ew   s-ew s-ew-n
eo   y-eo-man

Situation spelling — Long vowel *(oo)*

LONG V	INITIAL	MEDIAL	FINAL
o			to do
oo	oo-ze	b-oo-t t-oo-th	t-oo bamb-oo
wo			t-wo
ough			thr-ough
oe			sh-oe can-oe
ou		s-ou-p gr-ou-p tr-ou-pe	y-ou
ui		fr-ui-t s-ui-t j-ui-ce	
ew		s-ew-age	dr-ew r-ew fl-ew cr-ew
ue			tr-ue fl-ue bl-ue
u		fl-u-te ch-u-te fl-ue-ent tr-u-ant	

oeu –   man-oeu-vre

Situation Spelling — Long Vowel *(or)*

LONG V	INITIAL	MEDIAL	FINAL
or	or, or-b, or-bit or-der, or-al, or-chestra	sp-or-t sw-or-d	f-or, n-or oor = d-oor/fl-oor m-oor/sp-oor
ore	ore	fore-head	expl-ore st-ore, bef-ore theref-ore,c-ore
oar	oar	ab-oar-d h-oar-d	r-oar, s-oar
aw	only 5 words aw-l, aw-ning, aw-kward, awe, aw-ful	followed by single l, n er cr-aw-l, d-aw-n dr-aw-er	l-aw, j-aw str-aw, cl-aw dr-aw, th-aw
au	most other words *(or)* au-thor, au-tograph	= au h-au-nt	never (or)
ough	only ough-t	th-ough-t br-ough-t, b-ough-t s-ough-t, f-ough-t	[final ough = *(oh), (oo)* or *(er)*]
augh	only 1 augh-t	only 6 words c-augh-t/n-augh-ty h-aught-y/d-augh-ter t-augh-t sl-augh-ter	never

ar   –   w-ar, w-ar-m, w-ar-n, w-ar-d
a   –   a-ll, f-a-ll, sm-a-ll
our   –   y-our, p-our, f-our
ort   –   m-ort-gage
orps –   c-orps
aur   –   dinos-aur

PLURALS

Most children know that the plural form of nouns is made by adding 's' to the base word. Words ending with the fricative sounds 's,' 'z,' 'sh,' 'ch,' 'ss' and 'x,' add 'es' for the plural form:

buses, bushes, benches, bosses, boxes, buzzes.

Words ending in 'y,' obey the rule that 'y' changes to 'i,' unless preceded by a vowel. The new base then adds 'es': copy – copies.

All words ending with 'o' preceded by a vowel, add single 's' to form the plural:

radio – radios,   cameo – cameos,   folio – folios.

However, most nouns ending with 'o' preceded by a consonant add 'es':

potato – potatoes, tomato – tomatoes, volcano – volcanoes, buffalo – buffaloes, tornado – tornadoes.

'Imported' words ending with 'o,' add 's' to form the plural:

solo – solos, piano – pianos, photo – photos.

All proper names ending in 'o,' add 's': Eskimos, Filipinos, Romeos.

Some words change the vowel to form the plural:

man – men, tooth – teeth, mouse – mice, foot – feet.

Some words keep the same form for both singular and plural:

sheep, deer, fish.

Compound words add 's' to the last part where the word is solid, but to the most important word in a compound hyphenated word: spoonfuls, mothers-in-law.

PART THREE

'BORROWED' PREFIXES AND SUFFIXES

Changes for euphony.

This area deals with the addition of Latin and Greek prefixes to base words, and the changes that make for the easier pronunciation of the words that are formed.

The final letter of a suffix sometimes changes to a 'lip sound' to blend with the first sound of a base word e.g. ad+pear = appear; con+pose = compose.

Latin, Greek and Anglo-Saxon prefixes and suffixes may be listed, to enlarge the pupil's vocabulary and develop an interest in the history of our language.

For the same reason, lists of 'borrowed' roots may be supplied with their meanings. Exercises given, in which the pupil must underline either the prefix or the suffix of a word and indicate any changes made to the prefix, help the pupil to understand the reasons for the doubling of consonants in 'borrowed' words, and also increases the range of words within their written vocabulary.

PART FOUR

Homographs, with their alternative meanings, and exercises to place the stress mark on the syllable to indicate the correct meaning of a word, enhance the ability of the student of language to express himself to his full potential.

> abstract – existing in thought rather than matter
> abstract – take out – remove

Homophones with the single letter missing which changes the meaning of a word, is another way to stretch the understanding of the subtlety of language.

> advi-e – to recommend
> advi-e – words offered as an opinion.

GAMES

Games are an enjoyable way of reinforcing a rule. They can be made up on blank cards to suit the rule being taught.

PAIRS. Words are written on duplicate cards, can be either spread out face down to be picked up in matching pairs, or which dealt to two or more players, each receiving ten cards, the remainder being held in a central pack. The first player asks for the card he/she needs to complete the pair, and if it is 'not at home', selects the top card from the central pack. The words may be sight words, or words that need reinforcing.

DOUBLE, ADD or DROP. This deals with the addition of suffixes. The game is played on a noughts and crosses grid, so that the player who gets three cards with suitable words in a row is the winner. Words such as hot + er, help+er, bake+ed, are printed on the cards which are dealt to the two players. The players must build up a row of three cards which illustrate the same spelling rule i.e. three cards with doubled consonant words, or three where the suffix is simply added to the base word.

SWITCH. In this game, the cards are divided into three or four groups of eight or so cards, and the words printed on them deals with a sound, not necessairly with the same spelling. The first group of cards may have the words 'cook, stood, shook, wool, took, pull, push, full, put'; the second group may have the sound (oo) 'threw, chew, grew, blue, true, canoe, two, through.' (If preferred, all the endings may be the same to reinforce a spelling.) All the cards are numbered one to eight and may be printed using different colours. The first player must put down a card reading the word aloud and stating the number, the second player must either cover the card with the same sound, or duplicate the number stating the new sound. There are three master Switch cards in the pack which is dealt to the players, and any player holding a Switch card may change the sound by laying down the master card and stating his/her preference, to suit his hand.

CROSSWORD

A crossword may be built using a chequers board as a base. (A Scrabble board is too busy for the young dyslexic.) A spelling that needs reinforcing may be laid out as the first word, using the letter tiles from the Edith Norrie Letter Case, and other words are then built on to this frame. If appropriate some letters may be left blank and the pupil must fill in the blanks with a suitable letter.

c

t a u g - t

u

d - - ghter

h

na - g - ty

In conclusion, when teaching a pupil, I make a point of going back to the beginning, by assuming that the child has not previously grasped any of the basic rules of spelling, knowing that if he does know the rule, he will soon make me aware of the fact, and I can use this as a basis to build on.

My maxim is: 'Expect not and thou shalt not be disappointed!'

REFERENCES

Edith Norrie Letter Case (1973). Obtainable from The Helen Arkell Dyslexia Centre, Frensham, Farnham, Surrey GU10 3BW.

Words in Colour (1962). Cuisinere Co. Ltd., 11 Crown Street, Reading, RG1 2TQ.

Wood, Elizabeth (1982). Exercise Your Spelling. Hodder & Stoughton.

SPELLING –
DIAGNOSIS AND STRATEGIES

CATRIONA COLLINS
and JEAN C. MILLER

INTRODUCTION

'I'm not a good speller.'

This oft heard statement is made by children and adults from all walks of life, including many who are highly articulate and very well educated. Is there then a common denominator in this situation other than the belief that this is an unhappy fact of life which must be accepted? Spelling is undoubtedly an area of the curriculum which has been subject to varying teaching approaches, from the total emphasis on phonics to the opposite end of the spectrum where spelling errors were barely corrected, allowing freedom of expression unfettered by any pressures for accuracy. It is not uncommon for pupils to perceive spelling in a rather negative fashion.

SPELLING DIFFICULTIES

The inability to spell worries many dyslexic children very much and they may have experienced considerable humiliation in the classroom. Frequently their work has been returned liberally marked with red ink and often with comments about their spelling. No wonder they need courage to continue to write! What is the solution to that negative approach? What we need to do is to tick words that they have spelt correctly and gradually highlight one or two important words which, if given help, they can learn to spell and, hopefully, reproduce correctly in their written work.

How should we tackle the teaching of spelling? To begin with we must recognise that there are a number of reasons for students experiencing difficulty with spelling.

- **Visual Factors**

Poor spellers with weak visual recall have a fairly clear idea which symbol represents which sounds, but they are not always able to remember how the word should look and become confused when they try to write it down.

•   **Auditory Factors**

Children suffering from weak auditory analysis are often unable to say which letter symbol represents which sound. They are not able to hear some of the sounds within words and make wild guesses and often miss out syllables. 'Giraffe', for example, can be written as 'girf', 'suddenly' as 'sudnile', 'rescued' as 'rsood', etc. Before we can begin to work with poor spellers, we must try to decide to which group each child belongs. It is not an easy task – some have a 'foot in each camp'.

DIAGNOSIS OF THE DIFFICULTY

Spelling difficulty may be caused by poor performance in a number of areas. Diagnostic testing and scrutiny of the nature of the errors will pinpoint the problem. Necessary support may be planned using a variety of different strategies to support the student.

Where the difficulty arises from an aural problem, it will be important to bear in mind that careful articulation by both teacher and pupil is crucial, and to link aural to visual representation.

More commonly, the difficulty arises because the pupil is unable to recall the sequence of letters which go to make a word. A mistake of the type – I 'bot' a card – suggests that a purely phonetic attempt (indeed phonetically correct) has been made but that there was no visual recognition/recall of the word 'bought'. Moreover, 'bot' suggests some recall of the word, but difficulty with the letter string 'ght'.

MULTI-SENSORY ASPECTS

It is now well established in the teaching of spelling that multi-sensory skills are involved in the acquisition of the ability to spell well.

Knowledge of phonics is acquired via a systematic programme and visual skills using word games and most of all by seeing the written word. Many sounds in the English language may be written in two or even more ways, e.g. p(ear: p(are: p(air: and in this situation visual recall is used. It follows that exposure to spoken language and to the written word are very significant. It is very important that children write correctly, right from the beginning, those words which are most frequently used in their own work which do not follow phonetic patterns e.g. they, where, their, two, etc., as the more often these are written wrongly, the more difficult it can be to correct. Good spelling habits with these familiar words should be encouraged from the very early stages.

Such approaches are employed in, for example, 'Spelling Made Easy' by Violet Brand, published by EPL, with 'Remedial Spelling' aimed at pupils who have difficulty. Much emphasis is placed on the multi-sensory nature of spelling to listen, to say, to write, to look, and to link together common patterns and families of words so that spelling vocabulary can be encouraged and expanded, building on those words which the pupils can comfortably spell.

SPELLING SKILLS

The auditory discrimination of initial sounds, word endings, medial sounds, and rhyming words can be enhanced by means of listening games. Visual discrimination can be developed by means of sorting – matching type activities, motor skills by drawing, and handwriting activities as part of the programme to ensure fluency of writing. Where there is an established mis-spelling identified in a diagnostic test, it is helpful to re-train in the motor aspect of the spelling as well as the visual and aural. The handwriting programme of study can be consciously structured in such a way as to ensure practice in the letter strings or combinations of letters and to concentrate upon the visual and motor knowledge which is to be reinforced.

SPELLING RULES

Pupils should also learn the spelling rules, especially those simple ones which are most commonly seen in use and can be most helpful e.g. 'i' before 'e' except after 'c,' dropping of final 'e' before adding 'ing,' changing 'y' to 'i' to make plurals as in baby – babies. These spelling rules can be taught in a structured way and there are many commercially produced schemes using this approach. Pupils learn groups of words and use them in exercises to reinforce the visual and motor aspects. These rules do cover a great majority of the words in the English Language. For pupils with spelling difficulties these common rules as applied to the most frequently used words can be very helpful.

Spelling rules can be taught but much later than is often considered. Boys and girls in their third year in the Secondary School will ask about and appear to enjoy and understand some of the spelling rules which, to them, are logical.

The ultimate aim is to help the child to become aware of words, to be unafraid to write, and to use words regardless of spelling. Many children have devised their own way out of their failure. The teacher's task is not to be constantly correcting mistakes but to be helping children not to make so many the next time.

SPELLING AND READING

Spelling is not the same as Reading. It is a different skill and indeed fluent, able readers may be very poor spellers. Spelling has to be taught in a structured way, building upon skills using a variety of approaches to foster confidence in the use of the written word. It must be extremely unusual for a parallel progression to take place in the development of reading skills and of writing and spelling and the majority of pupils can read materials at a much more difficult level than the writing they produce.

Frith and Frith (1980) made an important observation: they argued that there was a difference between reading and spelling. Reading, they felt, was a recognition process, whilst spelling was a retrieval process. Thus reading can proceed using 'partial cues'. In contrast, spelling requires the use of 'full cues'. To spell well, words must be represented in a detailed way in the mind of the speller and this memory image must be recoverable. In the absence of spelling knowledge, an individual will be forced to spell words according to the way in which they sound. In the English orthography, reliance on a sound strategy is unsatisfactory (Snowling, 1985).

AIDS AND STRATEGIES

Pupils with spelling difficulties may be helped by work focusing on 'family grouping' of words containing the same letter strings. These letter strings do not necessarily always have the same sound e.g. gone: done: bone.

Another helpful activity is to look for words within words, e.g. **train**ing.

The use of cursive handwriting exercises linked into letter strings e.g. ch: ing increases fluency in writing these frequently used strings whilst also reinforcing the sequencing of the letters.

The keyboard is another aid found to be useful in reinforcing knowledge of letter strings. Pupils look for the key on the keyboard and then check the printout when using it for word processing or using such programmes as 'Eye for Spelling' or producing lists.

The visual dimension of spelling is further strengthened by means of the look, say, cover, write, check technique (which includes oral and writing aspects) to ensure consistency of the multi-sensory approach to spelling. The oral aspect reinforces work in the listening and phonic skills: the ability, where appropriate, to use the syllables of the word.

For those pupils who may already have built up anxieties about spelling, it is very important that correction of work be supportive and positive. Where the error is only one letter or one syllable, only that part should be indicated and the pupil praised for what is correct whilst their attention is drawn to the part which is not correct. To a pupil who has difficulties in either visual or aural discrimination, it is daunting and discouraging to have to search through a string of letters or syllables to find the error.

A spelling problem is not easy to remedy, despite a range of methods of teaching. Poor spellers are a constant reminder that teachers must continue to devise new ideas. Some strategies which could be considered include the following:

1   **Typing** enables the pupils to work slowly, finding the correct letters as they type, and it reinforces and strengthens their poor visual recall for words. If they have weak fine-motor control, using correct typing skills strengthens their fingering and improves their handwriting.

2   **Dividing Word into Syllables** can be a difficult task but some like the challenge of this skill. Finding two words from a compound word can be an excellent activity.

else where	where ever	be gun
hat red	dough nut	news paper

3   **Fitting Words into Shapes**

(see over).

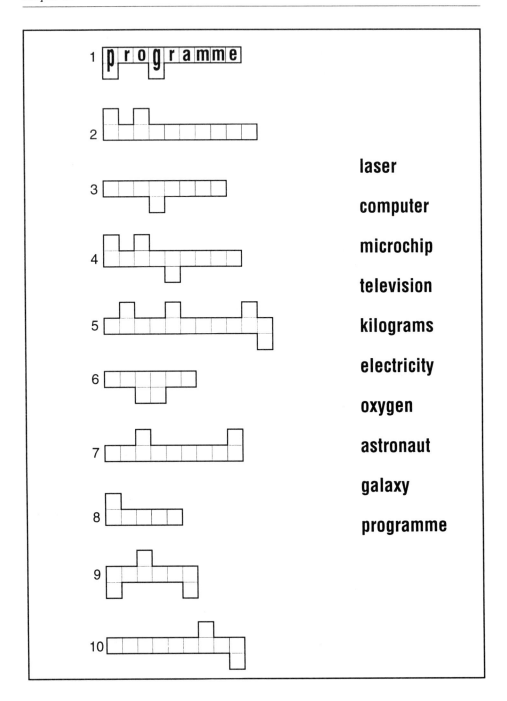

1. programme

2.

3.

4.

5.

6.

7.

8.

9.

10.

laser

computer

microchip

television

kilograms

electricity

oxygen

astronaut

galaxy

programme

4   **Growing words** have a fascination. Inventing patterns, working alone or in pairs, is ideal. Here is one example:

new

wall

link

kitchen

never

reached.

5   **Proof-reading** is a very useful exercise provided the pupils are presented with short sentences and the number of errors is stated. If this work can be linked with spelling just taught, it will reinforce the work.

6   **Anagrams** are very successful but must be based on the pupil's own experience. Pupils should be able, if they wish, to work in pairs for this activity.

7   **Crosswords** can be a teaching aid, reinforcing words being taught.

Teachers are often asked about spelling books, but there is no book or list of words that can be used regularly for children with specific learning difficulties. They have to develop their own list, so that for checking purposes they can refer to their own alphabetical indexed books. This enables each child to look up a word quickly when it is needed.

CONCLUSION

It is also important to remember that dyslexia affects areas other than reading and spelling. A child's difficulties with literacy result in anxiety and concern to that child, the parent and the teacher. Society demands a certain degree of competence in reading and spelling and therefore it is essential that, as teachers, we give due consideration to the assessment and the development of strategies in spelling to facilitate the development of literacy skills.

Spelling is a skill which those who have good visual recall, good aural skill and a wide experience of language, including listening, talking and seeing written language, are most likely to acquire easily. For those who have difficulty the school can provide opportunities to experience language, and varied techniques to help and support the learner in the acquisition of skills. Teachers should be positive and encouraging and employ a variety of teaching aids, activities and text.

REFERENCES

Brand, V. (1989). *Remedial Spelling*. Egon Publishers.

Brand, V. (1992). *Spelling Made Easy*. Egon Publishers.

Frith, U. and Frith, C. C. (1980). 'Relationships between Reading and Spelling' in Kavanagh, J. F. and Venezky, R. L. (Eds.). *Orthography, Reading and Dyslexia*. Baltimore: University Park Press.

Snowling, M. J. (1985). *Children's Written Language Difficulties*. NFER, Nelson Publishing Co.Ltd.

SPECIFIC DIFFICULTIES AND MATHEMATICS

CHARLES WEEDON

SPECIFIC DIFFICULTIES

A specific difficulty is one that stands out in contrast to the apparent potential of the individual. Sometimes it may be more precisely labelled – for example, the terms 'dyslexia', 'dysgraphia' and 'dyscalculia'. These carry with them an implication of neurological origin, and a certain intransigence in the face of intervention – but by no means all specific difficulties come into such categories. There may be a range of other, non-neurological explanations, and there is never any reason why intervention should not be successful, at least to some degree.

Difficulties can be highly specific, affecting in an obvious way only one area of activity; they can be specific, but manifest themselves in a wider range of activities; or they can be quite general difficulties. This last grouping, of quite general difficulties, often tends to be equated with an overall low level of intellectual functioning – but often these general difficulties are a function of specific difficulties that affect a range of activities wide enough to give an impression of a generally low level of 'intelligence'.

There can be difficulties that are specific to any human activity – use of written language is one, Mathematics is another. Any sophisticated activity demands access to a wide range of skills and processes, in complex interaction. Every activity draws upon and builds from certain clusters of skills and processes. A localised dysfunction anywhere in the prerequisite skills network, unless successfully circumvented, may finally lead to a specific disability in that area of endeavour.

The degree to which the resulting disability is specific to certain areas of activity will depend upon how task-specific is the skill or process concerned. If very specific, it may lead to a disability that manifests itself on a very narrow front. But if the skill is one that is needed in a wider range of activities, then it seems likely that there will be some difficulty manifested, in some form, in each of these activities.

REACTIONS TO SPECIFIC DIFFICULTIES

The most discussed and written about specific difficulties are those that manifest themselves mainly in the area of language. Not surprisingly – language is arguably mankind's most powerful tool, rendered many times more powerful when made permanent by means of writing.

The tension a specific difficulty creates is proportional to the perceived importance of mastery in that area. At one end of the continuum, a particular weakness can be easily dismissed: poor performance as a pole vaulter would not upset most of us; and while we might regret an inability to sketch well, we have little difficulty in rearranging our lives around that shortcoming. At the other end, no-one laughs off an inability to read or write or spell – it does matter so very much. And somewhere in between the two lie Mathematics and number manipulation: it's common enough to hear people declare, with a kind of perverse pride, that they 'could never do Maths', but there is a certain amused defiance in the declaration – because it does matter. The handling of number, shape and quantity does pervade a great many human activities and any specific weakness in this area is disabling in that it closes many doors, shuts off many areas of activity.

SPECIFIC DIFFICULTIES AND MATHEMATICS

There is a range of specific difficulties that might contribute to difficulties within Mathematics. Dyslexia, dysgraphic-type difficulties, spatial and organisational difficulties, and sensory or motor disabilities may all have implications for Mathematics performance. There may, too, be difficulties whose centre of gravity seem to be primarily mathematical or arithmetical (Lewis, Weedon, 1992). Where these are deemed to be neurological in origin, the syndrome may be termed 'dyscalculia' (Kosc, 1986; Sharma and Loveless, 1986; Sharma, 1979, 1986).

There is little doubt that there are learners who are competent elsewhere in the curriculum, sometimes highly competent, while finding Mathematics or Arithmetic difficult (Share *et al.,* 1988, Lewis, Weedon, 1992). Among children otherwise competent in the classroom, Arithmetic disability is quite commonly a correlate of reading disability, but certainly may exist on its own (Share *et al.*, 1988). From the sparse research to date, however, no typical cross-curriculum performance patterns can be identified among such pupils. They appear to share little more than their unexpected weakness in Mathematics: their strengths are quite various (Weedon, 1992).

SOURCES OF DIFFICULTY WITH MATHS

Those competent with Mathematics and numbers have long been bewildered by the incompetence of others: an HMI in 1876 felt it was 'a subject . . . beyond the comprehension of the rural mind' (McIntosh, in Floyd 1981).

Difficulties with Mathematics are not rare. They can stem from a number of factors, separately or together; social and educational factors, the individual's cognitive performance, neurological make-up, personality and learning style, all interacting with each other and with factors intrinsic to the nature of the subject.

In the same way that explanations of dyslexia tend to draw upon a neurological aetiology, so must a dyscalculic explanation of difficulties specific to Mathematics depend upon the exclusion of contending explanations, and rely upon congenital inheritance. As will be seen, the contending explanations are many and convincing.

Webster's Dictionary includes the entry (perhaps significant when considering why people might find it so hard): 'Mathematical: . . . rigorously exact, perfectly accurate . . . being beyond doubt or question'.

Its rigour combines with its abstraction. Mathematics is inherently abstract. The processes of abstracting and classifying are central to it (Skemp, 1971), and the very essence of Mathematics is that it abstracts to a stage beyond words. Mathematical thinking exists as a distinctive entity partly because it explores areas of thought beyond the easy control of words. It has developed and makes use of a whole different symbol system to express ideas and relationships that cannot easily be put into words, in a very compressed and precise way.

The purpose and essence of Mathematics is to solve problems. It demands the acquisition of, organisation of and access to knowledge, rules, techniques, skills and concepts with the aim of providing solutions to novel situations. It is both an organised body of knowledge and a creative activity. For some learners this may imply an internal tension: creativity involves independence, judgement and a readiness to take risks. School Mathematics with its apparent logical certainties pays little attention to these features (Polya, 1957; Lansdown, 1978; Plunkett, 1979; Giles, 1981).

'Algorithms' play an essential and central part in this. These are the formal routines that we learn and depend on so much, the 'rules, techniques and skills'. They are the mathematician's tools, his way of compressing and of providing a short cut.

As will be seen, algorithms are essential to success in Mathematics, but probably contribute more than anything else to confusion and lack of understanding. Too often the algorithm tends to take central place, a tool wielded by someone with little understanding of its function. The underlying meanings are left behind: 'the smaller number goes on the bottom line'; or in later years, 'turn it upside down and multiply'. In Ausubel's terms (1968), learning has become rote. It is not meaningful and the learner's mind quickly becomes a cluttered mess of confusing rules.

It is helpful in other ways to see mathematical thinking as having two main strands. Crudely these might be summarised as the distinction between skill and knowledge, between procedures and concepts (Polya, 1957; Floyd, 1981; Hiebart, 1986). Hiebert and Lefevre (Hiebert, 1986) think of mathematics in terms of 'procedural knowledge', dominated by rules and algorithms, and 'conceptual knowledge', a connected web of knowledge where the links themselves are as important as the pieces of information they link together.

The question of which of these two kinds of knowledge is most important, and what should be the appropriate balance between them, lies at the heart of most debates about Mathematics teaching.

'MATHEMATICAL ABILITY'

In Mathematics perhaps more than in other subjects there is a feeling that you need to be born with the right **kind** of intelligence, 'and plenty of it' (Giles 1981).

Cluster analysis, however, suggests that Mathematics ability is not a single ability, but a cluster of several. That they are gathered together under the purely convenience heading 'school mathematics' is an arbitrary function of school organisation (Joffe, 1980).

Often, the skills needed in Mathematics are seen as forming two main groups. For example, verbal abilities may be contrasted with visual abilities or spatial with linear (Joffe, 1980). For Joffe, spatial skills are needed in understanding shape, symmetry, and relative size and quantity, while linear skills contribute to understanding the kind of sequential and ordered symbols and representations found in the number system and algebra.

Recent factor-analytic studies have yielded separate factors for mathematical inference and mathematical knowledge independent of general intelligence or verbal skills, suggesting that mathematical ability is, statistically at least, an independent cognitive entity (Spiers, 1987).

Spiers goes on to consider a question important to a neurological perspective of Mathematical ability: whether calculation is a higher cortical 'function' that can be localised within the cortex, and if so, where; or whether it is better seen as a 'performance', a secondary process based upon other more fundamental functions? He suggests that in the sense that we regard language as a higher cortical function, so should we define calculation.

DIFFICULTIES CAUSED BY SCHOOLS AND TEACHERS

It is a frequently recurring theme that Mathematics failure is school induced (e.g. Ginsburg, 1977; Plunkett, 1979; Giles, 1981; Dickson *et al.*, 1984; Liebeck, 1984; Larcombe, 1985).

Certainly success levels in Mathematics are generally very low. If teachers test a skill taught and practised some time ago, probably they do not expect a generally high level of competence. Given our recognition of the rigorously linear nature of Mathematics, we teach with a remarkably high tolerance of failure, often even an expectation of failure.

With failure built-in in this way perhaps it is not surprising that Mathematics is associated with varying degrees of boredom, dislike, anxiety, alarm, fear and other emotions that accompany expectation of failure (Giles, 1981; Allardyce and Ginsburg, 1983; Orton 1987).

These institutional features stem from trying to convey a great deal of highly abstract content in a relatively short space of time and are the factors that cause us to rely so much on the short cuts provided by formal algorithms.

It may be that much failure is due to learning tricks in place of conceptual understanding. Children sometimes seem to think of mathematics as an isolated game with peculiar sets of rules and no evident relation to reality (Ginsburg 1977). Many writers (e.g. Ginsburg, 1977; Plunkett, 1979; Giles, 1981; Allardyce and Ginsburg, 1983; Dickson, 1984; Liebeck, 1984) suggest that standard algorithms are short cut devices introduced before the child has any real grasp of what is involved. As such, they conceal the underlying logic, specially from the less able. Any initial glimpses of reason will be lost through this process of mechanising. Seen this way, schools are suppressing an intuitive mathematical ability, rather than building on it.

LANGUAGE BASED DIFFICULTIES

These have received a lot of attention from researchers (e.g. Floyd, 1981; Cockcroft, 1982; Harvey *et al.,* 1982; Dickson *et al.* 1984; Shuard and Rothery, 1984). Quite apart from any other reading difficulties the extensive and significant, but often subtle, differences between Mathematical English (ME) and Ordinary English (OE) have been identified as the source of considerable difficulties. They have been well explored, and need not be documented in detail here.

DIFFICULTIES DERIVING FROM PERSONALITY FACTORS

Probably there are aspects of Mathematics that appeal to one individual while repelling another, functions perhaps of preferred styles of study and personality. The affective and the cognitive interpenetrate.

It has been seen that skills and abilities are not evenly or uniformly distributed. Within one individual certain clusters of skills may dominate, and this can sometimes be seen in terms of distinctive learning styles (e.g. Pask, 1976; Chinn, 1992), applicable to Mathematics as well as other areas: for example those who prefer to build their understanding step by step contrasted by those who prefer a more holistic approach.

Certainly school Mathematics tends to be a socially-isolated activity and one that does not demand the revealing of emotions in the way that other subjects may. Further, it is an area of certainties, with all the sense of beauty and completeness this can bring to some. It is often viewed as highly competitive, satisfying to some and unpleasant for others. Similarly some like the fact that answers are 'right' or 'wrong'; while those who thrive on discussion and debate may not find this aspect pleasing.

It seems helpful to see a personality continuum relevant to Mathematics success or failure, ranging from the very impulsive, through the reflective, to the ultra-reflective (Orton, 1987).

On the left the impulsive learner is too ready to take risks and will not be consistently successful. In the middle the reflective learner is prepared to take limited risks and is more likely to be successful. On the right is the far too cautious learner, terrified of failure and unable to take any risk, again leading to lack of success.

The 'right/wrong' nature of most responses to mathematics makes it easy to damage the self esteem of the learner, and many writers suggest that this happens again and again to too many of us (e.g. Allardyce and Ginsburg, 1983; Dickson *et al.*, 1984; Orton, 1987).

A HEMISPHERIC PERSPECTIVE

The hemispheric construction of the brain has been widely discussed in relation to mathematics. (Krutetskii, 1976; Wheatly, 1977; Sharma, 1979; DeLoche and Seron, 1987).

Sharma identifies two types of Mathematics learners: the Quantitative and the Qualitative mathematics learning personality (Sharma and Loveless, 1986; Chinn, 1992). Those with a left hemispheric orientation are good in language, verbal expression, problem solving bit by bit, quantifying, quantitative operations, and anything that builds up sequentially, such as counting, addition, multiplication. When given a word problem, they look for a familiar algorithm.

Those with a right hemispheric orientation look at problems holistically and explore global solutions. They are good at identifying patterns, both spatial and symbolic. They are creative and faster at solving 'real-life' problems.

As well difficulties that might arise from uneven hemispheric performance of this kind, there may be a problem in moving information from one hemisphere to other during processing. Further, there may be a problem in overall control by the left hemisphere (Sharma and Loveless, 1986)

DYSCALCULIA

There is on-going interest in neurological explanations of learning difficulties (e.g. Krutetskii, 1976; Farnham-Diggory, 1978; Sharma, 1979; Joffe, 1980; Orton, 1987).

Gonzalez and Kolers (1987) distinguish between the cognitive and neurological approach by suggesting that while the neuropsychologist is most interested in associating particular impairments with particular lesions, the cognitive psychologist is concerned with the mental operations that underlie particular performance. As the debate between 'function' and 'performance' implies, however, the two disciplines interpenetrate.

There are many ways a learner can encounter difficulties that cannot be attributed to his or her school experiences. While they may be seen as cognitive, they imply a congenital, neurological origin. They include (Bley and Thornton, 1981) visual and auditory perception problems, spatial and temporal disabilities, or motor deficits. There may be memory deficits, in working memory or long term. Visual deficits may make copying difficult, while auditory deficits lessen the ability to learn from oral drills. When dealing with word problems, memory deficits impede easy retention of items in order to operate on them, especially for longer problems. There may be sequencing deficits – much Mathematics involves sequencing; or there may be integrative deficits, a difficulty in pulling information together. In all of these, the cognitive/neurological borderlines are not clear and probably not important.

The principles used to define dyscalculia are similar to those used to define dyslexia: developmental dyscalculia is a special difficulty with numbers, not due to poor teaching or low IQ (Allardyce and Ginsburg, 1983; Sharma, 1986) . . . A neurological cause is implicated.

Developmental dyscalculia is neurologically defined as a disorder of the maturation of mathematical abilities which has its origin in a congenital or genetic disorder in a specific area of the brain (Kosc, 1974). When there is a pronounced inability for mathematics a low level of functional maturity of the inferior parietal region of the cortex and its connections with other sections of the brain is observed (Krutetskii, 1976; Sharma, 1986).

Studies of acquired and developmental dyslexia have provided each other with valuable data and insights, while also illuminating the normal functioning of the unimpaired user of language. There has been less interpenetration in the area of mathematical cognition (DeLoche and Seron, 1987), and apart from Kosc's work (1974), the neuropsychological studies that have taken place provide much of the sparse empirical evidence available in this field.

LINKS BETWEEN LANGUAGE DIFFICULTIES AND MATHEMATICAL DIFFICULTIES

While there is no clear evidence yet that arithmetic processing can be functionally localised in the brain (Spiers, 1987), calculation can best be conceptualised in terms of a network of several component processes, each perhaps with a distinct localisation in a certain site, and mediated at different levels within the nervous system. Such a 'network model' allows explanation of why language and calculation deficits sometimes overlap and co-exist while in other cases clear dissociations are established (Spiers, 1987).

Often a pupil identified as dyslexic will manifest mathematics problems: the characteristic signs of dyslexia include such things as an inability to subtract, unless with concrete aids, and difficulty with tables (Joffe, 1980). Mycklebust and Johnson (1962) placed dyscalculia in sixth place on their list of common features found among their sample of 200 dyslexics.

Joffe's study of dyslexics' Mathematics performance (1980) suggested that 60% of the dyslexic sample were retarded in arithmetic to some extent, the problem being severe for 50%. However, 10% excelled in all aspects of school mathematics, apparently by adopting alternative strategies to cope with numbers and problems. She found that calculation tended to be the major area of weakness, particularly multiplication and division, and attributed this to the dyslexic's characteristic difficulty with verbal labelling and using short-term memory. Spatial aspects and concept understanding she found to be usually unimpaired.

Joffe points up a range of extrinsic factors that might exacerbate the mathematics difficulties of a dyslexic: apart from the obvious need for reading skill, considerable emphasis may have been put on improving language skills, at the expense of other skills; or to avoid putting extra stress on the dyslexic learner, mathematics may not have been emphasised.

INCIDENCE OF SPECIFIC DIFFICULTIES IN MATHEMATICS OR ARITHMETIC

The data is sparse and sometimes ill-defined. While referring often to 'Mathematics' it tends to focus upon difficulties in arithmetic and calculation.

While acknowledging that most Mathematics difficulties arise from other factors, Kosc's influential Bratislavia study (1974) suggests that more than 6% of normal 11 year olds show signs of development dyscalculia.

Kosc's study does not, however, supply data upon the reading abilities of the pupils concerned. Rourke and his colleagues (1978, 1983) considered pupils with arithmetic problems, reading problems, and arithmetic-and-reading problems, and suggested that arithmetic disorders fall into two categories: specific arithmetic disabilities where pupils showed visuo-spatial and tactile-perceptual skills relatively poorer than their verbal skills; and arithmetic-and-reading disabilities where non-verbal skills were better than verbal skills. However, their population of children referred for learning difficulties gave no indication of incidence in the general population.

Epidemiological data is available from a New Zealand study reported by Share *et al.*, (1988), suggesting that while 6.4% of children show an arithmetic-and-reading disability, 4.8% have a specific arithmetic disability.

A recent study by Lewis, Hitch and Walker (unpublished at time of printing) used a population of over a thousand 9-10 year olds to explore the incidence of arithmetic disability within the general population in UK. Their rigorously defined criteria of pupil performance indicated that 3.9% of their sample had a reading-only disability, 2.3% an arithmetic-and-reading disability, and 1.3% on arithmetic-only disability.

SPECIFIC DIFFICULTIES AND MATHEMATICS: HOW THEY AFFECT THE LEARNER

As can be seen, specific difficulties do manifest themselves in Mathematics, for a range of reasons and in a range of ways. Certainly there are learners whose performance elsewhere should imply significantly greater success in Mathematics (Share *et al.*, 1988; Lewis, Weedon, 1992).

To date, there has been very little close analysis of the classroom performance of such pupils. While studies such as those of Share and Lewis and their colleagues (*op. cit.*) sought to measure typical incidence through paper-and-pencil testing, Weedon (1992) sought to access the perceptions of teachers. It was felt that their experience represented a considerable and relatively untapped source of understanding. In addition, their perceptions drew upon long term and typical performance rather than providing the kind of single episode and perhaps atypical analysis that is offered by paper-and-pencil testing.

Weedon's project sought to explore the existence and nature of difficulties specific to Mathematics, and to consider the extent to which provision reflected adequately the learning needs thus exposed.

The resulting data contained patterns of sufficient clarity to allow answers of some confidence to the questions posed:

(i) Teachers' experiences and understanding did suggest quite clearly that pupils who are otherwise competent may experience significant difficulty in aspects of Mathematics; and

(ii) The needs stemming from these difficulties can be met only in part by the types of provision and delivery currently in common usage.

The research questions were operationalised into a number of more focused strands of investigation.

Firstly, teachers were interviewed to explore in some detail how they perceived and understood mathematical difficulties. The resulting picture suggested that while teachers recognised the unnecessary pitfalls and hindrances caused by social, pedagogical and institutional factors, the main difficulties arise from the ways in which some fairly fixed attributes of the learners (e.g. their memory, certain personality traits, their ability to relate the abstract to the actual) interact with demands that stem from the intrinsic nature of Mathematics (e.g. its abstraction, its linearity). From this wide range of experienced practitioners, there was a clear sense that, for most pupils experiencing significant long-term difficulty in part or all of their Mathematics, their level of performance probably offered a fair reflection of their level of potential.

Secondly, teachers' understanding of difficulties specific to Mathematics were explored. It emerged quite clearly that relatively few were sceptical of their existence, attributing them to a range of factors centred about the pupil, again, fairly fixed factors stemming from the interaction between the nature of Mathematics and the attributes of the particular pupil. Most conspicuously, many teachers emphasised the distinction between difficulties with Mathematics and those with arithmetic: number-based difficulties, dysfunctions with calculation and with the very understanding of numbers, were seen as separate from difficulties with other areas of Mathematics, and often more severe and more widespread. It is difficult to provide a precise definition that distinguishes comprehensively between arithmetic and Mathematics – but evidently there are distinctions that are clear enough in teachers' minds to see difficulties in the two areas as separate phenomena.

The profiles of identified pupils confirmed the existence of these difficulties specific to Mathematics, suggesting not a unitary phenomenon but the kind of variable, multi-factor syndrome that we expect with dyslexic learners. Performance patterns and descriptions confirmed that while different kinds of difficulties may often overlap and interpenetrate they may too exist independently: for example, pupils may have specific difficulties in language alone, in language and Mathematics, or in Mathematics alone. While the project did not seek to quantify incidence, the data gave the impression of a relatively low level of incidence.

Throughout, there was a pervasive sense that these difficulties relate to pupil attributes that are relatively fixed – as with dyslexia there was a sense that specific difficulties with Mathematics tend to be relatively intransigent and inherent features of the pupil's profile as a learner of Mathematics. They might be lessened or coped with – but probably they will not be eradicated.

Given the picture that emerged it was not easy to be optimistic that provision currently available in schools could maximise the mathematical potential of these pupils. There was a strong sense that individualised schemes had been developed quite rigorously and effectively as the only means of curriculum delivery that might hold out hope – but that even at their best, it would be hard for them to provide adequately for pupils with specific difficulties in Mathematics.

IMPLICATIONS FOR OUR CURRICULUM PHILOSOPHY

The project claimed access to no objective realities – only to those insights to be gained from accessing the extended experience and understanding of teachers. These were, however, felt to be of considerable ecological validity: teachers alone, among all other education professionals, have an intimate and continuous experience of both the delivery of the curriculum and the ways in which pupils respond to it. Their views should carry some weight.

The views gathered during this project, expressed in the quite extensive interviews, left an abiding impression of measured pessimism: teachers saw these difficulties as enduring and unlikely to be righted easily. Such a view has curriculum implications: where difficulties seem deeply rooted and intransigent, be they specific or otherwise, then our emphasis upon common curricular goals for the whole mainstream population may need some reconsideration. While the views emerged from the consideration of specific difficulties in Mathematics, it seems likely that their implications apply equally to specific difficulties of other kinds too. It may be that, for a small number of pupils under some circumstances, two of our most important current curriculum orthodoxies may be unhelpful. Both are valid and both have been powerful agents for beneficial change. But both have limits beyond which they become unhelpful.

The first concerns the concept of a continuum of difficulty. Since Warnock (DES, 1978) it has been argued, with good effect and for obvious reasons, that it is unhelpful to categorise and label. Instead, we think of difficulties as lying along a continuum, from the very severe to the less severe. The Specific Mathematics Difficulties project demonstrated, however, something long apparent to those concerned with dyslexic-type difficulties: that there is no single continuum; that serious intellectual difficulties in one or more areas may be balanced by adequacy or even excellence in others. A single continuum can in no way represent this – it seems likely that for these learners, and perhaps others to a lesser extent, a complex mesh of overlapping continua would be needed. Such a model becomes too complex; and whatever the dangers of labelling, the right label, at the right place, may allow a very real difficulty to be identified and responded to.

The second and related concept is that of the curriculum-deficit model of learning difficulties. Like Warnock's continuum it has been a powerful and helpful concept. Its implication, that all pupils are able to move in the same direction, albeit at different speeds and by differing pathways, has allowed positive and responsive curriculum development with effective and realistic differentiation. The notion of an intellectual ceiling is rejected, as is the idea that some pupils need to be extracted – removed from their peers and provided with experiences that are essentially different in some respects. It also has been a powerful agent for change. But taken too far it too can become, for probably a small number of learners, thoroughly counter-productive. Where learning difficulties are both specific and severe, it may sometimes be necessary to adapt and modify the curriculum, to divert sometimes from the mainstream direction. We have learned to be suspicious of a pupil-deficit model of difficulties, usually rightly so – but if 'pupil-deficit' means to take as the starting point the pupil and his difficulty, then for these pupils that may sometimes be the only way forward.

Any change, however, needs to be undertaken with great care – these curriculum orthodoxies have been powerfully successful and have succeeded in diminishing the ill-effects of institutional labelling and segregation. But both can become absurd if taken to an extreme for which they were not designed.

There are no alternatives that are immediately obvious. The ideal of extended one-to-one tuition is not a realistic option; nor would extended extraction be helpful or appropriate.

The challenge is to find ways of building upon the hard-won strengths and advantages of our current provision while developing, at the same time, an organisational and curricular flexibility where it is needed.

Where there are serious specific difficulties, then certainly it does seem that it is needed.

REFERENCES

Allardyce, B., Ginsburg, H. (1983). 'Children's Psychological Difficulties in Mathematics' in *The Development of Mathematical Thinking*. Ginsburg, H., (Ed.). Academic Press.

Ausubel, D. (1968). *Educational Psychology: A Cognitive View.* Holt, Rhinehart & Winston.

Badian, N. A. (1983). 'Dyscalculia and non-verbal disorders in learning' in Myclebust, H. R., (Ed.) *Progress in Learning Disabilities,* Vol. 5, New York.

Bley, N. S., Thornton, C. A. (1981). Teaching *Mathematics to the Learning Disabled.* Aspen Systems Corporation.

Carpenter, T. P., Moser, J. M., Bebouth, C. (1988). *Representation of Addition and Subtraction Word Problems,* Journal for Research in Mathematical Education 19 (4) 345-357.

Chinn, S. J. (1992). 'Individual Diagnosis and Cognitive Syle' in Miles, T. R., Miles, E., (Eds.) *Dyslexia and Mathematics.* London, Routledge.

Choat, E. (1978). *Children's Acquisition of Mathematics,* NFER.

Cockcroft, W. H. (1982). *Mathematics Counts,* HMSO, London.

Critchley, M. (1970). *The Dyslexic Child.* London, Heinemann.

DeLoche, G., Seron, X. (Eds.) (1987). *Mathematical Disabilities: a Cognitive Neuropsychological Perspective.* Hillsdale, N.J. Erlbaum.

Department of Education and Science (1978). *Special Educational Needs* (The Warnock Report). London, HMSO.

Desforges, C., Cockburn, A. (1987). *Understanding the Mathematics Teacher.* Falmer.

Dickson, L., Brown, M., Gibson, O. (1984). *Children Learning Mathematics.* Schools Council Publications.

Farnham-Diggory, S. (1978). *Learning Disabilities.* London: Fontana/Open Books.

Floyd, A., (Ed.) (1981). *Developing Mathematical Thinking.* Open University Press.

Giles, G. (1981). *School Mathematics under Examination: Part 3, Factors Affecting the Learning of Mathematics,* University of Stirling, Department of Education, DIME Projects.

Ginsburg, H. P. (1977). *Children's arithmetic: how they learn it and how you teach it.* Austin, TX:PRO-ED, 1982.

Gonzalez, E. G., Kolers, P. A. (1987). 'Notational Constraints on Mental Operations' in DeLoche, G., Seron, X. (Eds.). *Mathematical Disabilities: a Cognitive Neuropsychological Perspective.* Hillsdale, N.J. Erlbaum.

Hartje, W. (1987). 'The Effect of Spatial Disorders on Arithmetical Skills' in DeLoche, G., Seron, X. (Eds.). *Mathematic Disabilities: a Cognitive Neuropsychological Perspective.* Hillsdale, N. J. Erlbaum.

Harvey, R., Kerslake, D., Shuard, H., Torbe, M. (1982). *Language Teaching and Learning: 6 Mathematics.* Ward Lock Educational.

Hiebert, J. (Ed.). (1986). *Conceptual and Procedural Knowledge: The Case of Mathematics.* Lawrence Erlbaum Associates.

Joffe, L. (1980). *Dyslexia and Attainment in School Mathematics: Part 1.* Dyslexia Review, Vol. 3, 1 Summer.

Joffe, L. (1980). *Dyslexia and Attainment in School Mathematics: Part 2,* Dyslexia Review, Vol. 3, 2 Winter.

Joffe, L. (1990). 'The Mathematical Aspects of Dyslexia: a recap of general issues and some implications for teaching,' *Links,* Vol. 15, No. 2. Spring 1990.

Kosc, L. (1986). *Developmental Dyscalculia,* Journal of Learning Disabilities, 7,3, 164-77.

Kosc, L. (1986). 'Dyscalculia – a special issue on the work of Dr. Ladislav Kosc' in *Focus on Learning Problems in Mathematics,* Summer/Fall 1986, Vol. 8, Nos. 3 and 4.

Krutetskii, V. A. (1976). *The psychology of mathematical abilities in schoolchildren.* University of Chicago Press.

Lansdown, R. (1978). *Retardation in Mathematics: a consideration of multi-factorial determinant,* Developmental Medicine and Child Neurology 20.

Larcombe, T. (1985) *Mathematical Learning Difficulties in the Secondary School.* OUP, Milton Keynes.

Lewis, C., Hitch, G., Walker, P. (unpublished at time of printing). *The Prevalence of Specific Arithmetic Deficits and Arithmetic-and-Reading Deficits in 9-10 year-olds.* University of Lancaster and Lancaster Polytechnic.

Liebeck, P. (1984). *How Children Learn Mathematics.* Penguin.

Lumb, D. (1987). *Teaching Mathematics 5 to 11.* Croom Helm.

McCloskey, M., Caramazza, A. (1987). 'Cognitive Mechanisms in Normal and Impaired Number Processing' in DeLoche, G., Seron, X. (Eds.) *Mathematical Disabilities: a Cognitive Neuropsychological Perspective.* Hillsdale, N.J. Erlbaum.

Myklebust, H. R., Johnson, D. (1962). 'Dyslexia in Children,' *Exceptional Children 29, 14-25.*

Newton, M. J., Thomson, M. E., Richards, I. L. (1979). *Readings in Dyslexia,* Wisbech: Learning Development Aids.

Nisbet, J., Shucksmit, J. (1984). *The Seventh Sense,* SCRE, Edinburgh, (1987). *Learning Mathematics: Issues, Theory and Classroom Practice.* Cassell.

Pask, G. (1976). 'Styles and Strategies of Learning,' *British Journal of Educational Psychology,* 46, 128-148.

Plunkett, S. (1979). 'Decomposition and all that rot,' *Mathematics in Schools* 8, (3), 2-5.

Polya, G. (1957). *How to solve it.* Doubleday Anchor.

Pritchard, R. A., Miles, T. R., Chinn, S. J., Taggart, A. T. (1989). 'Dyslexia and Knowledge of Number Facts,' *Links,* Vol.14, No. 3, Summer 89.

Rourke, B .P., Finlayson, M. A. J. (1978). 'Neuropsychological Significance of Variations in Patterns of Academic Performance: Verbal and Visuo-Spatial Abilities', *Journal of Abnormal Child Psychology,* 6, 121-123.

Rourke, B. P., Finlayson, M. A. J. (1978). 'Neuropsychological Significance of Variations in Patterns of Academic Performance: Motor, Psychomotor and Tactile-perceptual Abilities', *Journal of Paediatric Psychology,* 3, 62-66.

Rourke, B. P., Strang, J. D. (1983). 'Subtypes of Reading and Arithmetic Disabilities: A Neuropsychological Analysis' in Rutter, M. (Ed.) *Developmental Neuropsychiatry.* New York, Guildford Press.

Rutter, M., Yule, W., Tizard, J., Graham, P. (1966). 'Severe reading retardation: its relationship to maladjustment, epilepsy and neurological disorders' in *What is Special Education? Association for Special Education,* pp. 280-94.

Schaeffer, B., Eggleston, V. H., Scott, J. L. (1974). 'Number development in young children', *Cognitive Psychology,* 6, 357-379.

Share, D. L., Moffitt, T. E., Silva, P.A. (1988). 'Factors associated with arithmetic-and-reading disability and specific arithmetic disability' *Journal of Learning Disabilities,* 21, 313-320.

Sharma, M. C. (1979). 'Children at risk for disabilities in Mathematics,' *Focus on Learning Problems in Mathematics,* Vol. 1, (2), 63-64.

Sharma, M. C. (1986). 'Dyscalculia and other Learning Problems in Arithmetic: a Historical Perspective' in *Focus on Learning Problems in Mathematics.* Summer/Fall 1986, Vol. 8, Nos. 3 and 4.

Sharma, M. C., Loveles, E. J, (Eds.) (1986). 'Dyscalculia – a special issue on the work of Dr Ladislav Kosc' in *Focus on Learning Problems in Mathematics.* Summer/Fall 1986, Vol. 8, Nos. 3 and 4.

Shuard, H., Rothery, A. (Eds) (1984). *Children Reading Mathematics.* John Murray.

Skemp, R. R. (1971). *The Psychology of Learning Mathematics.* Penguin Books.

Spiers, P. A. (1987). 'Acalculia Revisited: Current Issues' in DeLoche, G., Seron, X. (Eds.) *Mathematical Disabilities: a Cognitive Neuropsychological Perspective.* Hillsdale, N.J. Erlbaum.

Sutherland, P. (1988) 'Dyscalculia, Acalculia, Dysgraphia or Plain Innumerate? – a brief survey of the literature' *Journal of the Education Section of the British Psychological Society,* Vol. 12, No. 1.

Suydam, M. N., Weaver J. F. (1977). 'Research on Problem Solving: Implications for Elementary School Classrooms' *The Arithmetic Teacher,* 25 (2), 40-42.

Tansley, P., Panckhurst, J. (1981). *Children with Specific Learning Difficulties.* NFER Publishing Company.

Weedon, C. (1992). *Specific Learning Difficulties in Mathematics.* Report to the SOED, University of Stirling and Tayside Region.

Weinstein, M. L. (1980). 'A neuropsychological approach to Mathematics disabilities' in *Learning Disabilities: old dogmas – new directions,* (Update 1980). Boston University School of Medicine.

Wheatly, G. H. (1977). 'The right hemisphere's role in problem solving,' *Arithmetic Teacher* 25, (2), 37-38.

HOW TO BUILD A MATHS PROFILE OF THE DYSLEXIC STUDENT

ELIZABETH MACKENZIE

Over the last few years there has been increasing demand for numeracy lessons for dyslexics. My method of dealing with this situation has grown out of two things:

- My knowledge of nine years teaching literacy to dyslexic students using a cumulative, structured, multi-sensory approach.
- A course in Oxford with Mahesh Sharma. He is a Professor of Maths Education at Cambridge College, Massachusetts, USA, who has been very successful in teaching maths to dyslexics.

DO ALL DYSLEXIC PEOPLE HAVE DIFFICULTY WITH MATHEMATICS?

No – some dyslexics can become outstanding mathematicians.

Why? Some have an intuitive sense of numbers which they don't have for letters; some have very good visual and spatial skills.

However, data collected over 22 years of psychological assessment at the Dyslexia Institute indicates that about 60% of identified dyslexics have specific learning difficulties with maths. (See also Joffe's study of Mathematics Performance, 1980).

If one were to look at these *specific learning difficulties*, the implications that arise for the learning of maths would include the following . . .

Working Memory. Most dyslexics have inefficient working memory skills which can be auditory, visual or both. This will cause difficulty with:

- The learning of tables – give them a table square. (If some tables need to be learned then aim for 2, 3, 5 and 10 tables only.)
- The learning of number bonds—give them a number line, plus five minutes of number bond activities/games, every lesson.

- The learning of formulae – devise strategies for remembering, e.g. mnemonics . . . which can be pictorial or in cartoon or story form, or be funny or rude. Some dyslexics are excellent at drawing.

Research shows that not only are dyslexics slower at putting things into memory, they are slower at 'clearing' their memory 'shelf', in which case you can find 'perseveration' – a strange numeral popping up, perhaps, still stored from a previous sum.

If your dyslexic has, at any one time an auditory memory 'shelf' for holding only three or four items of information, the chances of doing the correct homework are slim; on the day you give it out orally as five items of information, e.g.:–

The So and So Maths Book,	pl7	chapter 5	3rd column	Nos 6-16
1st item	*2nd item*	*3rd item*	*4th item*	*5th item*

Visual Perception. The inter-connection between the eye and the brain is not accurate with some dyslexics.

They may see **2**, and write **5**.
They may see **6**, and say **9**.
They may see **E**, and write **3**.
They may see plus: '**+**', but write times: '**x**'.

Auditory Perception. Here problems can arise if dyslexics think you have said eighty and you have actually said eighteen, or one for none, or four for more, or seven for eleven. There may be problems with order of mention, i.e. you say *seven*teen, and they write seven . . . and then one. Or you say subtract nineteen from 84 and they write 19 – 84.

Slower than average speed of information processing. When most of the class is on question nine, a dyslexic may still be working through question six. He may get less work completed and as a result may get much less practice with numerical processes – this latter being vital if one has the poor working memory of a dyslexic.

Limited Attention Span. It is important to continually switch information processing channels between visual, auditory, kinaesthetic and visual, thus keeping concentration at the optimum level whilst still working on the same teaching point.

Poor Fine-Motor Control. Sometimes the handwriting and presentation of a dyslexic's work might resemble what we would produce writing with our feet, not our hands. And the effort with our feet would be as great as that for some dyslexics using their hands. Always give them squared paper, because this gives them a grid to align onto, and will help with keeping numbers in the correct order and in the correct columns.

Sequencing and Laterality. Dyslexics have great problems in remembering the correct sequence of the days of the week or the months of the year or the seasons, or tables or what comes after ninety-nine, or before 200. They find it hard to count backwards. Reading lines of words require you to scan from left to right and sometimes scanning from left to right is also needed in maths:

$$3 + 4 + 7 \quad =$$
$$21 - 7 \quad =$$
$$3 \times 2 \times 1 \quad =$$

. . . but in the following sums you are required to scan from right to left:

$$\begin{array}{ccc} 347 & 217 & 321 \\ +743 & -172 & \times 32 \\ \hline \end{array}$$

Problems of **remembering** the **sequence** and the **direction** of a sum makes life so much harder for a dyslexic who has difficulty with all of these.

HOW TO GET TO GRIPS WITH THE PROBLEM

First you need to *build up a profile of your student.* Why?

I consider assessment to be a vital prerequisite to teaching because it helps me to arrive at a point from which to start.

Bearing in mind that all dyslexics vary in:
* The range of cognitive strengths and weaknesses they bring to every mathematical task.
* The amount of numerical knowledge they are able to retain from previous teaching.
* The particular stages of mathematical concepts they are operating at.
* The degree of difficulty they are experiencing with maths.
* The attitude to maths and the motivation to want to learn maths.

I need to test the following in order to begin teaching from a known point – teaching that will be cumulative, structured and multi-sensory, but above all targeted to a specific dyslexic's needs.

A test of the student's:
- Level of maths achievement.
- Maths learning personality.
- Level of maths learning vocabulary/language.
- Visual and auditory memory shelves for numbers.
- 'Level of knowing' of mathematical concepts.

LEVEL OF MATHS ACHIEVEMENT

There are several tests available that will show up your student's level of maths achievement. Choose one that you as a teacher have confidence in and trust the scoring. I use the WRAT-3 maths test (Wide Range Achievement Test) as does Sharma, but the Gillham and Hesse maths test and Steve Chinn's Math's Inventory can also be used.

From these kinds of tests you can begin to pick out your student's ability to get some sums correct (and into memory); you can analyse his errors; and you can make note of his failure to comprehend certain maths concepts. You may also obtain a 'mathematical age' that can be compared with his chronological age in the same manner as a reading age.

MATHS LEARNING PERSONALITY

We all process maths information differently and uniquely. The difference defines the way we learn maths.

One way to find out how we individually process information is to administer the Rey-Osterreith Complex Figure test. This is a perceptive, visuo-motor test that has been widely used in the research of developmental dyscalculia.

Firstly, you are required to copy the figure from a model and thereafter to draw it from memory, three more times, at different intervals of time.

The figure is constructed in such a way that it requires only a minimum of graphic skills. Each detail is easily reproduced in isolation and the task is only to compose the details into the structured whole. The results are marked and then evaluated (see example in the case study below).

The test will determine whether you are a qualitative (whole to parts) or a quantitative (parts to whole) learner.

Children usually start school qualitatively (holistically) but often we, as teachers soon teach a quantitative (step by step) approach and most children learn to adopt this pattern. Children with specific learning difficulties/dyslexia often fail to learn this adaptive style.

A good mathematician needs to be flexible in both styles. A good teacher of maths needs to be flexible in both styles. A good teacher of dyslexics needs to remember that if the pupil can't learn the way he/she teaches, can he/she teach the way the pupil learns?

Quantitative or qualitative or somewhere in between?

Sharma suggests that most personalities lie on a continuum between the two extremes.

As a result of the Rey Osterreith Complex Figure Test, you can decide on the following:

- How will the pupil learn? (The quantitative learner when given the sum $3 + 4 + 7 + 6 + 8 =$ might start on the left and add up number by number in the order given. The qualitative learner is more likely to overview and pick out patterns e.g. link 3 with 7 or 6 with 4 or pick out 6, 7, 8 as equivalent to three sevens.)
- How will he receive the teacher if her style is different from his?
- Are there visuo-motor problems?

The scoring of the Rey-Osterreith Test will also reveal further implications for learning.

- If the score on the second drawing is lower than that on the first, then there is a short-term memory and processing deficit.
- If the third drawing equals the score of the second, then the working memory is good.
- If the fourth drawing is very different from the second or third drawings, there is a long-term memory problem.
- If the fourth drawing equals the score of the third, then the long term memory is good.

- If the fourth drawing reveals original details previously omitted in other drawings then the pupil has a good reflective memory. The important implication of this is that the *pupil will take longer* to answer (usually correctly) in a test.

LEVEL OF MATHS VOCABULARY/LANGUAGE

Maths thinking to a great extent, is dependent on mathematical language. Maths is a second language and therefore needs to be taught as such.

If you think in a language you learn it.

As you think in it, your 'thinking skills' develop.

e.g. 7 - 4 = C What does this mean?
Write a number story for it. (e.g. *I bought seven apples and ate four, how many are left?*)
Tell the story another way, etc.

To test for maths vocabulary, administer a 'Maths language inventory' i.e., devise a list of 100 mathematical terms/words that a child of a certain age in your class *should* know.

The child needs to score 80% for his age range. If less than 80% is known then vocabulary may be a contributory factor to his mathematical difficulty.

Do be sure that the pupil understands what you are asking.

For example, when a pupil was asked if he knew what a degree was, he answered 'yes, it's a small circle.' The questioner, unsure if the pupil was on the right track said 'show me what twenty degrees look like.' The pupil drew:

I have also had the answer – an award you got from university! For 'area' I have had the answer – the countryside. For 'product' – things like butter and cheese. For division – a part of the Football League.

I have found that giving 'memory prompt cards' is an extremely successful way of fixing maths vocabulary.

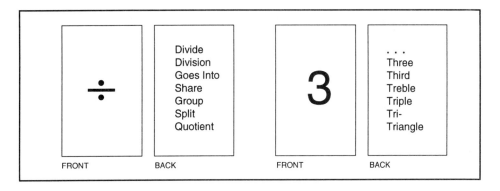

These cards need to be practised every night, to facilitate the transition from short-term memory into long-term memory. The student looks at the front of the card, says all the vocabulary on the back of the card (vocabulary necessary for his age range and therefore always being added to) before turning over to check that he is correct. The exercise in reverse is also important, i.e. if the adult says write the sign that means . . .

- Quotient the student writes +
- Product the student writes x
- Decrease the student writes −

VISUAL AND AUDITORY MEMORY SHELVES

How good is your auditory memory for numbers? Get a friend to say a string of numbers or give a mathematical calculation involving between four to eight numerals. Can you give these numbers back in the correct order of mention? Can you do so in reverse?

Where you faltered was the limit of your auditory memory shelf. If it was at five numerals you must strive for six next time. Remember that memory is like a muscle: it will improve with use. With practice, you or your dyslexic pupil can extend the auditory memory shelf. Memory skills need to be taught. Too often they are not.

Visual memory can be extended through the use of mnemonics. When I asked one of my students to remember the following calculation: $8024+1058+5390=$? (sixteen items of information) he was able to do so by applying the following strategy:

A spider with eight legs 8
ran over to a cushion 0
on which sat a man with 2 arms 2
who sat on a chair with 4 legs 4
Plus...+
He had 10 green bottles............................10
5 had pictures of spiders on them 58
Plus...+
Five had pictures of triangles....................53
He saw them on the 9 o'clock news...........90
What is that equal to? ....=

This particular student used the following code to remember numbers. In working out the properties of the numbers, he began to overcome one aspect of his very real 'maths phobia'—numbers became something concrete and began to be fun.

0 – head, cushion, splat!
1 – yourself (unique), the winner
2 – eyes, ears, (boobs)
3 – prongs (fork), triangle
4 – square-choc bar, playground
5 – fingers, toes
6 – eggs
7 – days of the week
8 – octopus, spider
9 – o'clock news
10 – green bottles!

'LEVEL OF KNOWING' OF MATHS CONCEPTS

As I mentioned previously, some dyslexics have an intuitive knowledge of maths – coming up with the correct answer but are often unable to show their *workings*. With each of your dyslexic students you need to discover at which level of knowing different maths concepts he is operating. Is he at the concrete or pictorial or abstract stages of knowing?

A brief description of each 'level of knowing' is given below:–

Intuitive: A child connects new concepts to those known. Start at intuitive level and teach at a level higher than the one being tested.
Concrete: If concrete materials are removed and the child cannot perform then the child is at this level.
Pictorial or Representational: If the child cannot do without a picture of a diagram they are limited to this level.
Abstract: The child can deal with symbols. Most teaching begins here although some children are not at this developmental stage.

CONCRETE OPERATIONAL REASONING TEST: EXAMPLES

Two motorcycle riders are racing each other in a field towards a small bush. They start at the same time and arrive at the same time. The rider on the first cycle followed the path shown by the solid line, while the second rider moved along the path shown by the dashes.

START

BUSH

Say which is the true statement:
1.   The rider on the path shown by the solid line had a higher speed.
2.   The rider on the path shown by the dashes had a higher speed.
3.   The two riders had equal speeds.
4.   Impossible to say.

A person using two different kinds of matchstick builds two roads as shown following:

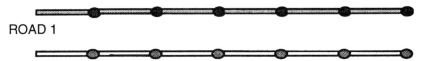

ROAD 1

ROAD 2
Suppose road 1 is left as it is, while Road 2 is changed into a zig-zag pattern as shown below:

ROAD 1

ROAD 2
Which of these statements is true for an ant walking from end to end after Road 2 is changed?

1.   Road 1 is longer for the ant.
2.   Road 2 is longer for the ant.
3.   Road 1 and 2 are the same length for the ant.
4.   Impossible to say.

Application: The child can apply maths concepts to the real world.
Communication: The child can give reasoning for methods and procedures.

I therefore first administer the Concrete Operational Reasoning Test, followed by the Logical Reasoning Test. The Concrete Operational Test is Professor Sharma's test of cognitive tasks where you teach no strategies but note how the task is done. The questions deal with:

- Conservation of number.
- Conservation of weight.
- Conservation of length.
- Conservation of area.
- Conservation of volume.

Other tests involve classification, spatial orientation, transitivity and the identification of variables.

Here are two examples of Professor Sharma's questions on the conservation of length, and two examples from his Logical-Reasoning Test.

LOGICAL REASONING TEST

In the diagram following, the line **XYZ** represents a wall. A ball is thrown at the wall so that it always hits at point **Y**. Angle **1** equals angle **6**, angle **2** equals angle **5** and angle **3** equals angle **4**.

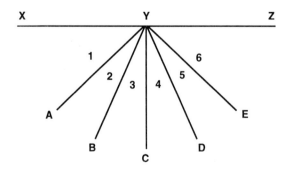

If a ball bounces from point Y to point B it must have been thrown from:

a) point **A**   b) point **B**   c) point **C**   d) point **D**   e) point **E**

LOGICAL REASONING TEST: IS TO . . . AS . . . IS TO

Lightbulb **is to**	(a) switch	**as**	(e) engine	**is to**	(i) boat
	(b) wire		(f) canoe		(j) engine
	(c) socket		(g) motor		(k) tractor
	(d) electricity		(h) stream		(l) paddle

(a) walk **is to**	*body*	**as**	*wheel*	**is to**	(e) roll
(b) toe					(f) machine
(c) knee					(g) bicycle
(d) foot					(h) spokes

(a) cow **is to**	*flock*	**as**	(e) soldier	**is to**	(i) bee
(b) horse			(f) swarm		(j) pig
(c) sheep			(g) pack		(k) regiment
(d) foot			(h) litter		(l) wolf

(a) brain **is to**	*head*	**as**	(e) spring	**is to**	(i) bedpost
(b) eye			(f) blanket		(j) ticking
(c) hat			(g) caster		(k) bed
(d) ear			(h) pillow		(l) summer

(a) music **is to**	*piano*	as	(e) chair	**is to**	*table*
(b) house			(f) leg		. . .
(c) stool			(g) eat		. . .
(d) tuner			(h) furniture		. . .

RESULT OF CONCRETE OPERATIONAL REASONING TEST

24 + correct	Completed concrete operational stage.
18 +	Cognitive development equivalent to a 10 year level.
10+	Functioning at eight year level of cognition.
Less than 10	He is in transition between the pre-operation stage and concrete operational stage i.e. functioning at lower than seven years of cognition.

If on each group (three questions on each concept and six on spatial orientation), three are correct, then that concept has been learned but if only two out of three are correct, then concrete experiences are still required.

Having completed all the above tests it is important to show the results in a report.

Here is a sample report on John H–, who is eleven years old.

JOHN H–'S ASSESSMENT

John H– is an eleven year old with a specific learning difficulty. With specialist tuition he has been successfully improving his literacy skills, but is having difficulty with his numeracy skills.

In his educational psychological assessment, he was found to be weak in visual memory and sequencing as well as in auditory memory and sequencing. These weaknesses will have quite an effect on his numeracy skills.

I carried out a series of tests in order to determine John's potential in learning mathematics, his mathematics learning style and his level of maths achievement. Thus, I hoped to provide remedial teaching suited to his specific needs.

MATHEMATICAL PERFORMANCE

John has quite a good understanding of basic number-line concepts and bonds. He is proud of his ability to do all his tables and to be able to tell the time. These are excellent achievements and all credit must go to John (and his mum!)

On the **Wide Range Achievement Test** I found John to be confident, speedy and correct in the oral part of the test. In the written part, his confidence was noticeably reduced. He misread a plus sign for a minus sign and correctly subtracted instead of adding. He panicked at H-T-U addition saying that it looked too hard, but proceeded to add correctly, but from *left* to *right*! He could not cope with remainders in the division sums, so he left them out.

His scores came out at the beginning of the 9 year level, which is lower than his chronological age.

COGNITIVE ASPECT

On the **Concrete Operation Reasoning Test** John H–'s performance on most of the activities indicated that he is operating at the beginning of the concrete stage, at only the 8 year level of cognition. This then is another of the reasons for his maths difficulty.

Breaking down the test into its sub-skills, I found that John has full marks for all the questions on conservation of number. This is a prerequisite skill for all numerical operations.

On conservation of area, length, volume and weight, John still requires concrete experiences. He also requires more practice in spatial orientation and organisation (games like Othello, Connect 4, etc. are useful for this.)

He failed to get any marks for the questions on identification of variables and relationships which is a pre-skill for abstract concepts and usually comes around eleven to twelve years of age.

MATHS LEARNING PERSONALITY

The results of the **Rey-Osterreith Complex Figure Test** would indicate that John has a qualitative approach to learning – i.e. a 'whole to parts' approach – and also has some problems with his long term visual memory.

Qualitative learners do better on geometrical concepts and the application aspects of Mathematics. They may have difficulty in following sequential procedures and they make, on the average, more careless mistakes than the quantitatively-oriented student. However, the learning of maths involves both quantitative and qualitative approaches so the elements of both types of learning styles need to be taught and integrated.

MATHS LANGUAGE

I administered the Mathematics Vocabulary Inventory and found that John scored less than 80% for his age, thus indicating mathematical vocabulary may be a contributory factor to his maths difficulties. As mathematical thinking is dependent on maths language to a great extent, it is important that John comes to grips with it as soon as possible. *This then will be my first priority in teaching provision.*

SUGGESTIONS AND RECOMMENDATIONS

- John H – is able to embark on a cumulative, structured, multi-sensory teaching programme that should include concrete experiences of conservation of length, area, volume and weight.
- He should be encouraged to play games that involve spatial orientation (Othello, chess, etc.) and to discuss the strategies involved. He needs to think about the reasoning behind certain moves.

- He should start a daily routine as described below. This will, in turn, give him the confidence to deal with addition, subtraction, multiplication and division sums of increasing difficulty. He needs at all times to learn to link facts and make explicit their relationships.

ACTIVITIES TO INCLUDE DAILY IN THE TEACHING PROGRAMME

- **Count** forwards, backwards, and by skipping numbers. Begin with simple numbers and proceed with numbers appropriate to the student's level. Approximately two to four minutes at first, then five minutes.
- **Try some oral number facts** (See Sharma's sample Arithmetic Fact Sheet, page 271). Just one page to start with, for approximately four to six minutes, building up to five to ten minutes.
- **Visualisation.** Begin with simple examples from the pupil's environment and proceed to mathematical problems.
- **Play a Game**. There are a lot of very good commercial games, such as Othello, Pass the Pigs, Four in a line, etc. Try to find some time to make sure you discuss the strategies that the pupil is using in the game, always asking the reason for certain moves and strategies, when the game is over.
- **Complete** one addition and one multiplication grid using the random process (e.g. complete every third box). Determine the response time for each table.
- **Auditory and Visual** sequential memory exercises with numbers can be useful.
- **Vocabulary 'Prompt Cards'**—practise, review and update.
- **'Fun Exercises'** involving logical reasoning—I like Critical Thinking Activities from Blackline Masters (Grades 4 to 6).
- **Follow up** any schoolwork, to either give more practice or a chance to talk things through for better understanding.
- **Estimation**. Begin with simple arithmetical operations of addition, subtraction, etc., at the pupils mathematical level. Approximately five to ten minutes.
- **Introduce a mathematical concept.** Develop related pre-skills and primary concepts, present concrete model of the concept, record and represent the concept on paper, help the pupil in the verbalisation of the learned concept in the written form of computation, review of the concept learned, application of the concept learned.

ADDITION FACT SHEET

The objective of the following activity is to develop the arithmetic facts but more importantly to help the child see the number of relationships and number patterns.

2+2=	42	92	52	72	32	62	82	12
	+2	+2	+2	+2	+2	+2	+2	+2
6+6=	46	96	56	76	36	66	86	16
	+6	+6	+6	+6	+6	+6	+6	+6
5+5=	45	95	55	75	35	65	85	15
	+5	+5	+5	+5	+5	+5	+5	+5
8+8=	48	98	58	78	38	68	88	18
	+8	+8	+8	+8	+8	+8	+8	+8
4+4=	44	94	54	74	34	64	84	14
	+4	+4	+4	+4	+4	+4	+4	+4
7+7=	47	97	57	77	37	67	87	17
	+7	+7	+7	+7	+7	+7	+7	+7
3+3=	43	93	53	73	33	63	83	13
	+3	+3	+3	+3	+3	+3	+3	+3
9+9=	49	93	59	79	39	69	89	19
	+9	+9	+9	+9	+9	+9	+9	+9

ADDITION

+	1	2	3	4	5	6	7	8	9	10
1	2	3	4	5	?	?	?			
2										
3										
4										
5										
6										
7										
8										
9										
10										

MULTIPLICATION

x1	1	2	3	4	5	6	7	8	9	10
1			3			6			9	
2		4			10			16		
3	?			?			?			?
4										
5										
6										
7										
8										
9										
10										

Addition and multiplication grids after Sharma.

Finally I sum up the factors affecting a child's ability to learn maths in the following table:

FACTORS AFFECTING A CHILD'S ABILITY TO LEARN MATHS

1. Cognitive

2. Mathematics learning personality:

Quantitative   *Qualitative*

3. Prerequisite and support skills
    a. Ability to follow sequential tasks
    b. Spatial orientation/organisation
    c. Pattern recognition
    d. Visualisation
    e. Estimation
    f. Deductive reasoning
    g. Inductive reasoning

4. Language of maths
    a. Linguistic
    b. Conceptual
    c. Skill of Process

5. Levels of knowledge
    a. Intuitive
    b. Concrete
    c. Pictorial/Representational
    d. Abstract
    e. Applications
    f. Communications

BIBLIOGRAPHY

Journals

Focus on Learning Problems in Mathematics. Centre for Teaching/Learning of Mathematics, PO. Box 3149, Framingham, MA 01701, USA

Math Notebook. Centre for Teaching/Learning of Mathematics, PO. Box 3149, Framingham, MA 01701, USA.

Dyslexia Review, Volume 3, 1980, 'Dyslexia and Attainment in School Mathematics' Part 1, Summer, Part 2, Winter, by L. Joffe.

Videos

The Teaching and Learning of Mathematics. Mahesh Sharma. Produced by Oxford Polytechnic. (Now Oxford Brookes University.) Available from Mrs P. Brazil, The Warren, Mapledurham, Reading, RG4 7TQ, UK. (All requests about Professor Sharma and his work should also be addressed to Mrs Brazil.)

Tests

Basic Number Screening Test (1987). Gillham, W. and Hesse, K., Sevenoaks, Hodder & Stoughton.

Graded Arithmetic – Mathematics Test (1986). Vernon, P. with the assistance of Miller, K. ,Sevenoaks, Hodder and Stoughton.

Mathematics Learning Style Inventory (1993). Chinn, S. J. and Bath, J. B., Belford, Northumberland: Ann Arbor (UK only). To be published.

Profile of Mathematics Skills (1979). France, N. Windsor: NFER-Nelson.

Test of Cognitive Style in Mathematics (1986). Bath, J. B., Chinn, S. J. and Knox, D. E., East Aurora, NY, USA: Slosson.

Test of Early Mathematics Ability (2nd edition) (1990). Ginsburg, H. P. and Baroody, A. J., Pro-Ed (8700 Shoal Creek Boulevard, Austin, TX 787589965).

Wide Range Achievement Test (revised edition) (1984). Jastack, S. J. and Jastack, G. S., Jastack Associates, Inc. (15 Ashley Place, Suite lA, Wilmington DE 19804).

Mathematics 8-12 (1984). National Foundation for Educational Research with Brighouse, A., Godber, D. and Patilla P., Windsor: NFFR-Nelson.

Games and Activities

Bolt, B. (1982). *Mathematical Activities. A resource book for teachers*. Cambridge University Press. 0-521-28518-6. (Also, *More Mathematical Activities*; *Even more Mathematical Activities*; *The Amazing Mathematical Amusement Arcade*).

Burton, L. (1984). *Thinking Things Through. Problem Solving in Mathematics*. Oxford: Blackwell. 0-63 1-1 3 8 1 3 -7

Kirkby, D. has written several books featuring games and activities including:
Starting Games (1993). Glasgow: Collins Educational 0-00312-5548. *More Games* (1993). Glasgow: Collins Educational: 0-00312-5556. *Go Further With Games* (1989) London: Unwin Hyman 0-0444-8099-7. Seymour and Beardlee. *Critical Thinking Abilities in Imagery and Logic, Grades 4-6* 0-86651-440-601815.

DYSLEXIA AND MUSIC NOTATION

EMMA VALLANCE

GENERAL INTRODUCTION

Research into music and dyslexia is a relatively new field of study. Much national attention seems to focus on music therapy projects and the development of tactile notation for the blind. By comparison, and without disputing the immense value of these initiatives, the role of music for dyslexic people is recognised by a mere handful of people.

Nevertheless, literature published and conferences organised during the last few years, suggest an increasing awareness of the difficulties which dyslexics may encounter learning music and especially its notation. With dyslexia, issues of notation and its difficulties, music and its benefits, seem to be entwined. How to unravel these difficulties to increase enjoyment and benefits further, is an obvious goal to strive for.

CLINICAL FACTORS

There is ample evidence to suggest that dyslexia has a neurophysiological basis. Post-mortem examination on the brains of dyslexic individuals has shown extraordinary cell arrangements. A study of the *planum temporale*, part of the surface of the temporal lobes on each side of the brain, has recently been undertaken (Galaburda, 1987). In 75 - 80 % of unselected brains the two plana are asymmetrical. However, in the eight brains of dyslexics examined, there was symmetry. An unusual balance of skills in the dyslexic seems highly likely. For instance, dyslexia is more likely to occur in individuals who are right hemisphere dominant; some have larger right hemispheres than normal. Sometimes functional and structural abnormalities occur in the left hemisphere, especially in the language areas. The following list shows some relevant functions of the two different sides of the brain:

LEFT	**RIGHT**
Language and Speech	Visuo-spatial tasks (non-verbal)
Mathematics, Sequencing	Pattern recognition
Use of symbols	Perception of colour
Analytical processes	Form, images
	Intuitive thinking
Music notation.	Most musical activities; art.

Whilst more scientific evidence is needed to support these claims, it seems appropriate and logical to relate alternative teaching methods (here, regarding music) to processes involving areas of efficient brain function, rather than to possible areas of abnormally and malfunction.

RESEARCH and LITERATURE

Documented research concerning music and dyslexia has a short history:

1983: Music Advisory Service at the Disabled Living Foundation, London, initiated a project exploring effects of dyslexia on reading, writing and performing music.

1987: Music and Dyslexia 'Working Party' formed.

1990: Working Party became part of the British Dyslexia Association (BDA).

1992: 1st 'Music and Dyslexia Conference' organised by BDA in Cambridge.

The *Cambridge Conference Proceedings* (1992) published by the BDA, represent the variety of teaching methods and research projects undertaken during the last few years, to promote an awareness and greater understanding of dyslexia and music. For example, papers covered topics of 'The nature of the difficulties', 'Teaching music to dyslexic children', 'Research at King's College School Cambridge' (and various projects undertaken by the Department of Experimental Psychology, Cambridge University) and 'Provision for dyslexic musicians'. Though other research has been carried out regarding music and dyslexia , the BDA is indeed a centre of much activity and information in this area. Members of its 'Music Working Party' include Violet Brand, a specialist in specific learning difficulties and music; Tim Miles, Professor Emeritus of Psychology, University of Wales; and Margaret Hubicki, former Professor of the Royal Academy of Music,

London. All three have published literature in the field of dyslexia and/or music. Margaret Hubicki's invention of 'Colour Staff' (a set of materials designed to overcome difficulties of music notation) and Helen McLullich's work with colour and chords, are particularly interesting.

Many non-dyslexics struggle with learning music notation. The written form of music combines symbols, words and numbers; together these may seem illogical and confusing. However, for someone with specific learning difficulties, it is even more likely that problems will be encountered. Every dyslexic child has different abilities and difficulties; it is important therefore when learning music to try and decipher the particular aspect(s) which are causing problems. A summary of some of these problems are given in Figure 1.

Fig. 1

Facts about music notation and possible areas of difficulty:

FACTS	**DIFFICULTIES**
1. **ALPHABET** Note pitches named after letters of alphabet, A-G	Coping with the same letters that are causing difficulties with literacy skills. Sequencing of alphabet and therefore of note names. e.g. Notes A-G but also Notes G-A *up* a scale.
2. **CLEFS** Notes of the same lines/spaces stave represent different notes when using different clefs.	Coping with a different clef.
3. **DIRECTION** Right hand side of keyboard = HIGH notes Left hand side of keyboard = LOW notes But, HIGH pitch = note at TOP of music stave LOW pitch = BOTTOM of music stave. Chords represented VERTICALLY against time represented HORIZONTALLY	Connecting these concepts. Remembering left hand from right hand etc. Eye movements along/ up/down page

4.	**BLACK/WHITE NOTES**	
	Black/white keys on piano/keyboard and Black/white representation of rhythmic values	
5.	**LANGUAGE**	
	Speed and style of a particular piece often in foreign language, esp. Italian	Memory. Confusion with other symbols when dynamics abbrev. to *f* etc.
	Words with ambiguous meaning in/out of musical context. E.g. notes, pitch, sharp, flat, key, up, down, 'piano,' etc.	
6.	**OTHER SYMBOLS**	
	Note values, rests, slurs, ties, staccato, dots, fingering, labelling strings, etc.	Added strain on memory

The rest of this chapter describes a 'Music in the Community' research project undertaken by the author focusing on dyslexic children in a large secondary school in Edinburgh.

Several dyslexic first year pupils were invited to take part in the Community project. Three twelve-year -olds showed a particular interest and agreed to attend the extra-curricular music sessions throughout the Spring term. Sessions were held in school on a one-to-one basis for 40-60 minutes each week. The aims of the project were:

- To enable each child to benefit more fully from the enjoyment and satisfaction of music, in a way most appropriate to their interests and needs.

- To progress school work in areas of learning the keyboard and understanding music notation

- To implement, devise or adapt alternative methods of learning, where appropriate.

- To assess the value of any alternative approaches undertaken.

The methods used to achieve these aims included:

- One-to-one tuition to assess specific areas of ability and difficulty.

- Hands-on approach of playing the keyboard and/or composing as a means of exploring concepts of notation.

- Multi-sensory approach to facilitate memory and to make connections between printed page and the sounded notes.

Brief descriptions of these children are as follows:

Lucy: difficulties with reading and particularly with spelling. At primary school had received learning support involving the use of spelling strategies, the development of phonic skills and access to a laptop and spellmaster. Dramatic improvement meant that although teachers were aware of her dyslexia, she no longer needed learning support at High School.

Ben: difficulties with spelling, also with maths and sequencing skills. Extra help at primary school but extra help not required at Secondary School.

Toby: specific difficulties with writing and spelling. (Tests e.g. Burt Vernon Word Test and Inglis Spelling Test indicating averages of 6.6 - 7 .9 year old.) A scribe recommended for school work. Orally competent. Requiring full time learning support.

The music curriculum for first year pupils of two one-hour class music lessons a week included musical performance (learning the keyboard and singing), composition, music history and an introduction to music theory. In the latter, the note names of the treble clef and basic note values had been covered. For the purpose of learning the keyboard, these were incorporated into a course of 'units'. Each child progressed through a folder of graded pieces at their own pace.

It was interesting to obtain the three children's perceptions about their own musical experiences and interests. Regarding instrumental lessons, all three children had been keen. Lucy had learned the recorder briefly at primary school, found it difficult, but had wanted to take up a wind instrument at Secondary School. Ben had started learning the drums out of school. Toby had learned the guitar for a year at primary school but was no longer having lessons.

After discussing the nature of my proposed music sessions with the three children, it was agreed that the keyboard would be used as a starting point for aspects of music performance, composition and theory, which they might wish to explore. Some of the key aspects which will be discussed here include: Creativity: Short-term memory: Co-ordination, and the Use of Colour.

CREATIVITY

During the first session with each child, I played two extracts of music. The first was from a recording of *Mars* from Holst's *The Planet Suite*; the second was *Venus*. Without revealing the title of the music, I asked each child to draw a picture of what the music suggested to them. From this short and simple exercise, I discovered some interesting information. All three children were good 'visualisers' (McLullich, H. and Palmer, S. *The inward eye: a personal investigation of mental imagery: The Art of Reading*, Ed. Hunter-Carsch, M.) and all three responded well to the contrasting extracts. Toby, in particular, had a vivid imagination. He drew a storm with shepherd and sheep pen for the first extract and a snowman/wintry scene for the second. However, his actual drawing skills – dexterity and co-ordination - were the least good. Lucy's and Ben's drawings were neat and precise but less personal. Possibly they had been more inhibited.

This was an exercise requiring creativity and imagination; literacy skills and a knowledge of music notation were unnecessary here and I felt it important to emphasise this. With pencils in hand, it seemed an appropriate moment to discuss some different ways that the extracts could be represented. We also discussed the reasons why people *do* notate music and the situations where it is important to have a 'universal' notation.

The point was made that music can be enjoyed without an understanding of its notation but that one's understanding of the music can be greatly enhanced when one starts to learn its notation. The first sessions, however, revealed that there were certain areas of difficulty or confusion for each child. These could be tackled during individual tuition, but inevitably and understandably had been overlooked in the context of a noisy music class.

Areas of confusion / difficulties with music notation, as observed in music sessions with Lucy, Ben and Toby, will be discussed under the following headings of 'Short-Term Memory' and 'Co-ordination'.

SHORT-TERM MEMORY

Most dyslexics have a poor short-term memory. Lucy, Ben and Toby were no exceptions. They could visualise and draw imaginatively but could they visualise and recall pitches and rhythms accurately? Although all three children had problems with reading and spelling, it was noticeable that the two boys had real difficulties remembering pitch and rhythmic notation, whilst Lucy did not. Lucy had learned to overcome the majority of her difficulties with spelling by applying strategies, rhymes and patterns. (This also proved useful when using colour.) She applied the same learning aids to music, for example:

Fig. 2

However, Beaumont (Cambridge Conference Proceedings, 1992) points out: 'It is crucial that theory is seen as secondary to understanding the concept which it serves to explain.' Mnemonics such as the E,G,B,D,F rhyme are helpful only when understood in relation to the larger sequence of pitch notation. Colour was used to show this relationship.

Lucy was able to recognise her own strengths and weaknesses with regards to learning and memory and this was a distinct advantage over the two boys. There was no easy solution to remembering pitch notation for Ben and Toby. However, I felt that the layout of the musical examples in the school keyboard units that we were using, were only adding to their problems. There was just too much visual information to deal with – counting aids, fingering, chord symbols and the note names all featured on the page – all this in addition to the actual notes, the time signature and key signature!

I dealt with this problem by rewriting some of tunes on strong card. This enabled me to include information relevant and helpful to each individual. As well as using tunes from the keyboard units, I wrote out some easy melodies from other music (for example, a few pop songs, TV theme tunes and a song from the musical *Joseph*). This provided variety and interest; I felt it important to avoid tunes which might insult their ages! Furthermore, I omitted the names of the notes as I felt this defeated the whole object of the exercise. With the keyboard units the tendency had been to read the letter names only. The result was that the stave was never once observed; rhythm and note values were thus meaningless. Rewriting the tunes also provided an opportunity to draw wider-spaced staves and larger note-heads. Neither Lucy, Ben nor Toby expressed any problems with visual discomfort or of notes 'jumping' lines on a staff, though I had noticed that the two boys often reversed a sequence of notes or repeated the same note twice.

I asked the children to recall new information (concerning the learning of pitch or note values for example) in as many ways as possible. 'Middle C' or a minim were therefore recognised from a page (sight), the note was played on the piano or the value clapped (hearing), the symbol was drawn on paper and traced with a finger (touch) and named out aloud. Hubicki and Miles (1991) referred to these principles in their paper on *Musical notation and multi-sensory learning*.

I also suggested the children could relate unfamiliar notation to something familiar. For example, a bar of music was like a bar of chocolate which could be divided down into a number of notes or a number of bits of chocolate.

In relation to pitch, I often asked the child to explain to me *how* they knew that the note they had played was a 'B' (for example). This enabled me to discover their thought processes, and to check whether they were playing a familiar tune by ear, by sight, or even by guess-work! Sometimes when a wrong answer was given or a wrong note played, the thought process initially had been correct. Particularly with Toby, this showed that a problem occurred during the processing of the information and was not due to a failure in remembering how to obtain the information. Sometimes a visual slip seemed apparent – he would count up two lines from E (the note he sometimes remembered as first on the line, first in the rhyme . . . 'Every') and tell me that a note on the middle line was 'F'. Sometimes however, I felt that Toby believed it was an 'F' because he *had* forgotten the sequence of the rhyme.

Also concerning repetition and multi-sensory learning, I decided to invent two memory games targeting rhythm. The first was for Toby, who needed the game to be kept as simple as possible. One and two-beat notes were concentrated on. (see Fig. 3).

Fig. 3

The 1-beat note was represented by a black mouse with long, black tail.
The 2- beat note was represented by a white mouse with long, white tail.

Similarities were pointed out between the mice and the music notation! To make the connection between colour, tail/stalk and rhythmic value, the white mouse scored two points, the black only one.

Both mice were hidden, one in each hand. The second player aimed to score highly by choosing the hand with the white mouse. After a number of goes, (the mouse was swapped between hands) the roles of guessing / hiding the mice were reversed.

Toby always kept score.

This memory aid drew on touch as well as sight, and made connections between a number, colour and shape / symbol. At this stage, because I felt Toby had enough information to deal with, the notes were referred to by their value only, rather than by their names of 'crotchet' and 'minim'.

Once one-beat and two-beat notes had been mastered, the mice could be given an 'eye' each! This represented dotted notes of one-and-a-half and three beats respectively.

Ben required a more sophisticated approach to learning rhythmic symbols. A game with mice would have probably insulted him and anyway he was already capable of coping with more than two rhythmic values! He could tap / play rhythms by ear with no problems, but reading them off a page was more taxing. Constant repetition of

in the form of an Origami 'fortune diamond' proved an ideal memory jogger: As shown in Fig. 4.

Fig. 4

> Four note values are placed on the outer four squares. Once the second player has chosen a symbol, the diamond has to be turned, x1, x2, x3 or x4 – testing a knowledge of the note values. If an odd number was chosen (MUSIC SCORE), the diamond reveals a set of inner triangles. Again these are labelled with different symbols for note values. After a number of choices / goes, the player then picks a symbol, states its value, checks the answer by lifting the flap and reading the reverse of the triangle . Here will be found the answer 1, 2, 3 or 4 (and, to make it more fun, a short 'fortune' message if the game is being combined!)

This enabled the dyslexic child to:

*   draw the symbols, label the note values (when making the fortune diamond),
*   point to symbols and say their value out aloud,
*   repeat the process and check answers (when playing the game).

Lucy, unlike the two boys, enjoyed number work. One week she was particularly frustrated by the fact that music notation involved the letter names which she hated in everyday life, and she suggested giving each note a number instead. Rhythm was to be notated as a fraction along a horizontal axis, and numbers for notes along the vertical axis.

She soon worked out the various possible drawbacks of her system and we spent time discussing other different notation systems and their drawbacks. However, Lucy's suggestion had been all the more illuminating because she *was* dyslexic. Again, she was pinpointing her own difficulties and finding her own solutions. This form of self-help is invaluable!

CO-ORDINATION

Toby and Lucy encountered particular problems with co-ordination. This was immediately obvious in their hesitant approach to playing the keyboard when confronted with a lot of information, and when asked to clap or play something rhythmically.

Simple exercises were tried, using clapping, a metronome or different rhythms on the keyboard. Toby found it particularly difficult to clap at half speed or double speed during a steady crotchet pulse, or vice versa. He could also play a piece on the keyboard using the rhythm selector and remain oblivious to the 'beat' throughout. It was merely a background noise. Perhaps Toby was unable to deal with this amount of information, and so to compromise, his brain had to shut out as much 'superfluous' material as possible. Rhythm fell into this category.

USE OF COLOUR

Colour was used to serve a variety of purposes and one of them was aiding co-ordination.

The use of colour with music notation is familiar to many people. Professor Margaret Hubicki developed this idea considerably with her invention of 'Colour Staff' in the 1960s. She uses colour both to identify different letter names and to demonstrate relationships between notes. It is, however, an aid to visual recognition of *patterns* rather than a specific memory aid. For example: a child is not expected to remember what letter names correspond to yellow, green and so on. This would only add to the problems of memory. Instead one can: (i) relate the *horizontal* format of a keyboard/piano (with its notes labelled in colour), to the *vertical* format of a pitch ladder (again with notes labelled in colour.) Similarly, one can: (ii) relate to notes an octave apart (labelled in the same colour), and (iii) also to patterns of octaves alternating between lines and spaces. (The latter is possible because colours are alternatively wide and narrow in shape. For example, Note A one octave above Middle C and two octaves above middle C is represented by wide and narrow green rectangles respectively.) (See Fig. 5.)

Fig. 5

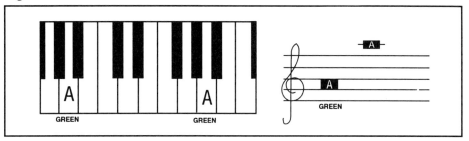

Developed for Hubicki's own pupils, some of whom were dyslexic, 'Colour Staff' highlights vital connections between page and keyboard, eye and ear. I found these principles particularly useful in sessions with Ben and Lucy. Rather than giving each note a colour however, I chose to use only three: C, F and G – using the colours red, green and blue respectively. The reason for this was twofold. Firstly, I wanted to keep the colour idea as simple as possible, (Hubicki's invention is designed to be flexible) and secondly, I wanted to tie in this idea with advice from Helen McLullich, author of the classroom teaching aid, *Music Alive*. McLullich used colour coding for chime bar accompaniments of songs. Though the idea was developed for children of infant school age, she suggested to me that something similar could be devised for dyslexic children of a wider age-group.

Rather than emphasising pattern, McLullich's idea emphasised co-ordination. For example, during the singing of a song such as *Skip to my Lou*, six children play an accompaniment with only two chords: F,A,C, (red) and C,E,G, (blue). When a red card is held up, three children play notes F,A and C ; when a blue card is shown, notes C,E,G are played. The children learn that a chord is achieved by members of the same group striking his/her chime-bar at the same time.

My version of colour as a notational aid combined elements of the two aforementioned ideas. I wanted to aid visual recognition of patterns for Ben and to assist with chord playing and its co-ordination for Lucy. Unlike the keyboard units' notation used by the school, where for example, the chord symbol 'F' was seen in large, bold type *above* the right hand melody, my version used coloured rectangles *beneath* the melody. (See Fig 6). This would familiarise the pupil with traditional positioning of the left hand/bass clef notation. It also represented the chord as a rectangular block, indicating that the notes should be played together, and it linked the coloured rectangle on the page to the group of coloured keys on the keyboard.

Fig. 6

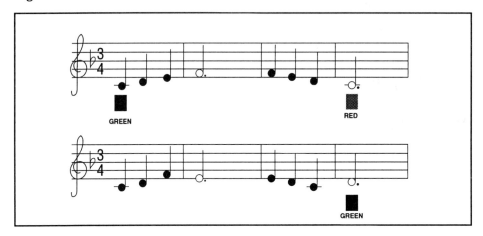

Though the keyboard units used a similar layout to the notation of guitar chords, I felt that for dyslexics children a chord could cause confusion when placed above the right hand melody. Furthermore, the symbol was yet another letter of the alphabet! Dyslexic pupils had enough of these to cope with already and, with the possible disadvantage of directional confusion too, I felt sure that one of Lucy's hang-ups was due to this conflicting information on the page.

With Ben, small, coloured stickers were stuck on keys in the lower register of the keyboard. Every F,A and C received green stickers, every C,E,G, was red and every G,B,D was blue. This was done only when he understood that the three notes were different, but that together they made up the same chord of F, C or G major.

The use of colours for chords aided Lucy's problem with co-ordination and undoubtedly improved her confidence and capability. In the early sessions, she was convinced that she could not play the keyboard using both hands at once, and wanted to use the right hand only.

Introducing colour to the music sessions was therefore an effective intermediary stage to chord learning. Lucy's initial problems had been due to a difficulty in processing large amounts of information quickly. This brought a lack of co-ordination, frustration and negative attitude. A particular problem was that she would depress the keys in one hand before the other, even when her fingers were in the right chord patterns over the notes. With quicker chord changes such as at a cadence at the end of a piece, she was unable to respond fast enough. Obviously this led to un-rhythmical playing as well.

With the introduction of colours, Lucy believed psychologically that the task of playing chords was easier, and therefore that she might be able to succeed. She now had less information to process and could concentrate on finding the notes of the right hand, the rhythm and depressing the keys simultaneously. As her confidence grew, she became more relaxed about the music. This again helped her co-ordination and rhythm. Soon, she could listen to the whole sound that she was creating, instead of devoting all her energy and concentration to the printed page. This meant that after repeated attempts at a tune, she could tell when she had played a wrong melody note or even a wrong note in a chord. Locating the slip at the keyboard, and relating it to the relevant symbol on the printed page, also increased her awareness of the notation and the vital link between sound and printed notes.

Learning a tune *with* the colours first had restored Lucy's confidence. She could then tackle the same tune *without* colour.

The next step was to learn a totally new tune without using colour at any point. The melody from Dvorak's *Largo* ('New World Symphony') was broken down into stages, again helping co-ordination and memory. For example,

> R.H. melody played with correct rhythm.
> L.H. chords were learnt separately (C,F,G).
> L.H. chords played in correct time.
> Lucy's L.H chords in time to my R.H melody.
> Final stage: both hands together.

This all took time but gradually worked with repetition and increased confidence. Many aspects of Lucy's playing improved as a result of this procedure, particularly in co-ordination.

Though the colour chords worked for Ben, co-ordination was not a specific problem. Instead the colours were more helpful as visual aids using pattern. As for Toby, rather than exploring the use of colours and chords (in fact we used no form of notation for his left hand at all, as there was more than enough information for him to process with the treble clef alone), it was decided to take a completely different approach to learning notation. Though Toby learned some keyboard pieces with moderate success, he suddenly progressed with leaps and bounds when a new found freedom in composition and improvisation was discovered! His imagination and creative talent revealed in the first session came into its own. He played me the start of a tune which he had written in class music. It was based on the pentatonic scale (the class had been looking at Eastern music around the time of the Chinese New Year) and it had a lot of potential for development and variation.

Enjoy first; notate later seemed to be the motto for Toby! This proved so important to his development as a person and as a musician. Music of this kind was one of the few areas of the curriculum which he enjoyed. The reason was that he was talented, and given encouragement in the right areas, was inspired and stimulated to progress and achieve. Once he knew he could achieve and that his effort was worthwhile, his confidence was boosted, his levels of concentration improved and his whole outlook seemed to be more positive.

The first few weeks were spent solely at the keyboard. Using his tune as a basis, we explored its sound at different octaves of the keyboard, using different instrumentation (the keyboard had a large selection), and using a different start note (transposing up to F sharp and using all black keys). A middle section evolved which linked a low version of the tune to a high version. Rhythm was also experimented with, though this proved less successful, mainly because tempo and rhythms seemed to change so dramatically in Toby's playing, even when a variation was not intended!

Later, the notation of Toby's piece was tackled. We could have devised an alternative notation, but, because an important aspect of the composition was to link up other work regarding pitch and rhythm, I decided to stick with the traditional system, however complicated. Nevertheless, it was kept as simple as possible. Rhythm, for example was distinguished only by long and short notes.

Again, composition provided a vital link between sound (created first) and the printed note (written second).

Perhaps the climax of Toby's composition was to see it finished on a piece of manuscript paper. The real test was, however, whether the notation meant something to somebody else. Though Toby had worked hard with the notation, we both knew that the tune was first and foremost in his head rather than visualised on paper. The composition was photocopied and presented to a group of students. Toby's face revealed such pleasure when he realised that his piece had been communicated to other musicians – via paper, and by his own efforts. With Toby at the keyboard, we then improvised as a group around his pentatonic theme. It gave him a chance to hear his piece on a clarinet, two violins and a cello, and to hear other ways of developing a musical idea.

Lucy and Ben had been much less keen to explore composition. Certainly they were more inhibited and so the idea was not forced upon them. Though improvisation was explored a little with Ben, he lacked the same creativity. His particular strength was rhythmical, and therefore the drums (being learned out of school) were ideal for him. A benefit of this instrument was that pitch notation would not need to be worried about! Coping with a drum kit would undoubtedly develop his co-ordination and overall confidence.

CONCLUSION

This study was based on observation of three dyslexic children at a secondary school. It highlighted the difficulties which dyslexic children show when learning music and its notation. Many of these were directly related to problems of short-term memory, directional confusion and co-ordination. As a result, a number of alternative approaches to learning music notation were explored. Several of these were rhythm games based on multi-sensory methods of learning. Using colour as an aid to the visual recognition of pattern and as an aid to co-ordination and chord playing at the keyboard was also successful. Notation was always studied in a practical way using performance or composition as a starting point.

Improvements were seen in several areas of each child's musical and personal development. These included a clearer understanding of the link between a sound and a symbol on a printed page, and improvements in some areas of short-term memory and co-ordination. Confidence and self esteem did seem to improve during the sessions. This was particularly noticeable in Toby, who despite suffering the most severe problems of dyslexia, showed extreme enthusiasm and commitment to the music sessions and a flare for composition and creative activities. The stages of composing, notating and performing his own piece stimulated and encouraged him towards higher goals of achievement, satisfaction and an obvious enjoyment of music.

Music and dyslexia is, clearly, an area ripe for further studies. Such studies should help to promote an awareness of the difficulties and benefits encountered by dyslexics when learning music. This is of relevance to the specific needs of the community, in its broadest sense.

REFERENCES

Galaburda, A. M., Corsiglia, J., Rosen, G. D., Sherman, G. F. (1987). 'Planum Temporale Assymetry: Reappraisal Since Geschwind & Levitsky'. Neuropsychologia, 25,6. In *The Nature of Difficulties*, Miles, T. R. (Ed). (1992). Music & Dyslexia: Cambridge Conference Proceedings, BDA.

Hubicki, M. (1963). *Colour Staff*. The Educational Supply Assoc. Ltd., Pinnacles, Harlow.

Hubicki, M. (1990). Learning Difficulties in Music. In Hales, G. (Ed.), *Meeting Points in Dyslexia*.

Hubicki, M. and Miles, T. R. (1991). Musical Notation and Multi-sensory Notation. In *Child language, Teaching and Therapy*, Vol. 7, No. 1 (1991). Edward Arnold.

McLullich, H. and Palmer, S. (1989). 'The Inward Eye: A Personal Investigation of Mental Imagery'. In *The Art of Reading*, Hunter-Carsch, M., (Ed.). Blackwell.

McLullich, H. (1979). *Music Alive* (Oliver & Boyd).

Ryden, M. (1989). *Dyslexia: How Would I Cope?* Jessica Kinglsey.

Reid, G. (1994). *Specific Learning Difficulties (Dyslexia): A Handbook for Study and Practice*. Moray House Publications, Edinburgh.

Springer, S. P. and Deutsch, G. (1984). *Left Brain, Right Brain*. Freeman: New York.

BDA Publications:
The Dyslexia Handbook (1993-4).
Music and Dyslexia (Rev. 1992).
Music and Dyslexia : Cambridge Conference Proceedings (1992).

ACKNOWLEDGMENTS

Special thanks go to Professor Margaret Hubicki, Helen McLullich, and Gavin Reid and to staff at Boroughmuir High School including David Dodds and John Clason.

SECTION 4

CURRICULUM AND
SUPPORT APPROACHES

ACCESS TO THE CURRICULUM

SYLVIA RUSSELL

INTRODUCTION

In the interests of brevity, throughout this chapter I have used the term 'dyslexia' rather than 'Specific Learning Difficulties'. Since the majority of primary teachers are female, I have used the pronoun 'she' and since the majority of dyslexic children are male, I have used the pronoun 'he'.

> *"By differentiation is meant the identification of, and effective provision for, a range of abilities in one classroom, such that pupils in a particular class need not study the same things at the same pace and in the same way at all times. Differentiated approaches should mean that the needs of the very able, and of children with learning difficulties are discerned and met".*

> SOED (quoted by Mary Simpson, Northern College)

Differentiation is synonymous with good teaching and is the process of assessing the needs of children and adjusting teaching methodology, materials, pacing and expected outcomes accordingly.

The most important feature of successful differentiation is good planning, firstly at whole-school level with senior management taking responsibility for curriculum support, and secondly at classroom level with the class teacher involved in a cycle of assessment, curriculum support and evaluation.

ASSESSMENT

Assessment is crucial to the implementation of an effective teaching programme.

> *"Assessment is inseparable from the teaching process since its prime purpose is to improve pupils' performance. It should help teachers to diagnose pupils' strengths and weaknesses; to match the work of the classroom to their capabilities; to guide them to appropriate courses and groups; to involve them in discussion and self appraisal . . ."*

> (D.E.S., 1985, p51, para 134)

Assessment, does not mean full scale examinations, reading and spelling tests every other week but a continuous analysis of **what** we are teaching and **why**, an observation of **how** our pupils are learning and the difficulties they are encountering. This will lead on to the devising of alternative strategies to enhance learning.

INTELLIGENCE

Dyslexic children are no more and no less intelligent than non-dyslexic children. You may find dyslexic children who are above average, average or below average intelligence. What will be noticeable will be the discrepancy between the child's expected and actual attainments (Siegel, 1989).

LEARNING STYLES

Like all children (and adults), individual dyslexic children will have individual preferred learning styles. Some children learn best when lessons are activity based and they 'learn by doing', some like to be teacher directed and use textbooks, some learn best by talking and discussing and some by discovery and problem-solving approaches. The good class teacher, through close observation, will have built up a picture of whether the child learns best alone, in a pair, with the teacher or in a reading group; whether he needs to move about or whether he needs to sit quietly without distractions; the time of day that is most suitable for highly concentrated study; the pupil's perceptual strengths and whether he learns best by auditory, visual, tactile or kinesthetic modes. The child's preferred learning style will have implications for the way that teachers teach different groups of children and the type of methodology that works for particular children but may not be appropriate for others (Carbo, Dunn and Dunn, 1986).

The variations in ability, learning styles and degrees of dyslexia make it impossible to write a prescription for differentiated teaching for dyslexic pupils. One can only write in the most general terms and the following suggestions will not meet the needs of all dyslexic pupils all of the time. These suggestions are intended to give busy class teachers some practical tips to allow dyslexic children access to the curriculum. The dyslexic child needs a highly structured approach which builds on what he already knows; in this he is no different from the majority of children. The dyslexic child, however, because of poor working memory; will also need a great deal of practice and revision before a lesson is mastered, and will need to be taught in a multi-sensory way.

IN-CLASS TEACHING OR EXTRACTION ?

Differentiation implies that the child will be taught within the classroom following the same curriculum as the rest of his classmates, but that the way in which he gains access to that curriculum may be different from his classmates. Whenever possible, the dyslexic child should be helped **within** the classroom. Withdrawal from the classroom places the child in a 'special' category, perhaps leading the class teacher to feel that she is not skilled enough to teach the dyslexic child and that he is therefore someone else's responsibility. That is not to say that extraction may not be necessary from time to time to work on specific skill areas. When this happens, it is important for both teachers to liaise closely so that there is a planned programme of learning objectives which both teachers are reinforcing. Time for this liaison is essential if both teachers are to co-operate on a structured teaching programme for the dyslexic child.

READING

Virtually all primary aged dyslexic children will first come to the notice of their teachers because of poor literacy skills. We often forget what a complex skill reading is. It involves the recognition of words, letters, and letter patterns, as well as sequencing, use of context, prediction, grammatical construction, punctuation and comprehension.

READING – EARLY STAGES

Most schools use early reading schemes which are largely 'Look and Say' but may also have a limited phonic element to them. Many dyslexic children have poor visual memories which can make 'Look and Say' approaches to reading very difficult. These children need early reading-teaching which has a heavy emphasis on phonics, and makes as light a demand as possible on visual memory skills. The dyslexic child will need much more practice and revision of phonics than the majority of his classmates and should be taught in a highly structured, multi-sensory way to compensate for his poor working memory and organisational skills.

Teachers will find the book, 'Specific Learning Difficulties (Dyslexia) : A Teachers' Guide' by Margaret Crombie an excellent source of ideas for multi-sensory teaching.

The dyslexic child need not be taught on his own as almost certainly there will be other children in his class who would benefit from joining him in such a structured approach.

Many schools have developed their own worksheets etc. for teaching phonics and some of these are better than others but most of them will not fulfil the criteria for structure and multi-sensory approaches. I would strongly recommend the Letterland Teaching Programme by Lyn Wendon which combines the structure, progression and multi-sensory teaching approaches that are so important for mastery learning and does it in a way that is great fun for young children. There are also excellent computer programmes for reinforcing phonics, 'The Animated Alphabet', (Sherston), 'A to Z' (IEC Software). One which I have found very useful is 'Concept Keyboard Matching' (Scetlander) which allows the teacher to make up her own concept keyboard overlays for alphabet matching exercises. This programme is also versatile enough to allow it to be used for any kind of matching exercise, at all ages, to reinforce vocabulary, number bonds, multiplication tables, foreign languages etc.

It is important that the dyslexic child is using a reading scheme which is appropriate to his age and reading level. It may not be appropriate for him to continue on the class scheme if he is unable to keep up with the other children and is becoming embarrassed by being on a much lower level than his peers. It would make sense to switch him either to an alternative infant scheme which has a graded, structured vocabulary or to try one of the many reading schemes aimed at children with reading difficulties. It is difficult to single out one as being better than another as so much depends on the child's preferences, but two which I have found particularly successful are 'Bangers and Mash' (Longmans) and 'Fuzzbuzz' (Oxford University Press). Both schemes have excellent reinforcement activities and are well structured. It is a good idea to reinforce the vocabulary of a reading scheme by preparing concept keyboard overlays. This allows the child to 'write' stories from a very early stage (Folio, Stylus, Prompt/Writer).

Obviously, if you are placing a child on a different scheme you are moving away from a differentiated programme of work to an individual programme. In my experience, it is usually possible to have the dyslexic child working as part of a group of children who are all trying to master early literacy skills.

Many dyslexic children have difficulty remembering the common 'abstract' words such as *the, this, who, why, and, of, does* etc. I have found that playing the 'Crocodile Game' helps them to memorise them. Children usually work in pairs and as it can be rather noisy, you may wish them to play in the corridor outside the classroom door. Write the words to be learned in large letters on large pieces of card (at least 25cm x 25cm). The cards are scattered at random over the floor and are stepping stones to cross a crocodile-infested river. Each child is given 3 lives and is told to jump on to the stepping stone that says for example 'this' and then to jump on to 'why' and so on until he reaches the other side of the river. Every time he jumps on the wrong word he loses a life. If he loses all three, he is eaten by crocodiles! Children find the game great fun and the large body movements involved in leaping from one stone to another seem to help 'fix' the words in the child's memory. The same game can be played with any sight vocabulary or phonic clusters that are proving difficult to remember.

READING – UPPER PRIMARY

The older dyslexic pupil may present a greater challenge to the busy class teacher. If the child's problems have not been diagnosed at an early stage he may have experienced years of failure and become totally turned off school in general and reading in particular. For such children, reading is very stressful and it is small wonder that they start to yawn, fidget and look for any excuse to avoid reading. It is important that the older dyslexic child is made to feel part of the class and work with his peers as much as possible. There is no reason why he should not take part in discussions and follow-up work on a novel that is being studied by the whole class. However, the teacher must be aware of the difficulties that he is likely to face and make alternative provision for them. It should be possible to tape record the story in advance. This can be done by the class teacher, parent helper or even other pupils. Make sure that the dyslexic child works in a group working at his intellectual level, for even though his reading and written work are of a lower standard, he will be motivated and stimulated by being in such a discussion/project group.

If worksheets are being used, the teacher must look very carefully at the language used and at the layout. It may be necessary to provide simplified worksheets or worksheets which have the key words marked with a highlighter pen to cut down on the reading load for the dyslexic child. It is also necessary to look at the follow-up work that is expected. The dyslexic pupil may find report writing and essays very difficult because of his poor handwriting and spelling, so alternative ways of recording his ideas should be found. This could be done graphically or recorded on a tape recorder to be transcribed or word processed later.

As well as taking part in the 'reading' of the class novel, it is important that the dyslexic child continues on a structured reading programme which will improve his reading fluency. This must be handled sensitively with older children who can be very self-conscious about their difficulties. It often helps to be quite open with the rest of the class and explain to them the types of difficulties the dyslexic child encounters and enlist their help. Most primary aged children are incredibly understanding and supportive of children with problems. Choose a reading scheme which is appropriate to the age, ability and interests of the pupil. The final choice is usually down to the child's personal preference and what is available within school or from the peripatetic support teacher. I have found the following schemes to be very useful : Wellington Square (Nelson), Skyways (Collins), Nick Dick Detective Series (Collins), Starpol Series (Ginn & Co.), Trog Series (Nelson), Rescue Readers (Ginn & Co.), Five Minute Thrillers and Tapes (LDA).

To encourage careful, accurate reading I have found two cloze procedure books to be invaluable, 'False Teeth and Vampires', and 'Astronauts and the Black Death' (LDA).

A Paired Reading approach should be used so that the dyslexic child is not put under pressure. It is also a good idea to let the child read into a tape recorder and then play the tape back while he follows the text in the book and tries to spot for himself any errors he has made.

Older children may still need to work on phonics to develop decoding skills for reading, and also to help with spelling. This can present a problem for class teachers beyond the infant stages who may not have any great understanding of phonic progression and the need to build on what is already mastered. Using a structured scheme such as 'Phonic Code Cracker' (Russell, S., Jordanhill College Publications) will give the teacher a package which includes assessments, precision teaching workbooks to encourage mastery learning, and a computer programme for reinforcement and revision. This phonics programme has been devised to need very little teacher time since most of the learning takes place either at home if parents are willing to help or in school through peer tutoring. The teacher is only needed for the 'Fluency Tests' which are timed with a stop watch and should only take 30 seconds or so each day.

As with Letterland for the younger children, phonics for the older children should encourage them to look at the patterns in words and should be presented in a way which is fun.

Much consolidation can be done through the use of games such as Phonic Rummy (Kenworthy Educational Services), Reading Games (Macmillan Educational), Betty Root series of reading games (NES Arnold), Help Games (H.E.L.P. Educational Games).

For children who have developed a real 'hang-up' about reading from books, I have found the computer to be a great motivator. There are many excellent programmes to reinforce phonics but teachers seldom consider the amount of on-screen reading a child has to do in order to complete some of the excellent 'Adventure' programmes such as 'Granny's Garden' (4 Mation), 'Flowers of Crystal' (4 Mation), 'Nature Park Adventure' (Sherston), 'Dragon World' (4 Mation), 'Fleet Street Phantom' (Sherston), 'The Worst Witch' (Sherston), 'Sellardore Tales' (Sherston) etc.

HANDWRITING

Many dyslexic children have poor handwriting skills. The letters may be poorly formed, wrongly sized, frequently reversed, interspersed with capitals and unjoined. Dyslexic children are often highly embarrassed by their messy, illegible handwriting and it can act as a deterrent to story writing. In the lower primary stages the teaching of handwriting should be done at the same time as the teaching of the letter sounds and multi-sensory methods should be used.

For example: the child **looks** at the letter, **says** the letter sound and letter name, **hears** the sound of the letter. The teacher writes the letter on the blackboard. The child, using different coloured chalk, **writes** over the top of the letter and then writes it again. He writes it on the desktop with his finger, he writes it with his finger on sandpaper (or in a sand tray) and finally he writes it on **lined** paper. Because dyslexic children have problems with letter sizes. I have found 'Tramline' paper (Philip & Tacey) to be excellent as children can see quite clearly that tall letters go above the line and tails hang down below. By paying close attention to correct letter formation and giving the child practice using large arm movements and 'feeling' how the letter is made, it is hoped that the child's muscle memory and kinesthetic memory will help him to retain the letter when his visual memory proves unequal to the task. Correct letter formation is essential if the child is going to join up his writing properly. I would recommend adding, as soon as possible, the necessary ligatures which allow the child to develop a flowing cursive style of handwriting.

| Example 1 | I hab a dab KoLb I WOS in my Peb |
| Example 2 | I had a bad kold. I wos in my bed. |

The first example was written by a bright, dyslexic 8 year old. The second example was dictated to him after six months' instruction in cursive handwriting. You will notice that although there are still spelling errors, the reversals have been eradicated and his work is readable.

When copying from the blackboard, make sure the dyslexic child is facing it and not having to turn round which may disorientate him. Teachers should also be aware that some dyslexic children find copying from the blackboard very difficult as they keep losing the place and have to keep re-reading and checking their work from the beginning. If this is the case, try to avoid asking the dyslexic to copy and allow him to have photocopied notes instead.

Some dyslexic children hold their pencils in strange, tight grips. This can be helped by sliding a 'Grippy' grip (L.D.A.) over the end of the pencil. This will encourage the child to place his fingers correctly (put it on upside down for left-handed children).

With older children I have found the answer to be to supply them with a script pen and treat writing lessons as art lessons. Once you have broken the initial feeling of failure so that the child can see that he can, on occasions, produce lovely work, it is easier to encourage him to practice this style and to begin to use it for general class work. As with the young children, multi-sensory approaches should be used, and tramline paper (with narrower lines) is again recommended.

SPELLING

Handwriting and spelling are very closely linked and many dyslexic children use poor handwriting as a way of disguising their atrocious spelling. In my experience, spelling is generally poorly taught in primary schools, with many children experiencing difficulties and being given no real strategies for learning. Children with good visual memories will usually be good spellers since they can visualise the word they want to spell and spot when a word looks wrong but many children, including dyslexic children, have poor visual memories and need to be given a structure for learning. There should be no difficulty in forming a 'spelling support group' in any classroom. This group will certainly need more teacher-input than the rest of the class but the extra work should show dividends. The teacher must have a clear idea of what she is trying to achieve and not just present words at random. As a general rule, teach word families which have the same sound pattern in them. Teach prefixes and suffixes and spelling rules since these can cut down considerably on the load of individual words to be memorised

('Logical Spelling' Collins). Teach the common, irregular words such as *done, any, was* etc. as the child will need these for written work. The 'Look, Cover, Write, Check' method advocated by Charles Cripps works well as does Lynette Bradley's 'Simultaneous Oral Spelling' technique. 'Cued Spelling' (Topping, Scoble & Oxley) is another useful teaching method and can be done by children working in pairs and supporting each other in a similar way to paired reading. 'Cracker Spell' (Russell, S., Jordanhill College Publications), uses the 'Look, Cover, Write, Check' approach and also has a computer programme for reinforcement. Using mnemonics can be a great help for children with poor visual memories. Children should be encouraged to think up their own mnemonics for their own 'bogey' words. 'Signposts to Spelling' by Joy Pollok and the series of photo-copiable masters, 'Don't Let Spelling Get You Down' (Tregear Publications), are packed with good ideas for this.

Some children will continue to have considerable problems with spelling, regardless of the amount of special teaching that they receive. It may be more realistic to accept that they will always have a problem and begin to give them strategies for coping. At the simplest level, they should be shown how to use a spelling dictionary such as 'The Pergamon Dictionary of Perfect Spelling' (Nelson) or the 'ACE Dictionary' (L.D.A.). The dyslexic child will need training in alphabetical order before he will be able to use a dictionary successfully. The computer programme 'Dyslexia Aid' (Edsoft) gives practice in alphabetic sequencing.

The 'Franklin Spellmaster' (Venture Marketing) is an electronic spelling aid which is little bigger than a pocket calculator. It will not be of much use if the child's spelling is totally bizarre but it can give a child great confidence when he is beginning to get to grips with spelling.

WRITTEN LANGUAGE WORK

Dyslexic children can be just as imaginative as the other children in the class. However, the teacher must be sensitive to the fact that writing a story follows on from having developed the ability to read, write and spell and these may prove an insurmountable barrier to good story writing. Initially, the child should tape record the story for transcribing later. A dyslexic child has the additional problem of sequencing difficulties and will almost certainly need training in working out a structure for his work so that he is able to put his ideas in a logical order. Younger children may be helped in this by giving them a series of pictures for which they have to write captions. 'Picture Writing Books' (Learning Materials Ltd.) are excellent for this or, alternatively, cut up comic strips and ask the child to stick them in sequence in his jotter and then write a caption for each picture. Older children can be helped by giving them a structure of steps to encourage logical sequencing. At its simplest level, this would be three steps – a beginning, a middle and an ending. By the upper stages of primary school, most children should be able to cope with a six part structure which includes :

1	Introduce the people.	2	Describe the setting/place.
3	Something begins to happen.	4	The exciting part.
5	Things sort themselves out.	6	The ending.

Children will need encouragement to pad out each section and it is helpful to give them the chance to do rough plans of the sequence of their stories and discuss these with them before they begin to write the actual piece of work. Proof-reading is another important skill which should be encouraged by the teacher. Train the child to self-correct his work when he has finished a piece of writing. He should be able to spot some spelling errors for himself and should also be encouraged to look at his sentence construction, at whether the story makes sense, and at whether he has punctuated it properly.

Allowing dyslexic children to use a computer to word process their work improves it considerably. Obviously, it is much less of a chore to correct mistakes on the screen than it is to rewrite a piece of work. For children with poor handwriting, the finished piece of work looks much better and the child is able to concentrate on the story rather than on the correct formation of letters and words. I have also noticed an improvement in spelling when a dyslexic's work has been word processed. One dyslexic boy explained this phenomenon to me by saying that the words 'looked wronger' on the screen so it was easier to see the ones he must correct.

Using a computer is also a great motivator for most children and the quality and quantity of their work also tends to improve. Many word processing programmes now include spell checkers which, though far from foolproof especially where homonyms are concerned, undoubtedly help. There are also programmes which will predict the word as the child starts to type ('PAL', for PCs, and 'PREDICTYPE' for the BBC computer, both from Scetlander Ltd., Glasgow). I have found 'STYLUS' (MAPE) a very useful programme for the BBC as it has a 'talk' facility. The child can type in his story and then ask the computer to 'tell' it back. The Dalek sounding voice greatly appeals to children and again, though not foolproof because of phonic irregularities in the English language, can help children to spot words that are obviously wrong. Children quickly become proficient at keyboarding skills and it does the dyslexic child's self-image no harm at all to find that he has become the class expert on the computer. With laptop computers tumbling in price many upper primary dyslexic children are now being given their own laptop with a spell checker which enables them to do all their written work on it without hogging the class computer. When this happens, it is important that the child, the class teacher and the parents are given training in the correct use of the laptop otherwise it can gather dust in a cupboard because no one is very sure how to operate it!

MATHEMATICS

The majority of dyslexic children also have difficulty with mathematics. Just as they have difficulty with letter recognition and orientation, dyslexic children will have similar problems with numbers. The same multi-sensory teaching strategies should be used. The mathematical symbols, + − x ÷ also cause confusion as indeed does the language which accompanies each process e.g. +, plus, add, count on, total, sum of etc.

These will all need to be carefully taught. It is helpful to give the child a small pack of cards as an *aide memoire*. The symbol is written on one side of each card and the vocabulary for that process on the other. The cards should be practised frequently and can be used by the child whenever he is unsure of a process. The teacher can help him by talking about what the symbol means and the method involved. The dyslexic child who has directional problems with reading from left to right will be even more confused in mathematics where division is worked from left to right but addition, subtraction and multiplication are worked from right to left. Putting in small direction arrows will help him to remember where to start. Using a jotter with boxes helps the dyslexic child to lay out his work neatly and makes calculations involving place value easier. He should also head his columns with Hundreds, Tens and Units and should be encouraged to talk himself through the place value of his answers so that he doesn't inadvertently put the numbers in the wrong columns.

A dyslexic child may have to rely on concrete material for a longer period of time than his peers since he will probably find it difficult to memorise number bonds. Showing him how to use a number line can speed up his work considerably. Many dyslexic children never master the multiplication tables though they can be helped to do so by using tape recordings of tables to music and giving them practice on the various computer software which is available such as 'Best Four Maths' (E.S.M.), 'Funfair' (Northern Micromedia), 'Monster Maths' (AVP) which reinforce 'almost learned tables' in a fun way. It may be more realistic to show them how to use a tables card or a pocket calculator efficiently.

For some dyslexic children, the mathematics presented in class is not a problem but because of poor literacy skills they may be unable to read and understand the instructions in their textbooks. This is the simplest problem to overcome as instructions can either be tape-recorded or the child can be paired with a good reader who can read the questions to him but must be instructed not to tell him the answers!

ORGANISATIONAL SKILLS

Most people appreciate that a dyslexic child has difficulty organising sounds and symbols into their correct sequence for reading and spelling, but it is not always realised that the dyslexic child's untidiness, poor concept of time, inability to remember more than one instruction at a time, and failure to remember to bring P.E. kit, football kit, swimming kit on the correct day are all part and parcel of the same problem. The dyslexic child may not have acquired a concept of time in its widest sense of days, weeks, months and years quite apart from learning to tell the time from a clock.

They find the sequencing of time difficult and may not be able to tell you what day it is, whether it is morning or afternoon. They may be thoroughly confused by *yesterday, tomorrow, next week, last week* etc. Teachers need to be understanding but at the same time must help the child to become more organised. Giving him a pictorial timetable where he can see clearly marked a picture of his football boots in the space for Tuesday afternoon and his swimming trunks on Friday morning can help but it is usually necessary to enlist the support of his parents so that they are reinforcing his organisation at home (see Christine Ostler's book, 'Dyslexia, A Parents' Survival Guide' for further help).

SELF-ESTEEM AND MOTIVATION

Self-esteem and motivation go hand in hand. Many dyslexic children have a very low self-esteem. They feel failures at school. Some may become depressed, some exhibit stress-related ailments such as headaches, stomach aches, exhaustion etc. and miss a lot of schooling. Others may, through frustration, begin to be disruptive in class and playground, or try to gain the esteem of their peers by being either the class clown or the 'hard man'.

The late-diagnosed dyslexic child may have experienced years at school of being called lazy, stupid, careless etc., and it is hardly surprising that dyslexic children tend to give up more easily than their peers. Confidence building must be a priority for the class teacher. Explaining the nature of dyslexia to the child and emphasising that it is not his fault and that he is not stupid can be helpful but it is vital to present class work in a way that ensures success. The teacher's maxim must be to minimise failure and maximise success.

The teacher must be ready to give praise and encouragement whenever possible and must be alert to situations which could prove difficult for the dyslexic. Give him praise for oral responses, mark his written work positively, give him credit for content and point out to him how many words he has written correctly and how many he has nearly got right. It is not necessary to dwell on his errors as he will already be more than aware of them, the teacher should be as encouraging as possible. Lawrence (1973) suggests that counselling in an uncritical atmosphere, providing opportunities for the child to talk about his family, friends, anxieties and aspirations, can build up self-esteem and enhance progress

Using a 'Records of Achievement' can be a good approach to building self-esteem as the child is able to keep a record of everything he is proud of, whether related to school work or not. He is then able to look back at the things he has succeeded at, a certificate for swimming 25 metres, a cub scout badge, a page of sums all correct, a good piece of descriptive writing etc.

LEARNING TO LEARN (METACOGNITION)

Explain to the child why he is learning certain things so that he has an understanding of the structure and progression of what he is doing. Too often, children do not see the relevance of certain lessons as they don't see where it fits into the big picture of education. Discuss with the child what he finds particularly difficult and ask him to identify what he would like to concentrate on next. Plan his next step with him so that he can see the relevance of his learning programme. If he can see that he is jointly planning his progress with you, his motivation will increase. Bringing the child to an awareness of his own mental processes, reflecting on how he learns, how to strengthen memory and how to tackle problems systematically will all help the child to 'learn how to learn' (Nisbet and Shucksmith, 1984). Children will learn more effectively if they have an understanding of how they learn best and have a strategy for organising their learning.

CASE STUDY

This case study is intended to help highlight some of the points discussed in the chapter.

THE PUPIL

Robert, when I first met him, was just beginning primary seven. He had recently been assessed by the Educational Psychologist and was in the average range of intellectual ability with a weakness in verbal skills and a significant immaturity in perceptual and motor skills. I assessed his reading using the Neale Analysis and the British Ability Scale Word Reading Test, and his spelling using the Vernon Graded Spelling Test.

His reading and spelling were both two and a half to three years behind his chronological age. His reading comprehension was one year behind his chronological age but when I reassessed his comprehension, having read the stories to him, his comprehension was three months in advance of his chronological age. I assessed his phonological awareness using the Code Cracker Phonic Test and found that he had large gaps in his knowledge and had great difficulty decoding multisyllabic words which he tended to telescope. He needed to follow a highly structured and cumulative programme and particularly needed practice in phonemic segmentation (Bryant and Bradley, 1985). His written work was almost unreadable, partly because of his poor spelling and reversal of letters but also because his handwriting was so poor with letters badly formed, unjoined and with no size consistency. His maths, though better than his reading, was being hindered by his difficulty in reading instructions and his inability to memorise multiplication tables.

Most worrying of all was his behaviour. He had become very lethargic in class, yawned a great deal, hardly put pencil to paper and was generally extremely poorly motivated. He was becoming increasingly aggressive with the other children and there were incidents when he tried to injure himself by punching a metal post until his knuckles bled or by banging his head on a wall. He was also receiving medical treatment for migraine headaches and bedwetting.

All in all, what I was seeing was a very unhappy and frustrated boy who had no confidence in himself, hated school and had given up on school work.

ACTION PLAN

After discussions with the Educational Psychologist, class teacher and mother, it was decided that I would work with Robert on a one to one basis for three 50 minute sessions a week . I would use part of one session to liaise and plan with the class teacher so that Robert's individualised learning programme would dovetail with the class work and she would also be reinforcing his programme in class. I also arranged to see Robert's mother, initially once a fortnight and then once a month, to keep her informed of progress and to ensure that she was supporting appropriately at home.

I had four main aims :–

1   Improve his self image.

2   Change his attitude to work.

3   Improve his behaviour with his peers.

4   Improve his reading, spelling and writing skills.

TEACHING PROGRAMME

The first few sessions were very difficult. Robert was totally demoralised over school work and his eyes glazed over whenever a reading book was produced. I decided to abandon formal work from books and use the computer instead. As a first step I presented him with various adventure programmes (see references). I wanted the sessions to be enjoyable and motivating yet challenging.

These were excellent for problem-solving and stimulating discussion. Most of the programmes had a great deal of 'on screen' reading, much of it too difficult for Robert but he was so keen to solve the adventure that he worked hard at decoding text on the screen which should have been too difficult for him.

He used the Phonic Code Cracker computer programme to cover the main gaps in his phonic knowledge (Russell, 1992).

Lawrence (1973) suggests that providing opportunities for the child to talk about his anxieties, aspirations, family and friends can build up self-confidence, self-esteem and enhance progress. By working one-to-one with Robert I was able to give him the opportunity to talk about himself. We discussed dyslexia and what it can mean for children and adults. I told him about other dyslexic people I knew and how they were coping with their difficulties. I emphasised at all times that being dyslexic did not mean that you were stupid (Siegal, 1989) but that you had a specific problem just as some people are deaf or have poor eyesight etc. I used the term 'dyslexia' rather than specific learning difficulties since the mother was happier with the commonly-used terminology.

I also used a metacognitive approach to help him become aware of and take responsibility for his own learning (Nisbet and Shucksmith, 1984). Hunter-Carsch (1990) suggests that we should be giving children strategies for learning and that the emphasis in teaching should be on *'de-toning anxiety and building confidence through self-awareness'.*

LIAISON WITH CLASS TEACHER

During my consultations with the class teacher, we looked at parts of the curriculum that were causing problems for Robert. I assisted the class teacher in providing differentiated worksheets for various lessons and projects that were being done. These were useful for many more children than Robert and he found some success in class at last and was able to work with a group. The class teacher was very co-operative and was willing to allow Robert to sit beside a 'buddy' who would read instructions for him but not give him the answers to questions; she marked written work for content rather than spelling; she allowed him to tape record his stories for transcription later; he used a multiplication/division table card for maths; most important of all, she tried very hard to find something positive to say about every piece of work that he did.

LIAISON WITH HOME

At our regular meetings I was able to convince mother that she was doing more harm than good by drilling phonics, spelling and tables every night. I encouraged her to be more positive with him and to concentrate on helping Robert to become more organised. She began to encourage him to join clubs such as the Boys' Brigade and a karate club and to socialise more. She bought him a BBC computer for his birthday and most of his homework then tended to be related to that.

REVIEW

After 4 months we reviewed his progress. Everyone agreed that his behaviour had improved and his mother reported that he was wetting the bed and having migraine attacks less frequently. He was also showing more interest in his school work. I was anxious that Robert did not become too dependent on one-to-one support and I felt it was important that Robert worked on the same curriculum as his classmates as much as possible so for the second half of his primary seven year I dropped one of the individual teaching sessions and worked co-operatively with the class teacher. This was invaluable as I could link his individual lessons more closely to his class work and it also allowed me to work with Robert in a group of children, lessening his dependence on one-to-one support.

CREATIVE WRITING

I now decided to begin more formal work with Robert. Still using the computer, he used the 'Keyboard Skills' programme (SCET) to speed up his typing and began to use the 'Folio' wordprocessing workbook package (NCET). Robert was still very reluctant to 'write' his own stories. The breakthrough came after he had been to a computer camp with his class. He was so stimulated by this that I persuaded him to write a report for the local newspaper. His report was published and he glowed for a week. He became a more enthusiastic writer and produced more written work than he had ever done before. The quality of his wordprocessed writing was much better than his handwritten stories. He spotted spelling errors more readily and found it easy to edit text when the sequence of his story was wrong.

Chris Singleton (1991) confirms this and states that the editing flexibility of wordprocessing helps dyslexics to overcome their difficulties with organising ideas and structuring written work. He also stresses the motivational value of computer-assisted learning which increases the time that children are willing to practise academic skills so that mastery learning can take place.

READING

I wanted him to begin to read from books again. His reading was slow and stilted and he still tended to yawn excessively when asked to read. He lost the place frequently, had difficulty with visual tracking and misread many of the 'little' words. I used the Ann Arbor visual tracking exercises to reinforce left to right tracking. Initially, I used the 'Skyways Readers' (Collins Educational). I stressed that we were reading for enjoyment and the story needed to be read fluently if we were going to enjoy it. We experimented with ways of speeding up his reading – for example, using a stopwatch. I would time him reading a page and then he would read it two or three times more, trying to beat his time on each reading. He responded very well to this approach and we then took turn about at reading alternate pages.

He became very interested in the 'Nick Dick the Detective' books from the 'Skyways Series' and another opportunity for writing came when, having read one particular book, he was very annoyed with the ending as he felt there was not enough proof to incriminate the gardener! I encouraged him to write to the author to complain about the weak story line in this particular book. He was highly delighted to receive an apologetic reply from the author enclosing a book from another series as compensation. This meant of course that he had to write a thank-you letter as well. By selecting his reading books very carefully, he continued to improve in reading fluency and comprehension. He particularly enjoyed the 'Starpol Series' (Ginn and Co.) and the 'Trog Series' (Thomas Nelson). To encourage careful, accurate reading, Robert used two close procedure books, 'False Teeth and Vampires' and 'Astronauts and the Black Death' (LDA)

HANDWRITING

As Robert's handwriting was so poor I had to re-teach letter formation using cursive script. Because his letters were poorly sized, I used 'tramline' paper to make it easier for him to see that tall letters go above the top tramline and tails hang down below the bottom tramline. I felt that teaching cursive script would eliminate the b/d and p/q reversals which were such a feature of Robert's written work and would also encourage a more flowing style. Robert was very negative about this to begin with as he complained that it was too slow but after timing me writing a passage in unjoined infant script and then again in cursive script he had to agree that once he had mastered the new script his writing should be much neater and faster. He worked enthusiastically through a set of cursive script workbooks. Within a few months his handwriting improved dramatically and for the first time in his life, he had some of his written work displayed on the classroom wall.

SPELLING

Robert's visual memory was very poor. He could spell the same word in three different ways in a short passage of writing. He tended to spell phonetically and had little or no knowledge of spelling rules or common letter combinations. Robert needed to use a multi-sensory approach to spelling and I used a combination of the 'Look, Cover, Write, Check' method advocated by Margaret Peters and the 'Simultaneous Oral Spelling' technique used by Lynette Bradley. Again much work was done on the computer using the 'Cracker Spell' programme (Jordanhill College Publications). Teaching word families and spelling rules using 'Signposts to Spelling' (Heinemann) and 'Logical Spelling' (Collins) helped Robert to see that there was a pattern to language, and for words that he just could not remember we devised pictorial mnemonics. As spelling will continue to be a problem for Robert, I thought that it was important that he should develop skills for coping.

Before his transfer to Secondary School he was given a Tandy WP2 laptop computer with a spell checker. Much of his individual teaching time during those last few weeks of term was devoted to making sure he could operate the laptop competently as we hoped that he would do most of his written work in secondary on the computer. He was delighted with this and quickly mastered the intricacies of the machine. It was quite a potent status symbol for him as it made him feel grown up and important.

LIAISON WITH SECONDARY STAFF

The principal teacher of learning support was invited to join the class teacher and myself to observe Robert's difficulties and to plan how best to support him when he transferred to S1. It was not felt to be appropriate to continue with one-to-one teaching but the Secondary School made sure that Robert would be in a class that received a great deal of extra support through co-operative teaching. All subject teachers were made aware of Robert's specific problems and were asked to co-operate on using a standard correction code and not penalising Robert for poor spelling or asking him to read aloud.

The use of a 'Buddy' to help him read questions on worksheets or textbooks would continue and the school would photocopy notes for him instead of expecting him to copy them for himself as he found this very difficult. The Secondary School was already running a successful paired reading project involving sixth year pupils as tutors for first year children. Robert would be included in this and his 'tutor' would be carefully chosen and given some insight into Robert's specific difficulties. Robert was also given a 'consultation' time with the learning support teacher each week when he would be able to discuss with him any problems that he was facing.

CONCLUSION

At the end of the year when Robert was re-assessed, his reading age had improved by eighteen months and his spelling age by 12 months. His handwriting was neat and well-formed. However, everyone felt that the greatest gains were in the three other original aims:

1   His self-confidence was markedly improved, the bed wetting had stopped and the migraine headaches were infrequent.

2   He was now well motivated in class and was prepared to 'have a go' at most things.

3   His aggressive behaviour had ceased. He was now the class 'expert' on the computer and the other children asked him for help which was a great boost to his self-image.

The success of this intervention was largely due to the holistic perspective adopted. This has been highlighted in this chapter and includes addressing the child's needs, examining the curriculum content, differentiating the mode of teaching and learning, utilising the available resources, and consulting with other professionals and, very importantly, the parents.

REFERENCES

Bradley, L. (1980). *Assessing Reading Difficulties : A Diagnostic and Remedial Approach*. Macmillan Education.

Carbo, M., Dunn, R. and Dunn, K. (1986). *Teaching Students to Read through their Individual Learning Styles*. Englewood Cliffs, NJ: Prentice-Hall.

Crombie, M. (1990). *Specific Learning Difficulties (Dyslexia) – A Teacher's Guide*. Jordanhill College Publications, Glasgow.

Department of Education and Science, (1985), *The Curriculum 5 to 16*. HMSO.

Henderson, A. (1989). *Maths for Dyslexics*. St David's College, Llandudno.

Lawrence, D. (1973). *Improved Reading through Counselling*. Ward Lock.

Nisbet, J. and Shucksmith, J. (1988). *The Seventh Sense*. SCRE.

Ostler, C. (1991). *Dyslexia, A Parents' Guide*. Ammonite Books.

Pollok, J. *Signposts to Spelling*. Heinemann Education.

Simpson, M. (1989). *Differentiation in the Primary School : Investigations of Learning and Teaching*. Northern College, Aberdeen.

Siegel, L. S. (1989). 'IQ is irrelevant to the definition of learning disabilities'. *Journal of Learning Disabilities*, 22, 469-78.

TEACHING MATERIAL

Astronauts and the Black Death and *False Teeth and Vampires*. Learning Development Aids.

Bangers and Mash. Longmans.

CRIPPS CHARLES, *A Hand for Spelling*. Learning Development Aids.

Five Minute Thrillers and Tapes. Learning Development Aids.

Franklin Spellmaster. Venture Marketing.

Fuzzbuzz. Oxford University Press.

Help Games. H.E.L.P. Educational Games, Didcot, Oxon.

LIDDICOAT A., *Don't Let Spelling Get You Down*. Tregear Publications, Ickenham, Middlesex.

Logical Spelling. Collins Educational.

ACE Dictionary. Learning Development Aids Ltd.

Nick Dick Detective Series. Collins Educational.

Pergamon Dictionary of Perfect Spelling. Thomas Nelson & Sons Ltd.

Picture Writing Series. Learning Materials Ltd.
Phonic Rummy. Kenworthy Educational Services.
Reading Games. Macmillan Educational.
Rescue Readers. Ginn & Co.
ROOT BETTY, *Reading Games Series*. NES Arnold.
RUSSELL S., (1992), *Phonic Code Cracker*. Jordanhill College Publications, Glasgow.
RUSSELL S., (1992), *Cracker Spell*. Jordanhill College Publications, Glasgow.
Skyways Series. Collins Educational.
Starpol Series. Ginn & Co.
Grippy Pencil Grip. Learning Development Aids.
Trog Series. Thomas Nelson & Sons Ltd.
TOPPING, SCOBLE and OXLEY, (1988), *Cued Spelling*. Kirklees Metropolitan Council.
Tramline Writing Paper. Philip and Tacey.
Wellington Square. Thomas Nelson & Sons Ltd.
WENDON L., *Letterland Teaching Programme*. Letterland Ltd., Cambridge.

COMPUTER PROGRAMMES

(BBC 'B'/ Master, though many now also available for other machines.)
Animated Alphabet. (Sherston).
A to Z. (IEC Software).
Concept Keyboard Matching. (Scetlander).
Cracker Spell. (Jordanhill College Publications).
Dragon World. (4 Mation).
Dyslexia Aid. (Edsoft).
Flowers of Crystal. (4 Mation).
Folio. (ESM) and *Folio Workbook* package (NCET).
Funfair. (Northern Micromedia).
Fun School. (Europress Software).
Games For Dyslexic Children, (IEC Software).
Granny's Garden, (4 Mation).
Fleet Street Phantom. (Sherston).
Monster Maths. (AVP).
Nature Park Adventure. (Sherston).
Phonic Code Cracker. (Jordanhill College Publications).
PAL (predictive adaptive lexicon for PCs). Scetlander Ltd., Glasgow.
Predictype. Scetlander Ltd., Glasgow.
Sellardore Tales. (Sherston).
Stylus. (MAPE).
The Worst Witch. (Sherston).

DIFFERENTIATION
IN THE SECONDARY SCHOOL

DAVID DODDS

INTRODUCTION

Differentiation has become a widely used term for a wide variety of teaching approaches, taking different forms in different subjects, so it is as well to be clear at the outset what is meant by the term.

The Scottish Office Education Department defines differentiation as:
'. . . The identification of, and effective provision for a range of abilities in the classroom . . . Differentiated approaches should mean that the needs of the very able and of children with learning difficulties are discerned and met'.

This definition clearly implies that the starting place in planning to differentiate a course or unit has to be the pupils and their abilities. This will determine the contexts and content to a large extent, rather than having the content determine what it is that pupils will be expected to do.

ROLE OF THE SUBJECT TEACHER

Considerable skill and expertise exists within learning support departments in direct teaching methods that contribute to improving the language skills of pupils with specific learning difficulties. Equally, in advising subject teachers on appropriate teaching strategies or the suitability of materials, learning support teachers have a great deal to offer in supporting such pupils. Subject teachers, on the other hand, often feel particularly challenged by such pupils and lack confidence that their training or subsequent experience has equipped them with the skills necessary to teach them.

It is, however, no more appropriate to seek the solution of such difficulties principally within the pupil than it is for pupils with other difficulties. If the curriculum is differentiated to allow for the full range of ability and structured to take account of young peoples' learning needs, then pupils with specific learning difficulties will have difficulty gaining access to the curriculum in only the most extreme cases.

In fact the subject teacher has a crucial role to play. The vast majority, if not all, of the time spent in school by pupils with even the most severe specific learning difficulties will be spent in subject classes being taught by subject teachers working alone. The subject teacher's expertise is also invaluable for developing the skills, approaches and insights of the subject in all pupils. At a time when the curriculum is crowded as never before, the justification for including a subject is very often its distinctive approach or methodology, and it is therefore of great importance that that approach is embodied in the activities of all pupils.

It should always be borne in mind that the teacher is the most readily available information source in any classroom and the use of a carefully planned class lesson as a stimulus to a sequence of activities should not be underestimated. A short exposition possibly (using visual aids, but making full use of tone, emphasis and careful pacing, then developing understanding with open-ended questioning and responses to pupil questions) remains a powerful tool of the classroom teacher.

As stated earlier, different subjects would, and should, approach teaching and learning situations differently, with each emphasising the particular skills and methods that characterise that subject, and it is possible that some subject teachers may feel that the approaches suggested here are not particularly relevant to their subject.

The maths teacher might have doubts about the use of discussion techniques but in fact, mathematical language is least like everyday language and will pose many problems for learners. The option of removing language completely and presenting the pupil with a page of examples is likely to make the situation worse rather than better, as it leads to an all or nothing dependence on algorithms. If these are not recalled accurately, there can be no possibility of success. In fact, anyone spending time in maths classes, particularly mixed ability, cannot fail to be struck by the high level of 'informal peer tutoring' that arises naturally, with pupils explaining processes to each other quite readily. This is an aspect that can be fostered and developed, to take account of the needs of the learners to deploy their own spoken language in attempting to understand a problem. Pupils might not only be encouraged but also required to explain what they are doing, to their peers. The increasing use of problem-solving approaches also lends itself naturally to discussion.

A modern languages teacher might point out that discussion in English is, in fact, counter-productive and discussion in a foreign language is not possible till late in the development of the language. This may be so but the main factors in learning remain unchanged and need to be taken into account. The kind of vocabulary and situations used to develop the modern language will need to reflect closely the kind of language and situations the pupil is familiar with in his own language. Also, critical listening is extremely important in developing spoken language. Where pupils are working in pairs, the listener can often be passive. By requiring the listener to identify and correct errors made by the speaker, both partners can be involved throughout the activity. Equally short or closed assignments, with their emphasis on right or wrong answers, can be very discouraging. Pupils are much more likely to respond to more open-ended assignments where absolute precision comes second to genuine communication.

MATERIALS AND APPROACHES

To develop resources for pupils with specific learning difficulties, an appropriate starting point can be an examination of existing materials with a view to adapting them to meet the needs of the pupils concerned. It might be anticipated that this would be a process of simplifying text, providing tape recorded text where necessary, and simplifying written assignments or altering them to provide alternatives to writing. It may, however, be necessary to substantially revise units of work to alter the sequence of activities or to change the emphasis in a particular assignment.

This possible need to substantially redraft can be due to the emphasis on presenting information leading to an individual written outcome as the organising principle of the unit. Although units may certainly cover the topic area, it is much less certain that it would be learned. Polling a study of a number of such units I found little evidence of a consistent view about the nature of the learner or how learning took place. The underlying assumption was that exposure to the materials would be sufficient in itself. This appeared to be confirmed by the findings of recent study Allan, Brown and Munn, 1991) that subject teachers were concerned to try to ensure that pupils **learned the same content.**

Where the content is the starting point for course design, the options for differentiation are likely to be reduced. Differentiation is often attempted either by having all pupils doing the same things but at different rates, e.g. all pupils work through the topics covered in a specific textbook but work individually and with different levels of support, or pupils follow courses at different levels of difficulty but covering the same areas in terms of the topic covered. On this model, pupils working on the lowest level might be expected to complete a blank-filling activity or word-search while pupils at a higher level might give single sentence answers to questions, and at a higher level still, might have to write a paragraph. The information leading to the pupil response would be presented at differing degrees of reading level and complexity

A common approach to course construction that combines both elements is the core plus options model where all pupils in a class work through a common core which is followed by a criterion-referenced test. The results of this test determine whether pupils go on to carry out extension or remediation activities before completing another final test. In practice, such a course is extremely difficult to construct. Problems tend to arise on what should constitute the core. If the core is limited as far as possible, then the time spent by pupils on separate extension or remediation activities can increase to such an extent that it would be difficult to describe pupils as following the 'same' course. If, on the other hand, a wider view of the core is taken, then the possibilities for meeting the needs of the least and most able decrease. Underlying this approach is the concept of mastery learning, and defining mastery for a set of tasks can be problematic as can testing for it. Nevertheless, such an approach can offer many pupils the opportunity to work on appropriate texts and at a suitable pace, and there are many examples of departments running successful courses along these lines. The structure in itself is, however, no guarantee that differentiation will occur. Teaching and learning approaches are the key to differentiation, whatever course structure is adopted.

PRINCIPLES OF DISCUSSION

In developing units and courses it is essential to take account of:

(i) Pupils' language skills;

(ii) Pupils' existing knowledge.

It is essential both to recognise and to capitalise on the highly developed language skills of all pupils, and to bear in mind that even pupils with reading and /or writing difficulties have considerable oral language skills. It is also important to keep in mind that the pupil's understanding will depend on how well he can assimilate new input with what he already knows. The most effective way of allowing pupils to bring to bear both their existing knowledge and their oral language skills is to give a high priority to talk and discussion as part of the learning process. Talking and listening to talk, being able to rehearse and examine ideas using their own language, are the most powerful tools and occasionally the only effective tools that pupils are able to bring to bear in understanding the curriculum.

THE PEOPLE OF SOUTH AFRICA

INFORMATION CARD

When it was elected in 1948, the Nationalist Government passed laws to support its policy of APARTHEID. Apartheid means separate development for people of different races. The government thought that it was best for each race to live separately. This would allow them to keep their own language, customs and traditions.

- Look carefully at all the information below. Now complete the graphs on the sheet called, 'SOUTH AFRICA'S PEOPLE: FACTS AND FIGURES.'

TABLE 1: SOUTH AFRICA: POPULATION

Racial group	Population	% of Total
WHITE: People whose ancestors came from Europe English or Afrikaans (a kind of Dutch)	5.0 million	13.7%
AFRICAN: Blacks who are descendents of the people who lived in Southern Africa before the whites arrived	28.0 million	75.0%
COLOURED: 'Mixed Race' Descendents of early marriages between blacks and whites	3.2 million	8.7%
ASIAN: The people whose ancestors came from India to work for the British on the railways they built after they arrived in South Africa	1.0 million	2.6%

TABLE 2: INCOME, PENSIONS, SPENDING ON EDUCATION, PUPILS PER TEACHER

	WHITE	BLACK	COLOURED	ASIAN
INCOME PER PERSON (RANDS per year)	15,000	1250	3000	4600
OLD AGE PENSIONS (RANDS per month)	280	180	230	230
SPENDING PER PUPILS (RANDS per year)	1300	500	1300	2600
PUPILS PER TEACHER	19	40	22	20

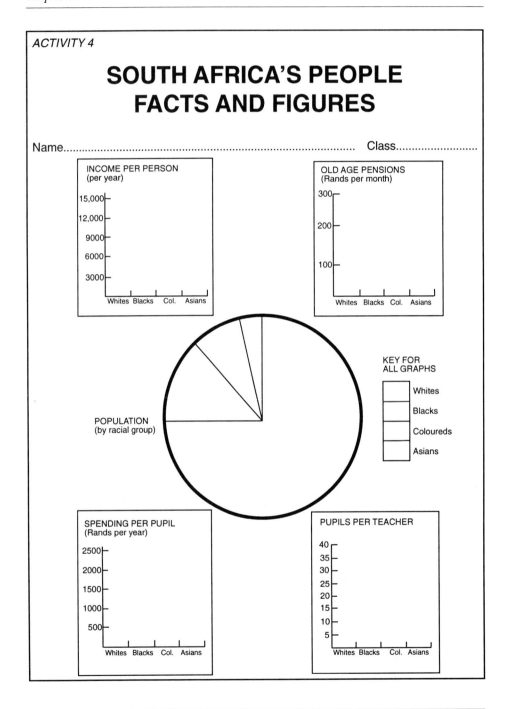

ACTIVITY 4

SOUTH AFRICA'S PEOPLE
FACTS AND FIGURES

Name.. Class..........................

INCOME PER PERSON
(per year)

15,000
12,000
9000
6000
3000

Whites Blacks Col. Asians

OLD AGE PENSIONS
(Rands per month)

300
200
100

Whites Blacks Col. Asians

POPULATION
(by racial group)

KEY FOR
ALL GRAPHS

Whites
Blacks
Coloureds
Asians

SPENDING PER PUPIL
(Rands per year)

2500
2000
1500
1000
500

Whites Blacks Col. Asians

PUPILS PER TEACHER

40
35
30
25
20
15
10
5

Whites Blacks Col. Asians

ACTIVITY 4   *Fig. 1*

SOUTH AFRICA'S PEOPLE
GROUP DISCUSSION SHEET

Name.. Class........................

- Look at your sheet 'SOUTH AFRICA'S PEOPLE: FACTS AND FIGURES'
- In groups of AT LEAST FOUR, discuss the information then complete the following
  table:

Standard of Living	Racial Group
HIGHEST	
↓	
↓	
LOWEST	

- Write the words ASIAN, BLACK, COLOURED and WHITE on four pieces of paper.
  Fold them up and get each member of the group to pick one.
- How do you feel about your choice? EXPLAIN WHY

- If you could, would you change?
  If YES, which group would you have chosen? WHY?

- In your groups, try to explain why the living standards of the racial groups are so
  different. Write your ideas in the space below.

GROUP DISCUSSION

Encouraging pupils to work together on discussion tasks in small groups or even in pairs can be a means of providing support for less able group members and allowing groups of differing abilities to tackle complex tasks. An example (fig. 1) taken from an S2 Modern Studies unit on South Africa illustrates how this approach might work in practice. In the original class, the sequence was as shown, an information card, followed by completion of the graphs and then the discussion. By altering the sequence so that the discussion activities precede the completion of the graphs the activity becomes much more accessible. The information card is extremely dense, containing a great deal of complex information. For many pupils working individually on this sheet would be a daunting prospect, but taking part in a group discussion, hearing the ideas re-phrased in familiar language, and being required to offer their own understanding of the material to the group allows pupils of all abilities to profit from the process, either in the support it offers or in the demands it makes not only to understand the material but to explain that understanding to others.

Groups are not seen as being fixed but would vary from task to task, on occasions, being pupil-selected or perhaps teacher-selected for a particular purpose, perhaps to group together children who were felt to be hesitant in offering ideas or to ensure a balance between different levels of ability. Where a particular topic or idea is felt to be of central importance, the teacher might decide to make use of tutorial groups within the class, either teacher led, or led by a pupil combining a good understanding of the ideas being discussed with the ability to lead a discussion.

In addition to promoting understanding of the topic under discussion, the group situation can be used to assess understanding by use of reporting back. Individuals can report back to small groups, or groups to the whole class, orally, perhaps using visual aids.

If group discussion is to play a central role in the learning process, it follows that the process itself, rather than just the outcomes of the process, must be taught and assessed within the context in which to be used. While many of the processes that shape group discussion, such as the ability to listen critically and to develop an argument, will be common to all subjects, the type of task undertaken will vary from subject to subject and should reflect the skills and priorities of that subject. A discussion in Science might well centre on the variables that need to be controlled if an experiment is to be reliable, while a discussion in History might centre on the interests (and therefore the reliability) of a particular source. In each case, the criteria to be used will need to be taught and developed. There will be occasions when a teacher may wish to emphasise only these subject-specific aspects of a task and may group pupils by their understanding in that particular aspect of the work, to ensure that pupils are able to develop through working with others at a similar level.

While working in groups on discussion-based activities will allow pupils of differing abilities to cope more efficiently with information, another important factor in developing understanding is the use to which the information is put.

ACTIVITY 6   Fig. 2A

THE HOMELANDS

Name... Class.......................

INDIVIDUAL WORK

- Get a copy of THE HOMELANDS INFORMATION CARD

- Read the information and look carefully at the map

- Complete this passage:

When the Nationalist Government divided South Africa, the areas for black people were

known as .... Where they were sent depended on

the home of their .... Families were often ....

because some people worked for whites in the.. These

people lived in ....outside the cities.

An example of a HOMELAND is..

An example of a TOWNSHIP is ....

This example (fig. 2A) from the same Modern Studies unit shows a fairly typical type of pupil activity. The pupil, having read a section of text, is required to fill in the blanks in this paragraph to ascertain whether or not he has understood the original information. A number of points arise out of this activity:

    (i)   Taking into account what has been said earlier, I would argue strongly that requiring the pupil to deal with the text individually is

---

much less effective than using the text as the basis for group discussion activities.

(ii) Even allowing for the fact that the missing words are supplied and that they all represent key ideas for this topic, a pupil cannot begin to cope with the exercise as a means of checking understanding of the ideas involved unless he can cope with the exercise as a piece of reading. This type of exercise requires the pupil to understand the context of the missing word as well as the word itself and is always likely to prove problematic for any pupil with reading difficulties, even though the words and the ideas behind them are well enough understood. If the pupil realises that the missing word has the same number of letters as there are dashes in the blank, the activity can be completed without understanding either the original text or the comprehension check. (In practice, pupils presented with this type of activity will frequently reduce it to a letter count, just as presented with a worksheet giving a text followed by numbered questions they will often begin reading at the first question, using the test only as a 'mine' from which correct answers are to be extracted).

Fig. 2B

GROUP WORK

- In your groups, discuss the HOMELANDS INFORMATION CARD.

- Complete the table below: use ALL the information

THE HOMELANDS	
Advantages to Whites	Disadvantages to Blacks

(iii)   This is a good example of an activity likely to ensure coverage, rather than learning of a group of ideas. The paragraph for completion is similar to the original text in which the terms were presented. All that is really required of the pupil is literal comprehension. Provided the paragraph is understood, the missing terms can almost be transposed from the original text. The information does not need to be reorganised in any way. The sequence of activities is intended to introduce information for pupils to read as individuals and to demonstrate their understanding individually before moving to group discussion. In practice, the group discussion activity (fig. 2B) makes the blank filling exercise redundant and it would be more effective for the group discussion to be the means for developing the understanding of the ideas in the original text. Individual follow-up from the discussion might have required the pupil to re-organise the information or to use it in another context, eg writing a script for a radio broadcast or writing as a black South African to explain to a Scottish teenager what the Homelands mean at a personal level. Compare this sequence of activities with the earlier sequence (fig. 1) where the pupils were required to represent the information in graph form. (Even here, opportunities for further differentiation exist by allowing pupils to opt for producing suitable graphs without the templates)

WRITTEN RESPONSES

The nature of individual written responses, as illustrated by fig. 2A is extremely important from the point of view of differentiation of the curriculum; in that example or in the type of 'text followed by questions' activity, even where care is taken to go beyond purely literal comprehension questions, the room for differentiation of responses is extremely limited. If all that is required is a sentence, then the difference between the 'best' possible answer, an adequate answer and an unsuccessful answer is very small. A pupil who has fully understood is denied the opportunity to display the extent of that understanding and the pupil who has not understood may not reveal the nature of source of his failure to understand. Written assignments need to be as open-ended as possible to allow pupils to extend their understanding in their completion.

Pupils should be given the opportunity to:

Re-organise information, e.g. changing events from chronological order to their order of importance;

re-present information, e.g. present it in the form of a graph or table;

evaluate information, e.g. in history to consider the reliability of a source; in Science to consider the validity of an experiment;

respond imaginatively to information, e.g. to write as one of the protagonists in a situation;

relay information, e.g. to 'teach' a new concept to a peer or group of peers, or to younger children.

This is by no means intended as an exhaustive list. Subject teachers will undoubtedly be able to offer further alternatives for their particular subject, and the balance of activities might alter from subject to subject, but every subject offers opportunities to develop understanding that goes far beyond literal comprehension.

THE USE OF TEXT

The use of printed text as the main or even sole source of information has limitations even when group discussion activities are being used as a means of allowing access to the material. In terms of involving pupils directly in a situation it requires a leap of imagination on the part of the readers even with the highest quality of written text. Much more direct access to information about a problem or situation, can be given by using video-tapes, audio-tapes or indeed talk by the teacher or other individual with first-hand experience. In the unit on South Africa already referred to, the second half of the unit is organised around a commercial video-tape based on the experiences of four British teenagers living for a month with South African teenagers. This allows complex and often difficult issues to be explored in a very direct and powerful manner. The sequence in the film that contrasts the opulent lifestyle of the white South African family with the black teenager collecting water to wash in from a standpipe illustrates inequality with a power that would be difficult to achieve even with the best of textbooks or worksheets.

In setting assignments, we need to allow pupils sufficient opportunity to bring what they already know to bear on the task and to extend their understanding, before setting a task that requires them to rework the input in some way that will allow us to measure how their understanding has grown.

CONCLUSION

In seeking to differentiate the curriculum in the secondary school, it has become common to try to provide different levels of printed input or to require different levels of written response while at the same time setting strict limits on the length and nature of the response. In short, it has been an attempt to differentiate on paper, to adjust the input and the output. If we are to meet a wide range of learning needs within the same subject class, we need to concentrate on the area between the input and output – the learning skills and processes that pupils are expected to develop through the activities on offer. It is here that pupils with specific learning difficulties can develop skills in learning, often in collaboration with others, to develop and refine the characteristic skills and perspectives of each subject area.

REFERENCES

Allan, J., Brown, S. and Munn, P. (Eds). (1991). *Off The Record: Mainstream provision for pupils with non-recorded learning difficulties in primary and secondary schools.* Scottish Centre for Research in Education, Edinburgh.

LEARNING SUPPORT PROVISION WITHIN A MAINSTREAM SECONDARY SCHOOL

DAVID BLAIR, AVRIL MILNE, MAGGI FENTON, MORAG GIBSON, JANICE MASTERTON, ISOBEL TRIAY and ANNE MORTON

THE SCHOOL

The school is a non-denominational, co-educational, six year comprehensive Secondary catering for about 1760 pupils. Opportunities are also available to adult students to undertake study within the curriculum. As well as the Learning Support Department, the school has a Department for Hearing Impairment and a Support Centre which caters for pupils with social and emotional difficulties.

The Learning Support Department has 5.5 members of staff, one of whom is Principal Teacher and one Senior Teacher. Three members of the department hold the Diploma of Professional Studies, Special Educational Needs – Secondary while remaining staff are undertaking the Moray House modules on Specific Learning Difficulties (Dyslexia).

The Department occupies two linking rooms. One room is used mainly as a Staff Base, Resource Centre and extra Tutorial Room, while the other is a Tutorial Room and Resource Centre.

The school operates a Year Head system with additional duties assigned to individual members of the Board of Management. The direct line to management for Learning Support is through the Assistant Headteacher whose responsibilities include Special Educational Needs and Guidance.

The Regional Framework

Learning Support staff in Fife are directed to support schools in identifying needs and arranging provision for pupils within the local mainstream setting. The focus for provision is through the curriculum and therefore support through consultancy, co-operative teaching and the staff development roles takes up the major part of the Learning Support timetabled time.

Where there is a need for a particular literacy, Numeracy, organisational or counselling programme, there may be a need for one-to-one teaching outwith the curriculum involving Learning Support. Regular reviews of programmes and evidence of successful transference of skills would be required for the programme to be extended long-term.

A balance is sought in term of progress in learning within context and progress in basic skills acquisition. All schools have guidelines for assessment and record-keeping along with guidelines on specific learning difficulties/dyslexia.

This school has been instrumental in recent years, in highlighting the need for more consistent record-keeping, related to support for learning, across Primary and Secondary. Because of the size of the school there is a particularly onerous task in monitoring and reviewing pupil progress.

Departmental Aims

The aims of the Department are:

*   To be a whole-school resource which helps to provide appropriate education for all pupils.
*   To respond to the needs of the school population by annually establishing which departments and individuals require Learning Support help.
*   To prioritise and plan provision according to the departmental resource and the 'Whole-School Policy for Appropriate Learning'.
*   To be as flexible as possible within this framework in order to respond to requests for help when they occur.
*   To act as a source of information on pupils, the curriculum, teaching styles and methodology and to circulate that information, where appropriate, to subject department or specific teachers.

Establishing Priorities

At the start of each term, a written communication is issued to indicate the focus of the department for the term. The communication keeps all staff informed of the on-going work of the department (see Figure 1).

Fig. 1

FOCUS OF SUPPORT – Session 94-95

TERM 1

FIRST YEAR

In-class support, as a means of monitoring S1, will be the focus of the Dept. until the 'October Break'. During the period, a paired reading programme will be set up for S1 pupils.

SECOND YEAR

The focus is to continue to support/monitor identified pupils or classes through in-class support, direct tuition, reading and/or scribing assessments and paired reading as appropriate.

STANDARD GRADE PUPILS

In S3 and S4 the focus of support will be the on-going monitoring of pupils especially those with Specific Learning Difficulties in line with S.E.B. Guidelines.

Support will also be given to the development and evaluation of a Spoken English course through Consultation and Co-operative Teaching.

From Monday 24th October, the work of the LSS Department will focus on the following:

- Curriculum/Pupil support for identified S2 classes in mathematics
- Curriculum support for delivery of S2 Earth Forces in Geography with identified classes.
- Continued curriculum/pupil support for identified S1 classes in mathematics
- Establishing and supporting paired reading scheme for S1 pupils
- Support for Spoken English course in S3 and S4
- Curriculum support for identified pupils in S2/S2 (withdrawals)
- Curriculum support for identified pupils in S3/S4 Short Courses
- Curriculum support for identified pupils in S2 Taster Course
- Scribing for SEN pupils in S4 prelims
- Primary liaison to make initial visits to Primary seven to review pupils with SEN and also low achievers. Implement the passing on of information on present S1 pupils to respective feeder primaries.

The priorities outlined above all be in place until end of term. However, pupil referrals should still be made through the normal channels.

Allocation of Staff

Learning Support staff are assigned to associated primary schools and liaison takes the form of Primary 7 visits in the primary school from October and continuing through P7 until transfer.

At the start of secondary, Learning Support staff are assigned to classes and those pupils remain that teacher's responsibility throughout their school career. Careful placing also occurs at this stage, whereby a pupil may be placed in a class being supported by the Learning Support teacher who worked with that pupil in primary. Late arrivals and on-going referrals are then dealt with by the member of the Learning Support team responsible for that class.

LEARNING SUPPORT FOCUS WITHIN TRANSFER FROM PRIMARY TO SECONDARY

The liaison between the Learning Support Department and its twelve associated primary schools is part of the school's pattern of providing a continuous, coherent and progressive education for all pupils in the associated schools. The Department operates Primary/Secondary liaison within the framework of both Regional and School policies on Support for Learning and the 5-14 National Guidelines. The Learning Support staff work to the following framework:

General Aim

To establish a two-way exchange of information to facilitate:

- Ease of transfer, for all pupils, from P7 to S1.
- Awareness of pupils' needs through detailed documentation.
- Continuity of appropriate learning contexts.
- The development of curricular links within 5-14 Guidelines.

Practice – General

The above aim is realised through the following practices.

Members of the Learning Support:

- Are assigned to associated primaries.
- Spend part of a morning each week in the associated primaries, ideally beginning in October, to get to know all P7 pupils transferring to secondary school.

- Open and maintain record-keeping on identified pupils and inform and encourage Year Head/Guidance/Subject Teachers to consult these.
- Act as an administrative/curricular link between the Primaries and Secondary school.
- May be involved in the Primary Roadshow (where secondary management hold an informative meeting with P7 parents in their respective primary schools) and/or P7 Parents' Evenings.
- Manage and organise P7 pupils visit to secondary school during the summer term, when pupils follow a typical timetable for a day.

Practice – Specific

Members of the Learning Support:

- Work with all pupils, paying particular attention to those pupils identified as requiring support for learning.
- Be aware of pupils' preferred learning styles and stage of cognitive development.
- Use all channels of communication available in the associated primaries in order to establish/add to working records through consultation with the Headteacher, Class Teacher, Primary Learning Support, Psychological Services, Fife Summary of Intervention (i) and attendance of Standard Circular No 83 meetings (ii).
- Become familiar with the P7 Curriculum in context and communicate this knowledge to subject teachers, both formally and informally, thereby fostering stronger curricular overlap.
- Compile and issue an initial information sheet for S1 Year Head, Guidance and Subject Teachers about transferring P7 pupils with identified learning needs and any other appropriate information on transfer to secondary schools.

In-class support, as a means of monitoring S1 pupils across the curriculum, is a focus of the department from August to the October break.

Additional information held in the Learning Support Base is always available to all teaching staff. Teachers of pupils with specific learning difficulties/ Dyslexia receive detailed information including strategies and support proposed following meetings in the primary school. A meeting with the Guidance staff and the Year Head also takes place at this time.

(i)   The Fife Summary of Intervention is a working document about good school record-keeping to assist identification of needs, assessment and agreed provision at stage 1 or 2.

(ii) Standard Circular No. 83 is the regional documentation which leads schools through case conferencing from level 1 to level 3.

N.B. Further information is available by contacting the Advisory or Psychological Services in Fife.

Monitoring Transition from Primary to Secondary

During the initial eight week period in Secondary School, Learning Support staff undertake a monitoring/shadowing exercise with all S1 classes. Apart from the very rare exception, all pupils follow a common curriculum and during this period of time, Learning Support staff gain valuable information on how pupils with specific learning difficulties/Dyslexia cope with the varying demands of the curriculum. It also means they are usually at hand to support pupils with specific learning difficulties/dyslexia.

By the end of the monitoring period, Learning Support staff have built up a clear picture of the need and level of support that the pupil with specific learning difficulties/dyslexia will need. Most often this support will take place within the classroom with extraction from class for the course assessments to be read and/or scribed as necessary.

WHOLE SCHOOL COMMUNICATION AND RECORD-KEEPING

Effective record-keeping of all communication forms an integral part of the role of the Learning Support teacher. Specific departmental proformae are used to record the details of any communication, both formal and informal, and these proformae are then placed in the pupil's individual file held in the Department, or circulated as appropriate. When deemed necessary, photocopies of this information may be passed on to the Pupil Progress Record held in the Guidance base.

An on-going record is also kept of the individual's progress within the context of the curriculum and during the direct tuition which serves as a means of monitoring and evaluating the pupil's progress in both areas. This information may also form the agenda for meetings with parents and/or pupils.

Initial contact with a pupil experiencing specific learning difficulties/dyslexia and his/her parents is usually made during the period P7 liaison, although such a contact may begin earlier. At this point, the parents are actively encouraged to phone/come into the school to discuss any issues or concerns they may have with the appropriate member of staff in the Learning Support Department. This on-going communication helps to establish a positive framework within which a valuable partnership between home and school develops.

The Learning Support Department works closely with the Educational Psychologist assigned to the school. He visits the Department on a weekly basis to discuss with the appropriate member of staff information on pupils with whom he is currently working. He may also attend and/or arrange joint meetings outwith his weekly visit. Communication may also be required between the Learning Support teacher and other outside agencies, depending on the needs of the individual pupil. Links between the Department and the Careers Advisory Service and Special Needs co-ordinator of Further Education establishments are developed to ensure that the pupil's future provision is well-planned and in place.

A high priority is placed on communication within the school context – between the Learning Support Teacher and the pupils whom he/she supports and between the Learning Support Department and other departments in the school. Learning Support works in close association with Guidance to support the pupil with specific learning difficulties/dyslexia e.g. the Learning Support teacher may provide a valuable source of information and encourage an appropriate selection of subject choices for Standard and Higher Grades. Joint involvement may be required to use the Fife Summary of Intervention. Members of the Learning Support Department are responsible for maintaining communication outwith the department in many ways viz:

- Circulating information on pupils,
- Consultation,
- Standardised memos,
- Case conferences,
- In-service training,
- Contact with Advisory Services,
- Negotiating with Scottish Examination Board for special exam arrangements through the designated Assistant Headteacher.

In this way, effective communication allows Learning Support staff to develop and maintain a partnership with the school, pupils and parents. This may also involve other outside agencies, as in Figure 2, which shows the pupil-centred model of interaction.

Fig. 2

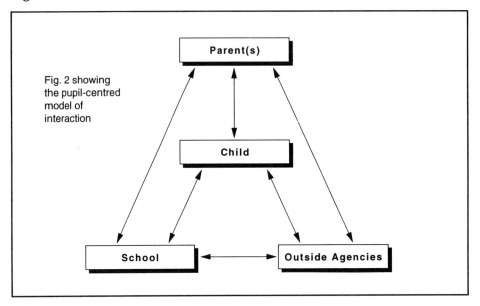

Fig. 2 showing the pupil-centred model of interaction

COMMUNICATION WITHIN THE LEARNING SUPPORT DEPARTMENT

This specific communication takes place via:

Departmental Meetings

These take place during Planned Activity Time (30 hours per session) and, in addition, one period per week. The meetings facilitate the dissemination of information and provide a forum for debate.

Members of the Department may place subject(s) for consideration on the agenda. Issues for general information are also presented. Minutes are taken and circulated to each member of the Department. An on-going record of all Learning Support Departmental meetings is filed, with a further copy being issued to the appropriate members of The Board of Management.

Circulars

Information arrives in the Department from a variety of sources, including minuted meetings within the school, Regional and National correspondence. The

Principal Teacher arranges for circulation within the Department. Each member initials the correspondence and, on return to the Principal Teacher, it is filed in the respective folder.

Referrals

Referrals to the Learning Support Department are processed according to the following procedure:

1. Referrals arrive in Learning Support via Principal Teacher (LSS) from Year Head.
2. Principal Teacher completes summary sheet in referral folder and transfers the referral sheet to the appropriate Learning Support teacher.
3. If possible, contact should be made with referring teacher within three school days.
4. Following consultation with the referring teacher, the Learning Support teacher should complete section 'Action Taken'.
5. The original referral sheet is returned by the Learning Support teacher to the Year Head, having retained a copy. The Year Head sends a copy to the referring teacher and files the original referral in the pupil's PPR.
6. Photocopies remain in the referral file until the end of the session, when they are transferred to the pupil's Learning Support file.

The summary of this procedure is outlined in the following flow chart (see Figure 3).

Fig. 3

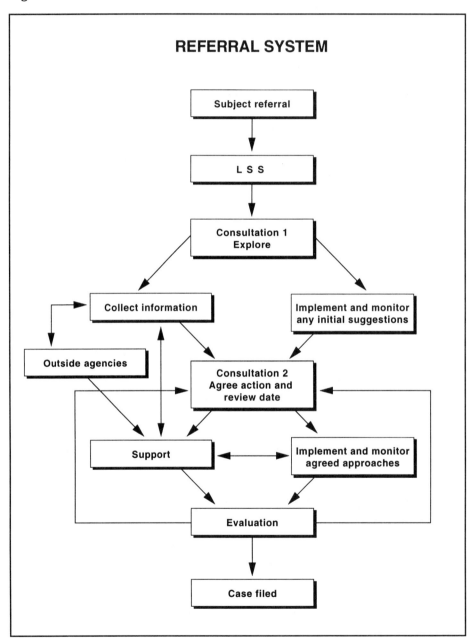

REFERRAL SYSTEM

SPECIFIC LEARNING DIFFICULTIES/DYSLEXIA AND ASSESSMENT OF NEEDS

Most pupils will have been identified through Primary Liaison whilst others will be identified on transfer. Their progress will be monitored through co-operative teaching and consultation during shadowing of S1 classes in term 1.

Learning Support teachers in Secondary Schools and the pupils they support must work within the curricula provided by 5-14, Standard Grade and Highers and make these curricula work for them. It is in these, and particularly in the exams which are their culmination, that parents, employers, institutions of further education and the children themselves measure their success. Underpinning both 5-14 and Standard Grade is the belief that pupils should be measured against their achievements within the curriculum. Thus, the most important forms of assessment in the Secondary School are curriculum-based. The child who excels in class discussion in Modern Studies but finds it impossible to communicate his thoughts on paper, the child who copes well in Maths but flounders in English, must be the concern of the Learning Support teacher.

For the Learning Support teacher and the pupil, perhaps the most important means of assessment is observation. Since the Learning Support teacher cannot always be available to the pupil in the classroom, it is of crucial importance to understand how the pupil functions there and to work with the subject specialist to ensure that both teacher and pupil understand each other's needs.

However, there is no one approach to assessment which will provide all the answers and staff need to be aware of a range of methods. Standardised tests provide reliability, validity and an understandable score. If used carefully they can also provide diagnostic information e.g. the Neale Analysis of Reading Ability can indicate a way forward.

PROVISION FOR SPECIFIC LEARNING DIFFICULTIES/DYSLEXIA

Throughout a pupil's school career support is offered either in class or by Direct Tuition. Within these broad approaches, several different pathways can be provided, tailored specifically to the needs of the individual child. (See case study).

The curriculum can be amended or restricted to articulate with pupil requirements and where this is not possible, alternative programmes can be provided either in class or through extraction. Paired Reading is offered with Direct Tuition to pupils in S1 and S2 utilising volunteers from the senior school. In S2, Curriculum Support is offered as one of a selection of Taster Courses which introduce pupils to possible Standard Grade choices. Pupils will preferably select this course themselves but may be encouraged to do so by Learning Support or Guidance. The content of the course is then articulated to the need of the child, focusing on specific aspects of the curriculum. As part of a diet of Short Courses in S3 and S4, the Learning Support Department again offers Curriculum Support to those pupils not following the full range of seven S grades. These courses are also curriculum-based, supporting pupils in aspects of courses which require independent study, such as investigations and Folio presentations.

The English department now offers a Standard Grade course in Spoken English. This was developed in consultation with Learning Support and its delivery is supported by the department. This course removes the written element for those pupils for whom it is inappropriate, develops strengths and encourages pupils to take responsibility for their own learning. All folio work and assessments are taped. The Talk element of Standard Grade English remains unchanged.

Pupils are encouraged to familiarise themselves with a variety of ways to access information and record their responses. In this way they may select their preferred methods of learning:

- Pupils may use a reader or listen to material taped by an auxiliary or senior school volunteer.
- Pupils may use photocopied notes from other pupils or teachers.
- Pupils may have work presented to them enlarged or on coloured paper.
- Pupils may use a scribe.
- The pupil's own work may be typed, with or without spelling corrections, by an auxiliary.
- Pupils may present their work assisted by technology available from the LS department: Spellcheck, Tandy, BBC, Applemac.

The pupil's access to the curriculum is greatly facilitated by the provision of auxiliary support. Auxiliary services may include the taping of course work for pupils to listen to, the transcription of pupils' taped responses and organisation of pupils' written work and practical tasks. After the pupil has experienced all the options and chosen the preferred methods of support, appropriate provision can be made for him or her in school assessments and national exams.

Although the Learning Support teacher will support the individual pupil appropriately, it is necessary to keep in mind that the subject teacher has ultimate responsibility for that pupil's learning. This can create problems and raise issues as indicated by the responses to a questionnaire issued to subject teachers, Guidance teachers and representatives of school management.

SPECIFIC LEARNING DIFFICULTIES/DYSLEXIA AND ACCESS TO PUPILS FOR DIRECT TUITION

Continuous access to a pupil with specific learning difficulties/dyslexia is provided through classroom support as agreed with subject teachers. When a decision is taken on the need for Direct Tuition, the old chestnut of 'where to take from' raises its head. In S1, agreement has been reached where access is available via time (2 x 40 minutes) from Classical Studies, which is a course accessed mainly through language. Any additional time to be found has to be negotiated with the subjects where support is sought. In S2, S3 and S4 it is not necessary to make arrangements for withdrawal from subjects because timetable provision allows access, viz the Taster Course in S2, Short Courses in S3 and S4 and module/study time in S5 and S6.

Problems and Issues

It must be stressed from the outset, that the pupil is never to be seen as the problem. The problem is ours, to adapt the system to cater for pupils' needs by modifying, adapting and providing alternatives. Pupils with specific learning difficulties/dyslexia depend on structured courses because they themselves lack organisational skills. Poor organisation has a 'knock on' effect in practical classes where they find it difficult to plan and carry out logical sequence. Lack of organisational skills can also affect completion of homework, bringing the correct equipment to school, planning essay structures or investigations and general management of the pupil's own timekeeping and resources.

The Way Ahead

A survey of class teachers was carried out and most of these teachers felt that problems/issues highlighted could, in part, be solved by addressing the need for in-service training providing a general background on the nature of dyslexia, as well as particular strategies to deal with individual pupils. The case conference model, which most suggested, would have timetabling implications which would have to be addressed as a whole-school issue. Consultation takes time but its value must not be underestimated and consultation with parents was seen by those surveyed as equally important. Planned Activity Time is already in place as part of the timetable and available to be used for meetings of interested parties.

Further links are being developed with the parents through the production of a specialist booklet which prepares the pupil with specific learning difficulties/ Dyslexia and their parents for transfer into secondary schooling.

The Authority promotes modular training on specific learning difficulties/ dyslexia at post-graduate level. It is anticipated that an in-service package will be available next session to schools, to be delivered to whole-school staff on awareness-raising of specific learning difficulties/dyslexia, enabling support service staff and class teachers to move on together in their understanding of dyslexia and the range of possible provisions.

CASE STUDY

James was identified as having learning difficulties in Primary 2 and had extensive time from learning support throughout Primary School. Continuity of support was provided on entry to Secondary School as the learning support teacher whom he met through primary liaison in P7 became his First Line Guidance teacher as well as the Learning Support teacher assigned to his class in S1.

His father is rather authoritarian and plays no part in the home/school dialogue. His mother provides this contact but confessed herself unable to cope with James' personality problems and poor social skills. Physically uncoordinated, he finds sport, especially team games, almost impossible. James enjoys practical tasks, often outdoors, such as mending a gate or constructing a fence. He can plan, organise and carry out quite complex pieces of building work or joinery.

Throughout his time at Primary School, James had become increasingly unhappy and isolated. He was distressed by being seen to be different and yet was not successful in working alongside others. He had poor social skills and became very negative and his home circumstances are not always easy.

Much of the support given to James in P7 had centred around the use of a Tandy laptop word processor, the intention being to steer him towards independent learning within the curriculum. Like many pupils with specific learning difficulties/ dyslexia he found organising his thoughts difficult and was physically unco-ordinated, leading to poor keyboard skills and information retrieval skills. Added to this, James hated being so obviously different from his classmates.

At Secondary School ,James had immediate problems coping with the array of subjects, the demands of particular subjects and the higher level of self management necessary to arrange homework, a timetable and movement around the school. James' anti-social behaviour was less easy to contain and control in Secondary School and this led to discipline problems due to truancy and personality clashes with teachers. It became a priority to deal with these aspects because until his attitude and motivation improved, little could be done for him within the curriculum. James began working regularly with teachers in the school's support centre on social skills, group work and talk. This was monitored in class in co-operation with the school's educational psychologist.

James had been withdrawn in S1 and S2 from his foreign language to work on programmes to improve his standard of reading, writing and to practise keyboard skills. This was changed in favour of counselling sessions and practising skills needed to use a reader and scribe effectively. In class, support Had been provided in most areas of the curriculum, but particularly in language-based subjects and also in Maths. This continued in S3 but in consultation with James' Guidance teacher, it was agreed that he should be encouraged to consider courses which would make support less obtrusive. James was happy to follow this advice.

James' Standard Grade Course was as follows:

Craft & Design	James had the skills needed to cope.
Maths	Foundation course with which James could cope.
History	James trusted his S2 History teacher and chose to work with him again.
Biology	Recommended for this course and placed with a member of staff with whom he had formed a good relationship in the school support centre.
English	James followed this course in Spoken English as a member of a mixed ability class.

One column was used to provide 5 x 40 minutes of direct tuition each week during which James had the privacy to tape work for his English course and had access to word processors to type his investigations.

James has had a very successful 2 years in Standard Grade and his growing confidence has led to improvement in his social skills and general behaviour. He has recently been applying for work in the building trade and his realistic attitude to the world after school and his place in it, suggests that in the end, James will be a responsible and contributing member of society.

INTEGRATED SUPPORT : WORKING ON THE SYSTEM IN THE SYSTEM

ROS HUNTER

INTRODUCTION

This chapter describes the process of supporting pupils with specific learning difficulties through the transition from Primary to Secondary School. It seeks to highlight approaches and issues that may be useful to the reader in reflecting on their own practice.

The context of the case study is that of a comprehensive High School of around 700 pupils with eight associate primaries in a highly rural catchment area. The school prides itself on high academic standards. It has a long-established Learning Support Department where the focus has been on support for pupils with moderate and severe learning difficulties. In recent years, increasing emphasis has been placed on support for learning across the mainstream curriculum, with some collaborative work on producing differentiated approaches to learning and teaching.

FIRST THOUGHTS

In the second term of the academic year prior to the transfer of the pupils focused on here, the Principal Teacher of Learning Support (PT:LS) began planning for the new intake with the Education Psychologist. Together, they noted that there were four pupils in various local Primary 7 classes with marked specific learning difficulties – three with Records of Need in process. Although there were some variations, they had broadly similar dyslexic-type difficulties with reading and writing and were of above average intellectual abilities. All four pupils received Learning Support in their primary schools and had made some use of word processing, two using computers supplied on a loan basis by the regional Learning Support Service through the microtechnology support teacher.

It was felt that the unusually high percentage of pupils with SpLD coming into S1 required support staff (LS teachers in both sectors; ancillary staff; the educational psychologist and regional advisory staff) to work together to assist in successful transition. It provided an opportunity to work with subject staff to extend their repertoire of skills and approaches to responding to SpLD. The work also helped with the development of regional guidelines for parents and for teachers on SpLD which were written by a Working Party and later distributed to **all** teachers throughout the regions in that session.

The development took the form of two distinctive but complementary approaches. Firstly, effective communication between key staff in each sector was established to ensure that action plans for transition were drawn up for each pupil. Carefully planned and well-attended review meetings were set up for each pupil **early** in the summer term, to which parents also contributed. The exchange of information was used to prepare jargon-free résumés of pupils' needs which were later distributed to **all** staff in the Secondarys School.

DEVELOPING THE STRATEGIES

One idea which emerged from these reviews was the need for a system to encourage the pupils to sustain and develop their use of word processing across the curriculum. This in turn promoted further thinking about raising subject teachers' awareness in order to:

- Encourage empathy,
- promote positive attitudes and
- develop practical classroom support.

Four strategies were adopted:

- Staff were issued with clear non-judgmental information about each pupil: for example, 'copying work from a blackboard/book is possible but slow and not always accurate. She can operate in terms of writing with acceptance of weak spelling. Reading of SPMG Maths material present difficulty in Primary.'
- At the same time, guidelines were provided for all staff on making the classroom curriculum accessible for pupils with specific learning difficulties (See Appendix 1 for extracts).
- A support system based on these guidelines was put in place by the PT:LS. It focused on the mainstream curriculum and provided up to four periods per week for work on individualised educational programmes for the continued development of reading, writing and spelling skills. Each pupil was also given access to a Tandy WP2 portable word processor based in the reprographics room (secure but accessible) where a printer sharer and printer were also based. Machines were dedicated to each user and could be taken home.

- Senior management bought additional Tandy WP2s. Training in the use of these was made available to **all** staff through the LS regional support staff (some 20% of staff opted for this).

- At a workshop, a teacher from a nearby Secondary School who has dyslexic difficulties spoke to staff about his own educational experiences – of failing his 11+, of being underestimated and understimulated at a Secondary Modern, of receiving help from a concerned teacher and of finally overcoming his difficulties and of his success at university. His talks were attended by more than half the staff.

- A structured programme to teach the use of the Tandy WP2 to pupils was developed by the PT:LS and the regional support staff.

Six Months Later

Six months later, a very informal piece of action research looked at the pupils' progress –through interviews with pupils, with a few subject teachers and with the PT:LS. Pupils were also shown a list of possible teacher strategies (Appendix 2) and asked to identify the most important *for them.*

It was apparent that all four pupils were relatively positive about their Secondary School experiences to date. There also appeared to be a strong correlation between their attitude to the school environment and their sense of success.

Laura

Laura, the only girl – aged 11 when she began Secondary School had a reading function of 7 years 9 months and spelling of 7 years 6 months, with handwriting difficulties. She was confident enough to describe herself as having dyslexia . . . 'I told my friends this and they were OK.' She was also confident about getting help with reading from friends.

Laura had extended her use of word processing over the six months using it regularly in Science and English, and occasionally for History work, especially at home. These were her favourite subjects. She had made positive use of the intensive support teaching and become committed to learning to touch type and to using spell-checking effectively. Her parents had shown their support for Laura and for the school's approach by buying her own Amstrad Notebook, which had the advantages of disk storage and a touch typing tutor as 'add-ons'.

The aspects of teacher support most important to her were:
- 'Making sure I understood the work.'
- 'Showing interest and encouraging me.'
- 'Not expecting too much reading and writing.'
- 'Letting me use computers, tape recorders and calculators.'

She did, however, perceive some subjects as 'too difficult . . . **because** you have to read and write a lot there' whereas it seemed that only the print elements were actually too difficult. This suggested that she was losing confidence in her intellectual abilities because of her specific difficulties. Asked about her one wish for school, she replied: 'to be brainier . . . well, to be able to do the work faster,' which seemed to sum it up!

Alex

Alex – aged 12 – was an interesting case. He was reported as having marked behavioural difficulties at primary school – destructive and dishonest – as well as his specific difficulties, with auditory and visual memory, with spelling (7 years 8 months) and with organisational skills. His initial programme of support therefore included structured monitoring of behaviour by support and guidance staff, together with access to a Tandy WP2 and some intensive tutorial support in a small group. He described his difficulties accurately: 'I've got problems with putting letters down the wrong way but my reading's getting better.'

Very quickly it became clear that Alex was doing well and so the monitoring was stopped and his support reduced to allow more time in the mainstream classes.

He made use of the Tandy WP2, mainly in English. Although he found it slow he felt he would continue to use it. In addition his parents sought advice about a dedicated spell-checker and purchased a Franklin Spellmaster for Alex.

In his favourite subjects he liked the work and found the teachers helpful. The aspects of teacher support most important for him were:
- 'Making sure I understand the work.'
- 'Finding extra ways of giving practice.'
- 'Showing interest and encouraging me.'

Generally, he felt he was doing well and experiencing success.

Colin

Colin was described to me as difficult and likely to be taciturn. In practice he was neither and was in fact very articulate (reflecting his high average performance in WISC tests). His major difficulties were described as organisational and in terms of attention span, and these difficulties appeared to generate problems for staff.

Interestingly, the support which he most valued was that which appeared most relevant to his needs - sixth year helpers in some subjects who 'stay with you, make sure you do your work properly and that you don't make mistakes.' He would have preferred shorter periods of tutorial support with 'more variety'.

The type of support he most valued was:

- 'Getting time to finish work.'
- 'Not being expected to do too much writing which can be hard going.'
- 'Teachers being interesting about their subject.'

The kind of flexibility which Colin wanted seemed more difficult to provide within the school structures.

THE TEACHERS' PERCEPTIONS

Classroom teachers' perceptions proved interesting. The staff development input had clearly had an impact . . . it appeared to have been sufficiently subtle, interesting and practical to raise staff awareness **positively**. The practical suggestions had been well received as being useful for a wider range of pupils experiencing difficulties. Attitudes to the use of the Tandys varied: generally speaking, staff who used more active learning approaches felt the Tandys enhanced pupils' work – again more widely than just for the pupils with SpLD.

The input by the teacher with dyslexic difficulties had been particularly well received as being both interesting and enlightening.

At the same time, even sympathetic teachers appeared to find it difficult to hold onto the fact that these pupils had **specific** difficulties rather than general learning difficulties. Did the superficial appearance of their work affect teachers' perceptions? 'One thing I would say, they are by no means the least able . . .' There was a concern that supporting readers and tapes should not encourage laziness! One otherwise sympathetic teacher was nevertheless committed to marking **all** spelling mistakes, despite advice to focus on common words and key subject specific terms: 'It can't help not to know they've got it wrong . . .'

One constant theme was the limited extent to which teachers felt they could respond to the particular pupil's needs in the interest of equity: 'I feel I owe equal allegiance to all the pupils.' As a result, they felt their contribution was limited. At the end of the day, most of their support comes from other pupils who help them through . . .'

THE ROLE OF LEARNING SUPPORT

The valued aspects of Learning Support were the provision of support materials, together with the opportunity to consult – flexibly. The Learning Support Teacher had found the introduction of the word processors a useful stimulus to his support. It provided a focus for the work done in extraction periods so that he went on to devise ways of using the machines to motivate pupils in doing routine and repetitive tasks necessary for improvement of basic spelling and reading.

He had become convinced of the value of teaching touch typing to pupils – provided they had the motivation. Ideally, he would have done this using the touch typing tutors now available in the newer generation of computers – including the Amstrad Notebook. In the absence of access to this facility, he had devised his own touch typing 'course' simplified from material supplied by Business Studies, and developed together with microtechnology support staff.

He had also worked at improving and refining the microtechnology support system. Firstly, IT support staff had ironed out practical operational difficulty between the Tandys and the printer. Then a simple system for recording use of the Tandys and the printer allowed the PT:LS to refine the system further.

It was also enhanced by the regional purchase of disk drives which allowed pupils to develop the habit of saving work. It became clear that if pupils were going to make more extensive use of word processing as they progressed into S3/S4 they needed to be trained in disk management at an early stage. This training was therefore introduced.

Whilst the development work had been a major undertaking, it was judged worthwhile because it had been very successful both in providing support for particular pupils and as a staff development strategy.

CONCLUSIONS

Issues and questions to consider:

*   Pupil attitude: how far is it influenced by the school ethos?
*   School ethos: are the messages conveyed to pupils by teachers important to the effectiveness of support?
*   Staff attitude: how can staff be encouraged to share support?
*   Back-up staff: how important is well-informed and well organised support?
*   Advice: does it help more if it is practical and jargon-free?
*   Manageable systems: is overall co-ordination and management important?
*   Developments: is a realistic timescale helpful?
*   Stimulus: is staff development more effective when linked to a real need?
*   Whole school strategies: does such focused work actually help develop the support system as a whole?
*   Communication: do these real needs make it easier for staff to ask questions and share strategies?

In conclusion, some of the key issues which came through were:

Tempering the ideal with the manageable.

Avoiding staff feeling guilty.

Working on the positive.

Raising the issue in a 'gentle' way.

Appendix 1

Departments are asked to choose those items from the following menu which would most closely fit the rationale of their S1 curriculum.

1. Provide pupils with photocopies of work sheets/work cards and allow them to write answers on the sheets. Accept limited responses to written work where response indicates understanding of content.
2. Provide photocopies of blackboard/OHP notes. (Special photocopying provision will be provided for 1 and 2 – please enter as Special Needs.)

3. Wherever suitable, encourage pupils to use Tandy Word Processors (with spell check facility) for written work or allow use of other word processors.

4. Accept oral answers on tape as substitute for written responses. Two Dictaphones are available.

5. Provide taped recordings of reading matter to enable pupils to follow class work. Three Walkmans are available from Reprographics and the Learning Support Department will get recordings done if approached.

6. Make use of sixth year volunteers as scribes/readers for recording.

7. Use a reader/scribes for assessment elements of a course. Approach Learning Support to arrange for scribe/readers.

8. Allow the use of a partner for reading and written work. Provide photocopy of the joint work.

9. Encourage the use of ring folders and the use of A4 lined paper rather than jotters for work. This will allow any photocopied material to be slotted in at appropriate place.

10. Allow the use of calculators or number squares.

11. Encourage use of Homework Diary as a means of communication between class teacher and home.

12. Keep in mind the predicament of these pupils. They may often feel stupid as a result of lack of writing or reading skills.

Can you add any other ideas? Please let Learning Support have a note of these for distribution.

Appendix 2

How Teacher Might Help

• Show interest and encourage you.

• Help you to be organised.

• Make sure you understand what you have to do.

• Give you TIME to finish work.

• Not expect too much writing.

- Find ways of giving extra practice.
- Write clearly.
- Give you a chance to use computer, tape recorder, calculator.
- Make sure others don't slag you.
- Let other pupils help you with work.
- Take time to explain to you.

Can you add any others?

Appendix 3

Laura

All about me.

I am 12 years old, and live on a farm. I love animals and I hat wherking on the farm. My hoday are cook and swimin. I kleked lots of things and, I have 2 dogs and 2 cats wich I love.

Alex

Myself

My name is Alex and I live at 8 Hig Street . . . I have live at . . . for 4 yers. I have a sitter. She is 9 yers old. She liks her hors. She gose hors riding on Sunday for six houre. My mum wurks in . . . She is a camunaty egacstion wurker. My dad is the regonal salls manger of . . . and his hobys are 4x4 driving he gos with . . . he wurks at . . . tyers. My hobys are 4x4 driving – train sets and bilding up bikes and riding them. When I am olde I want my job to be forastry manigmant.

SUPPORTING LEARNING THROUGH A WHOLE SCHOOL APPROACH

MORVEN BROWN

INTRODUCTION

This chapter focuses on the contribution that can be made by a Learning Resources Centre to the staff and pupils, including those with specific learning difficulties, of a large school catering for pupils of both sexes aged 5 to 18.

The Centre aims to provide not only for pupils with specific learning difficulties but also for any pupil who needs support, and to serve as a whole-school resource for every pupil and member of staff. The staff of the Centre includes experienced learning support teachers and an educational psychologist/teacher. This allows the Centre to offer a wide range of services to pupils throughout the school.

It is still too often the case that the facility (no matter how it is named) which exists in a school to support the learning of those who encounter difficulties is seen in a negative light, both by staff and by pupils. If the facility can provide a wide range of resources, seen as helpful to all pupils and staff, then a positive view should prevail. This can only be of benefit to those who have greatest need of its services.

The Centre is involved in the screening and monitoring of all pupils' progress; in the investigation of persistent difficulties; in the provision of teaching support; in the provision of materials to aid classroom support and differentiation; in the provision of counselling and emotional support; in liaison with parents; in liaison with outside agencies and so on.

Providing a Centre where support exists for learning and teaching (the two being inextricably bound together) across all areas and stages of the curriculum goes far in meeting the needs of many pupils including those with specific difficulties. The needs of pupils with any kind of learning difficulty cannot be met through specialist teaching/learning support alone. There is little point in pupils going to a special teacher if they have difficulties in learning or processing information and returning to an unenlightened classroom where the nature and implications of their problems are not acknowledged or accommodated.

An essential role of the Learning Resource Centre is, therefore, to provide staff in-service training. All teachers need help in acknowledging a fundamental cornerstone of their function, i.e. to support the learning of their pupils. Learning Support teachers and a Learning Support Department are still too often seen as existing to excuse or absolve the class or subject teacher from this essential task.

The functions that the Learning Resource Centre (L.R.C.) aspires to can be summarised as follows:

IDENTIFICATION

A major function of the L.R.C. is to be instrumental in the identification of pupils who require help or support. They fall into a number of categories:

1   Children with specific learning difficulties who:
    (a)   Can be anywhere on the range of intelligence from very superior to well below average.
    (b)   Can be anywhere on the continuum of difficulty from mild to severe.
    (c)   Can have any number of additional difficulties.

2   Children who have other types of learning difficulties:
    (a)   Sensory handicaps – visual, auditory, physical.
    (b)   Mild neurological impairment – for example because of illness, injury, epilepsy, premature birth etc.
    (c)   Emotional difficulties.
    (d)   Maturational delay, immaturity.
    (e)   Intellectual impairment.
    (f)   Language disorders.
    (g)   Behavioural disorders.

3   Children with disadvantageous educational history:
    (a)   Disrupted schooling.
    (b)   Inadequate teaching.
    (c)   Prolonged absence.

4   Children from non-English speaking background or whose language is impoverished for other reasons.

IDENTIFICATION PROCEDURES

L.R.C. staff can use a number of means at their disposal to identify pupils with difficulties:

1   Through objective assessment:
    (a)   School entrance tests.
    (b)   Annual screening tests carried out on all primary age children from P3 to P7 in reading, spelling and mathematics.
    (c)   National Tests.
    (d)   Internal tests and examinations.
    (e)   External examinations.

2   Through subjective assessment:
    (a)   Teacher observation and concern.
    (b)   Teacher reports.
    (c)   Parental concern.

3   Through more detailed diagnostic testing by the experienced Learning Support Teachers.

4   Through full assessment by the Educational Psychologist.

REMEDIAL ACTION

Once children are identified a number of measures can be taken:

1   Help can be provided within the classroom:
    (a)   From the class or subject teacher.
    (b)   From additional personnel in the classroom (e.g. another class teacher, trained auxiliary, parent or older pupil).
    (c)   From the L.S. teacher in classroom.
    (d)   Through the provision of additional teaching materials and aids.

2   Help can be offered outwith the classroom through:
    (a)   Extraction and specialised teaching help from the L.S. teacher.
    (b)   Tuition outside school.

3   There should be a full discussion with teachers and parents of the results of the identification procedure and of future implications.

This helps to ensure that the classroom situation is an enlightened one where teachers are aware of the nature of the difficulty and of how to support learning. It costs nothing but time and willingness to be flexible and creative – with the teacher as an enabler and a facilitator. Parents, if willing and supportive, can be encouraged to provide appropriate back up and emotional support.

4   Long-term monitoring:

(a)   Regular checks on progress through teacher comment and reports.

(b)   Careful record-keeping of L.S. history, reasons for identification and progress.

(c)   Regular checks that staff are aware of pupils' difficulties and the implications of these difficulties.

(d)   Automatic checking of all 'noted' names before the stage of sitting external examinations.

'HARD' RESOURCES

The L.R.C. offers a bank of resources and materials which can be used by staff for a wide range of pupils ranging from those with specific difficulties and those who are less able to those who are more able and require extension materials.

There is now an enormous range of photocopiable materials which cover extensive areas of the curriculum and a wide range of skills throughout the school age range. Many of these materials, some developed originally for pupils with difficulties, have relevance to the mainstream class and subject teacher. Many can be used effectively to achieve curriculum differentiation. Furnished with a range of such materials, the L.R.C. can provide a 'cafeteria' of choice from which 'customised' packages can be built for pupils. Obviously, close liaison with and monitoring by the L.S. teaching staff is essential.

The L.R.C. can collaborate with class and subject teachers in developing 'in-house' materials such as back-ups to course text books, audio-taped and video-taped information which can be used repetitively for those whose auditory or visual memory is poor and in building a bank of aids useful in many subject areas.

By combining proprietary materials and those developed in school, it is also possible to devise teaching modules to cover many of the areas which need to be addressed when helping older pupils with spelling, written language and number difficulties. This is of value when time is limited, and the curriculum full, but requires the commitment and self-motivation of the pupil and support at home.

Close links with the school library and technology centre are essential. Difficulties with learning are difficulties with processing and organising information and an essential role of the L.R.C. is in exploring effective ways of presenting and receiving information which will compensate for, or circumvent, any difficulties which pupils may have. The L.R.C. may be the first point in directing pupils towards back-up materials in the form of simplified texts, illustrated texts, video and audio-taped material, computer-based information sources such as CD-ROM and information about places to visit, outside sources of information and experience to explore.

The L.R.C. also provides a library of reference books and up-to-date catalogues of materials and books on all aspects of learning and teaching for staff, pupils and parents.

'SERVICE' RESOURCES

As well as a provider of 'hard' resources ,the L.R.C. can also be a repository of information and advice to teachers, pupils and parents about the learning process. Those of us who have the privilege of working with children with learning difficulties perhaps have a greater awareness of, and greater opportunity for, exploring the myriad range of individual learning and information processing styles used by children. In recent years, awareness of learning styles and approaches has heightened and there is an increasing wealth of explicit techniques aimed at enhancing learning. What is remarkable about many of these approaches is not their diversity, but the common thread which runs through them all (see Table 1) of self-awareness, self motivation and active involvement. Helping all teaching staff to become aware of these recurrent themes in learning theory and how they can be implemented is an important task of the L.R.C.

Knowledge and understanding of these learning and information processing approaches can enhance any learning situation. If such knowledge can be made easily accessible to all teachers and pupils in a school then benefits can be gained, not just for those with identifiable and enduring difficulties, but also for any individual who encounters difficulty in learning. There are few, perhaps none, of us who can claim to have negotiated the educational system completely free of difficulty.

As well as being a place where pupils receive direct teaching help, the L.R.C. should be a repository of information about learning and teaching techniques and a source of support for pupils and teachers who require it. It is therefore useful if L.R.C. staff can be involved directly in In-service Training so that awareness of learning/teaching techniques is heightened and teachers are clear about what is relevant for **them** and **their** pupils. There is no clear-cut border between the teacher and the learner or between the giver and the recipient of knowledge and a thorough understanding of the learning process seems a fundamental basis for effective teaching, no matter what the subject. The L.R.C. needs to provide an easy partnership with pupils and teachers in achieving this.

TABLE 1

Some Helpful Approaches to Learning and Their Communality.

(This summary is not intended to be comprehensive or definitive and is merely a personal observation of how these different approaches can be drawn together.)

Approach	Useful elements (stressing common threads)
Neurolinguistic programming	**Modelling** – analysing and understanding of successful learning strategies and applying them to new situations. Developing awareness through analytical observation of self and others.
Metacognition	Awareness of one's own thinking and learning processes, of the nature of a task and what is required to master it. Developing self-awareness and self-knowledge.
Educational Kinesiology (Brain Gym)	'Noticing' and being aware of one's state of mind and how situations affect one. The sensory integrative exercises may be helpful and the notion of balance, goal setting and positive attitude is central. Using the gestalt, creative brain, integrating the senses.
Instrumental Enrichment	Developing the capacity for storing, organising and using information.
DeBono's CoRT Thinking Programme	Developing thinking skills – evaluative and exploratory thinking. Creativity, looking at all aspects, gaining overviews.
Tony Buzan's Mind Mapping	Considering key concepts, overviews, planning using the gestalt.

	Exploring one's own memory and learning processes.
	Moving out into use of colour, images and representations – away from the restrictions of linear, language-bound learning.
	Stressing inter-relationships.
	Awareness of how information is processed, how memory works.
Multi-sensory teaching	Linking all the senses, exploring memory, becoming aware of every method we use to encode and stressing inter-relationships.
	Awareness of how information is processed.
Active learning	Acknowledgment of how learning occurs – the importance of doing, experiencing. Using all the senses, manipulating concrete materials.
	Active versus passive involvement.

STUDY SKILLS

One of the most important areas for those with specific learning difficulties, particularly for the older pupil, is the development of good study skills. The L.R.C. has a significant role in contributing to the whole-school policy on study skills. Almost every pupil who has had a history of specific learning difficulty will benefit from some explicit help on methods of study, memory techniques, time organisation and management, planning, drafting and redrafting written assignments, revision and note-taking and examination technique. There should be a whole school policy on study skills with its roots firmly established in the middle Primary School so that good habits are established gradually. However, it is often only in the upper part of the Secondary School that pupils develop the necessary maturity and self-motivation to implement advice effectively. Often the pupil with specific learning difficulties needs a 'short burst' of individual help tailored to his/her own needs when faced with the relatively sophisticated demands of the Higher syllabus. It is for this reason that long-term monitoring of those with difficulties is important. Even those pupils who appear to have coped well up to Standard Grade should be reviewed at the stage of commencing their Higher years.

The well-informed subject teacher, who is in tune with the demands of his subject, can be instrumental in ensuring that pupils are directed to appropriate help when required. The role of the L.R.C. in promoting a school climate which will encourage all teachers to be well-informed about learning and aware of subject demands on information processing skills cannot be sufficiently stressed.

EXAMINATIONS AND ASSESSMENT

We are indeed fortunate in Scotland in having an enlightened Examination Board who now offer a good range of concessions for those with specific learning difficulties affecting spelling and written language. Another important function of the L.R.C. is to identify those pupils for whom concessions should be applied.

The L.R.C. should also provide information to school staff about the nature and implications of specific learning difficulties and advice on assessment, correction and feedback to pupils. Though it may not be entirely desirable, much of our formal educational provision is assessment and examination-driven. If the Examination Board is prepared to offer concessions to candidates, then it is essential that school staff are made fully aware of these concessions.

The assessment of those who have difficulties in translating their thoughts and ideas into a written form is problematical. To separate evidence of an individual's knowledge, understanding and ability to manipulate information from his/her technical accuracy, presentation and performance under timed conditions is not easy. If, however, those who are teaching and assessing are not aware of the importance of separating these strands, then pupils with written language difficulties will be at an unnecessary disadvantage. The role of the L.R.C. in disseminating information about dealing with pupils who have such difficulties is therefore extremely important.

TECHNOLOGY

The importance of using word processors, data-handling programmes, and computer-based instruction and information-retrieval facilities cannot be underestimated for individuals with specific learning difficulties. Learning how to use a word processor proficiently may diminish the impact of the difficulty significantly and allow the individual to embark on courses, gain certificates and take advantage of tertiary educational opportunities which might otherwise be beyond his/her reach.

The L.R.C. staff should be able to ensure that all pupils who would benefit are given the opportunity of gaining that proficiency, preferably by having computers at their disposal.

A library of information about technological developments and opportunities with particular reference to special needs can easily be built up and kept current for almost no cost, and made available to teachers, pupils and parents for reference.

Software packages, designed to develop skills such as speed reading, reading comprehension, spelling, mathematical skills and so on, can provide valuable opportunities for consolidation of skills. A bank of back up and reference, video and audio-taped material can be built up for older pupils to use as required. The provision of audio and video tape players with earphones allows pupils easy and discrete access to information when they require it.

Dictaphones and tape recorders can also be a useful study or note-taking aid and can be borrowed for use in school. Such materials can be kept in the school library or technology centre as well as in the L.R.C. but a catalogue of them has to be kept in the L.R.C. so that L.S. staff can direct pupils, to them as required.

VOCATIONAL HELP

Often the pupil with specific learning difficulties needs help in planning his/her course, choosing subjects and investigating appropriate post-school placements. The L.R.C. can hold useful information to help in this and staff can discuss subject choices and implications for demands on reading skills and literacy. Advice can be offered about coping with the demands of post-school life, seeking help at college or university, and coping with later examinations and assessments.

EMOTIONAL SUPPORT

Almost without exception, pupils with specific learning difficulties need a good deal of psychological as well as educational support. The negative effects of specific difficulties on self-image and motivation are well publicised and the L.R.C. has an important role to play in minimising these effects. Providing support for pupils through allowing them to explore their own successful strategies, increasing their awareness of their strengths, celebrating their achievements, and encouraging them to take control and responsibility for their own learning is an integral part of the learning support teacher's job. It should be an integral part of every teacher's job. The desirable progression for all learners is towards independence. The whole process of education should be to promote skills in individuals which will equip them for the rest of their life and allow them to realise their full potential in every area, be it intellectual, emotional or psychological.

In an ideal world, young people should emerge from their years of compulsory education capable of thinking and functioning in the adult world to the best of their innate ability. Their educational experience should have promoted self-awareness and a positive view of themselves. Unfortunately for many pupils, particularly those with specific learning difficulties, their experience is a negative one. Through in-service training, L.R.C. staff can have the opportunity of encouraging all school staff to appreciate the importance of promoting a positive self-image and encouraging self-motivation.

RELATIONSHIP TO THE WHOLE SCHOOL

The relationship of the L.R.C. to the whole school must be a supportive one, beginning at an early stage and continuing throughout the years of education. A major aim of the L.R.C. is to ensure that the classroom settings in which children spend so much of their days are enlightened ones. The impact of any learning difficulty will be minimised if the educational setting is appropriate.

A partnership between the L.R.C. and the whole school can help in promoting conditions which will be conducive to effective learning for all, particularly for those with difficulty.

I have described above the major functions to which the L.R.C. aspires. I have stressed the benefits of a L.R.C. for a broad range of pupils but a major role is to meet the needs of individuals with dyslexic and specific learning difficulties. The summary below focuses, in more detail, on meeting their needs throughout the school age range

Nursery **Pre-school identification**

Children who may be at risk because of a number of factors (e.g. language difficulties; poor phonological awareness; immature speech; clumsiness – poor motor control; immaturity at school entry) can be identified and appropriate action taken to minimise future difficulties e.g. through nursery retention, referral to other agencies such as speech therapy, promotion of useful activities within the nursery setting, such as those to encourage language development, fine-motor control, co-operative behaviour etc.

Primary 1 Helpful approaches can be advocated such as extra activities to develop language and ensuring an integrated presentation of writing and reading.

Awareness of the development of literacy and language skills, of multi-sensory and other compensatory teaching approaches can be engendered. The importance can be underlined for all children, but in particular for those with difficulties, of a structured teaching approach from the beginning – in reading, written language (spelling, punctuation) and mathematics. Children can be helped to understand that written language is another means of communicating and the conventions and rules of written language are there to enhance that communication and need to be acknowledged from the beginning.

A metacognitive approach, awareness of the nature of the task and why things are done in a certain way, is not beyond the young child and can be advocated.

The importance of helping children to develop an easy and fluent hand cannot be over emphasised. On first entering an infant classroom children should be encouraged to hold a pencil properly (there are many pencil grips and specially shaped pencils available to help this). Developing an easy-flowing script should be an aim for all children. It is an appalling indictment of the educational system in this country that so many young people are unable to hold a writing implement efficiently and are condemned to a lifetime of writing in a contorted, awkward fashion. Motor habits are difficult to break once established and it is therefore essential to get the grasp correct in the beginning.

The L.R.C. staff can ensure that there is easy access to advice and materials from the Centre, and teaching help in or out of class if necessary.

The importance of early identification and appropriate help can be stressed. Pupils can be screened at the end of the first year to identify those with difficulty but staff can liaise with L.R.C. staff at any time if concerned.

Primary 2   A continuation of the above but with more teaching input, either from the Early Education Department or the L.R.C. staff within the classroom or through extraction. Close liaison with any others involved with the child (e.g. parents, speech therapist, educational psychologist) is encouraged.

Primary 3-5 Building on the above but there will be an increasing need for the child with dyslexic or specific learning difficulties to receive an individualised programme tailored to his specific needs.

Close contact between the class teacher and the L.R.C. is, of course, essential and help within the classroom is beneficial but there is no substitute for the kind of help which can be given one-to-one or in a very small group. Working alongside the child with a dyslexic-type difficulty in a relatively quiet and uninterrupted environment is essential if he is to be helped to gain awareness of his own successful strategies. It is essential that he receives positive feedback, experiences of success, credit for what he does well and careful explanation for what he has difficulty with. His teachers need to be fully aware that the way in which information is presented is of fundamental importance. It is so easy for a failing child to switch off and to stop trying. It is easy for the 'dyslexic' label to become an excuse for both the child and the teacher to expect less; for the child to stop trying and the teacher to expect little. Dyslexic children need to learn the unpalatable fact that they will have to work much harder than everyone else if they are to overcome their difficulty.

The correct balance between delivering praise and encouragement and promoting the need to strive and master difficult skills is tricky to achieve – especially for busy class teachers and harassed parents. They, also, need support from the L.R.C.

Primary 6-7 By Primary 6 the demands on literacy and other basic skills are increasing and continue to increase. There is a growing need to gain good reading skills – fluency, information retrieval, skimming and scanning, extracting key words, understanding nuance and style – all these skills which continue to develop throughout the remaining years in compulsory education.

The abilities to read and comprehend accurately, to infer and extrapolate, become increasingly important and without these skills youngsters become more and more disadvantaged in every area of the curriculum. In the same way, the skill of planning, drafting, redrafting and presenting a piece of written work becomes increasingly important. The early years should have given the opportunity to practise but few children are given sufficient experience for developing these skills adequately because of the extensive demands on curriculum content. This is difficult for all but disastrous for those with dyslexic-type difficulties. Like all skills – learning to punctuate, spell and express oneself coherently on paper improves with practice. While these skills can be taught in isolation, they need to be put to use in a concerted way as often as possible and the end result used effectively as a teaching aid.

Individuals with specific learning difficulties, more than any others, need to overlearn skills and it is the steady, repetitive, 'little-and-often' approach which usually pays off. It must also be noted that the heavy, repetitive slogging which often goes on for years may not bear fruit for some considerable time. As many teachers of children with specific learning difficulties will testify, they often cover the same ground year after year only to find the pupil making the same mistakes over and over again. Maturity may have an effect in that, often, there seems to be a spurt of progress when these seemingly tenuous skills 'gel' and reading, spelling and technical accuracy in written work suddenly improve.

In my experience this often happens around the end of second year in Secondary School but the importance of the earlier groundwork cannot be overestimated. The later help is offered, the less effective it will be and the importance of early identification and intervention is paramount.

Qualitatively, the teaching requirements appropriate to pupils with specific learning difficulties in the upper Primary School and lower Secondary School are very similar if they are within the normal range of intelligence and have received adequate teaching in the early stages.

By the last years in Primary School, and certainly by the early years of Secondary, pupils with specific learning difficulties should be given every opportunity to develop proficiency in the use of word processors and any other technological device which will allow them to cope with the demands of the curriculum more easily – e.g. hand-held spell checkers, tape recorders for notes and as a memory aid.

For many individuals, learning to use a word processor proficiently will greatly increase their ability to overcome their difficulties in later life.

Senior 1-2   While the needs of pupils with specific learning difficulties in the lower years of the Secondary School remain similar to those in the upper Primary, the demands of a more subject-orientated curriculum are very taxing.

The need for teachers to be fully aware of the learning process, the importance of how material is presented and the difficulties some of their pupils, particularly those with specific learning difficulties, have in processing information cannot be over emphasised. Close liaison with the learning support department is highly desirable but may be difficult to achieve. Time needs to be made available explicitly for the purpose of developing dual strategies with the learning support staff to provide the sort of support required by children with specific and other learning difficulties in each subject area. Discussion about presentation of information, back-up facilities, support material, addressing particular difficulties and so on is essential in every area of the curriculum. While each subject area has its own intrinsic set of demands, the three Rs remain their cornerstone. Only through developing the skills and knowledge of all teachers can the environment for those with difficulty be improved. Learning support can never exist in a vacuum and all teachers need to know how to support learning.

However, the current vogue for learning support only within the classroom is unlikely to meet the needs of the pupil with specific learning difficulties. Individuals with dyslexic-type learning difficulties require help outwith the classroom either on their own or in very small groups (no more than two or three).

Senior 3   This year is a transition between the Primary/lower Secondary School and the upper Secondary School which becomes more and more syllabus-driven. The demands of sitting examinations and coping with written assignments, reading for information and taking notes are very taxing indeed for the pupil with specific learning difficulties. If the arrangements such as using a scribe or reader in external examinations are likely to be required then practice in using them should begin in earnest. The full implications of using a scribe or reader need to be explored as it is always preferable for the pupil to develop strategies which allow him independence in later life. At this time, the development of mature study habits, organisational and planning skills become increasingly important. While the promotion of good study habits should begin in the middle Primary School and develop as an integral part of the curriculum, youngsters often do not gain the maturity or motivation to approach study in a routine, ordered way until much later.

The difference between a fifth or sixth year pupil bent on gaining Highers and moving on to tertiary education and a third or even fourth year pupil moving towards Standard Grades can be quite dramatic in terms of attitude and ability to implement advice.

Senior 4   Support during the demands of the examination year can often be extremely important and working through specific problems in any area of the curriculum may be required. The L.R.C. should be a source of support and advice to all pupils with specific learning difficulties – easily accessible to them as somewhere they can drop in and discuss any difficulties or queries.

In the same way, staff should be able to, indeed encouraged to, seek advice, help and materials as required. Ideally, there should be easy access to advice and materials e.g. word processors, audio and video taped material, practice exercises, back up to syllabus materials, examples of good practice, routes to information sources e.g. through the library or Technology Centre.

Pupils may need to be motivated through the exam years by being encouraged to consider appropriate and realistic post-school goals. The L.R.C. staff can seek appropriate exam allowances and offer help in preparing for the emotional demands of sitting exams e.g. through using self-help techniques like relaxation. Pupils with specific learning difficulties often need the reassurance that exams are not all-important and that there is almost always another route to a suitable post-school goal.

Senior 5-6   As well as continuing in the support for examinations there is an on-going need to help pupils prepare for life after school. While educational input and practical support is always required for the pupil with a specific learning difficulty the importance of nurturing a positive self-image can never be over stressed.

Those with specific learning difficulties will have the best chance of achieving their potential if they feel good about themselves, have developed self-awareness and the ability to be assertive and are in control of their own learning and thinking. They should not underestimate their potential but should avoid being over-ambitious. Brighter dyslexics who aspire to college or university may need careful support and guidance in seeking an establishment which will offer support for their difficulties and they will often approach the L.R.C. for advice and information about careers. As always, it is important to allow them to be in control but to give them the opportunity to make fully informed choices.

CONCLUSION

I have attempted to describe how a whole-school resource could be developed to embrace some of the learning, teaching and psychological needs of teachers, parents and pupils. The facilities offered by such a Learning Resource Centre are essential for those with specific or dyslexic-type learning difficulties, but many of the approaches and materials used with pupils who have difficulty in learning in a conventional setting are of benefit to a much wider range of individuals. Meeting the needs of those with specific learning difficulties in a positive setting where more, as well as less, able pupils can take advantage of what is on offer can only be of benefit to their self perception.

If staff, too, can freely make use of support for their teaching and find opportunities to enhance their skills and to develop their understanding of the learning process then the whole school community will benefit.

THE READING UNIT –
PRINCIPLES AND PRACTICES

ALISON FOX
and KATH WINN

PRINCIPLES

This chapter describes the principles and practice of a reading unit.

Reading Unit is a generic term describing an off-site provision for children with literacy difficulties. In West Lothian the Reading Unit is called the Literacy Unit. This is because some of the pupils have begun to make progress with their reading and attend the Unit to address the difficulties they have with the other literacy skills such as spelling, handwriting and writing. Throughout this chapter the two terms can be presumed to be synonymous.

Cedarbank Literacy Unit is situated within Psychological Services at Cedarbank Centre in Livingston, West Lothian. It is administered by the Principal Psychologist. The Unit serves West Lothian children with persistent and complex specific learning difficulties (dyslexia) who require highly intensive teaching.

Prior to placement at the Unit these children will have been supported in their own schools by their class teacher, trained learning support teacher and Neighbourhood Support Officer. If this support does not achieve the expected progress, further discussion leading to a full referral to the school psychologist takes place after parental permission is given.

If an assessment identifies the child as having specific learning difficulties (dyslexia), the psychologist notifies the Neighbourhood Support Officer and the child's name is noted for close monitoring. An individualised programme is constructed using appropriate materials according to the child's needs. This programme is regularly reviewed.

It is expected that early identification of specific learning difficulties (dyslexia) will be made. Lothian policy states that from nursery onwards, children with difficulties in responding to rhyme, in naming alphabetic letters and in discriminating speech sounds in words, are identified. They are given appropriate work to develop these skills and their progress is carefully monitored by the class teacher and learning support teacher.

While this level of intervention is enough to improve the skills of most pupils, a few may continue to struggle. So if, during a child's Primary 5 year, there is still serious concern about progress, then the possibility of a Literacy Unit placement is considered for Primary 6 and/or Primary 7. By then, it will be clear that specialist individualised teaching in literacy skills is necessary.

By that age pupils are generally mature enough to spend time out of their base school, and to cope with two school settings and the necessary travel between them. They are likely to benefit from meeting other children with severe specific learning difficulties (dyslexia) and to be able to assimilate work habits and study skills which will be of value in secondary school and beyond.

Pupils of average and above average ability with a large discrepancy between their chronological age and their reading and spelling ages are chosen by a selection panel consisting of the Principal Psychologist, Neighbourhood Support Officer and Literacy Unit Teacher. They are aware that specific learning difficulties (dyslexia) can be present in learners of all abilities and in the past have admitted to the Literacy Unit children of below average ability with specific learning difficulties (dyslexia). Such pupils have found the placement too intensive and despite working hard have not made significant lasting progress. For these children, work at a slower pace in their own school has proved a more successful route and further support is given to their school staff, e.g. visits to the Literacy Unit.

The selection panel considers detailed assessments of reading, spelling and writing skills provided by the school. Results of the psychologist's psychometric tests are also studied with particular emphasis on the sub-test profile. Information from the parents regarding birth, developmental and medical history is also considered. The children need to have the potential to become self-motivated. A Literacy Unit placement is very demanding for all concerned and emotional problems other than those which can be ascribed to feelings of failure interfere with learning and should be minimal. As continuity of learning is crucial, school attendance has to be regular. It is expected that parents and teachers will show concern and support for the child, and undertake to maintain this support during attendance at the Literacy Unit. Reports from any other agencies involved with the child e.g. speech therapy, occupational therapy are also considered.

In this way, pupils are identified for placement, taking account of the compatibility of the children in each possible grouping and the number of vacancies. The parents and child are then invited to the Literacy Unit for a pe-visit during school hours and the placement is explained. A video of the Literacy Unit in action may be borrowed by parents and schools for further study and discussion. The parents then decide whether or not the place is accepted.

PLACEMENT

There are sixteen places in the Literacy Unit and children attend in groups of four (three or four times a week) travelling to Cedarbank by supervised mini buses or taxi. Although various timetables have been tried, it is felt that these regular visits give the necessary continuity for learning. Care is taken to establish good liaison between the base school and the Literacy Unit to ensure sensitive management of the pupil's whole curriculum and minimise disruption caused by travelling.

The Literacy Unit teacher has two afternoons per week non-teaching, during which time she liaises with the Head Teacher and the class teacher at the base school. These meetings are informally minuted and circulated to the school psychologist and the Neighbourhood Support Officer once a term. A daily jotter aids positive on-going communication between the class teacher, the Literacy Unit teacher and the pupil.

Regular meetings between the Neighbourhood Support Officer and the Literacy Unit teacher occur and psychologists liaise as required. Liaison between the Literacy Unit teacher and Principal Teacher of Learning Support of the relevant secondary school takes place during the child's P7 year.

On very rare occasions, a child's placement at the Literacy Unit is terminated following a special review meeting. A placement may end because of, for example, undue stress in the pupil, unacceptable attendance records, or severe behaviour difficulties.

Liaison with parents

Partnership between parents and the Literacy Unit is crucial. To encourage this, the Literacy Unit teacher liaises with parents in their homes once a term, explaining her programme of work and listening to parental concerns. A home/ Literacy Unit diary is used for on-going communication. Parents' nights are also held taking the form of informal information evenings and formal consultations.

Review

In P6 there are no formal reviews but one can be called where necessary. In Primary 7 there is a formal review in the Spring term to which the parents and all relevant professionals, including secondary staff, are invited. The views of the pupil regarding perceived progress are sought prior to the meeting and are presented to the review meeting by the Literacy Unit teacher. A minute of the review meeting is circulated to all concerned and discussed with the pupil.

PRACTICE

The pupils who attend the Literacy Unit have a wide range of profiles and therefore differing educational needs. Their problems are generally well documented and these needs have already been identified. So the decision to be made by the teacher in the Literacy Unit is how best to meet these needs. Pumfrey and Reason (1991) emphasise that no one method is a panacea capable of alleviating the literacy difficulties of all pupils with specific learning difficulties (dyslexia) but fortunately, there are constructive strategies, many methods and a wide range of materials and media available.

Self-understanding

Perhaps the reason that there is no one method capable of addressing the needs of all pupils with specific learning difficulties (dyslexia) is that no two pupils are the same. Each pupil arrives at the Literacy Unit from a different school environment, with a different learning history and as a unique individual. Each one has been affected by failure and even the most supportive parent and school cannot totally compensate for daily setbacks and frustration. Therefore, a vital element of each child's programme is to increase their understanding of their difficulties and to begin to build in them a belief that progress can be made.

Self-esteem

Much has been written about the counselling approach to tackling literacy difficulties. Pumfrey and Reason (1991) review this literature and suggest that further research is necessary. However, they do quote Lawrence's study (1985) which found that children receiving remedial help with reading will show higher gains when this is supplemented with self-esteem enhancement. Therefore, underpinning all teaching in the Literacy Unit is the promotion of positive self-regard. Praise is an essential element of this but is only valued by children if it is valid praise.

Every day literacy and sequencing tasks

On admission, a 'teacher-made' criterion-referenced checklist is used to look at the pupils' abilities with everyday literacy and sequencing tasks.

- Can they write their name and address consistently and fluently?
- Do they know their birth date?
- Can they recite the days of the week, the months of the year, the alphabet?

These are achievable goals. Some pupils have to break down their address into very small parts, and they need to work on it every day for many sessions. However once mastered, this gives an immeasurable boost to self confidence. The same is true when mastery of the common sequences has been achieved. Dictionary skills are vital to these pupils and, of course, knowledge of the alphabet is a prerequisite.

Handwriting

Another area which has often caused problems for the child with specific learning difficulties (dyslexia) is handwriting. Again, positive change is achievable for the vast majority of pupils. Reason and Boote (1986) see good handwriting as neither as important nor as complex as fluent reading and accurate spelling. However, they go on to argue that it should be taught and claim that properly formed writing is quicker and that quick writing is an aid to good spelling. Brown (1990) describes the benefits of the use of fully cursive handwriting for pupils with specific learning difficulties (dyslexia) as it has a heavy emphasis on kinaesthetic learning. He also found that controlled cursive writing enhanced fluency of expression and was associated with enhanced self-image and confidence.

In the Literacy Unit, a looped cursive handwriting is taught (Chapman, 1990). While the main aim of this is to facilitate fluent legible handwriting and good presentation, it has been found to greatly increase the pupils' self-confidence. They see that improvement and success is possible with hard work and practice and that good presentation is often rewarded.

Reading/spelling

As said, each pupil has a different profile. Each one will be at a different stage in the often painful process of learning to read. Most programmes developed for pupils with specific learning difficulties (dyslexia) are multi-sensory in nature.

They involve over-learning and work to develop automaticity. They also tend to be highly structured, sequential, cumulative and are usually phonic based.

Ehri (1991) states that students who have difficulty learning to read are almost always deficient in their knowledge about the spelling system and goes on to suggest that instructional methods which facilitate the acquisition of reading skills are those that are effective in providing students with working knowledge of the spelling system. So the teaching of reading and spelling are very closely linked in the Literacy Unit.

Phonic awareness

Firstly, a child is assessed to find exactly what phonic knowledge they have. It is often necessary to go over the language of reading at this stage.

- Is the pupil clear about the difference between a letter and a word?
- Do they understand that each symbol has a name and a sound which are different?
- Do they have knowledge of vowel sounds, long and short?
- Can they differentiate between vowels and consonants?

Their ability with rhyme is also assessed. Adams (1990) states that on looking at all the evidence, letter knowledge and phonemic awareness are critical for the beginning reader. Bradley (1990) reports on the positive long-term effect of training children to appreciate the connection between rhyming and letter patterns and suggests that this is a particularly effective way to help children grasp the relationship between phonological awareness and the alphabet. So in the early stages at the Literacy Unit, the pupils who have difficulty with rhyme play games to increase their awareness of it. They make groups of rhyming words from plastic letters (Alphabeta letters) and are shown the relationship between each one.

Sound/symbol correspondence

A check is done to see if any sounds remain unmastered and work follows to address this. There are many different programmes which teach this in varying ways but the desired outcome of them all is that the child has an automatic oral response to the visual stimulus and can automatically write the symbol down when hearing the sound. In the Literacy Unit, no one programme is used exclusively. The Literacy Unit teacher selects whatever is appropriate from a wide variety of resources to meet the needs of the individual child. Many different teaching techniques need to be employed in delivering each programme, depending on the way the child is able to learn.

Plastic letters are used again, to allow the pupil to use their sense of touch, thus utilising their kinaesthetic memory. A blindfold and a bag of letters encourage a child with a weak visual memory to differentiate between similar letters. Drawing the letters in a sand tray or finger tracing them on sandpaper also uses a different sensory channel and can aid memory. Visual mnemonics are used extensively to help pupils differentiate between similar letters. Once a sound has been introduced and learned, it is written on a card with a key word and picture. This card is added to a pack of previously learned sounds and is practised daily to ensure mastery.

Phonic progression

Once the initial sounds are mastered, a progression is followed which should enable the pupil to begin to decode regular words and at the same time learn to build these words. This is not always as easy as it sounds. Some pupils need a great deal of work to help them to blend these sounds together and can get confused with the sequence of the sounds, despite having an automatic response to each symbol in isolation.

Different teaching techniques

For the child with specific learning difficulties (dyslexia), irregular words present a different challenge. Depending on whether a particular child has an auditory or visual strength, this can be approached in a different way. Again many methods have been developed which allow us to present information in a way best suited to a child's learning abilities.

The Edith Norrie Lettercase is used a great deal in the Literacy Unit and is especially useful for pupils who have difficulty with visual recall. This box of colour coded letters helps selection of the correct sounds. All vowels are red while consonant are black or green depending on whether they are voiced or voiceless. It further categorises sounds by where they are made in the mouth. The pupil therefore reduces the choice of symbol if it is known that, for example, the consonant sound is made by the tip of the tongue and is voiced. It is used to reinforce the sound that a symbol makes and is very useful when the pupil is beginning to build words.

A method used to help a child with a weaker auditory memory is the Fernald Kinaesthetic Technique. This helps the pupil who has trouble with blending and phonic analysis and encourages visual recognition of whole words. Gill Cotterell (1985) describes the technique in detail. Essentially, a basic working vocabulary is built up by this method. Each word to be learned is written in blackboard size cursive handwriting on a piece of card and the child traces over the word with his/

her dominant forefinger, while saying each part aloud as naturally as possible. This is repeated as often as necessary until the child can write the word independently, without looking at the original. The child should be encouraged to say the word when writing it. This is a writing approach to the teaching of reading which incorporates the skills necessary for reading, writing and spelling.

Other pupils benefit from auditory feedback when at the early stages of learning to read. The Language Master, which uses cards with audio tape on them, can be used to help reinforce unknown words. The visual stimulus is fed through the machine and the pupil is able to hear it being read by the teacher. They then record their own voice saying the word and can re-listen to this as often as is necessary, before writing it.

The ARROW system (Lane 1986) also allows this auditory consolidation. ARROW is an acronym for Aural-Read-Respond-Oral-Written. So the pupil listens, reads, responds orally, listens to their own voice then writes. The difference between an ARROW recorder and an ordinary one is that a child can rehearse on top of pre-recorded material without erasing it. This resource can be used in many different ways as suits the pupil.

Write Out Loud, used on the Apple Macintosh, reads what is written on the screen. This also gives a pupil auditory feedback. While it encourages children to write, it can also be used to reinforce new words. They can be written on the screen for a pupil to listen to, and copy as often as desired.

Simultaneous Oral Spelling is another technique which can be helpful to the pupil with specific learning difficulties (dyslexia) . It is described in detail in Reid (1994). It is a multi-sensory technique where each letter is named as it is written, using cursive script. The child receives kinaesthetic feedback through the movement of the arm and throat muscles. It reinforces sound/symbol association, sequencing and recall. A word has to be practised three times a day for five or six consecutive days. Once the correct motor pattern has been established, the naming can cease.

Automaticity

Once pupils start to build up a group of known words, it is important that they develop an automatic response to them. If each word has to be worked out every time, reading remains a painfully slow and difficult task. Research has shown that rapid word recognition speed aids comprehension. Mosely (1990) summarises this research and suggests that training and practice in rapid automatic decoding of isolated words is likely to be valuable. Phonic Code Cracker (Russell 1992) is a resource which incorporates timed fluency tests. The pupils at the Literacy Unit enjoy trying to 'beat the clock'.

Top-down approach

Much of what has been outlined so far can be described as a 'bottom-up' approach to the teaching of reading where the emphasis is on the phonic building bricks. However the 'top-down' approach is also used at the Literacy Unit. This approach stresses the importance of meaning and the underlying belief that we learn to read by reading. Pumfrey and Reason (1991) advocate a combination of the two approaches maintaining that neither can be adequate on its own or the other would have disappeared from teachers' repertoires long ago.

To encourage use of context when decoding unknown words, cloze procedure tasks are used. Which Word and Cloze Plus are two useful text books. LDA produces photocopiable sheets e.g. Corn Circles and Codswallop. Many of the passages have a high interest level and are also used at the Literacy Unit to do some reciprocal reading as described by Brown (1993). She notes that children who are passive and anxious learners become keen, active and enthusiastic when reading in this supported way.

Access to books

One of the purposes of reading as defined in English Language 5-14 is to gain imaginative and aesthetic pleasure. This is an area to which many Literacy Unit pupils have limited access. There are now many well produced commercial audio-stories and pupils are encouraged to listen to stories and novels. This allows access to the pleasure of stories and also allows them to extend their understanding of the nature, structures and conventions of language. As well as tapes, a great variety of reading material is on offer at the Literacy Unit. This ranges from comics and magazines to novels and information books.

Games

Over-learning is necessary for pupils with specific learning difficulties (dyslexia). The same ground has to be covered many different times. Motivation and interest can understandably wane, however, games can provide a fun way to consolidate. There is a huge number of commercially produced games on the market which cover most aspects of reading and, of course, teachers are renowned for their ability to produce games and variations of games to suit every teaching need. In the Literacy Unit, H•E•L•P Educational Games are widely used. Phonic Rummy is also a great favourite and has been found to be useful for reinforcing letter strings. There is much computer software available, such as Bangor Hi-Spell and Fun Phonics (Shelton 1987). These allow for drill and practice in specific areas of reading skills.

Strategies for spelling

Goulandris (1985) said that spelling is the weakest literacy skill and the most difficult to remediate. It often remains a weak area despite enormous amounts of work and effort. So it is important that each pupil is introduced to strategies to get round their difficulties. They are taught to use an aurally coded dictionary, the ACE dictionary (Mosely and Nicol 1986). They are also introduced to the electronic spellcheckers available, such as the Franklin Elementary Spellmaster. Spell it Yourself (Hawker 1981) and other more orthodox spelling dictionaries are also introduced. Depending on their own learning style, a preference for one of these aids usually develops.

Word processing skills

In the Literacy Unit, pupils have access to an Apple Macintosh. They are taught to use Claris Works and Write:Out Loud. These can be used in association with the predictive word processor, Co:Writer, and of course the spellcheck facility. Tandy WP-2 laptop word processors are also available and enable some children, freed from the effort of the mechanics of handwriting, to express themselves in writing more easily.

ISSUES

Integration/segregation

The debate rumbles on about whether it is best to receive such tuition in a small group or individually and whether children should be withdrawn temporarily from their own classroom to receive it. Riddell, Brown and Duffield (1993) report the continued demands from parents that their children receive expert tuition delivered on a one-to-one basis. While the parents are motivated by concern for their own child, the education authorities are obliged to balance the needs of the individuals against the wider group. In Effective Provision for Special Needs (1994), the Inspectors report that most pupils with special educational needs attend their local school but where it is not feasible to provide the exceptional levels of support required, then other more specialised forms of education will be necessary. The overriding concern must be to ensure that the educational provision takes account of a child's all round needs and does not allow them to become socially isolated.

Payne (1991) found that more children, when asked, chose to be assisted by extraction rather than support within the classroom. On looking at the advantages of extraction he thought that privacy was an important element. There is no question in our minds that the Literacy Unit provides that private safe place for many pupils, where they can learn skills that their classmates learned years previously. They can for example, sing the alphabet, play with plastic letters or begin to read aloud in the company of peers who have similar difficulties. They no longer have to lose their jotters to avoid anyone seeing their written work. Indeed, some pupils see the placement as an oasis in their desert of failure. Payne's research also suggested that children who were temporarily extracted to receive support for their learning worked harder on more appropriate work.

The importance of meeting with other similar children cannot be underestimated. One very anxious boy went home after his first day amazed, telling his mother that 'There's someone worse than me!' So peer group support is an integral part of a Literacy Unit placement. Lasting friendships are made.

It would be wrong not to mention that some children do find it socially difficult to come from their own school to the Literacy Unit. This can be due to the child and his/her peer group misunderstanding the nature of specific learning difficulties (dyslexia). It has been found that if the emphasis is put on helping pupils to understand this, the problem can be alleviated very quickly. It is very rare for a child to continue to feel a 'stigma' for any length of time. Indeed they can be instrumental in raising the awareness of their peers (and their teachers and parents) about specific learning difficulties (dyslexia).

Resourcing

Another criticism is that as Reading Units are primarily for pupils identified as having specific learning difficulties (dyslexia), they fail to address the needs of children with poor literacy skills who have not been thus labelled. Bryant (1987) argues the case that dyslexic children are not qualitatively different from other children who have difficulty with literacy, and that they do not need a different kind of teaching. However, he admits readily that this is an unpopular view and that most people involved in dyslexia insist on qualitative differences. Thomson (1991) states that most specialists in the field of specific learning difficulties (dyslexia) feel that dyslexic pupils require a specialist form of skilled teaching. We would agree with this view, and would argue that it is only the most severely affected dyslexic children who need the level of support and intense, specific intervention provided in Reading Units while the needs of most dyslexic learners are appropriately met in their own school.

Gender proportions

It is not thought that the criteria for selection to the Cedarbank Literacy Unit favours boys over girls and yet the ratio from the 1990 intake to the 1995 intake has been 52 boys to 8 girls. This is roughly 6:1. Thomson (1991) reports that there is a good deal of evidence that specific learning difficulties (dyslexia) is more common in boys than in girls. He quotes Goldberg and Schiffman (1972) who reviewed the literature and found that the ratio of male/female incidence varied from 3.3:1 to 10:1. The reason for the difference has not been agreed. Thomson suggests that it may be due to social and emotional differences but prefers the explanation that there is a difference between the sexes regarding relative cognitive skills as a result of maturation and development.

Intellectual ability

It could be argued that to exclude children with lower intellectual ability is elitist. However, as stated above, it has been found that these children find the intense nature of the teaching at the Literacy Unit very stressful. Many of the resources designed for children with specific learning difficulties (dyslexia) ask for the understanding of complex concepts which are demanding of bright children. For example, in the Kingston Programme (Cowdery *et al.*, 1984), which is described by its writers as being highly cognitively-oriented, children have to be able to understand complex linguistic concepts. Cowdery *et al.*, (1983) state that while only children with full score IQs of around 90 or more are accepted for referral to the Kingston Reading Centre, they prefer candidates in the high average range of 100-115.

This is not to say that pupils with specific learning difficulties (dyslexia), who are of lower intellectual ability can not be helped to acquire literacy skills but we would argue that different, less intensive methods would need to be employed and a Reading Unit may not be the most appropriate place to deliver such a programme.

Case Study

This is not a classic story of success. This case study describes a boy with complex specific learning difficulties (dyslexia) who progressed due to a great deal of hard work from him but who continues to have a long struggle ahead of him if he is to achieve his potential.

Colin attended the Literacy Unit for two years. He had had difficulties acquiring literacy skills and at the age of 9 years 5 months was assessed as having a reading and spelling age more than 3 years behind his chronological age.

The third child of three, Colin was seen by his mother as a bright, exciting child, quick to learn to walk and talk. Pre-school, his mother was not aware of any of the classic early indicators of specific learning difficulties (dyslexia). When asked if there was a family history of similar difficulties, she reported that she herself had had problems with 'wee words' but that this had sorted itself out. She described him as 'the opposite of clumsy'. He learned nursery rhymes easily. His strengths were doing jigsaws and building.

So while he did not appear to have a typical profile of dyslexic difficulties at the early stages, his profile of strengths coincided with those described by Jean Augur in the British Dyslexia Association booklet, Early Help, Better Future. Here she describes a child who is a quick thinker and doer, who has aptitude for constructional or technical toys and who appears bright but seems 'an enigma'.

His mother also reported that he enjoyed Primary 1 and 2. She only became aware of problems when they began to emerge in Primary 3 when it became clear that he was not acquiring literacy skills. From Primary 4 onwards, Colin began to display aggressive behaviour in the playground. His mother was very sure that he was not bad, 'just frustrated'.

Colin's school history showed that he had several teachers in Primary 1. He also had a prolonged absence in Primary 3 due to a broken leg.

There were fairly obvious discrepancies in Colin's performance. Reid (1993) outlines three main areas of discrepancies to be investigated when looking at specific learning difficulties (dyslexia). These are decoding/reading comprehension, oral/written and subject discrepancies.

In Colin's case, using a New MacMillan Reading Analysis, at 9 years 11 months, he scored as follows:

> Accuracy less than 6y 5m
> Comprehension Range from 6y 2m to 7y 11m

While this does not show a great discrepancy, his comprehension score was inevitably depressed by the decoding difficulties. Colin's performance in oral comprehension tasks as opposed to his slow and laboured word attack skills suggested a large discrepancy between his aural and reading comprehension.

Colin also showed a discrepancy between his oral performance and his written work. He was able to relate an interesting, well sequenced story orally but this became stilted and limited when put in the written form. Indeed, his written work was very poor.

In looking for discrepancies between Colin's performance in different subject areas, we saw that many of his strengths were of a creative nature. He was a talented actor, being able in that context to learn scripts and ad-lib with ease. He continued to be an able builder, enjoying working with technology materials at school and at home. He had good general knowledge and his oral work was greatly superior to his written output.

Despite his general ability being shown to be average on the British Ability Scales, the difficulties encountered by Colin were many. When first seen, his grapheme/phoneme correspondence was faulty. This led to inevitable difficulties with decoding and word building. Phonological difficulties were evident also. He found it difficult to isolate phonemes in a word though could identify syllables.

On using the Assessing Reading Difficulties test sheet (Bradley 1980) he was able to identify first and middle sounds which were different but on Condition 1, last sound different, his score fell outside the acceptable limit. Interestingly, Colin was able to recall, accurately, a nursery rhyme of his choice. This illustrated his greater ability with meaningful units of language. Using the Aston Index, he was found to have a poor visual sequential memory for symbols though not for pictures and particular difficulties with sound blending and auditory sequential memory.

Colin also had difficulties of an emotional nature. He was a very hurt boy. His need to defend himself from failure was very great. This fear of failure was a real obstacle to his progress. At one stage, he pretended he wore spectacles in order to 'forget' them at a later date. This was all an elaborate ploy to manufacture an excuse for his poor reading skills. His avoidance skills were many and varied.

Colin was a child who illustrated the maxim, 'nothing succeeds like success'. To maintain his motivation, it was essential to present tasks of manageable length and complexity, to minimise the chance of failure at all times. His difficulty in acquiring literacy had fostered low self-esteem and low self-expectation. A major prerequisite to his acquisition of literacy skills was to repair this damage.

Colin's programme was to be presented in a multi-sensory way and included working towards the mastery of grapheme/phoneme correspondence. This was achieved using many different resources. The Edith Norrie Lettercase was used and it was particularly useful in helping Colin sort out sounds which confused him. It allowed him to look at the letter, say it and work out how the sound was made in his mouth and whether it was voiced or unvoiced. At this stage, a sand tray and alpha-beta plastic letters were also used to further reinforce each sound using the tactile and kinaesthetic channels.

To help strengthen Colin's auditory memory and help him link sounds to written symbols, he used the ARROW system. This required him to look at a visual stimulus while listening to a teacher's voice reinforcing it. He then had to repeat the sound and write it. It was found to be most useful when used with his teacher's voice rather than using the commercially produced tapes.

At this early stage, work was also done on rhyming. This was seen as essential as understanding of rhyme can help reduce the workload when learning to spell. Games were used extensively. To help him improve his disjointed, untidy and laboured handwriting style, cursive handwriting was introduced at an early stage.

Fig. 1

Fig. 2

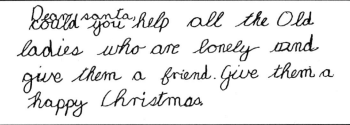

The benefits can be seen in the samples below, written fourteen months apart. This improvement undoubtedly helped Colin's all round self-confidence.

After much work on sound to symbol and symbol to sound, Colin began progressing through the phonic reading programme taken from Skill Teach (Shelton, 1984). To complement the phonic approach, cloze procedure work was incorporated in his programme. Reciprocal teaching (Brown, 1993) aided comprehension and also helped to increase his use of context when reading.

Work was also done using Phonic Code Cracker. This enable Colin to increase the speed of his automatic responses to words. Much over-learning and consolidation was required at each stage to encourage mastery. As his decoding skills improved, more emphasis was placed on developing comprehension.

Spelling was also taught in a multi-sensory way. After initial success using ARROW, this was utilised at several points to help consolidate words. He worked on a structured spelling programme, following his phonic reading programme and also simultaneously, worked on irregular key words. Progress was made using several methods. When introduced to a word, he made it, using plastic letters. He was then encouraged to find words which rhymed, thus visually reinforcing the similarities. On a personal spelling sheet, he looked at the word, said it, covered it and wrote it. Once he checked that he was correct, he repeated the task. This was repeated each session until the word was mastered. If the word continued to elude his long-term memory then Simultaneous Oral Spelling was used, further reinforcing the letter sequence using visual, auditory and kinaesthetic memory. He was taught to us an ACE dictionary and a Franklin Spellmaster. These enabled him to find a word independently or confirm his spelling if unsure

After two years at the Literacy Unit many changes had taken place for Colin. Most noticeable was his increased self-confidence and his decreased frustration level. It was now very rare for frustration to bubble over in either school or playground. His attitude to learning had changed as he learned to believe in himself. He began to enjoy writing, taking a pride in completed pieces of work. His spelling errors became less bizarre. He had failed to score on a Burt Inglis spelling test before coming to the Literacy Unit but now achieved a spelling age of 7 years 1 month. This illustrated his progress but also the struggle ahead of him.

His reading scores at age 11 years 11 months were now:

Accuracy Range 8y 6m – 9y 8m
Comprehension Range 10y 0m – 11y 9m

Still a long way to go with accuracy but his comprehension was almost age appropriate and his class teacher reported that he had become more able to cope with reading tasks across the curriculum. He was often paired with a more proficient reader or writer when working on a task where his good comprehension skills could be valued. Having been taught to do so, he was able to use the word processor and tape recorder to facilitate the recording of work while the latter gave him access to texts which he was still unable to decode.

This programme continued until his secondary transfer. Liaison with the Principal Teacher of Learning Support at his Secondary School allowed early decisions to be made about the provision which would be necessary. Elaboration of the curriculum was necessary as continued direct teaching of reading and spelling was still required. While he was equal to the same intellectual challenges as his peers, alternative methods of recording and support with reading material would enable him to show this. Differentiation of the curriculum as described in Support for Learning (1993) would be essential if Colin was to achieve his potential.

Without the intervention of the Literacy Unit, Colin's frustrations would have increased and his learning problems would have become overshadowed by his social, emotional and behavioural difficulties. As it is, good reports continue from the secondary school where he is displaying his ability and working towards achieving his potential.

This quote from Pumfrey and Reason (1991) perhaps sums up Colin's story to date:

"SpLD are not 'cured' or completely rectified by any means currently at our disposal. Such difficulties can be alleviated and their adverse effects reduced. There is no simple recipe to attain even this end but there are many promising lines of methodological development. The pursuit of literacy by the pupil with SpLD is demanding of the pupil, the parent and the professional. It is expensive psychologically and financially. It remains an eminently worthwhile objective."

REFERENCES

Adams, M. J. (1990). *Beginning to Read Thinking and Learning About Print.* Massachusetts Institute of Technology, Cambridge, Massachusetts.

Augur, J. (1992). 'Early Help, Better Future'. In *A Guide to the Early Recognition of Dyslexia.* British Dyslexia Association. Reading.

Bradley, L. (1990). 'Rhyming Connections in Learning to Read and Spell'. In Pumfrey, P. D. and Elliot, C. D. (Eds.) *Children's Difficulties in Reading, Spelling and Writing.* The Falmer Press, Hants.

Brown, E. N. (1990). 'Children with Spelling and Writing Difficulties: An Alternative Approach. In Pumfrey, P. D. and Elliot, C. D. (Eds.) *Children's Difficulties in Reading, Spelling and Writing.* The Falmer Press, Hants.

Brown, P. (1993). 'The Learner – Metacognition in Reading'. In Reid, G. (Ed.) *Specific Learning Difficulties (Dyslexia): Perspectives on Practice.* Moray House Publications, Edinburgh.

Bryant, P. (1987). 'The Question of Prevention'. In Snowling, M. J. (Ed.) *Children's Written Language Difficulties.* NFER-Nelson, Windsor.

Cotterell, G. (1985). *Teaching the Non-Reading Dyslexic Child.* LDA, Cambs.

Cowdery, L., McMahon, J., Morse, P. and Prince, M. (1983). *The Kingston Programme. Teaching Reading Through Spelling – Diagnosis.* Frondeg Hall Technical Publishing, Clwyd.

Ehri, L. (1991). 'The Development of Reading and Spelling in Children: An Overview'. In Snowling, M. and Thomson, M. (Eds.) *Dyslexia Integrating Theory and Practice.* Whurr Publishers, London.

Scottish Office Education Department (1991). *English Language 5-14* SOED, Edinburgh.

Goldberg, H. and Schiffman, G. (1972). *Dyslexia: Problems of Reading Disabilities.* Grune & Stratton, New York.

Goulandris, N. (1985). 'Extending the Written Language Skill of Children with Specific Learning Difficulties – Supplementary Teaching Techniques'. In Snowling, M. (Ed.) *Children's Written Language Difficulties.* NFER Nelson, Windsor.

HM Inspectors of Schools. (1994). *Effective Provision for Special Educational Needs.* SOED, Edinburgh.

Lawrence, D. (1985). 'Improving Self Esteem and Reading'. In *Educational Research* 27,3,194-200.

Moseley, D. (1990). Suggestions for Helping Children with Spelling Problems. In Pumfrey, P. D. and Elliot, C. D. (Eds.) *Children's Difficulties in Reading, Spelling and Writing.* The Falmer Press, Hants.

Pumfrey, P. D and Reason, R. (Eds.) *Specific Learning Difficulties (Dyslexia) Challenges and Responses.* NFER Nelson, Windsor.

Payne, T. (1991). 'It's Cold in the Other Room.' In *Support for Learning.* Vol. 6, No. 2, 61-65.

Reason, R. and Boote, R. (1986). 'Learning Difficulties in Reading and Writing. *A Teacher's Manual.* Windsor. NFER Nelson.

Reid, G. (1994). *Specific Learning Difficulties (Dyslexia): A Handbook for Study and Practice.* Moray House Publications, Edinburgh.

Riddell, S., Duffield, J., and Ogilvy, C. (1993). 'Interchange' *No 18 Specific Learning Difficulties: Policy, Practice and Provision.* Report to SOED.

Riddell, S., Duffield, J and Ogilvy, C. (1993). 'Specific Learning Difficulties, Learning Support Teachers and the Impact of Changing Policy'. In Reid, G. (Ed.) *Specific Learning Difficulties (Dyslexia): Perspectives on Practice.* Moray House Publications, Edinburgh.

Thomson, M. (1991). *Developmental Dyslexia Studies in Disorders of Communication.* Whurr Publishers, London.

RESOURCES

Alphabeta Letters, Belgrade Insulations Ltd. Dennington Road, Dennington Industrial Estate, Wellingborough, Northants, NN8 2QH.

Augur, J. and Briggs, S. (Eds.) (1992). *The Hickey Multi-sensory Language Course*, Whurr Publishers Ltd., London.

Bangor Hi-Spell 1,2 and 3. Xavier Educational Software Ltd, University College of North Wales.

Bradley, L. (1980). *Assessing Reading Difficulties: Diagnostic Remedial.* NFER Nelson, Windsor.

Chapman, P. (1990). *Handwriting for the National Curriculum. A Cursive Foundation Hand.* Berol, King's Lynn.

Claris Works II (1993) Claris Corporation, USA.

Co:Writer 2.1. (1992-94). Don Johnson Developmental Equipment, Inc.

Cowdery, L., McMahon, J., Morse, P. and Prince, M. (1983). *The Kingston Programme. Teaching Reading Through Spelling – Foundations of the Programme.* Frondeg Hall Technical Publishing, Clwyd.

Franklin Elementary Spellmaster (QES-90). Franklin Electronic Publishers, Mt. Holly, NJ 08060.

Hawker G. T. (1981). *Spell it Yourself.* Oxford University Press, Oxford.

H•E•L•P Educational Games, Didcot, Oxon.

Hornsby, B. and Shear, F. (1990). *Alpha to Omega..* Heinemann Educational Books, Oxford.

Hutchison, L. (1981). Which *Word? Graded Cloze Text and Comprehension Exercises.* Hodder & Stoughton,

London.

Hutchison, L. (1987). *Cloze Plus*. Hodder & Stoughton, London.

Jarman, C. (1992). *Corncircles and Codswallop Cloze Procedure Stories*. LDA, Cambs.

Lane, C. H. (1986). *ARROW System*. The Cambridge System Ltd., Huntingdon.

Language Master System, Bell & Howell, Middlesex.

Moseley, D. and Nicol, C. (1986). *ACE Dictionary*. LDA, Cambs.

Newton, M. and Thomson, M. (1982). *The Aston Index*. LDA Wisbech, Cambs.

Phonic Rummy, Better Books, Dudley.

Russell, S. (1992). *Phonic Code Cracker*. Jordanhill College, Glasgow.

Shelton, K. (1984). *Skill Teach. A Structured Reading Resource for Children with Learning Problems*. PAVIC Publications, Sheffield City Polytechnic.

Shelton, K. (1987). *Fun Phonics. A Structured Programme of Computer Games*. PAVIC Publications, Sheffield City Polytechnic.

The Edith Norrie Lettercase. Helen Arkell Dyslexia Centre, Surrey.

Write Out Loud (1993). Don Johnson Developmental Equipment, Inc.

INFORMATION TECHNOLOGY AND SPECIFIC LEARNING DIFFICULTIES

MARIE DOUGAN
and GEORGE TURNER

INTRODUCTION

Children with specific learning difficulties are children first and their needs are similar to those of all children. The need to exercise some control over their environment is one of these basic needs. It is this need which gives micro-technology its power. Microcomputers, with appropriate input devices and software, although internally complex, can be remarkably simple to control. Furthermore, unlike some of the humans the children come into contact with, they have a consistency in their performance and give feedback on the children's performance in an uncritical way, making their use in presenting educational material highly acceptable.

The last 10 years or so have seen significant advances in the development of microcomputer systems. They are now cheap enough to be accessible to children for educational purposes and powerful enough to meet many of their needs.

USING IT FOR SUPPORT STRATEGIES

IT has a unique contribution to make in the area of support for children with specific learning difficulties. It can provide support for organising of writing, for the writing itself, and for spelling and memory.

IT AND ORGANISING THOUGHTS

Many individuals with specific learning difficulties encounter problems when beginning to commit their thoughts to paper. Apart from any difficulties with handwriting skills, it is often difficult for them to commit their ideas in logical sequences – they are 'all over the place'. There are various planner and outliner packages available for computer systems which will allow pupils to type in their ideas in any order and subsequently link them together and add text to them under 'idea headings'. An example of a useful package in this area is **Thinksheet** [1], which allows 'ideas' to be manipulated on screen and text moved about visually.

Fig. 1 Example of Thinksheet screen

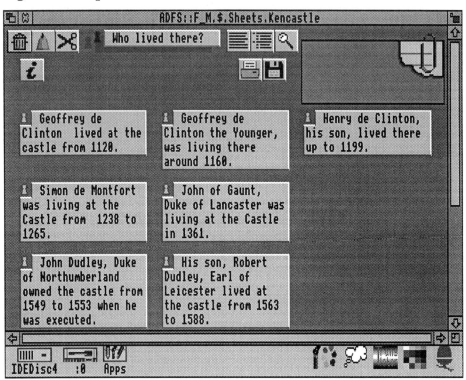

Many word processing packages also have the added feature of an outliner facility. This is, however, not so easy to manipulate visually because the ideas are being sequenced in a more linear progression. Many people find electronic personal organisers very useful and the memory-jogging and organisation support which they offer can be of immense value to those with specific learning difficulties.

SUPPORT FOR WRITING

Micro-technology offers huge benefits in this area for those with specific learning difficulties. Pupils who have experienced failure in writing throughout their school career often take a very natural step and avoid the process at every possible opportunity. For a large number of pupils, it comes as a great relief to be told that they can make as many mistakes as they wish in their writing when using a word processor.

Pupils using word processors often report feeling less apprehensive or stressed when approaching a writing task. The actual process of forming letters may constitute a block to writing and can be removed by access to a word processor. Word processors are particularly useful for those who have problems in the kinaesthetic-motor area. Often, removing this anxiety will have the effect of freeing them to concentrate on skills of composition, and may in turn lead to work which is of better quality and greater in quantity.

Touch typing skills, although very helpful, are not an essential requirement for using a word processor efficiently. Some keyboard familiarity is, however, essential, and opportunities must be provided to practise this activity.

Word processors offer the facility to edit text and move it around within the piece of writing. Some pupils prefer to have their work printed out at a draft stage, and consider the possible changes they make from their paper copy. Others find it easier to edit directly on screen and have no difficulty in moving the cursor around. Whichever technique is employed, there is no doubt that drafting using a word processor is much less laborious than redrafting and rewriting by hand. A good quality printed product gives the pupil a real sense of achievement and provides an opportunity for the work to be shared with others. Indeed, the process also lends itself to providing more opportunities for collaborative work and discussion and this is particularly important for those with specific learning difficulties.

Some pupils find it easier to read through their own work when it is printed rather than handwritten. In fact, the same applies to teachers who, on seeing a printed copy of a pupil's work, have commented, 'Now I can see what some of the difficulties are. At last the text is readable.'

There are facilities within most programs to change the typeface (or font) and it is often possible to vary both background and foreground colours. This is discussed in detail later.

Other support strategies may be incorporated within the word processor program. Word processors can be introduced at a very early stage by employing the concept keyboard (a touch sensitive pad) as an alternative input device – **Prompt Writer.**[2] Text may then be entered by pressing a picture to enter a word or phrase. There is also the facility to enter the actual text required by pressing the appropriate area on the concept keyboard. The flexibility of many of these programs in allowing the teacher to customise overlays for particular pupils is a great bonus. The overlays may be developed to allow the pupil to progress in small steps by gradually replacing the pictures by text, which can be built up into fairly complex language structures. Sometimes the only support required may be the availability of a wordbank or wordlist, and these are readily available within these programs. In addition, there are some concept keyboard programs which present the user with a sequencing activity resulting in the production of a piece of text. Such programs involve the user in pressing the areas in the correct order – thus providing further practice in sequencing skills as well as the production of text.

Fig. 2   Concept keyboard overlay for use with PromptWriter program

○ ◀NCET▶ Kaleidoscope Packs				**Albert's House Support Pack**					Program : Prompt/Writer ○ filename : Albert C.Hopkins & SMurty B.I.T. Team						
a	b	c	d	e	f	g	h	i	j	k	l	m	"	'	Caps
n	o	p	q	r	s	t	u	v	w	x	y	z	!	?	●
Here		There		This		The		Albert		Albert's		afraid		from	
I	He	is		hiding		can		see		mouse		has		and	
		white		little		big		cat		upstairs		long		a	
		hall		house		his		lives		downstairs			of	in	
		landing		bedroom		mousehole			lounge		← →		DELETE		
		the	garden		kitchen		bathroom		SPACE		↑ ↓		RETURN		

Recently more powerful support has become available through the use of predictive word processors. The user typically types in the first letter of the word which they wish to enter. A list of possible words are then offered on screen – based on the particular vocabulary used by the child, and often also based on a set of grammatical rules. Such systems include **PAL**[3] and **Co:Writer**[4].

One advantage of the **Co:Writer** program is that it may be set up in such a way that the pupil can point to the words offered with a mouse or other pointing device and have the word spoken back through the computer providing auditory feedback. In addition, there is flexibility over the way in which the words are

Fig. 3   Example of Co:Writer

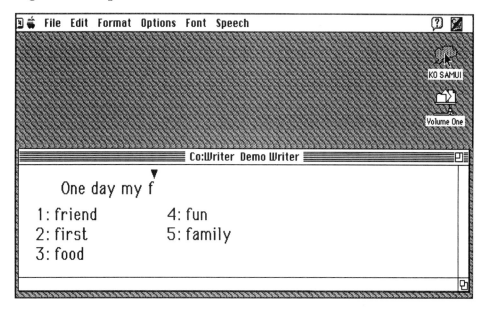

displayed on screen – the size of the letters, the font, whether they are arranged alphabetically or in order of the most likely first.

The computer 'learns' the new words the user types in and will begin to offer these also as predicted words. Great care has to be exercised by the teacher over this facility – it is very easy for the pupil to be offered his own misspellings as predicted words. There is usually some facility whereby the teacher can either switch this feature off or edit this new vocabulary and correct the spelling if required. The option of having the words offered according to grammatical rules is a powerful feature, particularly for those who have significant language problems.

The combination of a predictive program together with a talking word processor offers the opportunity for further auditory feedback. Such a combination might be **Co:Writer** with **Write:OutLoud**[5] .

SUPPORT FOR SPELLING

Support for spelling can be offered by using a spelling checker to encourage the pupil in independent self-correction. These can be a real bonus to some pupils but emphasis should be placed on the word 'some' here. Often teachers and parents clutch at the spelling checker as at a straw whereas, in reality, their use is not always appropriate.

Spelling checkers can be divided into two main groups – hand-held devices and those which are incorporated into a word processor used within a microcomputer. Of the former, the most common in use are probably in the **Franklin**[6] range. Usually, these are a cheaper option than buying a microcomputer with spelling-checker built into the software but suffer from the disadvantage that the user must either realise that a particular word has been misspelt or check the spelling of every word. The latter will normally check a complete document, highlighting only possible misspellings, and suggest alternatives. This has the effect of protecting the correctly-spelt words and saving the pupil with specific learning difficulties the frustration of examining correct spellings. In addition, such systems normally allow words to be added to the dictionary set giving a measure of personalisation. Some, like the **Tandy WP3**[7], give an optional audible warning of a possible misspelling.

Some points to bear in mind when considering a spelling-checker:

The keyboard on a hand-held device may not be large enough to allow comfortable typing.

The spelling-checker will highlight all words which are not in its dictionary set – including some which are correctly spelt e.g. proper names.

It will not pick out words which are correctly spelt but which are wrongly used in the context e.g. homonyms 'their' and 'there'.

It may suggest too many alternative spellings and create further confusion.

Most spelling checkers are designed specifically to highlight typing errors rather than spelling errors.

Some spelling errors may be too bizarre for the checker to cope.

Some are designed for the American market with, of course, American spelling.

Usually spelling checkers rely upon the user being able to read and recognise a suggested correction – not always possible for pupils with specific learning difficulties.

Software is now available on some systems which offers an option for the computer to 'say' the words which are given as suggested corrections and thus help those with poor reading skills to make a correct choice.

An example of this is the **Write:OutLoud** talking word processing package which is available for the Macintosh range of computers. The words offered can be spoken by the computer and also may be spelled out letter by letter.

Fig. 4   Example of Write:OutLoud

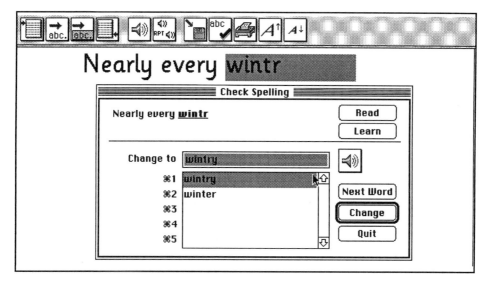

Franklin have also produced a speaking version of the '**Wordmaster**', one of the hand-held range of spelling checker devices. Unfortunately, at the present time, this is only available with an American dictionary option.

For a comparison of spellcheck effectiveness, it may be worth consulting **I.T. Support for Specific Learning Difficulties (1992)**.

SUPPORT FOR READING

The more powerful systems currently available are sophisticated enough to allow them to produce 'talking books' . Such systems incorporate the facility to display good quality graphics on screen together with good audio output. At the simplest level, this involves pictures being presented on screen and linked to recorded sounds which may be accompanied by highlighted text. It may be possible (noting copyright restrictions) to transfer pupils' reading materials to the computer. At a higher level, text may be scanned electronically and spoken by the computer.

Another strategy which may be employed is the use of programs such as **Developing Tray**[8] which require the pupils to predict letters and words in a hidden passage of text using both context clues and knowledge of the syntax.

SUPPORT IN THE PRESENTATION OF MATERIALS

The technology also permits schools to produce clear, well presented materials for pupil use. Word processors allow teachers to have control over the typeface used and the layout of the text.

Choice of typestyle is also very important when considering the readability of printed materials. Rosemary Sassoon (1993) has investigated this problem, spending a great deal of time working with and talking to children. She wishes ' to bring to everyone's attention the need to consider the requirements of different classes of readers, and also to highlight the implications for computer-generated letters in education in general'.

For instance, the ability to justify text is generally used for newsletters and textbooks, but justified text is actually harder to read than text which has a ragged right hand edge. In order for the text to have even margins on both sides, spaces have to be added into the text to make all lines exactly the same length. This causes more problems for those with reading difficulties, since it is more difficult to track easily from the end of one line to the beginning of the other.

A result of her work is the production of a typeface specifically designed for children called the **Sassoon Font**[9].

Fig. 5   Example of Sassoon Font

Nearly every winter my family makes cakes for the old folk. Kevin and my dad made fairy cakes and sponges.

Shorter lines are also much easier to read than lines filling the width of the page – when it is easier for a beginner reader to get lost.

```
This paragraph illustrates the difference in
using a font whose characters are not spaced
proportionally - the letter i takes up the
same width as the letter w.
```

The size of the printed type also has some bearing on the readability of text – small 9 point text is very tiring to read,

but much larger text requires the reader to read a much larger number of lines.

A good range of type size is between 12 and 18 point text.

Care also has to be taken over the **enthusiastic** use of **bold**, <u>underline</u> and *italics*, to avoid the print becoming very ***<u>cluttered and confusing.</u>***

Most word processing programs will also allow the spacing between lines to be altered to make the text more suitable for an individual reader.

These techniques can be used to create good quality worksheets for pupils with specific learning difficulties, for example with short lines, and with lists of keywords with phonetic spellings. Technology also allows worksheets to be presented electronically on screen, possibly even with auditory clues attached to some of the keywords.

IT AND REMEDIATION

There are computer programs around for all machine platforms, which aim to provide practice in particular skills. If used carefully, these programs can complement a structured teaching programme very well. Although the microcomputer may simply be offering the same old materials to pupils, they are usually very motivated to use them. A number of the programs have been specifically designed to follow closely a particular teaching programme. Again, many of the programs produced more recently offer a number of additional features, such as auditory feedback through both digitised and synthesised speech.

These programs can be used to provide additional practice and training in areas such as :

Letter recognition – **Fun Phonics**[10], **Hi-Spell**[11]
Auditory memory – sound pelmanism programs
Visual memory – **Picture Gallery**[12]
Sequencing skills – **CK Sequencer** [13]
Spelling patterns – **Starspell**[14], **Complete Speller**[15], **Soapbox**[16]
Reading skills– wordsquare programs, **Developing Tray**
Keyboard skills – these may be simply keyboard familiarity trainers such as **Keyboard Skills**[17] or typing tutors such as **Mavis Beacon Teaches Typing**[18]
Directional skills – **Alan Nixon Special Care**[19]

The highlighted programs are examples only.

Details of many other programs useful in these areas are available in **A Software Guide for Specific Learning Difficulties (1993).**

HARDWARE

At the time of writing, we are in a period of change as far as educational hardware is concerned. This is symptomatic of the over-riding difficulty in dealing with computer hardware – it is in a continual state of flux. No sooner has something been written about it than it is out-of-date. For many years now, schools have relied very heavily on BBC systems. Much of the development work on software has taken place with these systems in mind and many different access methods have been devised for pupils with special needs (e.g. concept keyboards, switches). Unfortunately such systems are no longer in production but they will continue to give good service in schools for many years to come. It is tempting for developers to turn their attention to exciting new systems with promising new features but it would be a mistake to forget the tried and tested equipment which plays such a useful part in classrooms all over the country.

Hardware can be divided usefully into two main classes – desktop systems and portable systems.

Desktop systems

Those in common use are:–

BBC – models B and Master
PCs from many different manufacturers
Apple Macintosh
Archimedes
RM Nimbus

Early systems were severely limited in terms of their ability to handle graphics and colour as well as having limited internal memory and this resulted in a plethora of text-based programs or programs with chunky graphics which presented children with pictures which were often difficult to recognise. Where the graphics were good, the programs frequently had the disadvantage of being very inflexible.

Clever design and techniques of mass-production have produced (in a price range which makes them accessible to schools) systems which are now better able to handle the graphic requirements of pupils, and which are still modifiable to meet individual needs. In addition, the advent of relatively inexpensive scanners and the ability of systems to make use of video images or still images stored on magnetic disk or CD ROM bring high quality graphics into the realm of educational software. Furthermore, and this may be of particular interest to those working with pupils with specific learning difficulties, modern systems are often capable of allowing the digital recording of sounds. Within appropriate software, this opens up the possibility of adding audio-help to passages of text, including screen-based worksheets, without having to resort to robotic, synthetic speech. It may be, however, that schools are still unable to afford these additional peripheral devices and this is one area where local information technology support units may be able to provide a helpful service for schools.

PORTABLE SYSTEMS

In some cases a portable system may be appropriate to meet the needs of an individual pupil. This is certainly so in the secondary sector where pupils are required to move from class to class. For some time 'pseudo' portable machines have been available but many of these have, in practice, been too heavy to be readily transportable – especially if they are required to be moved from school to home and vice versa. Others, although truly portable, have been limited in internal memory and processing power. Unfortunately, development of light-weight battery power has not kept pace with the developments in the processors themselves, resulting in limited time being available for computer use between battery charges. Furthermore, ignorance of the characteristics of rechargeable batteries has created serious difficulties in the management of power supplies for portable systems – particularly systems incorporating electromechanical devices, such as disk drives, which have relatively heavy power consumption.

Miniaturisation of components and reduction in moving parts should allow the advent of truly portable systems without reduction in processing power. Already, systems which rely on memory cards as external storage devices are becoming available at reasonable cost. Some schools are considering the use of portable, laptop machines as standard word-processors for classroom use. This seems to be a sensible idea in these days of financial restraint when perhaps four laptops could be purchased for the price of one desktop. Furthermore, there is usually relatively easy transfer of files from laptops to desktop systems. This spread in the use of laptops is gradually making it less likely that individuals are being singled out by their peers as pupils with special needs.

WHICH MICROCOMPUTER?

Choosing an appropriate machine can prove to be a frustrating experience. It is worthwhile trying to be as specific as possible about the reasons for investing in a microcomputer system and to be aware of operational difficulties which may occur once the machine is in use. It may be helpful to ask the following questions:

Who is going to use it?

What are they going to use it for?

What software is available to meet the needs of the users?

Are there any special problems of access that must be addressed?

What training is available in the use of the equipment?

Does it have an understandable and helpful handbook with a good index?

Who will repair it when it fails?

What will happen if a replacement is not available at crucial times and a machine fault occurs e.g. during examinations?

How will the Examinations Board view the use of the machine and software?

Who will be able to give support once the machine has been purchased?

What will it cost to insure against theft, accidental damage etc.?

Who is going to be responsible for the equipment?

Is the pupil familiar enough with the keyboard to make effective use of the machine?

In the case of the portable and in addition to the above:

How will it be powered?

What backup power is available?

Can the screen be read in different lighting conditions?

Is the keyboard the correct size for comfortable use?

Will there be ready access to any additional equipment in the various locations where the machine will be used e.g. printers

Is the pupil sufficiently literate to make use of a laptop? If not a concept keyboard and desktop system would perhaps be better option.

Schools are not the only purchasers of microcomputer equipment. Many parents seek help before investing in equipment for their children. In order to deal with such requests for help in choosing a microcomputer, the following may be worth considering:

Which computers are in use at school?

Is extra computing time at home really necessary?

What are the chances that the children will become bored by using programs to which they already have access at school?

Is the pupil sufficiently motivated to make good use of the machine?

If the computer is required for more than one purpose, then compromise may be necessary and neither user may get the 'ideal' system.

Whichever item of hardware is ultimately chosen, it is important to consider the specific needs of the individual and then to find appropriate hardware and software to meet these needs rather than start with the hardware and look around for a client to fit it. In addition, it should be stressed that additional items may be required – items often overlooked. In these days of emphasis on safety in the home and with more stringent rules of safety in the schools, a trolley with lockable wheels and fixed power block may be required. A disk storage system may be worthwhile in order to avoid frustrating delay in getting started on a program.

POWER MANAGEMENT AND PORTABLES

As mentioned earlier, many portable systems rely upon the use of rechargeable batteries for their power. Those with backlit screens and in-built disk drives may only be able to deliver 2 to 3 hours use between charges so it is important to make the best use of the power available. Some systems will power down automatically if not used within a specified period of time or if the display panel is closed. Some will give an audible or visual warning if low on power. Others offer full power management programs on chip as an integral part of the machine.

Most of the portables make use of Ni-Cad rechargeable batteries which require careful handling and the following should be especially noted:

The manufacturer's instructions should be followed regarding charging (particularly the first charge).

The first charge may take 16 hours and even then may only be charged to 80% capacity.

Two charges may be required to achieve full charge.

If batteries are recharged before reaching the level at which the portable gives a low charge warning, then they may develop a 'memory' for full charge which is less than their actual capacity.

In order to correct the condition above, the batteries should be discharged as far as possible before going through the procedure of recharging as for a first charge.

CONCLUSION

Although the use of technology is not a panacea for those with specific learning difficulties, it has great potential to assist in teaching and learning. Technology is changing very rapidly and it is important to keep the needs of the children in mind. Great care must be taken in choosing appropriate hardware and software to meet the needs of learners since it is all too easy to be led by the technology rather than by the needs of the pupils.

REFERENCES

1	Thinksheet	Fisher Marriott, 3 Grove Road, Ansty, Coventry CV7 9JD. 0203 616325.
2	Prompt Writer	NCET, Sir William Lyons Road, Science Park, Coventry CV4 7EZ. 0203 416994.
3	PAL	Scetlander 74 Victoria Crescent Road, Glasgow G12 9JN. 041 357 1659.
4	Co:Writer	Don Johnston Developmental Equipment, Inc. UK Supplier: Fairhurst Apple Centre Chester, Northgate Pavilion, Chester Business Park, Chester CH4 1LN. 0244 680 700.
5	Write:OutLoud	Don Johnston Developmental Equipment, Inc. UK Supplier: Fairhurst Apple Centre Chester, Northgate Pavilion, Chester Business Park, Chester CH4 1LN. 0244 680 700.
6	Franklin	7 Windmill Business Village, Brooklands Close, Sunbury-on-Thames, Middlesex TW16 7DY. 0932 770185.
7	Tandy WP3	Intertan UK Ltd., Leamore Lane, Walsall WS2 7PS. 0922 710000.
8	Developing Tray	North West Semerc, Fitton Hill CDC, Rosary Road, Oldham OL8 2QE. 061 627 4469.
9	Sassoon Font	Dr Rosemary Sassoon, 34 Witches Lane, Riverhead, Sevenoaks.

10	Fun Phonics	Pavic Publications, Sheffield City Polytechnic, 36 Collegiate Crescent, Sheffield S10 2BP. 0742 665274.
11	Hi-Spell	Xavier Software, Bangor Dyslexia Unit, Department of Psychology, University College of North Wales, Bangor, Gwynedd LL57 2DG. 0248 351151 x 2616.
12	Picture Gallery	Scetlander, 74 Victoria Crescent Road, Glasgow G12 9JN. 041 357 1659.
13	CK Sequencer	Ian Singer, Lothian Region.
14	Starspell	Fisher Marriott, 3 Grove Road, Ansty, Coventry CV7 9JD. 0203 616325.
15	Complete Speller	Northern Micromedia, University of Northumbria, Coach Lane Campus, Newcastle upon Tyne NE7 7XA. 091 270 0424.
16	Soapbox	Xavier Software, Bangor Dyslexia Unit, Department of Psychology, University College of North Wales, Bangor, Gwynedd LL57 2DG. 0248 351151 x 2616.
17	Keyboard Skills	Scetlander, 74 Victoria Crescent Road, Glasgow G12 9JN. 041 357 1659.
18	Mavis Beacon Teaches Typing	Software Toolworks Ltd., The Coach House, Hooklands, Scaynes Hill, Haywards Heath, W Sussex RH17 7NG. 0444831761.
19	Alan Nixon Special Care	NorthWest Semerc, Fitton Hill CDC, Rosary Road, Oldham OL8 2QE. 061 627 4469.

BIBLIOGRAPHY

A Software Guide for Specific Learning Difficulties (1993)

Day, Jill   Sir William Lyons Road,
NCET   Science Park,
                Coventry CV4 7EZ.

IT Support for Specific Learning Difficulties (1992)

Ed. Sally McKeown,   Sir William Lyons Road,
NCET   Science Park,
                Coventry CV4 7EZ.

Computers and Literacy Skills (1991)

Ed. Chris Singleton,
The British Dyslexia Association Computer Resource Centre,
Department of Psychology,
University of Hull,
Hull HU6 7RX.

Computers and Typography (1993)

Compiled by Rosemary Sassoon,
Intellect Books,
Suite 2, 108/110 London Road, Oxford OX3 9AW.

The diagram on page (Fig.2) is taken from Alberts House Support Pack by Chris Hopkins published by the NCET and is reproduced here with the permission of the publishers.

Figures 1, 3 and 4 reproduced by permission of the publishers.

USEFUL CONTACTS

NCET
Sir William Lyons Road, Science Park, Coventry. CV4 7EZ .
Tel 0203-416994.

Publications: A Software Guide for Specific Learning Difficulties – J. Day.
Special Update – Jan 1993.
Dyslexia Information sheet SEN 6.11.
Portable Computers and Special Needs SEN 6.21.

NERIS
Maryland College Leighton Street, Woburn, Beds. MK17 9JD.
Useful source of information on software and publications.

BRITISH DYSLEXIA ASSOCIATION
98 London Road, Reading, Berks., RGl 5AU.

Publications: Computers and Literacy Skills – Chris Singleton (Ed).
Using Computers with Dyslexics – Getting Started Series.

NASEN
> 2 Lichfield Road, Stafford. ST17 4JX.

SNUG
> Jeff Hughes, 3g Eccleston Gardens, St Helens. WA10 3BJ.
> Help and advice for users of technology.

BDA COMPUTER RESOURCE CENTRE
> Dept. of Psychology, University of Hull, HULL HU67RX.

Northwest SEMERC
> Fitton Hill CDC, Rosary Road, Oldham. OL8 2QE.
> A Source of useful software.

> Publications: Laptop Computers and Special Educational Needs – L. Mason.

CECC
> Prissick Base, Marton Road, Middlesborough, Cleveland. TS4 3R.
> A Source of useful software.

> Publications: Technology for Specific Learning Difficulties.
> A Parent's Guide to buying a computer.

SCOTTISH EXAMINATIONS BOARD
> Ironmills Road, Dalkeith, Midlothian EH22 1 LE.
> Guidance on the use of technology in examinations.

THE USE OF RESOURCES
TO ACCESS LEARNING SKILLS

ANNE F. PHILIP

INTRODUCTION

Irrespective of the debate highlighted in the research regarding the aetiology and the teaching of dyslexic children, the classroom environment would be extremely lack-lustre without a range of teaching resources. This chapter will focus on the variety of resource material which can be used and adapted by the teacher to develop a range of skills among dyslexic children and additionally to facilitate and enhance a positive self-concept.

WHAT IS A RESOURCE?

A resource can be defined as 'any supply which will meet a need'. Such a supply can include books, equipment, teacher-adapted materials, the teacher and the learning environment. Resources, however, should be placed within a context. That context includes both the needs of the learner, teaching methods and the classroom setting. Often, the dyslexic learner is a very bruised and damaged individual and this needs to be appreciated in developing and using resources. Additionally, the school policy, the environment for learning, the method of study, the demands of the syllabus, including the 5-14 programme in Scotland and the National Curriculum in England, and the primary difficulties experienced by the child also need to be borne in mind when identifying and developing suitable resources for dyslexic children.

THE TEACHER

The teacher is clearly a major resource. In an ideal world, the teacher should be interested, informed, enthusiastic, possess a sense of humour, display considerable patience, have a 'herculean constitution' and an ever-welcoming smile.

DEVELOPING RESOURCES

A Teaching Framework for Dyslexic Children.

Such a framework should include a number of different aspects all of which are important and need to be considered in the development of resources (Fig. 2).

Check List

(Fig. 2)

Alphabet
Name & Address
Units of Time - Money
Mathematical Symbols
Compass Points
Use of: dictionary
            atlas
            encyclopaedia
            library
Reversals (correction)
Cursive Writing
Auditory Perception
Visual Perception
Spelling Rules
Syllabification
Basic Sight Vocabulary
Social Sight Vocabulary
Outlaws
Reading with some competence
Writing with some competence
Sequencing
Orientation

The Alphabet

The sounding of the letters of the alphabet is of great importance. These letters are the tools of reading. There are many different representations of letters currently available, such as plastic letters and wooden letters (Galt). Letters can also be put on to cards and can be used in a variety of ways in the teaching process. The cards can be hung on a 'washing line' across the room so that not only can they be readily seen by the children, but they also can be moved together to form various kinds of digraphs and blends (see Fig. 3).

(Fig. 3)

Alphabetic order is also very important for the use of dictionaries, telephone books and other reference texts. If possible, the use of the actual resource, dictionary or telephone book is preferable. Dictionaries can be divided easily into four parts, for example: A-D; E-L; M-R; and S-Z.

The child can be helped to remember this division through the use of a simple mnemonic such as:

'Alphabetic Entry Makes Sense'.

(Fig. 4)

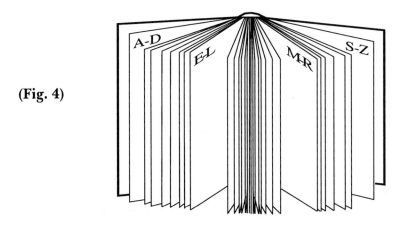

The use of the alphabet can be reinforced through the use of games. Such games can include arranging the children in alphabetic order according to their surname or Christian name.

Name and address

It is important that the child can spell his or her own name and address. This can sometimes prove difficult for dyslexic children and a card, like a credit card, can be made to help to reinforce the correct spelling of the child's name and address.

Units of Time and Money

It is sometimes necessary to reinforce units of time and money. There are many ways in which this reinforcement can be achieved. These can include:

- **An egg timer** instead of a clock. This provides the sense of time and highlights particular units of time, e.g. three minutes on an activity.
- **A festival folder** in which the months of the year are highlighted including the special events of each month.
- **Use of real money**. This can reduce any loss of learning which can occur when learning needs to be transferred to other contexts. The use of real money replicates real situations more readily than using 'toy money' or counters.

Mathematical Symbols

It is important to ensure that the child has a real understanding and appreciation of mathematical symbols. Graphics can help to make the meaning of symbols clearer to children. (For examples of this see 'Mathematics and Dyslexia' – Ann Henderson).

Syllabification

This process can make spelling easier because the word is broken up into syllables. It is important to highlight syllabification for dyslexic children, since this process can be quite difficult for them to acknowledge (Bradley, 1988).

It is useful, therefore, to ensure that the child is aware of the natural syllabic breaks in words. This can be done by actually marking them on the word or by breaking larger words into small ones e.g. 'fire/place'. The Stott Reading Programme provides many useful examples of strategies for syllabification.

Basic sight vocabulary

This is necessary, not just to provide the child with a working vocabulary which can help in the comprehension of reading passages, but also to give the child a degree of confidence from being able to read at least some words. This basic sight vocabulary should include words which can be described as a 'social sight vocabulary – some everyday commonly used words' (Fig. 5 and 6).

(Fig. 5)

a	for	make	she
about	from	me	so
an	get	more	some
and	go	must	that
are	goes	much	the
as	had	my	their
at	has	new	them
back	have	no	then
be	he	not	there
been	her	now	they
before	here	of	this
big	him	off	to
but	his	old	too
by	I	on	two
call	if	one	up
came	in	only	want
can	into	or	was
come	is	other	we
could	it	our	well
did	just	out	went
do	like	over	were
does	little	right	will
down	look	said	with
first	made	see	you

Outlaws (Fig. 5a)

In addition to Basic Sight Vocabulary is the list of Outlaws – words for reading and spelling which make life tough.

ache	else	please
across	enough	push
again	even	put
against	ever	queue
all	every	quite
almost	eye	ready
alone	few	school
also	friend	shone
always	find	such
among	four	sugar
amongst	fourth	their
answer	full	these
any	give	those
anyone	gone	though
away	half	through
because	height	use
beauty	how	useful
beautiful	instead	usual
become	island	very
behind	kind	walk
biscuit	learn	what
both	many	when
busy	money	where
business	most	which
buy	mother	why
caught	next	
child	none	
children	nothing	
deny	often	
door	once	
either	people	

Social Sight Vocabulary (Fig. 6)

DOCTOR	NURSE	CHEMIST	EMERGENCY
POISON	PRESCRIPTION	FIRST AID	SURGERY
Take three tablets twice per day		DENTAL SURGERY	
TOILETS	LADIES	GENTLEMEN	GENTS
VACANT	ENGAGED	PUBLIC	
PUSH	PULL	ENTRANCE	EXIT
WAY IN	WAY OUT		
WAIT	CROSS NOW	GIVE WAY	ONE WAY
STOP	GO	NO LEFT TURN	
OPEN	CLOSED	PAY HERE	
PAY AS YOU ENTER			
POLICE	STATION	RAILWAY	BUS
SCHOOL			
TELEPHONE	POST OFFICE		
PRIVATE	PARKING		
RESTAURANT			
Make up real life situations			
Where possible find true to life signs			

Writing

Some writing competence should be encouraged. An excellent framework for the development of such skills can be found in the 5-14 development programme (English Language). The use of a word processor can also be included in the resources for the development of written language.

Listening

It is unwise to assume that the pupil is listening. Brief exercises to strengthen listening skills can therefore be useful. Such exercises can include:

- The use of music at the beginning of a lesson to help children 'switch on' their 'listening ears'.
- Reading stories, particularly those constructed by the child.
- Dictation.

- Listening bingo.
- Asking the children to go outside to hear six different sounds.
- Listening to, and acting on, verbal instructions.

Talking

Talking and discussion can be a great strength and thus a source of success for the dyslexic child. It is important, therefore, that this should be fully utilised. This may be done by:

- Encouraging children to tell stories in small groups and tape them,
- reading sentences in rotation with a partner,
- providing a 'help sheet' which outlines a framework for a talk, thus encouraging the child to give a structured talk (see Fig. 7).

Title Help Sheet   (Fig. 7)

Title of Talk...

Jot down ideas at random - any how!
Select the best
Make up talk
Reduce to note form
Rehearse - aim to interest the audience -
         not to fill the Albert Hall
Tape yourself - how you sound
            - think of your audience
Enjoy yourself!

Reading

Reading has a variety of strands including information, enjoyment, silent reading and reading aloud. It is necessary for the teacher to become aware of the child's reading preferences – this may not be reading aloud – and to acknowledge this in order that some enjoyment may be possible from reading.

It is advisable to explain to the child different types of reading and their functions. These include:

- **S**kimming – a telephone book for numbers,
- **scanning** – selecting parts of a book for interest,
- **understanding** – scrutiny, reading carefully in order to, for example, follow instructions,
- **speed reading**

The pleasure in reading can come from activities such as:

- **News corner**

This might include a daily paper, some school information, extracts from the school diary, reading out events involving the child or even their daily diary.

- **Personal Anthologies**

A collection, made by the child, of those poems, passages from books, words and even jokes which have had some impact on them.

- **Vocabulary of reading**

   Helping the child to understand the vocabulary of reading, including:
   - Reading aloud,
   - silent reading,
   - top of page,
   - foot of page,
   - letter,
   - word,
   - sentence,
   - paragraph,
   - roman numeral,
   - index,
   - contents,
   - cover.

It is also important to ensure that the child's eye movements in reading are correct. It is possible the child may require some specific eye tracking exercises. There are a number of useful resources for this including the Word Tracking Series (Ann Arbor Publishers) which includes high frequency words and proverbs. Some of the activities to enhance scanning and eye tracking include writing particular words in lines of text.

Frameworks for Reading (Fig. 8)

Book Review

> Title ....
> Author ....
> Publisher ....
> Outline of Story:
> N.B. who, where, what, why, when, how.
> List most important characters
>
> Describe - looks: personality.
>
> Enjoyment level ....

Reading for Information / Comprehension

> Reading for Information / Comprehension
>
> 1.   Look at passage
>   N.B. Title: extract: author: illustration:
>   layout: type: shape: length of paragraph.
>
> 2.   Skim:
>   What is it about?
>   What is the purpose of writing?
>
> 3.   Read all questions
>
> 4.   Read again   (Big 6)
>
> 5.   Answer questions - follow the directions and
>   instructions.
>
> who   = person   how = in what way
> where = place   why = for what reason
> when = time   what = (many answers)

Character Sketch

> Character Sketch
>
> Book..
> Author...
> Name of Character...
> Age...
> Appearance..
>
> Would you like to meet him?
> Where in the book do you meet him?
> What was he doing / saying?

Writing

Important aspects of writing include the following:

- Functional,
- imaginative,
- personal,
- language,
- spelling,
- punctuation and structure,
- handwriting and presentation.

All should be given some focus. The child may need particular help with creative writing. Such help may include encouraging five paragraph essays; providing a list of possible opening sentences to each of the paragraphs; writing postcards; writing letters. Other useful writing activities include form filling and completing applications. Note taking is also a useful skill to develop (see Fig. 9).

LAYOUT OF NOTES: Pointers   (Fig. 9)

1   Notes may be laid out in graphic or linear style.

 2   Leave good margins.

(THESE BLANK AREAS CAN BE USED FOR AMENDMENTS OR ADDITIONS)

3   Use plenty of space.

Small undivided work is difficult to read.

4   To emphasise important points or equations or formulae:

(a)   CAPITALS   (d)   Highlighter pen

(b)   <u>Underline</u>   (e)   Coloured pens

(c) | BOX |

5   Legibility.

6   **Abbreviations** may help.

$=$	equals	$\&$	and
$\propto$	proportional to	N.B.	take note of
$>$	greater than	i.e.	that is
$\therefore$	therefore	$\neq$	is not equal to
e.g.	for example	$\not\propto$	not proportional to
cf	compare	$<$	less than
		$\because$	because

*when taking notes omit small words-
(a: the.........etc.)
Shorten words.*

Spelling

Spelling needs to be taught, where possible in context, or at least some reason needs to be given to explain why there is a need for functionally correct spelling. There are a number of aids available to assist with spelling such as the Franklin Spellmaster, dictionaries, and specific computer programmes such as PAL (Predictive Adaptive Lexicon) which can help with spelling, punctuation and structure. Spelling should be taught in some context which helps to emphasise the point that we write to communicate not spell. It can be noted that often awareness of being a poor speller can lead to reluctance to write.

Use of non-threatening words e.g. orthography instead of spelling and calling the Spelling Group Orthographers can be an advantage.

Handwriting and Presentation

It is important that the child develops a good, correct handwriting grip. Rubber grips and non-slip pencils can be useful to help with this. Some strategies which can help with handwriting include:

- Sellotaping along the margin which helps to provide the child with a starting point,
- the use of 'Braille paper' which allows the lines to be felt,
- a green spot on the page to indicate the starting position, and a red spot to show where one should stop.

Study Skills

For the dyslexic child study skills are an essential part of the teaching programme. A number of very useful publications exist on study skills, but the teacher can also employ some strategies which can also help. These include:

- Displaying information on graphic posters,
- use of mind maps,
- classroom pin board,
- the logging of information to help with recall,
- help with planning a daily routine (the dyslexic learner is often 'lost in time and space' so this time planning is essential),
- help the child to find the learning style most suited to him/her. For example, background noise, or no background noise, music, silence, bright light, dim light (Dunn & Dunn, 1992).

Resources are indeed a crucial component of any teaching programme for dyslexic children. There are many excellent commercially available resources, but additionally the teacher can adapt materials to facilitate the learning and teaching process for the dyslexic child. Any resource, however, must consider not only the content of a lesson or a skill, but the holistic needs of the child and therefore should aim to enhance and develop a positive self-concept – which in itself will facilitate learning.

Self-Esteem

As far as possible, the dyslexic learner should have self-esteem boosted. I have a 'Feeling Better' bag which is a collection of sayings, cartoons and poems to boost morale.

SOURCES AND RESOURCES

This list of books, publications and equipment can be useful to the teacher. The list is by no means definitive but I would hope that it would be helpful to those involved in teaching dyslexic learners. These resources are never complete in themselves but are more to be used, often in part, when they are relevant, when a different approach is needed or when all else fails. They are wonderful teaching tools and should be used accordingly.

General

Plastic letters: Galt clinging letters. James Galt & Co.
Letterland L. Wendon: Letterland Ltd.
Learning through Play: Jan Marzolla & Janice Lloyd. Unwin Paperbacks.
Entertaining and Educating Young Children: Robyn Gee. Usborne Publishing.
Early Childhood Resource Book: Merle B. Karnes. Winslow Press.
Building Auditory and Visual Perception Skills: LDA.
A Manual for the Training of Sequential Memory and Attention: Pruna S. Klein and Allen A.Schwartz.
     Academic Therapy Publications.
Gill Cotterell Check List. LDA.
Games to Improve Reading Levels: Jim Nicholas and Joe Guthrie. NASEN.
Stand by Series: Ken Blackford and John Humphries. Nelson (Short lesson plans).

Dictionaries and Reference

A Sentence Dictionary: Eric Neal. Hulton Educational Publications.
Collins First Dictionary: Collins (both give definitions by using the word in a sentence).
ACE Spelling Dictionary: David Mosely and Catherine Nicol, LDA. (Can be difficult for some children
     to use because of the reference method.)
Spell it Yourself: G. T. Hawker: Oxford University Press (very clear layout as a spelling check).
Oxford Children's Picture Dictionary: Oxford University Press (words presented as groups under
     themes e.g. fruit and vegetables).
Pergammon Dictionary of Perfect Spelling: Christine Maxwell. Wheaton.
Collins Concise School Dictionary: Collins. (clear layout).
Pocket Dictionary: John Grisewood. Kingfisher Books (clear and well illustrated).
Atlas: Folens Ordnance Survey World Atlas. Folens (very clear and concise – now with photo-copiable
     material).
Letter Tracking: Ann Arbor.
Globes of the World either as free standing or as transparent 'balloon' reproductions which can be
     suspended in a classroom.
Library and friendly librarian – an invaluable resource.
CD-ROM (Reading Only Material which gives access to information in encyclopaedias on computer,
     very often with illustration, animation and even voice over).

Listening

Oral comprehension: LDA.
Fast Forward: Joyce Dring: LDA.
Reading and Thinking tapes: LDA.
Warm-up Exercises Books 1-3: Rita Kisner and Brooke Knowles. Better Books.
Learning to Listen – William F. McCant: Better Books.
Is Your Bed Still There When You Close the Door: Dr Jane Healy: Better Books (great fun and
     stimulating).
Remedial Spelling: Violet Brand: Egon Publishers (part of the Spelling Made Easy series and an
     excellent source of dictation work).
Alpha to Omega: Beve Hornsby and Frula Shear: Special Educational Needs (Marketing) (for dictation
     exercises).
Books on tape which can be found in many good booksellers and record shops.

Talking

Springboards for Writing: Brenda McNeal: Academic Therapy Publications (lists of sentences and
paragraphs which can be used for oral work as well as part of a very good writing scheme).
Novels and stories to encourage talk: e.g. The Iron Man: Ted Hughes.
Any by Roald Dahl.
Help Yourself Stories: Nelson.

Reading for Information

(Some of these will obviously cover various strands of any programme but I have divided reading into two main
categories – for information and enjoyment).
Reading Alive and Library Alive: Gwen Gawith: A & C Black.
Headwork books 1-8: Chris Culshaw & Deborah Waters: Oxford University Press (books 1-4 are
particularly good containing cloze, matching, deduction, sequencing, classification).
English Headwork books 1-4: Chris Culshaw and Deborah Waters. OUP.
Way Ahead English books 1-4: Gareth Price: LDA. (includes – following directions, writing skills,
collecting information, the media).
New Treasury of English books 1-4: Eithne Roycroft: Folens (grammar, comprehension, nature study
all presented so clearly and with good illustrations).
Language Patterns books 1-6: ed. Donald Moyle. Cassell (includes stories for enjoyment as well as
workbooks and teacher resource books – a well laid out scheme for the smaller group).
Word Power books 1-4: Helen McLullich. Oliver & Boyd (with Wordpower Assessment Tasksheets
which are photo-copiable, this is excellent material).
The S.T.A.R Pack: Tricia Barthorpe. Desktop Publishing Club (wonderful collection of strategies to
assist reading).
Cloze procedure:
- Words for Living,
- Which Word,
- Words in their Places: Lynn Hutchison: Hodder & Stoughton.
False Teeth and Vampires: Astronauts and the Black Death: Christopher Jarman: LDA.
Fact Finders: Wendy Body and Julie Garnett: Longman.
Reading Comprehension: Jane Givin. Better Books (graded, all various subject matter).
Reading: 92 Gripping Stories: Kim Marshall. Better Books. (American spelling: well laid out.)

Prediction

Start Thinking.
Keep Thinking.
Stories for Thinking: Lynn Hutchison: Hodder & Stoughton.
Directions: John Cooper: (all books in this series cover essential reading skills – skimming, scanning,
speed reading, prediction, reference skills, study skills, also photo-copiable material) Oliver &
Boyd.
What's that You're Reading: Sandra Gilfeather: Edward Arnold (comprehension exercises using
pictorial material).
Tests in English Comprehension: Betty Kerr: Macmillan.
Reading for Meaning books 1-4 George A Carr: Hodder & Stoughton (old fashioned but good short
passages).

Primary Language Programme books 1-7: Masson, Monoghan, Thomson: Heinemann.
I See What You Mean books 1 & 2: Kilpatrick, McCall, Palmer: Oliver & Boyd.
What's the Idea: Graham R. White: Oliver & Boyd: (for summary and report writing).

Reading for Enjoyment

Books of pupil's own choice.
Anthologies and collections are an excellent way of getting the flavour of a book and perhaps
    encouraging the child to read more.
I Like This Story: Puffin.
Meet my Friends: chosen by Kaye Webb: Guild Publishing (characters and their adventures).
Openings: ed. Roy Blatchford: Antony Rowe Ltd. (good collection of stories with follow on activities
    included at the end of the book).
Reading 2000. 1-5. Oliver & Boyd (good novels and back-up activities).
Headwork Stories 1 & 2: Chris Culshaw: OUP (good stories and questions).
Twists: Gordon Hogg: Hodder & Stoughton: (stories with a twist in the tail – there is associated work
    but good for the stories alone).
Usborne Puzzle Adventures (various) Usborne Books.
The Black Knight, The Longship Invaders etc: Michael Thomson: LDA.
Learning with Letts: Letts (to quote – English activities with additional maths and science based on an
    exciting adventure story: different, well presented and fun).
Sea Hawk Main Readers: S. K. McCullagh: E. J. Arnold.

Poetry

Lizard Over Ice: Gervasse Phinn: Nelson.
Any collection by Brian Patten: Roger McGough.
Choral verse where the effect of group reading can support weaker readers – chosen from A. A. Milne:
    T. S. Eliot's 'Old Possum's Book of Practical Cats'.
A Second Scottish Poetry Book: Alan Bold. O.U.P.

Writing

Really Useful Picture Series: Learning Materials Ltd.: (several books with pictorial material for
    encouraging writing).
My Book About Myself: Learning Materials Ltd. (excellent framework for personal writing).
Finish the Story. Books 1-4: Kate Fitzsimmons: Learning Materials Ltd.
Tell Tale: Gordon Hogg and Graham Turnbull: Edward Arnold.
Brain Waves photo-copiable material.
Using the Newspaper to Teach Social Studies: Marilyn Olson: Dale Seymour Publications (useful
    different approach to writing and reading making use of newspapers).

Spelling

Spelling and Tables: Folens: (concise lists with dictation).
Exercise Your Spelling books 1-3: Elizabeth Wood: Hodder & Stoughton (also excellent photo-
    copiable material).
Spelling Made Easy. Books 1-3: Violet Brand: Egon Publishers Ltd.

Super Spelling Book books 1-6: Charles Cuff: Longman.
Alpha to Omega: Beve Hornsby and Frula Shear + Activity Packs: Beve Hornsby and Julie Pool: Heinemann.
Space to Spell: More Space to Spell: Frula Shear: Special Educational Needs (Marketing).
Attack: Jean Richards: Reeves Hall Hepworth Norfolk (very good associated material).
Catchwords books 1-6: Charles Cripps: Harcourt Brace Jovanovich.
Hand for Spelling: Charles Cripps: LDA.
Sounds O.K. books 1-3: Tony Walsh: Folens: (very clear presentation).
Step-by Books: Constance Milburn: Arnold Wheaton (a source of fun activities).
500 Word Book: Learning Materials Ltd.

Spellbound: Elsie T. Rak: Educators Publishing Service (structured phonic programme).
Put it Right: Violet Brand (Egon Publishers Ltd. (proof reading).
Franklin Spellmasters: small computer aids to spelling: FLS Services, Fareham.
Spelling in Context: Margaret Peters and Brigid Smith. NFER, Nelson (excellent material for linking writing and spelling).

Structure and Punctuation

Teaching Written Expression: Diana Phelps-Terasaki: Academic Therapy Publications (different and effective way of looking at sentence structure).
First Aid in English: Angus Maciver: Robert Gibson.
Mind Your Language books 1-4: U. E. Palmer and Peter Brinton: Oliver & Boyd (well illustrated and fun grammar).
Master Your English: Punctuation: Davies, Dillon, Egerton-Chesney: Basis Blackwell (very handy little book).
Punctuation in its Place: Don Shiach: Hodder & Stoughton.
Language and Languages: Derek Strange: Oxford University Press (good activities).
Introduction to Language: Aphir, Crawshaw, Roselman, Williams. Hodder & Stoughton (should the dyslexic learner study a modern language – this provides good and interesting background).

Handwriting

Handwriting Activities books 1 and 2: Thomas Barnard: Wardlock Educational.
Building Handwriting Skills in Dyslexic Children: Ed. John I. Arena: Academic Therapy Publications.
Handwriting: a second chance: LDA.
Pencil grips: LDA and Early Learning Centre.
Hand Huggers: Berol (John Menzies).
Penmaster: Phillips: Phillips High Street Oxford: (handwriting guide).

Study Skills

Basic Study Skills: Charles Milward: Macmillan.
Research Skills book 1-3: James McCafferty: Edward Arnold.
Improve Your Study Skills: Doug Humphries: CRAC.
Super Student: Carel.
Learning to Learn: Gloria Freuder. Better Books (strengthening study skills and brain power).
Study Skills Bk. 1-4: Charles Cuff: C.U.P. (variety of skills covered in a fun way).

Thinking Skills

Critical Thinking Activities: Dale Seymour Publications.
Reading and Thinking: Arthur Evans and Looking and Thinking: Arthur Evans. Learning Materials
   Ltd.
Basic Workbooks for Everyday books 1-4. Arnold Wheaton (good variety of material).
Brain Busters: Peter D Thoms: Arnold.
Electronic games such as Simon.
Reasoning and Reading 1 & 2: Joanne Carlisle. Better Books.

Exercise

Sensorimotor Activities: Academic Therapy Publications.
Motor Education and Perceptual Training: A. E. Tansley: Arnold Wheaton.
Switching on: Dr Paul E. Dennison.
Graded Activities for Children with Motor Difficulties: James Russell: Cambridge University Press.
Sensory Integration and the Child: Jean Ayres: Western Psychological Services.
Tracking Books: Ann Arbor.
Take Time: Mary Nash-Wortham and Jean Hunt: Robinswood Press: (fascinating variety of activity).

Mathematics

Ginn Mathematics Scheme: Ginn (clearly laid out).
Mathswise books 1-3: Ray Allan, Martin Williams: Oxford University Press (good book for practice
   exercises).
See the Maths books 1 & 2: Sandra Gilfeather: Edward Arnold.
Dyslexia: basic Numeracy: Vicki Burge: Helen Arkell Dyslexia Centre.
On the Track to Problem Solving: Margaret McDougall, Rae Cook: Nelson: Blackie.
Number Practice books 1-4: A. J. Stables: Schofield & Sims.
Visual Maths: Educational Insights: (for number bonding up to 10).
Maths and Dyslexics: Anne Henderson: St David's College, Llandudno: (this book contains very good
      graphics on mathematical symbols (page 29.)
Tables Teacher: Early Learning Centre: (marvellous pencil case which revolves to provide answers to
      the tables).

Self-Esteem

Every Letter Counts: Susan Hampshire: Bantam Press: (collection of letters from those with dyslexic
      problems who have survived.
Unicorns are Real: Barbara Meister Vitale: Jalmar Press.
Free Flight: Barbara Meister Vitale: Ann Arbor: (both contain a fresh approach and numerous sayings
      which help boost the confidence).
Breakthrough Learning: Barbara Given: George Mason University, USA.
No Easy Answers: the Learning Disabled Child: Sally S. Smith, US Dept. of Health Education and
      Welfare.
Self-Assessment Forms: writing, reading, listening, Folens: (all photo-copiable).
Language User's Handbook: Tony Ramsay: E. J. Arnold (for older pupils at the end of their tether –
      good for dipping into).
Computers, computer aids e.g. PAL, word processors.

I Can: Easy learn (photocopiable material).

A Rainbow of Words: Jeanne Holloway, NASEN (activities to promote listening and speaking – great variety of aproach).

Boxes of Ideas

Unique Reading Games.

The Reading Box.

Aston Portfolio.

Building Receptive and Expressive Language Skills.

Getting the Main Idea et alia (good 'no book approach').

Mathsteps: LDA.

Microtechnology

(See chapter 28)

For Older Pupils

Writing Workshop: Richard McRoberts: Macmillan (an excellent guide to the craft of writing).

English Plus: T. McSweeney and M. Elam: Longman (a practical scheme of work for the examination years – essays, punctuation, spelling, spoken English, comprehension).

The Oxford English Programme National Curriculum Stage 3: J. Selly, F. Green, D. Kitchen. Oxford University Press.

Subject Spellchecks. Spelling for Exams. E. G. Stirling.

Help for the Dyslexic Adolescent: E. G. Stirling: Better Books.

Highlight English books 1 and 2: Susan Duberly + Teacher's Resource Pack: Heinemann.

Enjoying English books 1-3: (extracts from novels, plays, poems well presented in themes).

Enjoying Poetry: More Enjoying Poetry: Appreciating Poetry: (an excellent selection of poetry and a superb teaching book). All by Sadler, Haylar, Powell. Macmillan.

Look it up: Peter Forrestal: Nelson: (a good handbook for help in the conventions of writing).

Take any Book: Richard Bain and Ali Cooper: GCSE (very good for book reviews).

Spelling it Out: R. Pratley: BBC Publications.

Word Mastery: J. Conlan and M. Henley: Oxford University Press.

Spelling Matters: Bernard R. Sadler: Edward Arnold.

Mathematics Foundation Skills 11-14 yrs: Michael Ashcroft: Letts.

Problem Solving Pack: Edward Arnold.

Writing Skills for the Adolescent: Diana Hanbury King. Better Books. (American pub. structured and interesting).

And Not Forgetting

Learning Difficulties in Reading and Writing: A Teacher's Manual: Reason & Boote: NFER Nelson.

Specific Learning Difficulties: Dyslexia: Margaret Crombie: Jordanhill College of Education.

Fantastic Ideas for Frenzied Teachers: Christine Syme: Collins Educational.

Special Needs Information press: a monthly publication with very pertinent articles. 23 Saxholm Way, Southampton.

This Book Doesn't make ~~sens~~ ~~cens~~ ~~sns~~ ~~scens~~ sense. Jean Augur: Antony Rowe Ltd.

Reading Problems: Identification and Treatment: Peter Edwards: Heinemann.
Monaco Hang UP a/V Storage: Don Cresswell (for displaying the pupils' 'Best Work').
Differentiated Ideas: Tricia Barthorpe: Desktop Publishing club.
Dyslexia in Schools: Multi-sensory learning (excellent source of photocopiable information).
Dyslexia: How would I cope: Michael Ryden. Jessica Kingsley Publishers.

REFERENCES

Bradley, L. (1988). 'Rhyme Recognition and Reading and Spelling in Young Children' in Masland, R. L. and Masland M. R. *Pre-School Prevention of Reading Failure.* Parkton, Maryland. York Press.
Dunn, R. and Dunn, K. (1992). *Teaching Elementary Students Through Their Individual Learning Styles.* Allyn & Bacon, Massachusetts. (1992).

SECTION 5

CONTINUING EDUCATION

ADULT LITERACY WORK – DIFFICULTIES AND NEEDS IN READING AND WRITING

DON MACKIE

Estimates of literacy needs in the adult population range from 10% to over 40% and, in a sense, the spread of estimates, is actually more interesting than attempts to pin needs down to figures. There seems to be no disagreement that millions of adults in Britain do experience difficulties with reading and writing; clearly the actual figure will rise or fall depending on the measure that is used and different people have different opinions about when a difficulty is a problem. Large scale measures tend to look at performance against general indicators, regardless of what any particular individual may need or wish to do and consequently tend to measure ability rather than needs or aspirations.

As yet relatively uninfluenced by the need to relate its work to any particular dimension of outcome – jobs, national certification, academic success, income, crude numbers attending, or use of facilities – local authority Adult Basic Education provision in Scotland still operates within an area where need is the problem owned by the individual rather than difficulty perceived by a system. Further, because of its location within the Regional Community Education Services, Scottish ABE has been uniquely placed to capitalise on community development and local access opportunities, as well as benefiting from a network of professional staff skilled in process focused work with adults.

Attendance at ABE remains in any terms non-compulsory, offering neither financial incentive to the unemployed nor, largely, time off work to the employed, and its immediate value is clearly measured by its usefulness to the individual rather than to any external functionalism. The needs addressed are those felt independently by individual adults and are dissociated from absolute levels of ability as might be measured by reading age or other tests.

By responding to the needs of those who request help, ABE schemes find themselves working with adults at a range of levels, from beginning reading through writing difficulties of all kinds to support for students already in further education who are struggling with the written components of the work (composition, structure).

In most cases, the particular lack of skill will be long-standing, but equally, in many cases, this will be of minor practical relevance until the actual skill is needed for a specific purpose. By and large, the majority of adults are, if not happy with, at least resigned to their abilities in reading and writing, measuring their needs in relation to day-to-day activities; it is typically only at the point where discrepancies emerge between the individual's day-to-day level of ability and what he/she needs or wishes to do that literacy needs are perceived.

From a practitioner's viewpoint, it is arguable that, in these terms, ABE needs do not exist until circumstances in the adult's life have generated them. Rather than being absolute, needs increase and decrease with changes in an individual's life; some changes (new forms/regulations/unavoidable changes of circumstance) are enforced and can create real crises of need, stress or loss of self-respect but other changes may reflect the individual's aspirations to develop and to take on challenges (wishing to go to college, self-expression, keep up with the children's education) and, consequently, ABE is required to be more than simple compensatory education for those who would show up as having difficulty.

While ABE students appear at many levels of skill, for the student, needs are defined by their situation rather than ability: solutions to situations are the real need for many of the students rather than any particular wish to be more literate and, as a rule, ABE is perceived as a means to an end rather than as an end in itself, success being measured by students in their own terms.

The improvement of literacy skills is more likely to be an aim in its own right for adults who are poor readers, yet, by the same token, such adults are, on an almost daily basis, confronted by potentially exposing, even threatening, situations which are hard to avoid while still living a reasonable quality of life. Taking up a new interest, hobby or sport, shopping, playing the lottery or choosing the chef's special pub lunch all carry enough potential for ridicule or exposure for the poor reader, but difficulties will also tend to be spotted and commented upon by staff in the Job Centre or Benefits Agency, social workers and health visitors, so that, in a manner of speaking, life can be a series of recurring situations with literacy as the issue.

In many – probably most – cases, embarrassment, dignity or a sense of personal privacy will prevent adults with reading difficulties from coming forward for help and many adults appear to be getting by, relying and depending upon a friend, relative, husband or wife and seriously limited as independent individuals. A poor grasp of reading may be enough to create a semblance of choice - choosing packaged food by brand recognition, but possibly missing out on new or less distinctive cheaper products; buying baby food, pain killers or carpet shampoo easily enough but not being too sure about amounts, doses or proportions when mixing. Close scrutiny of the contents may be a reasonably normal activity to those who are environmentally-aware or health conscious and literate enough, but for large numbers of adults who are not literate enough, the issues will not be things which they can have realistic choice in. In fact, the issues may never become issues because there is never anything clear enough to choose between. However, at times, particular life situations can rise in prominence, generating, perhaps for the first time, a powerful and urgent motivation for learning: choosing a meal from the menu or selecting the right record on a juke box can become extremely important where a new relationship is at stake.

One of the most common situations which brings adults with reading difficulties forward for help is when their first child starts school. The potential loss of self-respect or of being seen as inadequate in one's own child's eyes can amount almost to crisis when the child brings home his or her first reading book.

Crisis characterises so many of the situations described by new students, where many years of not coping very well may be focused on a single activity or incident. It is known that adults can become skilled in strategies for covering up weaknesses or avoiding situations involving reading or writing: poor eyesight, lost glasses, not having time at the moment or preferring to take the form home to fill it in will often see people through but, pressed in a threatening situation, adults can appear to become unco-operative or aggressive, or suffer from feigned or even genuine illness. For some, the crisis will be an awful moment such as a bad interview, being laughed at by workmates or appearing to be stupid in a shop; for most, it will be part of a wider life change, such as the loss of a job, the introduction of new procedures at work, loss of the partner or relative who gave support or the breakdown of a marriage. At times, positive changes and opportunities – a new relationship, marriage, a new job or the chance of promotion – can bring new pressures.

Indeed, one of the reasons that Adult Basic Education has worked so well within local authority Community Education Services is that community education processes are designed to open opportunities for positive change through involvement in a variety of activities; because priority has been given to attracting traditional non-participants, many potential literacy students have gained access to education by a positive route. Community education workers are conscious that literacy may present problems for those taking on new challenges and will work in a sensitive way, generally supporting those with difficulties but also making discrete links to ABE when appropriate. By being involved in activities such as computer groups, cookery classes, issue or discussion groups, adults can come to need literacy skills in a positive way and are also given the context and purpose to use them.

Literacy difficulties are generally not observable in day-to-day life and, because of the popular assumption that everyone, through school, has got to grips with the skills of reading and writing, there is an instinctive impression that it is very rare for a normal adult to have problems. Indeed, as we all do, adults with difficulties almost conspire in this by pretending to be more able than they are. And we all – even those with difficulties – start off with the assumption that everyone is fully literate. Unlike children who may be at a similar level of literacy ability, adults with difficulties are treated as readers and writers until their cover is blown, after which they are treated as inadequate.

It is not surprising, therefore, that it may take a serious personal crisis to bring people out and, even then, a fair amount of courage and commitment to set out to describe what, until that point, has been felt to be a private and personal problem. Indeed, over the years, many students have described how they almost came forward once – maybe several times – before. Some have sat in the car outside the Centre for a while, watching who goes in and who comes out to see whether they look odd or normal, others have walked round the block a few times as they tried to build up the courage to come in, and many have phoned up to make an appointment but have not come along.

By the time a new referral reaches ABE, lack of confidence and lack of self-belief may actually be more of a problem than the literacy difficulty. At this point, the worker will need to reassure the adult returner that he/she has made a positive step forward rather than (as may be felt) a step back. For adults returning to education for the first time, memories of school will, most probably, be very strong; certainly, memories will be those of childhood experiences and of the learner in a child's role in a system and there will be a tendency for returners to conform to their own expectations. Differences, hopefully, will be obvious, although it is unfortunate that so much adult literacy provision is based in old school buildings and parts of existing schools, and the worker does need to emphasise by manner, conversation and general relationship, that things are indeed different and that now the learner is in control of the situation.

For most new ABE students, memories of education itself will tend to be memories of failure and it may be hard for potential students to believe that there can be improvements, but feel, rather, that they owe it to themselves to go through it once more - regardless of how painful it may be. Generally speaking, while they may be clear enough about what causes them problems, students dramatically underestimate their general ability and it is common for students (whatever their ability) to open by saying that they will 'need to start from the beginning' and there are substantial benefits in establishing with students what they are already able to do. This may well be the first time that the student has ever discussed or really considered their abilities, and school rather appears to leave people with the impression of what they were not good at.

Initial assessment in ABE work will normally take the form of an informal conversation with the emphasis on process. It will be assumed that the student actually wishes to describe as accurately as possible what the difficulty is and the ABE worker's job is therefore to assist in this rather than to root out an arcane diagnosis or arrive at score of ability.

Consequently, tests are redundant as well as being threatening and are never used in this process. Materials at hand – posters on the wall, magazines and leaflets – can enable the adult to illustrate what he/she is able to read or spell. The ABE worker may have a mental checklist of ability as a reference (read own name and address; read signs; basic reading; newspapers; instructions; simple form; write shopping list; write a note to self; to someone else; write down message; simple letter and so on) but the conversation will focus on the student's opinions and feelings about different activities:

> 'How do you think that you'd get on if you had to write [a particular word or sentence from a poster or leaflet] without copying?'

> 'Can you read any/most of the words on the poster. Where do you think that you'd get stuck?'

> 'If you wanted to find out what time a particular programme is on television, do you think that you'd be able to find out from the newspaper?'

But, ultimately, beyond establishing a somewhat crude estimate of overall ability, the worker (and student) will be more interested in concentrating on the immediate need which has brought the student in.

In realistic terms, there is little value in a precise assessment at this point: typically, ABE can offer a couple of hours tuition each week and relies for success principally upon individualised learning programmes which focus directly upon practical situations and rather a lot on the student's motivation to achieve a tangible change. At the early stage at least, motivation will rest on early rewards, and goals need to be short-term, achievable and visible.

The ABE worker may appear to be more interested in when the problem is rather than what, but, by establishing the context, a work programme can be set out to achieve the earliest practical results. For example, an adult who referred himself because of spelling difficulties was also a painfully slow reader who would give up at the first difficult word and was unwilling to write even the simplest original sentence. The man had been employed for almost twenty years as a machine operator and had coped with the weekly job of filling in a stock sheet by using a small notebook with a list of the twelve or so regular words that were needed. In the conversation with the ABE worker, it emerged that difficulties were most felt when he needed to take his pay out of the bank: until relatively recently, he had been paid by a weekly pay packet but when the system changed to a monthly credit transfer he needed his wife to complete his bank withdrawal form. In essence, the man had lost direct access to his own money, although, most probably, it was his wife's growing irritation rather than this disempowerment which had driven him to ask for help.

In terms of immediate success, taking his own money out of his bank account was of more importance to the man than, say, improving his reading or beginning to express himself in writing. As a starting point for tuition, therefore, an accurate assessment of general ability would be of less use than a closer look at his specific abilities in relation to the practical job of completing and submitting the bank withdrawal form. In this whole task analysis, we would check out the basic skills needed to achieve the task:

- Familiarity with the geography of the form and where to write what,
- writing of numbers in figures,
- writing of numbers in words,
- convention for writing sums of money,
- spelling the word 'pounds',
- writing the date,
- signature,
- knowing the name of the branch (and meaning of 'branch'),

- writing the name of branch,
- where to find the account number/sorting code number,
- reading/understanding the abbreviation A/c No.,
- reading other words on the form.

This checklist applies to a specific Royal Bank of Scotland form and, clearly, it would be necessary to use the appropriate form from the appropriate bank, rather than from Bank of Education or Bank of Nowhere samples, as the words, layout, conventions, colour and questions will differ.

While the main need may appear to be for the spelling of numbers, the student's current abilities – already able to spell 'ten', 'forty', 'fifty' and 'sixty' – would let us concentrate on 'pounds', the branch name and where particular numbers need to go. For this student, the actual skills needed to withdraw forty pounds from his account were mastered in a few weeks, although the confidence to actually carry out the task took longer to gain. In the meantime, he extended the range of numbers that he could spell and began to practise writing for the postcards that he would like to send from Blackpool later in the year.

In fact, practical short-term achievements can prove to be springboards for new ambitions in the student's mind. One student, who arrived for help with his joined up writing because he had felt embarrassed when he'd been asked to sign some papers by his lawyer, came to discover that he enjoyed creative writing and the writing process and soon moved on to Further Education to do national certificates. Another student who came with the specific aim of brushing up English for a Forces entrance test found that he enjoyed studying for its own sake and abandoned the idea of joining up, going on to academic studies instead. There are many stories of individuals whose personal horizons have opened out by discovering what they can achieve. Very often, women who have been at home for a number of years, bringing up a young family, can feel completely disarmed by the complex of skills which would be needed for them to return to work or to become involved in community activity. For many, social competence, the mysteries of new technology, their own social background and memories of inadequate literacy skills become combined into an insurmountable barrier and, without the opportunity to measure their own abilities in a secure setting, it can be impossible for them to see their own potential or worth. We have seen many people whose ambitions, in this way, have become limited to holding their own as parents (keeping up with child's homework, writing a note to school) but who, after joining a group to improve their basic writing, have begun to sense new possibilities for themselves.

It would be misleading to give too much emphasis to development in terms of gross outward achievements – qualifications, college, university, jobs – because it is the growth of the individual in relation to their own starting point that has made the difference for so many students. Adults at the level of beginning reading will have achieved very little against the major markers of success in life, and if literacy work is seen too much as the early stage of academic achievement rather than as an empowering lifeskill, potential can be stifled. If we value success only in terms of objective standards of literacy, there is a danger that we set the goals for the student along a single dimension (say, of reading continuous prose) and, as a consequence, we may find tutors doing little more than paying lip service to literacy. We have met significant numbers of adults whose problems with reading would appear to be insurmountable if worked with in the context of high (or normal) literacy aspirations and yet, if worked with from the starting point of what would be of realistic and practical use, can achieve personal goals and, all the while, remain rewarded and motivated. Rather than automatically putting the non-reading student into a (child-oriented) learning programme that assumes development of fluent reading over time – graded readers, key words or a phonic approach – the adult literacy worker, without the constraints of a standard curriculum, will set out to find practical activities in the individual student's life where success and rewards may be quickly attained and the activity itself will carry built-in reinforcement.

By establishing personal interests, routines and lifestyle and, at the same time, beginning to draw up an agreed personal word list (similar to a social sight word list but more interesting to the student) the worker will begin to set out a learning plan which has its coherence in the personal life and interests of the student. Agreed learning objectives will be short-term, achievable and probably very practical: the student may wish to read the handwritten titles on cassette tapes or videos and, to the student, it may be more relevant to recognise 'Schwarzenegger', 'Cruise' and 'Kostner' before worrying about more generally common words. The student who usually prefers lasagne in a restaurant can feel quite a sense of empowerment in being able to recognise for himself whether they have it on the menu – even although, at first, he might not be able to tell whether lamb chops is a realistic alternative when lasagne isn't there. For many non-readers in institutions, choosing from the menu can be a major statement of independence. For other students, being able to read their own football team's score, or the names of the scorers each week, can provide motivation and, again, increases the chances of reinforcement and practice.

For many reasons – early rewards, adult oriented learning, adult vocabulary, the fact that cognitive developments are not a major factor – the adult literacy tutor will concentrate heavily upon instantaneous whole word recognition, reading with meaning and relevance and, importantly, putting enjoyment into reading. Much of the tutor's energy, especially in early reading work, will go into finding effective, varied and interesting ways for the student to be able to learn manageable amounts. As said, the materials are the real materials of adult life, the focus is on practical situations and tasks: mini one-to-one role play might give the student practice with buying from catalogues, choosing the shampoo for dry hair, checking supermarket receipts, ordering from a menu; the student and tutor will certainly go for coffee together. Games such as Scrabble and word snap might punctuate the session; new technology has added the important dimension of educational games; word-processing reinforces the mood of going forward in skills (rather than going back) and, as well as saving on the drudgery of re-writing, provides a motivation for writing and encourages re-reading of text.

Up to a certain point, the close, individualised support of the literacy tutor cannot be substituted and, surely, in itself, is one of the main reasons why so many adult returners succeed. But the computer has proved itself to be a valuable tool in the encouragement of independent study and self-directed learning. From very early days, in the emphasis on community education/community development processes through to the wholehearted adoption of language experience activities and approaches, features of adult literacy work in Scotland have reflected a belief that the fundamental purpose in literacy skill development is the promotion of independence and self-reliance in its students. And this principle is reflected in all aspects of its practice. The objective in spelling work cannot be the teaching or rehearsing of large numbers of words but rather finding and passing on strategies and tricks which work for the individual student and which can be of transferable use to the student in improving his/her own spelling.

Beyond the undoubted literacy benefits in language experience work of emphasising the student's ownership of the language, respect for the student's vocabulary, easy access and individual relevance of the language content, every other aspect of the worker's approach should be coloured by the goal of handing over control and developing choice and self-direction in the student. We would strongly emphasise to our tutors that the educational process is not limited to the acquisition of literacy skills and that it is not necessarily their job to make choices for their student, select books from the library, collect the keys to the room, order the coffee for both and so on.

Nevertheless, a growth in self-confidence or self-reliance without an improvement in literacy skills would rarely be regarded as a success in our work and, most probably, would not satisfy the student who will have already identified an aspect of literacy improvement as a goal. The real measure of a successful worker is the ability to develop the independent learner through the methods and approaches used in literacy teaching. While students improve the skills of reading or writing, they should also learn about their own abilities to learn. Our example student learned to spell a few crucial words which enabled him to take on a new task for himself but more importantly he learned that he could learn and that the skills of learning – the spelling routines, techniques and tricks – could be applied independently of the tutor and adult literacy.

DYSLEXIA IN FURTHER AND HIGHER EDUCATION – A FRAMEWORK FOR PRACTICE

ALISON CLOSS
SIONAH LANNEN
GAVIN REID

INTRODUCTION

This chapter will focus on a number of practical issues relating to dyslexic students undertaking further and higher education courses of study. The number of dyslexic students accessing such courses is increasing (Singleton, 1994) and some colleges and universities have recognised this by providing special provision and additional support to help dyslexic students throughout their courses (Beloff in Closs, 1993; Gilroy, 1991) This clearly touches on equality issues and should ensure that dyslexic students are not discriminated against because of their difficulties.

It is important, therefore, that assessment and support facilities are available and that course tutors have some awareness of the difficulties associated with dyslexia. Factors such as the nature of the difficulties the dyslexic student displays, self-concept and learning styles, and how these aspects can be dealt with by student, tutor and the further education system, are all of considerable importance and will, therefore, be discussed in this chapter.

• Awareness

The reality of dyslexia in further and higher education is a relatively new phenomenon. It is not surprising, therefore, that awareness of the difficulties and how dyslexic students can be supported, is also relatively low. Some guidance has been provided (SHEFC, 1994) but this form of assistance needs to be understood and implemented by tutors. The general view obtained from a recent international conference on Dyslexia in Higher Education (University of Plymouth, 1994) was that in the main, staff at colleges and universities saw the difficulties experienced by dyslexic students as being outwith their experience and felt that they lacked the skills to deal with this type of problem. It is important that all subject lecturers and tutors are aware of individual students' difficulties – and indeed of their abilities and aspirations – so that the student may be supported by appropriate differentiation of teaching and learning approaches, by positive non-discriminatory assessment and by encouragement. However, in many educational establishments it may be in students' and lecturers'/tutors' interests that a designated learning and personal support tutor be available to give more specialist advice and to act as an intermediary or advocate for the student, should the need arise.

Such an arrangement should not preclude, or reduce, the development of student independence, and indeed, this should be one of the aims of any learning support service. The support tutor and the student should normally discuss the key issues of whether the student wishes and would benefit from further help which focuses on remediating specific literacy difficulties, or whether the focus should be on enabling learning within the subjects being studied. For many students in Further Education, and for most in Higher Education, the latter is generally true, but it may often be combined with some measure of the former kind of help, in addition to the deployment of other coping strategies such as the use of a scribe, or of microtechnology.

It is necessary to heighten the awareness among responsible staff as to the nature of dyslexic difficulties and the needs of students. This would help tutors in the preparation of lectures and tutorials, and also in the type of feedback which would be most helpful to students following, for example, written assignments.

It is important for tutors to recognise some differences between students who are perhaps 'rusty' in written work, but will improve with practice, and those students who have dyslexic difficulties, and need some extra consideration from the subject tutor, or from a designated support tutor.

The tutor, therefore, should attempt to identify the nature of the difficulties which the student is experiencing in written assignments, and how these difficulties may be evidenced in their work. Useful questions are listed below:

- What kind of assignment generates most (or least) difficulties?
- Can student choice of assignment be negotiated?
- Are there particular circumstances in which errors are made (e.g. in timed exams rather than in continuous assessment tasks?
- Does the student make syntactical errors and if so, is there a pattern to these errors?
- Is there evidence of semantic errors?

- Why are these errors occurring?
- Has the student understood the text?
- Is there a pattern to the misspellings – is the same word consistently misspelt?
- Are words which look alike used in the wrong context?
- Is there evidence of reversals of letters or letters in the same word out of sequence?
- Is the piece of written work badly organised? Is it too long or too short?
- Are points not fully explored or explained?
- Is there evidence of wide reading or an over-reliance on a limited number of texts?
- Is there an over dependence on quotations from other texts, without accompanying discussion
- Does the student use simpler vocabulary in written work than in normal conversation or oral responses to questions?

These points can provide the tutor with a summary of information, which can help provide useful feedback to the dyslexic student and to his other lecturers/ tutors, and a good source of information if the student is to be referred for further assessment.

ASSESSMENT

In some cases it may seem necessary that the student's difficulties should be assessed more fully. However, these students may already have been assessed many times. Data from such assessments, if available, should therefore be scanned for useful information which would still have current validity in the new context. If, however, further assessment is still thought to be necessary, then it should be undertaken as early as possible in the student's course. The ideal is pre-course assessment, so that the student would not experience early failure or receive negative feedback from tutors, demoralising experiences for a student with dyslexic difficulties.

Assessment should include a range of informal and formal strategies:

- ### Informal Assessment

Because of the likelihood of previous assessment throughout their school careers, students may well be aware of their specific difficulties and it is therefore important that they are asked how:

(i)   They, themselves feel about their difficulty.

(ii)   They have sought to compensate for their difficulties.

(iii) They perceive their strengths and weaknesses.

(iv)   They deal with the parts of the course which they find difficult.

From the initial interview, one is attempting to obtain some information about a number of factors, including the level of the student's self-concept and particularly how they view the course in relation to their perception of their own abilities. It may be necessary to undertake further assessment, if it is felt more information concerning the student's strengths and weaknesses is required. It should be remembered, however, that formal assessment is time-consuming and may not necessarily reveal any additional factors which could help in the development of support strategies for the student. A great deal of information can be obtained from talking with the student and structuring a study skills programme with the student.

- **Formal Assessment**

A formal assessment should be as comprehensive as possible. It should, therefore, include tests of reading and spelling accuracy; analysis of reading and spelling errors; reading comprehension, reading fluency; and if possible, an intellectual assessment which can provide a full cognitive profile.

In reading and spelling accuracy, one is looking for the attainment level of reading and spelling. It is important, however, to consider the student's self-esteem when confronting him/her with long tests of words to read. The Wide Range Achievement Test (WRAT-R, Jastak and Wilkinson, 1984) is appropriate for use with adults, but because it involves the presentation of ninety words on a page, it may have a demoralizing effect on some students.

When analysing the types of reading and spelling errors, one is looking for a distinctive pattern such as words consistently mispronounced, which can indicate a phonological difficulty. Further evidence of a phonological difficulty can be obtained from a non-word reading test through observing the accuracy of reading and spelling of word endings.

Elbro, Nielson and Peterson (1994), in a study of dyslexic adults, found that phonological difficulties were a significant factor and even some comprehension difficulties were explained by phonological difficulties. Their study also suggests that dyslexics possess less distinct phonological representations of spoken words. Pennington *et al.* (1990) found that dyslexic adults struggled with words which they had not come across before. Such findings, therefore, confirm the view that the pattern of reading difficulties commonly found in dyslexic children is also found in dyslexic adults. Pennington's research has particular relevance for students in further and higher education entering new areas of study which may require the acquisition and use of substantial new vocabularies. In a study, however, of over 100 dyslexic children and adults (Lannen and Lannen, 1995) the researchers found that phonological difficulties were not the most obvious problem of dyslexics, but rather short-term auditory memory and 'suspected visual problems' were more prominent. This underlines the need to conduct an assessment by using a variety of formal and informal strategies including observation and analysis of written work.

In a comprehensive assessment, other factors such as visual difficulties, omissions, reversals and sequencing errors would also be considered. 'Refusals' in relation to reading may indicate a lack of confidence, or perhaps a lack of comprehension. Usually, a reader would make a reasonable guess at a word if the passage is understood. Reading comprehension, therefore, is an important aspect of an assessment and this can be addressed in a variety of ways, including taping or reading the passage to the student, or by allowing the student to read silently and then ask relevant questions.

Reading fluency is important because it is likely a dyslexic student will read slowly and therefore may need some additional guidance in relation to recommended course texts. The dyslexic students reading may have to be more selective than other students, so it is important that the most useful books, or indeed chapters, are selected to guide the students reading.

• Intellectual Assessment

It may be appropriate to obtain measures of the student's cognitive skills and obtain standardised scores from an intellectual assessment. The debate concerning the use of intelligence tests in the assessment of dyslexia is well documented (Conners, 1994; Reid, 1994; Stanovich, 1991 and Siegal, 1989).

The test most commonly used is the Wechsler Adult Intelligence Scale – Revised (WAIS-R). It is a normative test and can be used with individuals from 16 to 74 years. It consists of eleven sub-tests, six representing a verbal scale, and five forming a performance scale (see Fig.1).

Fig. 1:

A brief description of each WAIS-R sub-test:

Information:	General knowledge, long-term memory.
Digit Span:	Recall of information (numbers), short-term auditory, memory, concentration.
Vocabulary:	The ability to express ideas verbally, word knowledge, long-term memory.
Arithmetic:	Attention, concentration, short-term auditory memory, numerical reasoning.
Comprehension:	Interpret social situations, make practical judgements, common sense reasoning, long-term memory.
Similarities:	Concrete and abstract reasoning skills, categories and relationships, long-term memory.
Picture Completion:	Visual alertness to environmental details.
Picture Management:	Non-verbal reasoning, sequencing of information.
Block Design:	Spatial visualisation, analysis of whole into its component parts.
Object Assembly:	Part-whole integration, analysis of parts into a whole.
Digit Symbol:	Paper and pencil task requiring the duplication of abstract designs, visual motor integration, speed of information processing, visual tracking, short term visual memory.

In the diagnosis of dyslexia, some sub-tests would be more important than others. The digit span, for example, is a test of working memory and consists of digits forward and digits reversed. In the latter test, the examiner repeats a series of digits and the examinee is required to repeat them backwards. Many dyslexic adults would find this difficult while, on the other hand the sub-test – comprehension – would tend to reveal higher scores (see Fig. 2). For students who have not mastered reading to a level where it is undertaken other than for essential tasks, scores on the information sub-test may be affected because of poor general knowledge of the kind acquired through wider reading.

Fig. 2:

WAIS-R RESULTS

On the Wechsler Adult Intelligence Scale – Revised, W. obtained a verbal, a performance and a full scale score in the high average (bright) range of intelligence.

Verbal IQ	113
Performance IQ	114
Full Scale IQ	114

VERBAL SCALE		PERFORMANCE SCALE	
Information	10	Picture Completion	10
Digit Span	8	Picture Arrangement	14
Vocabulary	14	Block Design	8
Arithmetic	8	Object Assembly	8
Comprehension	16	Digit Symbol	17
Similarities	9		

(Average scores = 8 - 11   Range 1 - 19)

VERBAL SCALE: Strengths:

Relative to performance on the verbal tasks of the WAIS-R, significant strengths (in the very superior and superior ranges respectively) were on measures of ability to interpret social situations and make practical judgements and the ability to express ideas verbally.

A score in the average range (50th and 37th percentiles respectively) was obtained on measures of general fund of information and concrete and abstract reasoning skills.

Weaknesses:

Relative to the performance on the verbal tasks of the WAIS-R, significant weaknesses (in the average range – 25th percentile) were on measures of ability to recall auditory information in proper sequence and detail and numerical reasoning.

PERFORMANCE SCALE: Strengths:

Relative to performance on the visual perceptual tasks of the WAIS-R, significant strengths (in the very superior and superior ranges respectively) were on a paper and pencil task requiring the duplication of abstract designs and non-verbal reasoning skills when dealing with social situations.

A score in the average range (50th percentile) on a measure of visual alertness to environmental details was obtained.

Weaknesses:

Relative to a performance on the visual perceptual tasks of the WAIS-R, significant weaknesses (in the average range – 25th percentile) were on measures of spatial visualisation and non-verbal concept formation (analysis of a whole into its component parts) and part-whole integration (analysis of the component parts into a whole).

SUMMARY OF RESULTS:

The results of the WAIS-R indicated a high average cognitive potential.

Scores on the tasks of the WAIS-R which required short-term auditory memory processing were weak. These tests measure the mental manipulation of information in short-term auditory memory and suggest a comparative weakness in this form of processing. However, performance on the aforementioned tasks can also be adversely affected by distractability and/or anxiety.

Note: when short-term memory tasks are present visually, a well developed processing ability of (97th percentile) is evident.

There were weaknesses in the area of spatial analysis and perceptual organisation. Students with weaknesses in these areas are often referred to as field-dependent and find visual figure-ground and visual discrimination activities difficult. They may not naturally structure stimuli when they are dealing with perceptual and verbal materials.

To sum up, this student is presented with specific learning difficulties due to an interaction between the following factors:

- A significant weakness in the area of short-term auditory memory processing (adversely affected by distractability and/or anxiety).

- A weakness in the area of spatial analysis and perceptual organisation skills.

- Mixed laterality which can cause difficulties in terms of orientation and visual tracking often resulting in reversals, loss of place and lack of fluency in reading. Difficulties may also occur in the area of eye, hand and body co-ordination.

- Possible visual difficulties.

Source: Lannen and Lannen, 1995.

It must be appreciated, however, that the same pattern of difficulties is not always obvious in the cognitive profile of dyslexic adults. Therefore it can be misleading to look for consistent patterns from the profile obtained from the WAIS-R scores. For example, in many cases the digit symbol sub-test would present considerable difficulties for dyslexic children (McLoughlin, Fitzgibbon and Young, 1994), but it is possible, as the extracts from the educational reports show (see Fig. 2), that dyslexic students can perform well in this kind of task, particularly if they have visual strengths and have developed compensatory strategies.

The assessment, therefore, should provide information which can be fed back to the student to help him/her become more familiar with their learning style and how they can use their strengths to help deal with their difficulty. It should also help the course tutor's awareness of the student's difficulties and the type of approaches which may be best suited for the student.

The next section of this chapter will focus on how the student can be helped to minimise the effects of their difficulty.

• Dealing with the Difficulty

There are a number of ways of helping students deal with their difficulties. Many of the commercially available reading or spelling programmes are inappropriate as the content does not relate to the age or interest of the adult. It can also be de-skilling for students in higher education to return to basic reading programmes. However, some very simple approaches, such as a list of subject specific vocabulary for spelling practice, can be very effective, especially if they can be part of a computer assisted learning support programme. Students in a Further Education or Higher Education establishment with open access computer resource facilities may readily use personalised disks for this necessary, but otherwise tedious, practice. Advice is obtainable from a variety of sources on appropriate software (Singleton, 1994; Pottage, 1994; McKeown, 1992).

As far as possible, suggested remedies should involve the student taking as much responsibility as possible for their own learning. Study skills programmes and strategies which make the student aware of their own learning styles are particularly important. These should provide the student with a positive approach to learning, utilise the student's own learning preferences, help the student develop self-awareness and provide some guidance on appropriate study habits (Reid, 1994).

An effective study skills programme, therefore, should focus on the student's individual learning style, attempt to establish an appropriate learning environment for the student, enhance the student's self-esteem, and attempt to develop skills in information processing through memory work, building up concepts of schema and practice and recording and summarising information.

Fig. 3 below, which is part of an educational psychologist's report on the student referred to in Figs. 1 and 2, illustrates some of the above points.

Fig. 3:

Reading/Reading Comprehension

W. needs to develop her reading and reading comprehension skills. 'Taped' reading (following the text while listening to a tape) is an excellent way in which to gain more experience in reading and helps to develop word identification, mediated meaning and fluency. It is also an excellent way in which to develop the visual tracking/scanning skills which are crucial to reading and studying.

Four concrete strategies aimed at comprehending a section of text are questioning, clarifying, summarising and predicting (Baker and Brown, 1984). These have a dual purpose in that they are both comprehension fostering and comprehension monitoring. That is they enhance comprehension whilst allowing the reader to check whether it is occurring.

The individual reads the chapter/section of the book and then asks herself questions about the content. She then clarifies the meaning of the chapter, summarises (this could be written down in mind maps etc.) and attempts to predict upcoming content in the text.

The following procedure is also recommended for studying a chapter/ piece of text in depth:

- First, go to the back of the chapter to see if there is a summary. Often the reading of a summary will make the reading of the entire chapter unnecessary. The salient ideals are summarised for you, read them carefully and decide if you would like to read some more about them within the body of the chapter. If not, you've no need to read the chapter!

- The next thing to look for, still at the end of the chapter, is for a set of questions. If there are questions listed at the end of the section, you may not have to prepare your own review questions but use the ones from the book instead. By reading the questions, you can re-test yourself. Find out how much you already know about the subject matter. The kind of questions will also be a very good indication of the level of difficulty involved in the mastery of the topic – this can effectively adjust the intensity of your approach to suit the material at hand.

- Once you've finished with the preliminary survey of the chapter, get a piece of paper and a pen, or a word processor, and start reading. As you go along, you'll find that the information consists of two kinds of words: the key words, sometimes called the concrete words and expressions, and the fillers, which make the text readable. The key words are the ones that carry the ideas. They are usually nouns and verbs which, when activated in your memory, will help you to recall the entire body of information you saw when you collect the key words. Once you've realised this fact, there is hardly any point in attempting to copy sentences and even entire paragraphs from a book. Collect the key words and arrange them in their proper relationship (pattern notes, mind maps, flow diagrams etc.). Recording the key points and playing them back while you're travelling etc. will strengthen your learning.

In advocating a 'study skills' approach it is important to remember that such approaches are best incorporated within all subjects and aspects of a student's programme, rather than 'bolted on' as an additional part of the programme. This is more readily achieved in school age education and in some kinds of further education than it is in higher education, where such skills are often assumed to have been acquired already. Without such a systematic earlier approach to study skills, students may have acquired a range of idiosyncratic coping mechanisms of variable effectiveness, to which they may cling even when offered alternatives.

AUDITORY MEMORY

The results of the report, in Fig. 3, indicate that the student's short-term auditory memory skills are weak.

Short-term memory difficulties can be overcome by repetition and rehearsal of materials. This form of over-learning can be achieved in a variety of ways and not necessarily through conventional, and often tedious, rote learning.

In order to maximise the effect of repetition of learning, it is important that a multi-sensory mode of learning is utilised. Repetition of the material to be learned can be accomplished through oral, visual, auditory and kinaesthetic modes. The learner should be able to see, hear, say and, if possible, touch the materials to be learned. This reinforces the input stimuli and helps to consolidate the information for use, meaning and transfer to other areas. There are implications here for multi-mode teaching, e.g. the use of drama, to enhance the kinaesthetic mode of learning.

Simple mnemonics can also be utilised. These can be auditory or visual or both auditory and visual. Auditory mnemonics may take the form of rhyming or alliteration while visual mnemonics can be used by relating the material to be remembered to a familiar scene such as the classroom, supermarket or the student's favourite room in his/her house. When using mnemonic strategies as a memory aid, students should be encouraged to think up their own. These can be used to help in all areas of the curriculum. Memory research has shown that the more unusual we imagine an item to be, the more likely we are to remember it. For example, if we wish the student to remember how to spell a word such as 'Beautiful', allow him/her to devise a mnemonic such as 'Big Elephants Are Unusually Timid in Following Useless Lions'. The more ridiculous the mnemonic, the more likely it is to be retained. Encourage the use of both mnemonic and visualisation techniques and, if possible, both together (e.g. visualising the above mnemonic).

Because the student in Fig. 3 has well developed visual memory skills, she should be encouraged to use these abilities to help her retain, remember and recall information, e.g. using mind maps, spidergrams, concept diagrams, etc. (Buzan, 1993). Although mnemonics may be useful for some students, for others they may be perceived as just one more difficult memory task.

Mind mapping is now widely used and helps the learner remember a considerable amount of information. It encourages students to think of, and develop, the main ideas of a passage or material to be learned. Essentially, mind maps are individual learning tools and one person's map/diagram may not be useful to another. It is important, therefore, that students should create their own mind maps. This will help with both the understanding of key concepts and the retention and recall of associated facts. Mind mapping can also help to organise information, for instance in preparation for essay writing, and this exercise in itself can aid understanding. Elaborate versions of mind maps can be constructed using pictorial images, symbols and different colours.

When constructing mind maps it is a good idea to make letters in printed capitals. In writing down ideas they tend to arrange themselves quite naturally with the main ideas near the title, which is usually at the centre of the page. The subdivisions of the first order come next, then the smaller, less significant divisions near the perimeter of the notes. If a major idea occurs belatedly, another main branch can be generated issuing from the centre. Mind mapping can also be undertaken in some word processing packages.

WRITING/SPELLING SKILLS

In many cases, dyslexic students' verbal skills are well in advance of their ability to express themselves on paper. For written work to make sense, working memory has to operate at an acceptable level as the individual has to be able to think up what s/he wishes to say, put his/her ideas into a sentence and retain it for long enough to get it down on paper. Individuals with these difficulties often lack any kind of structure for their ideas and this can lead to a tendency for written work to be disjointed and incomplete, as well as a source of frustration to them as they struggle to maintain their flow of thought. Words which students fear they may misspell are often avoided and alternatives – not always accurate or appropriate – are used. All of these factors lead to students being unable to demonstrate the level of their understanding and knowledge through the medium of written language.

Dictating presentations on to a tape recorder and then transcribing can help students to get their thoughts and ideas down on paper, or into a word processor. The work can then be organised and edited. In word processing, a word or concept which requires further thought, in terms of spelling or expression may be marked with a particular symbol, passed over quickly to maintain momentum and coherence in the narrative, and returned to later for further refinement. The marking symbol may be traced through the word processing package to facilitate the editing of all such 'problems' in the text.

Dyslexic students should also be encouraged to use metacognitive strategies to help them to structure their written work. For examples, questions such as those shown below should be encouraged:

- Did I leave out an interesting part?
- Did I use the most suitable words I could find?
- Did I use punctuation and capital letters correctly?
- Did I stay on the topic?
- Are my ideas in a logical order?
- Will readers feel the way I want them to feel?

The following suggestions are also designed to help students put their ideas into a logical order when writing assignments:

- **Introduction**

In the introduction, define the terms of the question. For example, if asked to compare and contrast 'Psychodynamic Theory' with 'Behaviourism', begin by giving the definitions of the two theories; how the assignment is to be tackled; the areas to be discussed; and why the assignment should be approached in this way.

- **Exposition**

This is the bulk of the assignment when notes are used and would perhaps include:

- Review of the positions,
- description of the methods used and their restrictions,
- discussion, analysis and argument giving facts, ideas, theories, concepts and data providing examples as illustrations,

- details of the difficulties, limitations and successes,
- summary of points for and against an argument presented in a logical order.

- **Conclusion**

State the conclusion, based upon the evidence given. Describe the outcome of the argument. Refer back to the question, remind the reader of the ways in which the topic has been dealt with and provide some reflection on the method of tackling it. New facts should not be introduced at this stage.

Students would need encouragement to pad out each section of written assignments and it is helpful to map out the sequence of their work with them and discuss these before they begin to write the actual piece of work.

Study does not have to be isolated. Friends and family can be involved in the study process. They should therefore be encouraged to open a discussion on their current area of study and to listen to the views and ideas of others. Discussion of ideas will help to strengthen thoughts and perceptions.

Information Technology such as word processing packages with a spell check facility or the hand-held Franklin Spellmaster would also help students become more confident in terms of using more sophisticated vocabulary in their written work. Research (Clayton, 1994) confirms that the editing flexibility of word-processing helps students with specific learning difficulties overcome their problems with organising ideas and structuring written work. The appearance of the work improves greatly and the students no longer have to concentrate on the physical skill of handwriting. Spelling seems to improve when students see the image on the screen. The motivational value of computer-assisted learning is also important.

LEARNING STYLE

The assessment should reveal some information about the student's learning style. For example it may suggest the student will learn better when auditory information or instructions are accompanied by visual aids (video-tape, labels, diagrams, mind maps etc.).

The assessment of the student referred to in Fig. 1-3 would suggest that she would benefit from:

- Time to integrate and consolidate learning,
- positive contact with peers,
- opportunities to make choices,
- being able to use imagination,
- divergent questions.

Teaching strategies which can therefore be recommended for this student's preferred learning style include:

- Structured learning,
- use of checklists,
- opportunities for creative writing,
- choice of working alone or with others on projects,
- providing tactile and kinaesthetic resources for learning,
- providing creative art activities, opportunities for making displays and scrapbooks,
   dramatic presentations, oral reports and group sharing,
- encouraging solving old problems in new ways, open-ended discussions, self-expressive activities e.g. designing an experiment, keeping a personal journal, acting etc.

WORKING WITH STUDENTS WITH SPECIFIC LEARNING DIFFICULTIES (DYSLEXIA): SOME ISSUES IN GUIDANCE AND COUNSELLING

Longitudinal studies, which follow dyslexic children into adult life or studies of adults with specific learning difficulties indicate that, while coping mechanisms improve and some aspects of difficulties in literacy become less problematic, some difficulties do persist beyond childhood into mature adult life (Closs, 1987, 1991: McLoughlin, Fitzgibbon and Young, 1994). This is particularly true for those whose difficulties are most pronounced. For those adults, success is hard won.

Closs (1991), reporting on the personal perspectives of young adults with specific learning difficulties on their educational 'careers' in primary, secondary and tertiary education and in employment, noted the following issues:

- Many subjects gave responses indicating overall low or fragile self-esteem and a need for continuing support.

- Some young adults appeared to have become 'addicted to struggle' and were rarely satisfied with their achievements.

- Modular courses and those which involved continuous assessment seemed to have offered greater opportunities for successful learning than did more traditional courses in secondary and tertiary education.

- Of the young adults in Higher Education, those experiencing most difficulty either had the minimum entrance requirements, or had underestimated the literacy requirements of the course.

- Some young adults had overly ambitious or unrealistic vocational aspirations.

- Those who seemed most content and whose self-esteem appeared to be strongest were those with realistic and supportive families and those with particular talent or abilities in a vocational area.

- A few subjects reported adequate educational and vocational guidance.

This last issue has a bearing on the others. As with all young people, it is important that those with specific learning difficulties receive guidance and support which enables them to access opportunities which are commensurate with their aptitudes, abilities, interests and aspirations. Nonetheless, guidance which fails also to address the nature of their learning difficulties, and the educational and vocational implications of such difficulties, is flawed. It may lead young people to frustration and failure and to further damage to their fragile self-esteem (Wszeborowska-Lipinski, 1995).

In order that dyslexic students in further and higher education succeed, they should have ready access to a system of guidance and on-going learning and personal support which covers their transition from school to tertiary study, the period of study itself and finally their transition from study to employment.

Students at some further and higher education establishments may have to draw on a selection of unco-ordinated services such as Secondary School guidance, the careers service, voluntary associations including the Dyslexia Association, occupational psychologists from commercial or government agencies and literacy support tutors from a variety of sources. Other establishments provide a comprehensive 'single door' service which is plainly preferable.

PRE-ENTRY GUIDANCE AND SUPPORT

It is hard for all young people to know for sure what they wish to study, and how they want to earn their living subsequently. They may have no clear route through their perhaps confused pattern of interests and abilities. Guidance prior to school leaving should involve a thorough assessment of interests, possibly using an interests inventory or profiling system, the outcome of which should be discussed with the young person. Counselling approaches to this discussion should aim to allow the individual ample time for reflection and self-assessment.

While McLouglin *et al.* (1994) suggests that the focus of careers counselling should be on enabling dyslexics to acquire the strategies which would allow them to study and work in their areas of greatest interest, it is also appropriate at this stage to discuss with young people their ability in terms of their 'capacity to perform' in their areas of interest. While many dyslexics may indeed under-achieve in relation to their full potential, young people must weigh up the costs to themselves in terms of extra time and effort spent in study, if their usual level of performance is to improve.

They are also likely to be moving away from home, and will therefore not be able to access the parental support which plays an important part in the lives of many successful dyslexics of school age. The route between overly ambitious aspirations and potentially boring lower targets is not easily found.

Stereotypical guidance on subject and vocational choice – 'Don't take a foreign language', and 'Why not catering – it is so practical?' should be avoided. Young people are, however, entitled to information based on reality to make an informed choice. Some arts and social science subjects in higher education require students to read in such quantity and at such a pace that dyslexic students start at a huge, and sometimes insurmountable, disadvantage. Some traditional academic courses involve end-of-term and session exams while others have continuous selected samples of reading material, access to lecturers' notes, etc. and assessment. Some courses are very practical. All such information is relevant and must be available.

Choice of a particular course should relate, therefore, not only to young persons' interests in subject areas, but also to courses' compatibility with their pattern of strengths and weaknesses, and to their styles of learning.

Potential students need to know in advance what kind of support may be made available to them while on courses, so that they may judge whether it is appropriate and sufficient. They may also need advice on micro-technological aids, such as wordprocessors and related software. They will certainly need guidance on sources of funding for such aids and for payment of scribes or readers if appropriate.

GUIDANCE AND SUPPORT THROUGH STUDY

The need for on-course support is significantly reduced by appropriate pre-course guidance. Nonetheless, most students, even when a suitable choice of course has been made, will require help from time to time. Any deficit in pre-course guidance and counselling will almost certainly have to be made good at some point during the course on which they have enrolled.

For more able students with a lesser degree of difficulty this may involve only intermittent monitoring contact and encouragement. For those with more severe difficulties, or those who have selected courses which require them to function at the upper limits of their competence, support may involve some or all of the following:

- General support for organisation regarding workload.
- Scheduling of extra subject-based tutorials and/or literacy support tutorials.
- Negotiation for additional lecturer notes.
- Negotiation on access to fellow students' notes.
- Guidance on appropriate and more accessible texts.
- Advice on best use of micro-technology to aid study and to produce assignments.
- Extension of course length.
- The making of special arrangements (extra time, scribing, transcription etc.) for examinations or other forms of assessments.

When a student shows signs of struggling to cope, the possibility of changing courses should be discussed, especially if support is already at its optimum level. Some students may either, as already mentioned, have received inadequate advice, or have persisted in a misguided choice. Some educational establishments show greater flexibility than others in allowing students to transfer. Obviously this is more readily, and happily, effected early in a student's career, where it is a matter of choice rather than compulsion following failure.

POST-COURSE SUPPORT

It is easy in the pressure of a final year or term of study to focus exclusively on successful completion and to see this as an end in itself. While this is in part true and success should be savoured, the next stage has to be addressed with, if anything, even greater reflection than the earlier stages, since the rest of the young adult's life will be affected by the career decisions made now.

Many pupils and students with specific learning difficulties – and their parents and teachers – have put enormous effort into the successes achieved. In considering their working lives, students will have to weigh up not only the skills and knowledge they have acquired, but also the fact that support as they have known it in education will not be available in employment. Career choices, therefore, have to be made on the basis of what individuals can do, and sustain, by themselves. They should also consider wider issues, such as time for leisure and recreation, and the overall quality of their lives. Do they, can they, sustain the effort which some have put into their educational careers? What could offer them enduring satisfaction along with ample opportunities for demonstrating their competence, and minimised demands on their areas of enduring weakness?

The greatest need, therefore, at this time is for a wise and knowledgeable careers counsellor who will enable the dyslexic adult to find his way to making decisions, and who will offer support in the processes of making job applications and preparing for interviews. Those dyslexics going through the process need to know that while 'prominent figures' such as Jackie Stewart, Susan Hampshire and Michael Heseltine have indeed gone before them, so have large numbers of motor vehicle repairers, computer operators, nurses, scientists, engineers, general managers, artists, shop assistants, charity workers, accountants, craftspeople . . . who also have fulfilled social and personal lives and who are therefore successful human beings.

REFERENCES

Baker, L. and Brown, A. (1984). Metacognitive Skills in Reading. In Pearson, P. D. (Ed.) *Handbook of Reading Research*. New York: Longman.

Beloff, H. (1993). Making it at a university: academic and social development. In Closs, A. (Ed.) *Special Educational Needs Beyond 16*. Moray House Publications.

Buzan, T. (1993). The Mind Map Book – Radient Thinking. London: BBC Books.

Clayton, P. (1994). *Access Students and Dyslexia – A Guide to Good Practice*. University of Kent at Canterbury.

Clayton, P. (1994). *H.E.F.C. Project on Access/Foundation Students and Dyslexia*. Paper presented at International Conference, Dyslexia in Higher Education, University of Plymouth, October 31st-2nd November 1994.

Closs, A. (1987). One Long Struggle: 'Career' Perceptions of Young Adults with specific learning difficulties. M.Ed Dissertation. University of Stirling.

Closs, A. (1991). *Still Struggling: A Follow-on Study of the Career Perceptions of Young Adults with Specific Learning Difficulties*. Research Report. Moray House Publications.

Connors, M. J. (1994). Dyslexia (Specific Learning Difficulties): Assessing Assessment. In Educational Psychology in Practice. Vol. 10, No. 3, Oct. 1994. 131-140.

Elbro, C., Neilson, I. and Peterson, D. K. (1994). Dyslexia in Adults: Evidence for Deficits in Non-Word Reading and in the Phonological Representation of Lexical Items. In *Annals of Dyslexia*. Vol. XLIV, (1994). Orton Dyslexia Society, Baltimore, USA.

Gilroy, D. (1991). *Dyslexia and Higher Education*. Bangor University College of North Wales.

Jastak. S. and Wilkinson, G. (1984). *Wide Range Achievement Test* – Revised Los Angeles CA: Western Psychological Services.

Lannen, C. and Lannen, S. (1995). *Psychological Assessment of Dyslexic Students*. Unpublished Study Educational Psychology Services, Riyadh, Saudi Arabia.

McKeown, S. (Ed.). (1992). *IT support for specific learning difficulties*. NCET.

McLoughlin, D., Fitzgibbon, G. and Young, V. (1994). *Adult Dyslexia, Assessment, Counselling and Training*. Whurr Publications, London.

Pennington, B.F., Van Orden, G. C., Smith, S. D., Green, P. A. and Haith, M. M. (1990). Phonological Processing Skills and Deficits in Adult Dyslexics. In *Child Development 61:13:53-78*.

Pottage, T. (1994). *Using Computers with Dyslexics*.

Reid, G. (1994). *Study Skills – A Positive Approach to Success – Converting Deficits to Differences*. Paper presented at International Conference, Dyslexia in High Education, University of Plymouth October 31st-November 2nd 1994.

Scottish Higher Education Funding Council (1994). *Access to Success for Students with Disabilities in Higher Education in Scotland*.

Siegal, L. S. (1989). IQ is irrelevant to the definition of learning disabilities. *Journal of Learning Disabilities*, 22, 469-78.

Singleton, C. (1994). *Dyslexia in Higher Education*. Paper presented at International Conference, Dyslexia in Higher Education, University of Plymouth. October 31st-2nd November 1994.

Stanovich, K. E. (1991). Discrepancy Definitions of Reading Disability: Has Intelligence Led Us Astray? *Reading Research Quarterly*, XXVI/I, pp. 7-29.

University of Plymouth (1994). *International Conference*. Dyslexia in Higher Education. Dartington Hall, Devon, UK. October 31st-2nd November 1994.

Wechsler, D. (1981) *Wechsler Adult Intelligence Scale (Revised)*. New York: Psychological Corporation

Wszeborowska-Lipinski, B. (1995). *Dyslexia in Poland*. Research Report. In Bridges, Vol. 2, No. 2, p.35.

NOTES ON CONTRIBUTORS

* **Donna B. Ayres** is a facilitator and programme manager for the US Army Corps of Engineers in Alexandria, Virginia. She helps work groups and task forces in the Corps in the Washington D.C. area design and run strategic planning and problem-solving meetings and also serves as the programme co-ordinator for the Corps' Alternative Dispute Resolution Program. Her professional background is eclectic. Donna has worked in the National Capitol Region for the past 10 years of her 21 years in government. Prior to that, she served as the Chief of the Office of Organisation Development and Planning and as the Organisational Effectiveness Officer for the Army's Finance and Accounting Center in Indianapolis, Indiana; as a research psychologist for the Army's Soldier Support Center, specialising in leadership programme and curriculum development; as a director of student housing at a women's college; as an interior designer, and as a psychology intern at a mental health centre. Donna has a BA in Sociology from St Mary's College, Notre Dame, Indiana and an MS in Industrial/Organisational Psychology from Purdue University, also in Indiana. She is currently a doctoral student in the Ph.D in Education Programme at George Mason University in Fairfax, Virginia, specialising in curriculum and instruction, assessment, and programme development and evaluation in the field of thinking skills, particularly metacognition.

* **David Blair** has held the position of Principal Teacher of Learning Support at Queen Anne High School since 1985. His training in special needs was the Secondary Remedial course at Dundee followed by a place on the initial D.L.D. at Moray House. He has served on several Regional Working Groups and at present is a member of Area 5-14 group.

* **Gordon Booth** is a consulting educational psychologist with a long-standing interest in the problems faced by dyslexic children and their parents. He regards it as a particular achievement to have been instrumental in setting up in 1978 the first of several special Learning Units for children with specific learning difficulties in Grampian and in having been associated with the specialist training of teachers in this field.

* **Morven Brown** is Learning Resources Co-ordinator at Daniel Stewarts and Melville College and the Mary Erskine School. A psychology graduate, she trained

as a primary teacher and then worked for the Child Guidance Service in Lothian Region as an educational psychologist until 1980; since this time she became interested in dyslexia and specific learning difficulties. She has been involved with the Edinburgh Dyslexia Association since the early 1980s. Her present post involves the development of support for learning throughout the school-age range.

* **Claire Bedford-Feuell** recently completed her post-graduate training in educational psychology at University College London after working as a primary school teacher. She is a full-time mother of twins.

* **Helen Calcluth** has 20 years experience in teaching at Primary and Nursery levels. In 1987, she completed the British Dyslexia Diploma course. Over the last eight years, she has developed the PASS Programme to tackle the problem of specific learning difficulties in the mainstream classroom situation. The Programme is a multi-sensory, structured phonics programme which can be effectively used as an intervention programme in the whole-class situation or a remediation programme in the individual or group situation.

* **Alison Closs** is a lecturer in Special Education at Moray House Institute of Education. She was previously Head of Special Needs at Stevenson College of Further Education, Edinburgh. She has undertaken research into the perceptions of young adults with specific learning difficulties of their educational and vocational careers.

* **Dr Catriona Collins** is a part time lecturer at Napier University and also actively involved in research into auditory dyslexia. She is also currently a tutor for the RSA Diploma course for teachers of pupils with specific learning difficulties in Edinburgh, and is a external verifier for the RSA.

* **Margaret Crombie** co-ordinates a team of specialist teachers dealing with children with special educational needs in mainstream schools in Renfrewshire. She also lectures part-time for Moray House Institute and Heriot-Watt University. Author of *Specific Learning Difficulties (Dyslexia) – A Teachers' Guide*, she has contributed to a number of other books and has written several articles on dyslexia for educational journals. She has researched into the effects of specific learning difficulties (dyslexia) on the learning of a foreign language in school.

* **Vera Dearnley** has been a tutor for the past 10 years, with the Edinburgh and South East Scotland Dyslexia Centre. After a year's secondment at the Institute of Education London, she ran a centre for children with learning difficulties, under

the aegis of the Child Guidance Service, Barnet, for eight years. She joined the Helen Arkell Dyslexia Centre, London, as a tutor for five years before moving to Edinburgh.

* **Fernando Almeida Diniz** is Head of Department at Moray House Institute of Education, Heriot-Watt University and Chairperson of the Advisory Committee for the Centre for Specific Learning Difficulties. After teaching in special and mainstream schools, he lectured at the University of Greenwich, London, where he was Head of Division and Reader in Special Needs in Education. He has extensive international experience and has held visiting professorships at universities in Germany and Spain.

* **David Dodds** is currently principal learning support special needs teacher at Boroughmuir High School. He has worked in secondary learning support since 1980, before which he was a primary teacher. He developed an in-service package on supporting pupils with specific learning difficulties/dyslexia in the secondary school while on part-time secondment from 1990/92.

* **Marie Dougan** is Senior Teacher – Learning Support (Information Technology) – Lothian Region. She graduated from Glasgow University with a degree in Biological Sciences, and taught Biology and General Science in secondary schools before moving into the Special Education sector in 1978. She has held her present post with responsibility for microtechnology and special education for seven years. She has completed the Post-Graduate Certificate in Specific Learning Difficulties at Moray House and is currently course tutor for the Microtechnology component of the Moray House course in dyslexia.

* **Alison Duncan** works as an educational psychologist in Angus having previously taught in secondary and primary schools both within Scotland and in East Africa.

* **Maggi Fenton** is a member of the Learning Support Department at Queen Anne High School. After four years teaching Home Economics, she took a 14 year career break to bring up a family. She has taught in her current school for eight years except for one year at Moray House to gain the Diploma of Professional Studies. SEN (Secondary).

* **Alison Fox** has taught in the Literacy Unit in West Lothian for the past five years. After gaining a degree in Psychology and Sociology from Glasgow University, she taught infants in Paisley before spending five years as a teacher in the Department of Child and Family Psychiatry at Yorkhill Hospital. She then moved into learning support, teaching in a variety of schools in Orkney and West Lothian.

She has completed the Post-Graduate Certificate in Specific Learning Difficulties at Moray House and is also a course tutor for the Moray House Post-Graduate Course in Dyslexia.

* **Dr Norah Frederickson** is Course Director of the MSc in Educational Psychology at University College London and Senior Education Psychologist in Buckinghamshire County Psychological Service.

* **Sarah Geiger** is an educational psychologist currently employed in Buckinghamshire Psychology Service. She taught as a primary teacher and special needs co-ordinator before moving to a large secondary school where she worked as Head of Learning Support with responsibility for developing teaching and learning styles and support for students with special needs and English as a second language. She completed her post-graduate training in educational psychology at University College London.

* **Morag Gibson** is a part-time teacher of Learning Support at Queen Anne High School. Initially trained as a teacher of Home Economics, she gained an additional teaching qualification in Primary Education in 1991 and is currently completing the Certificate in Specific Learning Difficulties (Dyslexia).

* **Dr Marcia Henry** is Professor Emeritus at San Jose University in California, USA. She is currently President of the Orton Dyslexia Society and on the editorial board for two international journals. She is the author of the 'Words' teaching programme and has other published work in the area of reading and spelling instruction for students with dyslexia. She was Fulbright Professor at the University of Trondheim in Norway in 1991.

* **Ros Hunter** is assistant adviser in Borders Region with responsibility for Learning Support and Special Educational Needs. She is currently seconded to the Scottish Consultative Committee on the Curriculum to work on a national project promoting differentiation.

* **Dr Sionah Lannen** is Director of Educational Psychology Services, Riyadh, Saudi Arabia. She was previously an educational psychologist with Lancashire Education Authority. Following teaching training at Dundee, she taught in Fife Region as a primary teacher, and learning support teacher. She then embarked on post-graduate training in educational psychology at Glasgow and Edinburgh Universities before taking up posts in Canada, at Ottawa University and Western Quebec School Board. She has had a long-standing interest in specific learning difficulties in relation to teaching, assessment and teacher training.

* **Karen Laws** is currently Acting Senior Area Educational Psychologist in Aylesbury Vale, Buckinghamshire. She previously worked in Kent as a classroom and peripatetic teacher for pupils with special educational needs. After completing professional training at University College London in 1992/93 she returned to Kent working as an educational psychologist in the North/Mid team.

* **Rosemary McGhee** is Principal Teacher of Learning Support at Lossiemouth High School. Initially she trained as a Home Economics teacher and has completed RSA Diploma for Teachers of Children with Specific Learning Difficulties.

* **Elizabeth Mackenzie** is Principal Teacher of the Dyslexia Institute in Scotland. She had a Froebel training before teaching in London and Scotland. After her daughter was assessed as dyslexic, she trained for the Dyslexia Institute Diploma and also for the British Dyslexia Association Diploma. She has done a course in Oxford with Professor Mahesh Sharma on the teaching of maths to dyslexics, and has just finished working for a post-graduate degree in Education and Management. She is currently the Course Director on the Post-Graduate Course (Kingston University with the Dyslexia Institute) in the teaching of students with dyslexia, for Dumfries and Galloway Local Education Authority.

* **Don Mackie** is an English graduate from the University of Dundee and a Community Education graduate from the Northern College. He has worked in Adult Basic Education in Tayside since 1980 as a tutor, Community Education Worker and, since 1989 as ABE Organiser. Over the years, his main interests have been the development of educational resource materials and computer aided learning.

* **Janice Masterton** has an M.A. in History from Edinburgh University. She joined Queen Anne High School eight years ago as a part-time teacher of Social Subjects and helped in the setting up of the school's A.W.A.R.E. scheme. For the last five years she has been a teacher in L.S.S. and is currently completing the Certificate in Specific Learning Difficulties (Dyslexia).

* **Jean Miller** has been Headteacher of Portree Primary School in the Isle of Skye since January 1991. Prior to that she was Headteacher of a large primary school with a special class for pupils with moderate learning difficulties and a Special Education Unit for pupils with severe and profound learning difficulties. She was very active in promoting the integration of SEN pupils into mainstream and was a member of a Highland Region Working Party on Integration.

* **Avril Milne** is a Senior Teacher, Learning Support at Queen Anne High School. She trained and taught as a teacher of Physical Education before taking a break to bring up a family. For the last 15 years she has been working in Learning Support in Fife. She holds the Diploma of Professional Studies, Special Educational Needs (Secondary).

* **Karen Kiesel Morrison** is an educational diagnostician at George Mason University, Virginia, USA, where she also teaches an assessment course to special educators. She has worked as a special education teacher and psychologist in the public schools and has experience administering neuro-psychological evaluations at Children's National Medical Centre in Washington, D.C. Karen is presently working on a PhD in Special Education and School Psychology.

* **Anne Morton** is Adviser for Learning Support across primary and secondary schools in Fife. Prior to this, she was Principal Teacher in Learning Support at Glenrothes High School for eight years following an earlier career in primary class teaching across several regions in Scotland. She holds the Diploma of Professional Studies, SEN (Secondary) and is currently completing the Moray House Post-Graduate Certificate in Specific Learning Difficulties (Dyslexia).

* **Dr Anne O'Hare** is Consultant Paediatrician, Community Child Health, Senior Lecturer, Department of Child Life and Health, University of Edinburgh and Honorary Consultant to the Neurology Department, Royal Hospital for Sick Children.

* **Anne Philip** is specialist teacher responsible for students with specific learning difficulties at the High School of Dundee. Since joining the staff at the High School of Dundee in 1980, she has established a Learning Skills Centre which serves both as a resource base and a support classroom for students with specific learning difficulties. Anne has made a number of conference and seminar presentations on dyslexia and the use of resources.

* **Dr Rea Reason** is Associate Tutor to the MSc course in Educational Psychology at Manchester University and Senior Educational Psychologist with Oldham. Contact address is Centre for Educational Needs, School of Education, University of Manchester, Oxford Road, Manchester M13 9PL.

* **Gavin Reid** is Co-ordinator of the Moray House Centre for Specific Learning Difficulties (Dyslexia) and Course Leader for the Post-Graduate Awards in Specific Learning Difficulties. He has been instrumental in the development of the M.Ed Award in Specific Learning Difficulties and is the author of the course text 'A

Handbook for Study and Practice' and editor of this two-volume course reader 'Dimensions of Dyslexia'. He has made a number of presentations at conferences and universities, both in the UK and the United States: published journal articles and is a member of a number of national consultancy groups. He has had lengthy experiences as a class teacher and as an educational psychologist.

* **Sylvia Russell** is the Co-ordinator of Learning Support Services for Lanarkshire. She ran a Psychological Service Reading Centre for many years before changing to a peripatetic school based service. She is author of the Phonic Codecracker Programme and is currently completing the Moray House Post-Graduate course in specific learning difficulties.

* **Dr Chris Singleton** is a Chartered Psychologist who lectures in Educational and Developmental Psychology at the University of Hull, and is Director of the Dyslexia Computer Resource Centre at Hull, working in collaboration with the British Dyslexia Association. He is most well-known for his internationally pioneering research which has resulted in the creation and validation of a computer-based system for early identification of dyslexia. He is also chairman of the National Working Party on Dyslexia in Higher Education, which is investigating the assessment of, and provision for, dyslexics in higher education across the country. He is author of many articles on dyslexia, as well as editor of two books, including the latest *Computers and Dyslexia: Educational Applications of New Technology* (1994). He is co-editor of a practitioners' handbook on the assessment of reading soon to be published by Routledge, and has recently been appointed Editor-in-Chief of the *Journal of Research in Reading*.

* **Isobel Triay** has been a teacher of Learning Support at Queen Anne High School since 1992. After working as a Biology teacher in Lothian and Fife, she left teaching for several years to bring up her family. During this time, she continued to work closely with young people. She is currently studying modules towards a Certificate in Specific Learning Difficulties (Dyslexia).

* **Mark Turner** has recently completed his Masters in Educational Psychology at University College London and now works for Kent Psychology Service. Mark is interested in developing the LARC materials for use with children with a variety of Special Educational Needs. He hopes to be able to continue with research while providing a psychological consultation service to schools in the Hoo and Stroud area of Kent. He can be contacted at Educational Psychology Service, Compass Centre, Chatham Maritime, Chatham, Kent, ME4 4YN.

* **Emma Vallance** studied music at Edinburgh University, graduating in 1995. Part of her degree involved a 'Music in the Community' course and she chose to work with several dyslexic children in a local secondary school.

* **Dr Charles Weedon** is Principal Teacher at George Watson's College, Edinburgh. After leaving the Royal Navy, he took an Edinburgh B.Ed., then worked as an English and Maths teacher, and taught in Shetland, Fife and Tayside. His M.Ed. and Ph.D research focused on writing and reading skills.

* **Kath Winn** is currently a neighbourhood Support Officer in West Lothian responsible for promoting the integration of pupils with special educational needs into mainstream schools, acting as a resource person to management, teaching staff and non teaching staff across all sectors. Trained in learning support with a special interest in specific learning difficulties (dyslexia), she was involved in setting up the West Lothian Literacy Unit.